An' then the world came tae oor doorstep

To darling Michael

14th November 2011

All my love

C x

Lockerbie Air Disaster Memorial Window, 21st December, 1988

The stained-glass windows in Lockerbie Town Hall that represent the 21 bereft nations of the disaster. John Clark was the artist and it was unveiled in December 1991.

An' then the world came tae oor doorstep
Lockerbie Lives and Stories

Jill S. Haldane

The Grimsay Press

The Grimsay Press
an imprint of
Zeticula
57 St Vincent Crescent
Glasgow
G3 8NQ
Scotland.
http://www.thegrimsaypress.co.uk
admin@thegrimsaypress.co.uk
First published 2008

Cover:
Timed photo of crater site, from a hole in the roof of a house on Sherwood
Crescent, taken one day and four years after the disaster. The photographer is
Euan Adamson, whose family still live in the same house. © Euan Adamson
2008. http://www.euanadamson.com

ISBN-10   1 84530 063 7 Paperback
ISBN-13 978 1 84530 063 0 Paperback

This book is dedicated to the guid folk o' Lockerbie

Acknowledgements

I would like to take this opportunity to thank the following people for their help and support in writing and compiling this book. Your assistance was greatly appreciated.

My particular thanks go to Hugo Manson, historian (New Zealand and Scotland) and my Mum and Dad, Yvonne & Jimmy Haldane.

In Lockerbie, to
Mr Herbert, Lockerbie Academy; Jim Rae; Douglas Lipton; Arthur Johnson; Dumfries Archives Service; Hannah & Ted Hill; Margaret & John Montgomery; George Shankland; Geoff Creamer, Lockerbie Library; Euan Adamson, Photographer

At Aberdeen University
Terry Brotherstone, Dr Ben Marsden

In New Zealand
Cheryl Frost; Scott Kendrick; Gavin Frost; Ola Frost; Girvan Frost

At Massey University, New Zealand
Dianne Haist; Marie McCambridge; Geoff Holland; Helen Thomson; Sharon O'Sullivan

Transcribers, New Zealand
Sue Shirrifs; Jennifer Lawn; Lorna McGibbon; Anne-Marie Clarke; Brian Johnston; Leigh Sargent

At Alexander Turnbull Library, New Zealand
Linda Evans, Curator; Bronwyn Officer, Sound Specialist

All the interviewees who participated in the book and project – thanks for the memories.

Jill Haldane, July 2008

The field at Tundergarth, where the nose cone of the Flight 103 fell.
(© James Haldane)

Plaque set into the wall of the Dedication Room at Tundergarth.

"THERE ARE THREE
THINGS THAT LAST:
FAITH, HOPE AND LOVE
AND THE GREATEST OF THESE IS
LOVE"

Contents

Memorial Garden at Dryfesdale Cemetery

List of Illustrations

The remaining contents of a garage in Sherwood Park, after the disaster.
(© Dumfries and Galloway Regional Council, 2008)
Typical airline activity above the Lockerbie skies, March 2008.
(© James Haldane)

Foreword

The only previous book of which I am aware which is devoted to recording something of the social life of the town of Lockerbie is *Lockerbie: A narrative of village life in bygone days* (Lockerbie: Herald Press, 1937) by Thomas Henderson, Solicitor, of the law firm Henderson & Mackay (which exists to this day) . The author's intention was to record with historical accuracy (albeit in a loose, fictionalised narrative form) what was known about life in the town at the time of the Napoleonic wars, while there were still people around who had heard first-hand accounts from parents and others who were alive at the time. My copy contains a clipping of a lengthy and laudatory review (probably from the local newspaper, *The Annandale Herald*) by the then minister of Dryfesdale Parish Kirk, Rev John Charlton Steen MA (who, incidentally, some ten years later, baptised me) .

At least part of JH's aim in the present book is not entirely dissimilar: to record accounts by inhabitants of Lockerbie of the recent event with which the name of the town has become indissolubly linked and to reflect on how that seminal event may have changed, for good or ill, the life of the town and its indwellers.

Here, in brief, is my, and my family's, story.

In 1988, both of my parents were still alive and living in the town's Hillview Street. I was due to join them there on 23 December to spend Christmas and the New Year.

The first news of the Lockerbie disaster came to me through BBC radio. I was at my home in Edinburgh preparing my evening meal with, as usual, my wireless tuned to Radio Four. The first reports were, inevitably, sketchy and, I remember, suggested that Langholm too had been affected. But as soon as it was indicated that a plane had crashed on the town, my immediate thought was that it must have been one of the RAF jets that used the locality for low-flying exercises, to the great concern of the local inhabitants who often predicted that there would one day be a tragedy.

I immediately tried to telephone my mother, but all the lines were down and I could not get through. Shortly after 8pm a university colleague phoned me. Her first words were: "Bob, are you sitting down?" When I said that I wasn't, she said "I think you should." She then said that television programmes had been interrupted to announce that a plane had crashed on Lockerbie. Knowing that I did not have a television set (and twenty years later I still don't) she assumed that I would not have received the news.

As the gravity of the incident became clearer, so my concern for the safety of my mother and father increased. However, at around 8.15, I received a phone call from my niece, at that time a nurse in a hospital in Glasgow. It transpired that she had actually been on the phone to my mother when the plane came down and, because the line was not cut until a few minutes thereafter, was able to confirm that her grandmother and grandfather had not been killed or injured. At the actual moment of impact, my father had been outside the house, posting a letter in the pillar box just across the road. He rushed to the alleyway between the houses and sheltered there while small items of debris rained down on the street.

When I drove in to Lockerbie on 23rd December, I was asked by the police what my business there was and, having convinced them that it was legitimate, was instructed to take a circuitous route to Hillview Street because the direct route was closed. That route would have led through Park Place which, of course, was one of the locations (other than Sherwood Crescent) most affected by debris from the plane.

Hillview Street itself had not been damaged. But a short distance away, just beyond Lambhill Terrace, the local golf course was one of the main sites from which bodies were recovered. Indeed, the main immediate impact that the disaster had on my family's daily life was that it prevented my father from taking his daily walks over the golf course with his elderly next-door neighbour's equally elderly dog.

The most obvious signs to me over the next few days that all was not normal were: the presence of multitudes of strangers in the town; the prevalence of baseball caps [not at that time a common item of headgear in Scotland] among the [presumably American] incomers; and the constant noise of helicopters.

My parents – typically, I think – did not then, or in the years that followed, talk a great deal about the event. Nor did their friends and neighbours. These were not people who wore their emotions on their sleeves. Scorn and distaste were, of course, expressed for the disaster groupies who felt compelled to visit the principal sites of destruction and gawk. But apart from that, reticence was the keynote of local reaction. And while there may well have been some citizens of the town who made use of the counselling services provided, on the whole the denizens of Lockerbie did not provide fertile ground for trauma counsellors.

My personal involvement in the aftermath of the destruction of Pan Am 103 began in early 1993. I was approached by representatives of a group of British businessmen whose desire to participate in major engineering works in Libya was being impeded by the UN sanctions that had been imposed on Libya in attempt to compel the surrender for trial in Scotland or the United States of America of their two accused citizens. They asked if I would be prepared to provide (on an unpaid basis) independent advice to the government of Libya on matters of Scottish criminal law, procedure and evidence with a view (it was hoped) to persuading them that their citizens would obtain a fair trial if they were to surrender themselves to the Scottish authorities. This I agreed to do, and submitted material setting out the essentials of Scottish solemn criminal procedure and the various protections embodied in it for accused persons.

In the light of this material, it was indicated to me that the Libyan government was satisfied regarding the fairness of a criminal trial in Scotland but that since Libyan law prevented the extradition of nationals for trial overseas, the ultimate decision on surrender for trial would have to be one taken voluntarily by the accused persons themselves, in consultation with their independent legal advisers. For this purpose a meeting was convened in Tripoli in October 1993 of the international team of lawyers which had already been appointed to represent the accused. This team consisted of lawyers from Scotland, England, Malta, Switzerland and the United States and was chaired by the principal Libyan lawyer for the accused, Dr Ibrahim Legwell. The Libyan government asked me to be present in Tripoli while the team was meeting so that the government itself would have access to independent Scottish legal advice should the need arise. However, the Libyan government expectation was clearly that the outcome of the meeting of the defence team would be a decision by the two accused voluntarily to agree to stand trial in Scotland.

I am able personally to testify to how much of a surprise and embarrassment it was to the Libyan government when the outcome of the meeting of the defence team was an announcement that the accused were not prepared to surrender themselves for trial in Scotland. In the course of a private meeting that I had a day later with Dr Legwell, he explained to me that the primary reason for the unwillingness of the accused to stand trial in Scotland was their belief that, because of unprecedented pre-trial publicity over the years, a Scottish jury could not possibly bring to their consideration of the evidence in this case the degree of impartiality and open-mindedness that accused persons are entitled to expect and that a fair trial demands. A secondary consideration was the issue of the physical security of the accused if the trial were to be held in Scotland. Not that it was being contended that ravening mobs of enraged Scottish citizens would storm Barlinnie prison, seize the accused and string them up from the nearest lamp posts. Rather, the fear was that they might be snatched by special forces of the United States, removed to America and put on trial there (or, like Lee Harvey Oswald, suffer an unfortunate accident before being put on trial.) .

The Libyan government attitude remained, as it always had been, that they had no constitutional authority to hand their citizens over to the Scottish authorities for trial. The question of voluntary surrender for trial was one for the accused and their legal advisers, and while the Libyan government would place no obstacles in the path of, and indeed would welcome, such a course of action, there was nothing that it could lawfully do to achieve it.

Having mulled over the concerns expressed to me by Dr Legwell in October 1993, I returned to Tripoli and on 10 January 1994 presented a letter to him suggesting a means of resolving the impasse created by the insistence of the governments of the United Kingdom and United States that the accused be surrendered for trial in Scotland or America and the adamant refusal of the accused to submit themselves for trial by jury in either of these countries. This was a detailed proposal, but in essence its principal elements were: that a trial be held outside Scotland, ideally in the Netherlands, in which the governing law and procedure would be that followed in Scottish criminal trials on indictment but with this major alteration, namely that the jury of 15 persons which is a feature of that procedure be replaced by a panel of judges who would have the responsibility of deciding not only questions of law but also the ultimate question of whether the guilt of the accused had been established on the evidence beyond reasonable doubt.

In a letter to me dated 12 January 1994, Dr Legwell stated that he had consulted his clients, that this scheme was wholly acceptable to them and that if it were implemented by the government of the United Kingdom the suspects would voluntarily surrender themselves for trial before a tribunal so constituted. By a letter of the same date the Deputy Foreign Minister of Libya stated that his government approved of the proposal and would place no obstacles in the path of its two citizens should they elect to submit to trial under this scheme.

On my return to the United Kingdom I submitted the relevant documents to the Foreign Office in London and the Crown Office (the headquarters of the Scottish prosecution service) in Edinburgh. Their immediate response was that this scheme was impossible, impracticable and inherently undesirable, with the clear implication that I had taken leave of what few senses nature had endowed me with. That remained the attitude of successive Lord Advocates and Foreign Secretaries for four years and seven months. During this period the British government's stance remained consistent: United Nations Security Council Resolutions placed upon the government of Libya a binding international legal obligation to hand over the accused for trial to the UK or the US authorities. Nothing else would do. If Libyan law did not currently permit the extradition of its own nationals to stand trial overseas, then Libya should simply alter its law (and, if necessary, its Constitution) to enable it to fulfil its international duty.

However, from about late July 1998, following interventions supporting my "neutral venue" scheme from, amongst others, President Nelson Mandela, there began to be leaks from UK government sources to the effect that a policy change over Lockerbie was imminent; and on 24 August 1998 the governments of the United Kingdom and United States announced that they had reversed their stance on the matter of a "neutral venue" trial.

Although many within the governments of Britain and the United States and within the media were sceptical, the suspects did eventually, on 5 April 1999, surrender themselves for trial before the Scottish court at Camp Zeist. That trial, after lengthy delays necessitated by the defence's need for adequate time to prepare, started on 3 May 2000 and a verdict of guilty was returned against one of the accused, and of not guilty against the other, on 31 January 2001.

I feel a measure of pride in the part that I, a Lockerbie boy born and bred, played in resolving an international impasse and in bringing the trial about. I have reason to suspect, however, that the United Kingdom government feels no sense of gratitude towards me. And I feel no pride whatsoever in the outcome of the proceedings. The conviction of Abdelbaset al-Megrahi on the evidence led at the trial constitutes, in my view, a flagrant miscarriage of justice, and one that I hope to live to see rectified as a result of the reference of the case back for a further appeal by the Scottish Criminal Cases Review Commission in June 2007.

Many in Lockerbie hoped, I think, that the twentieth anniversary of the tragedy would signal an end to the town's exposure to the eyes of the world. Regrettably, because of the Crown's delaying tactics, it looks as if the new appeal will not be concluded before 21 December 2008. But the town's wish will surely be fulfilled before the twenty-first anniversary and Lockerbie will be permitted to sink back into decent obscurity. But future generations will be grateful that, before that happened, JH had the vision and the persistence to find a way of ensuring that the voices of the people of Lockerbie were heard and preserved.

Robert Black, QC FRSE
Professor Emeritus of Scots Law
University of Edinburgh

Introduction

Lockerbie is my hometown, the small place I identify as home. I've had many homecomings in my life because I've lived away from my home town and my first family for 22 years now. As a student and in my working life, I have lived in a few places. I was in Aberdeen as a student, then I lived and worked in the capital, Edinburgh, for a few years, coupled with a short stint in the Isle of Arran, off the west coast of Scotland, and a year and more at college in Carlisle. Once I left the shores of the UK and crossed onto the continent of Europe, I found a new and exciting life, so never returned to live in the UK. I was lured to the other side of the world in 1999 and thus consolidated my self-imposed exile from my homeland and hometown.

Of course, I returned frequently from domiciles in Scotland and over the border, to visit family and friends. I came back less frequently from Europe, and now only once every five years from my current home in another continent, Oceania: another island country, New Zealand. So I know something about homecomings!

I am always welcomed warmly by my family; my first family, the family that I started with, before I made a second family of my own. Yet, I know that the expectant feeling of excitement and anticipation of my family, and the scale of the homecoming celebration, increases with my proximal distance and length of absent time: when living in Carlisle, my trips home were every weekend, so there would be a nice meal waiting, a catch-up on news, and the washing clean for my departure.

When in Poland, I would get back to Scotland three times a year: these homecomings were a special occasion in the family home, full of stories of new people and ways of doing things, now and in the past, in unknown places. In comparison to my return visits from New Zealand with my new family - anticipated weeks beforehand, with celebratory plans and preparations to the house, larder and events itinerary - there is a spatial distinction directly related to the scale of the celebration upon return.

As a student in Scotland, returning home for the holidays was a small matter; another marker of the year's progression and an indication of exams passed or impending. Another year chalked up and another year of student loan looming. Going back home for Christmas, Easter or Summer was part of the yearly cycle. The Lockerbie Disaster occurred on one of these trips home for Christmas holidays. I was never more than a few hours away from home in the UK and returned every so often: still in the realms of proximal interest, still in the security of the homeland. The diet's the same, the weather, the accommodation, the language – my life experiences, from that distance, were still identifiably common and familiar.

Once I departed the national perimeter and crossed borders, seas, oceans, great stretches of mountains and desert plains, the homecomings took on another dimension. You have to reverse that distance - retrace your steps - to return. It's a journey of the mind as well - scaling those mountains and plodding through seering deserts and swimming those vast oceans to get back home. That's how important home is.

Remember Dorothy in The Wizard of Oz? She makes unexpected friends, commands whole nations of munchkins, fends off the Wicked Witch of the North and experiences a whole new world of colour down the Yellow Brick Road. At the end of the day, she wants to pack it all in because there's no place like home. And I know what she means – faced with a 24 + hour flight from the bottom of the globe to the top, I wish I had a pair of clickety red high-heels. Or a handy, pocket-sized portal.

Well, there's always a meal waiting, there's beaming smiles and chatting and catching up, exchanging photos and stories, a few drinks. My family have me home again. On one occasion, after relatively far distance and long time away, and with many life-changing experiences, I was welcomed home with a party; a get-together of friends and family long removed by the intervening distance and time.

It's always special to come home, a special time we all remember fondly. I feel special too, because I've been on a journey of the mind, a tourist of consciousness. The people at home - aunties, sisters, grandparents, nephews, school and family friends - are all unified by common life threads which they share. Once I pick up the same threads after a few days, tourist me has unpacked the baggage and I feel "at home" again, as if I'd never left, moulding and shaping myself into the environment and its constituents again. Blending in.

Home and Away is Near and Far. Home cannot be qualified without an Away experience: the further away you go and the longer you're away, the more significant home, the associated people, and its physicalities become. Inherent in the perception of home is an awareness that it is the preferential state, where familiarity is expedient to unfamiliar otherness. This semantic dichotomy stimulates contradictory language, with intrinsic value judgements conveyed in the meanings. The values are embedded in the language which, in turn, is semantically opposite: them and us, good and bad, right and wrong, top and bottom, north and south, front and back, rich and poor, now and never.

Home symbolises many feelings – warmth, security, belonging, truth – and the expression of home is signified in such language as home and dry (definitely safe and successful) ; homely (unpretentious and caring) ; home-made and homegrown (traditional, crafted, genuine); homespun (plain and unsophisticated opinions and philosophies) ; home truths (the cold hard facts told out of concern for another) ; home rule (in charge of your own affairs) ; in the comfort of your own home (the ultimate place of sanctity) and words in the modern lexicon such as homepage (the origin of a web environment, where it all starts) ; homeboy or homie (friend).

"An Englishman's home is his castle." Home is a social construct, relative to disparate socio-cultural systems, and reflective of economic expectations. Compare the trailer parks of the mid-West to the Malibu mansions in the US; the high-rise apartments in Poland, accommodating professionals and factory workers; or the nomadic tribes of the Gobi desert.

Home, with capital 'H', also exists in the consciousness of Humanity – we feel 'homesick' when we first leave our family and familiar environment; exiles feel profound grieve of separation from their homeland and culture, and mild offenders are granted privileges in home-detention.

Semantically, the word "house" gives us dwellings - building for animals, theatre, business operations, halls of residence. But the word "home" brings us family group, birthplace, native habitat, place of origin, safe place, place of assistance. Native, principal and domestic are all adjectives associated with the word "home".

There are so many types of homes throughout the world and they each house a different type of resident. Whether an igloo, a caravan, mudhut, houseboat, apartment, tent, mansion, castle or converted garage, the nature, form and function of any domicile is quantifiable by the socio-economic structure of the cultural community. It shows how stratums of that society live, from the very rich to the very poor. No matter how lowly, the home is the castle, to be protected above all other. Home invasion, therefore, is right up there with personal violation on the serious crime stakes for the very reason that the domestic space is sancrosanct.

In NZ, an increasing number of middle-class baby boomers have a second home for holidaying: little wooden beach huts called the bach. Bach living in 2008 is now the reserve of the privileged strata, since coastal property in this style, however rustic, is reminiscent of past times of inflated innocence, now vastly inflated in price. The majority of wage-earners, however, are struggling to afford one home, which is more often a contemporary brick bungalow compared to the traditional weatherboard and tin roof structure of the 1950s and 60s. The urban environment can be apartment living or the period-style wooden colonial character home. Owning a home is the prime social and financial goal for millions in the developed world and the largest single debt-inducing capital purchase for the middle-classes.

This may sound like a value judgement of the middle-class, to which I belong socially but not culturally: to clarify, my upbringing and life expectations regarding education, employment, travel, and family are socially standard. Yet, personally, I do not exhibit fiscal characteristics of middle-class behaviour in terms of disposable income, expenditure and consumer behaviour, interpersonal customs or milieu. Deductive assumptions about other cultures are common- we don't have a full awareness of another people, but we know we don't share this or that trait. Therefore we feel we know them, based on discernible contrasts and never mind the indiscernible similarities – this attitude is synonymous with semantic polarisation, adapted into stereotypes. Yet, cultural presumptions are made about people based on their living environment and dwelling as it relates directly to social stratosphere and the cultural link is implicit.

How do I know that? For example, I have never lived in a tree house, and I don't know anyone who lives or has been brought up in a tree house. I've never been to the jungle and I've never seen a tree house [other than a makeshift children's one] So whilst I cannot comment with any veracity on who lives in a tree house, I'm sure they don't work in the city, drive an SUV, watch a flat screen TV or send their kids to ballet lessons. More to the point, I know that tree house dwelling is not a recognised structure of European Western culture. I know that because I have similar European cultural mores, milieu and traditions.

Home is a universal notion, modelled by the family unit or a substitute framework of fundamental support. As such, it's an effective starting point for the reader to experience the desecration of the principal familial, social, cultural, spiritual and communal structure in one's Life. Through the narratives of the people in Lockerbie, the reader has access to the pervading ethos of the stories – historically and moving forward, home, family, community relationships, communication and cultural understanding are all that matter. Feelings, thoughts, opinions, beliefs, presumptions and their intrinsic meanings are transmitted through personal life histories of Lockerbie folk. Resident and non-resident, the impact of the disaster on these individuals, and on the wider community, is framed by my commentary on circumstantial aspects of the disaster's legacy, such as the function of ceremonies; flying; faith; family relations; the nature of the community; stress; the stigma of Lockerbie's profile; the Twin Towers disaster, fate and luck and Lockerbie today.

Lockerbie stories tell of the absolute incomprehension of something as alien as hunks of aeroplane and associated detritus falling through the roof of the home from aerospace above, penetrating the security of the family and exposing the self to chaos and despair, inverting life's experience from relatively familiar to discrete. The grief and trauma that followed, dealing with veil of death and destruction as victims and their belongings rained on homes, gardens and streets, together with the shock and upset involved in evacuation from your home and disruption of your routine. The frustrating inability to communicate with family and friends out with the community; the violation of all pre-conceived representations of Christmas and the descending swarm of strangers. To see your wee space on the planet, on the screen and beamed to innumerable other homes across the world. The silence then the noise: the sound of people and busyness was deafening to the quietude of the town and the echo reverberated for a few years.

This is not a comparative study of how the Lockerbie bombing compares to any other disaster, natural or premeditated. By nature, disasters are variously horrific for the people directly and indirectly involved. Writers bang on in superlative style about the worst or the most in connection with Lockerbie. From my experience, the Lockerbie bombing was distinctive because it is the only disaster I have been involved in it. Yet, one of the participants has been a police officer and has witnessed carnage and tragedy on a professional basis, while two of the participants recall the war years of their childhood. Disasters are tragic for all parties drawn into the trauma and, once experienced, mitigating the effects of that trauma becomes the overarching and principal operation. That said, the most I can wish for is that neither my family nor I is drawn into another disaster in life.

This disaster certainly has a duality of form – it was a terrible catastrophe for the people on the ground, but the victims on the aircraft were subject to terrorist action. One superlative can be levelled at the people of Lockerbie – with the exception of the sadness and grief caused by the 11 fatalities in Sherwood Crescent, Lockerbie was the luckiest wee town to survive a crash of that magnitude with the major proportion of residents unharmed.

If you are tucked up in bed right now reading this, or sitting quietly by the fire, rest assured that's the kind of relaxed and homely thing the residents were doing when the implicit structure of their community, and their conscious part in it, was penetrated by winter wind, metal and concrete, soaked with aviation fuel.

The million-to-one likelihood of an aviation disaster of this type, coupled with the odds of it happening in your town, takes it to trillion-billion-to-one. So the juxtaposition of incredible misfortune to be living in Lockerbie at the time, whilst being exceptionally lucky to survive begins its introduction and then you can see the oscillating effect of happenstance on the psyche. Nonetheless, this book is testament to an awareness that the narrators were more than considerably lucky. There is a mismatch of fortune for Lockardians, and it is living with this disharmony that pervades the stories.

The intervening twenty years since the Lockerbie Disaster is a significant period of time in which to forget the circumstances of the events that night in December, 21 1988. It is enough time for a generation of Lockardians to have been born and grown up without living memory of the events of their town. It is enough time for the town itself to alter considerably, in terms of population, capital development or infrastructural decay. Twenty years can be an historical reference point: a stage of the journey along the road, when we can look back to see how far we've come and the type of terrain that has been travelled: a time to check the signposts, uncritically and with full understanding that the road continues on through.

'History repeats' is a common phrase and this is my perspective of how our reality passes through time to inform the present and the future. Oral transmission empowers people with the ownership of their own history in their own words as opposed to an historian who interprets what happened from his academic standpoint, or a journalist who pedals the agendas of the news media agency.

Is it the time lapse that creates historical from contemporaneous, or the importance of the events in the past to the present? Does the fire at the Tower Chip Shop, Lockerbie, in 1973 constitute history? Of the town, certainly, because it was a significant event on the timeline of the community. Yet the Lockerbie bombing was significant to twenty-one countries at a familial, communal, national and international level.

Twenty years allows individuals, the community and the environment to change. As change takes time and time passes, does it follow that the events in Lockerbie that night, and the myriad of consequences and outcomes, become History? One participant describes the approach of History on the contemporaneous past as a "creeping osmosis" [*D. Wilson, personal communication, March 27 2008*]

Barak Obama will be President of the United States of America. The first black president in the history of American politics: his success against the other Democratic presidential candidate, Hillary Clinton, was announced on the news media as history in the making. The question, why is it history? is answered with two substantiations – because he is unique, as the first non-white candidate, and it has never happened before, in the chronological progress of America. Secondly, the racial tensions that marked American history in the 1960s and 1970s have been overcome to the extent that presidential office is open to an ethnicity that was the underclass just 40 short years ago. This is a significant success for American social policy and the American people. It is also significant for the global population since Obama's racial status, as well as his democratic political ideology, could have a direct influence on the policies and directives of the Superpower's administration There may be a sea change in the world, driven by America, which would be in stark contrast to its current reputation. So Obama makes history by being uniquely significant on a familial, communal, national and international level.

The Lockerbie bombing also has a wider geo-political context, the ramifications of which are still debated today. The consequential changes to Scottish judicial procedure and the unique orchestration of the method of legal trial make Lockerbie a significant entry in the chronicles of legislative history. The book on local authority and organisational emergency planning and disaster preparedness has been revised to include the dos and don't in response to the Lockerbie disaster. As a direct result of the disaster, the principal American luxury airline carrier no longer operates. These examples illustrate Lockerbie as a significant historical event, both nationally and internationally; yet for those involved, it was a terrible personal experience and this book gives them voice.

But 1988 was a busy year in History: we stood at the threshold of great changes in Civilization then – peeking through the keyhole on the cusp of a new decade was glasnost and the fall of the Berlin Wall; the first invasion of Iraq by the US; computerised living, and laissez-faire political Conservatism. If you were around then, do you remember, 'Don't Worry, Be Happy' because the song took the Grammy award for the biggest-selling record in the US that year; do you recall that Australia celebrated its bicentenary in 1988? Or that a cruise missile fired from the USS Vincennes shot down at Iranian airliner, IR655, between Dubai and Bandar Abbas in July of that year?

Lockardians had to deal with how our home town fitted into the global timeframe of those events – wee Lockerbie, whom no-one outside of Scotland ever knew about. In the UK at least, along with the Piper Alpha Disaster and the Clapham Rail Junction Crash, it was the news media item of 1988. It catapulted the regional broadcasting of BBC Scotland out of parochial and into the international realm of operations. That may just sounds like words to you right now, but consider this statement after the list of other formidable 1988 international happenings.

On January 1, perestroika, the programme of economic reform, began in the Soviet Union under Mikhail Gorbachev. In February, the Winter Olympics were held in Calgary, Canada. March was a newsworthy month, with Colonel Oliver North and Vice Admiral John Poindexter charged with defrauding the US in the Iran-Contra incident; a Colombian airliner, Boeing 727 crashed into a Venezuelan mountain, and killed 143, and George HW Bush wins the Republican presidential candidacy over Robert Dole.

In April, the movie, *The Last Emperor*, won nine Oscars, and the World Expo was held in Brisbane, Australia. In May, the Soviet Union commenced withdrawal of troops after eight years of fighting in Afghanistan. Nelson Mandela, the then imprisoned ANC leader, celebrated his 70th birthday in absentia at Wembley Stadium.

Mid-year was marked by the Piper Alpha oil rig disaster in the North Sea, killing

167, while on the other side of the world in Malaysia, a ferry terminal bridge collapsed in Butterworth, and more than fifteen hundred people were killed or injured. The 8888 Uprising, on 8th August that year, saw thousands of anti-government protestors killed in Myanmar, while the 'Terminal Man', Mehran Karimi Nasseri, began his 8 year diplomatic detention at De Gaulle Airport in Paris.

The Summer Olympics were held in Seoul, South Korea, in September, and Hurricane Gilbert devastated Jamaica and the Yucatan Peninsula in Mexico. October saw women allowed to study at Magdalene College in Cambridge for the first time ever, and men mourned the change with black armbands. Voters in Pakistan, in November of that year, chose the popular Benazir Bhutta as Prime Minister. The year ended with horrendous loss of life from natural disasters - a cyclone in Bangladesh, that left 5 million people homeless and thousands dead, and the Armenian earthquake, 6.9 on the Richter scale, whose litany of dead, homelessness and injuries reached the hundreds in thousands.

They are important to a concentrically-widening circle of interest as the years pass – some events effected great enjoyment and there is significant nostalgia in revisiting personal memories of past times, events and people, while the new generation can discover the mistakes of the past, hopefully with a fresh perspective.

Yet it is facile to conclude that Lockerbie has a distinctive classification in the history books, in comparison to Obama's ground-breaking achievement. An explanation of divergent social aspects, political viewpoints, economic considerations, cultural expectations, along with emergent generations and their perspectives and the wisdom of retrospection, is required to argue that Lockerbie does not inhabit the same shelf in the archives as Obama. The stories of Lockerbie lives open with a discussion on why that point is academically self-evident but elitist, by considering the nature, form, structure, style, scope and of History: how it has developed in conjunction with Humanity's passing of time, and the different aspects and perspectives of discursive hermeneutics that have developed as Civilization has continued to experience itself. Historiography has advanced from eccleciastical and secular schisms in the past millennia, where philosophical questioning, combined with historical determinism and the human will to progress, has created specialised branches of history to springboard the contemporary age into future advancement.

The key that turns the lock on History is the aspect of human fallibility, symptomatic of Time and its degenerative properties: our capacity to forget, or our failing to remember. History is a cognitive response to human frailty. Memory is derived from consciousness, and the Lockerbie narratives fit within a framework of discussion on how spatial and temporal memory operates in a mutual relationship with history and cultural experience.

The participants' experiences are forged from a system of historiography or historical enquiry that is defined by the nature of their oral and aural transmission. Telling the stories empowers people with the ownership of their personal and communal history, using their voices to express events, feelings, thoughts and significance of meaning, as opposed to an historian interpreting from an external academic standpoint, or a journalist who defines the context to fit the gist of the article. When removed from the commercial engine of the media, or the intellectual dissection of the researcher, the process of narrating stories becomes like chatting over the fence, nattering on the phone or lying on the therapists' couch.

The people's stories have valid integrity since they are sourced, reside in and issue forth from residents and non-residents, whose continuum of consciousness is ever-changing. The stories have been and continue to be recounted today, just as they were recorded in late March and early April 2008. They will form part of Lockerbie individuals' oral tradition of telling stories about their life history including the communal event known as The Lockerbie Disaster. Owing to their status as living memories, and due to the lack of inference by a third party, these transmissions resonate with authenticity: they are a vocal expression of the past, just as the participant is a living embodiment of that same past.

At this juncture in time- 20 years after the event - a retrospective of the events and the intervening two decades could been termed an historical legacy: what is left as a result of past events. Yet these stories are not dried parchments or faded diaries – they emanate from living, sentient, contemporary sources whose organic nature is fluid and robust. I consider this publication, at this time, to be a referential hook on which the historical events of Lockerbie can be hung.

As a community, Lockerbie can share in the guardianship of these stories, yet they are not the definitive history of Lockerbie or the time of the disaster. There is no conclusion to this episode of the town's history – the consequences are limitless. (In addition, the grief of personal loss, the consequences of the Lockerbie Disaster, per se, emit political, legislative and diplomatic outcomes that are not for this book.)

Memories, recollections and stories do not cease; oral accounts become layered, to develop the texture and colour that shapes the fabric and design of the incoming generation of Lockardians, to pick up the threads and to begin their stories.

Background to project

I exhibited a retrospective collection of photographs of the marae [meeting house] complexes of the iwi [tribe] of Whakatōhea in the Eastern Bay of Plenty of New Zealand in 2006. The exhibition comprised old and new photographs of the 8 marae of the tribe. Local people came to see the display in the town centre, and from that came an issuing of stories by elder family members, some never heard by the younger generations. This is a considerable outcome, as Māori is an oral culture, and kōrero [oracy] is part of the kaupapa [custom] and the tikanga māori [Māori cultural tradition].

Simple stories are common-place and they are always there, but not uttered by their owners until an objective voice strikes up the question: Why don't you tell us about..... It's also about people coming together, to share the past and communicate orally, and that happens less and less in the developed world. The Whakatōhea stories had never before been heard because the conditions and circumstances of the photographic exhibition had never before been present, in that style and forum, and presented from that perspective. At the pōwhiri [blessing] for the opening of the display, the kaumātua [elder] of the entire iwi [tribe] commented that the collected display may mark the beginning of the development of a collective iwi archive. He said it took a female non-Māori from Scotland, also tribal in its indigenous socio-historical composition, to collate and assemble images from which kōrero on the history of the complete tribe may emanate. It was a new dynamic.

I listened only. Collation of these stories by me was culturally inappropriate. I was intrigued to instigate a project where oracy was the vehicle, the stories of the past were the driver, and a greater understanding or consolidation of individual and collective consciousness was the destination, and where I had implicit cultural approval to do so. I could do this in no place other than the community from whence I came, that being Lockerbie.

Simple stories are beyond headlines, the counterpoint to sensationalism. The same is true with Lockerbie, as it is with Whakatōhea. There are many simple stories, owned by self-effacing voices, that stay mostly silent because the narrators don't have a reason to share them in the busy world of 2008.

In mid 2007, I was drawn to starting a plan for an oral history project – a series of extensive interviews about living in Lockerbie, then and now, which covered different demographics of the community and built a comprehensive profile of opinion and commentary on this place Lockerbie in this timeframe: the living memory of the chosen narrators. Standing amidst the participants, with commonality of experience, self-deprecation, and historical awareness of the community in Lockerbie, I could juxtapose my physical distance from Lockerbie for the past 22 years with my experiential proximity and relative identity with the participants. This internal standpoint was particularly important to me because the objective of the oral history project was not just to transfer narratives onto tape for perpetuity, but to approach the subject matter with multiple aspects: specifically to achieve strong and resonant, open and detailed narratives through my prior interpersonal connections with the participants.

It has been recognised by the townspeople in Lockerbie that the commemoration this year, to mark the 20th anniversary, will be the ultimate occasion of public acknowledgement of the disaster. Thereafter, memorial activities will be individualised and should allow for personal expressions of remembrance, irrespective of the town and the authorities. My thoughts were similar and I reckoned that this year was the ultimate opportunity to allow the definitive public record on the disaster to rest with the people who know.

The intrinsic value of the stories themselves, as oral historical records, is not their context or the subject - part of the oeuvre of documented accounts on the Lockerbie Disaster - but the distinctive perspective and format in which they were gathered. The people own the experience by laying down their stories so they resonate in years to come, when living memory passes into historical chronicle. The stories were told me as part of known relationship and they were told to me as an insider, a fellow experiencee. That relationship is blended into the speaking and the listening of the narrative – a two-way conversation. The interface laces together the stories surrounding the event and the relationship between aspects of speaking, asking, responding, hearing and understanding that subject matter.

The event of Lockerbie was a one-off occurrence while the stories that surround that event change day to day. Oracy and aurality have been the human mode of remembering and retelling pre-writing. The electronic revolution has created parallel communities in cyberspace to the point where terrestrial reality starts at the familiar sound of the human voice and listens with an inquisitive turn of the head, like a dog hearing a high-pitched inaudibility. The method of using narratives to demonstrate how we handle the passing of time provides a framework on which to develop the factors of time and space in a comparative study of personal ability to remember and the public contrivance to commemorate.

Factual accuracy of the commentary and veracity in the participant's chapters is not my prime concern, nor is it the major aspect of oral history. Subjectivity confers the individual as a medium of historical dialogue and this is what is heard by the oral historian. There is no objectified discourse to be researched and analysed for exactitude. Alessandro Portelli says:

"...oral history has made us uncomfortably aware of the elusive quality of historical truth itself. Yet, an aspiration towards 'reality', 'fact', and 'truth' is essential to our work: though we know that certainty is bound to escape us, the search provides focus, shape, and purpose to everything we do".

To me, the way in which dialogue is constructed from types of memories, and the voice of those remembrances, is the focal consideration. It is the idiosyncracies of memory that makes the stories sparkle.

I could not ignore that the twentieth anniversary of the disaster, a major spike in the town's historical timeline, was approaching, and that a retrospective engagement would be timely and relevant. The subject of the Lockerbie Disaster is full of superlatives and platitudes, while the objective of this project and book is to divorce itself from the usual rhetoric and excessive images. The commonalty speaks, without embellishment or abridgement, and the images have never before been published.

Simplicity has to be the response to an historical retrospective on the disaster – it's been reiterated by the people as their preference of style of commemoration. It is antithetical to the media scrum – one speaker, one voice. Yet the resounding message in the multiple voices resonate more today than ever – home and family are the priority, and let the past be the past, as it naturally is.

The people of Lockerbie are not victims of Fortune – they are variously strengthened or accepting of the experience, or unchanged by it. Their stories are universally recognisable, not by the experiential event but by the feelings, thoughts and meanings expressed by the people, with which we can all relate.

By archiving the oral history project, generations of people will be able to access Lockerbie's history through the words of its people. By collating and publishing the transcripts, generations will be able to share the stories first-hand.

A second volume, to be published in 2009, will deal with the mechanics of this volume's narrative compilation. The methodology of oral history used here, in *An' then the world came tae oor doorstep: Lockerbie Lives and Stories* is discussed in the context of a dialectic on traditional forms of historical research. Chronological history, cultural history and oral history square off to identify the dimensions that each methodology brings to its subject of enquiry. Authenticity and the search for truth pervades all historiographical works: *An' then the world came tae oor doorstep: Lockerbie Lives and Stories*, whilst dealing with first-hand experiences and life histories, is no different in that regard.

Throughout my research and oral history interviews with participants in Lockerbie Lives and Stories, the recurrent question was silently pitched: What do I remember and why? As our memories are subjective until we share them, I began to inquire into aspects of remembering that allows the conscious mind to reconstruct actual time and space that has passed into memory. But what shape do those memories take and will they metamorphose with the passing of time and the layering of experience? The second volume, likely to be called *Dimensions of Historiography and The Consciousness of Memory: Methodology and Research in Lockerbie Lives and Stories* looks at the conscious perception of memory, including false memory; the veracity of first-hand rememberance; the role of memorials in our community, and the vital conditions of time and space for perceiving the past.

Jill Haldane,
Levin, New Zealand
October 2008

Te Riaki AmoAmo, elder of Whakatōhea tribe of east coast, New Zealand, outside his ancestral marae (meeting house) named Tutamare after the father of the hapu (sub-tribe)

An old pre-railway print of the centre of the town. Horse Market Street is known today as Bridge Street because of the railway bridge built across the lines in the late 1840s. The post in the centre is the thief's muckle post, as mentioned in the town's declaration. (© Dumfries and Galloway Regional Council, 2008)

The High Street looking south, between 1889 and 1922, when the War Memorial was erected. (© Dumfries and Galloway Regional Council, 2008)

High Street, Lockerbie.

Lockerby Toon

***Extracts from* Lockerbie and the Surrounding Area through the Ages**
John H D Gair, Dryfesdale Lodge Visitors' Centre Trust, n.d.

Today, Lockerbie and the environs comprise of small townships and villages, with farms and smallholding scattered in the pastoral countryside. The largest town in the district in Dumfries, 12 miles to the south west, located on the River Nith. Lockerbie lies in the rolling Annandale valley, before the land rises to the steeper southern upland hills of Moffat and Beattock. The Esk Forest flanks the area to the east, heading over to the rugged Border country of Hawick and Langhom. [Gair, n.d.p.10] 10 miles to the south is the town of Annan, on the river Annan, and 15 miles away is Gretna Green and its town, famous for its blacksmith anvil, over which eloping English couples were wed. A few miles further down the M74 - the English border.

Like much of the northern parts of Britain, Lockerbie has historical links to the Roman period of invasion and settlement, in the form of encampment sites and forts. Hadrian's Wall is to the south of Lockerbie and the Antonine Wallis to the west.

Evidence of Roman settlements in the form of forts and campsites still remain in the region and the Romans carried out raiding parties against the Caledonian people, and the Picts, in the proceeding two hundred years; for example, the distinctive flat hilltop of the Burnswark hill is a former Roman site and hillfort of significant archaeological interest [*Gair, p.8*] .

In the early 1100s, the Lord of Annandale was Robert be Brus. There was a cluster of such de Brus support and corresponding manor houses with moats around the Lockerbie area: the Johnstone, the Jardine and the Corrie families all occupied timber mottes [Gair, P.10] The Johnstone family line continued to predominate in the Annandale district, building considerable tower houses to honour their status as chiefs of Annandale. A Johnstone tower house in Lockerbie was removed to provide a building site for the new police station in 1967 [Gair, p.13] The Johnstones became earls in the district and baronets in Nova Scotia, Canada [*ibid*]

The Locards or Lockharts are thought to have been supporter of the de Brus lairdship at the end of the 12th century. They were gifted land in the Annandale valley; antecdotally, they occupied a laird's motte or a working farm on the ridge of contemporary Mains Street in Lockerbie. Epistemologically, the place name of Lockerbie may originate from "Locardebi", likely to mean the farm of Locard or Lockhart. [*ibid*]

A slightly different derivation sees the name, 'Lokardebi' first recorded around 1300, and thought to be an old Norse word, meaning Loki's village.

" By 1750 Lockerbie had become a significant town, and by the 1780's was a staging post on the carriage route from Glasgow to London. During the 1700's agriculture was also important to the town's development and Lockerbie held Scotland's largest lamb market. Lockerbie grew rapidly after the construction of Telford's Glasgow to Carlisle Road in 1818. And from 1847 the Caledonian Railway brought further growth and increased the scale of the town's crossborder sheep trade. The railway also brought access to cheaper coal enabling a gas works to be built in 1855."

The Census in 2001 accounted for 4009 people resident in Lockerbie. Indicated industrial activity in Lockerbie favoured the manufacturing or the wholesale/retail sectors, with most people claiming skilled trades or elementary skills occupations. Seven years ago, the majority demographics were the over 60 year olds and the 25-44 age range. The weekly income then was three thousand pounds sterling lower than the average Scottish weekly income, with just slightly less than the mean Scottish average going on to higher education from Lockerbie.

Extracts from Recollection of Lockerbie

Thomas Henderson, 1937, The Herald Press, Lockerbie,

Thomas Henderson was a solicitor and he wrote autobiographical accounts of his early life and days spent as a resident of the town, just after the Crimean War in the late 1850s, until the 1880s. It is entitled Recollections of Lockerbie, and was published in 1937, in the town by The Herald Press. It provides a first-person narrative on society, culture, working life, and the operations of the town in Lockerbie. One aspect of life that Mr Henderson doesn't mention is religion and the Church.

Mr Henderson's lawyers office operated in 1904 from Station Road. Henderson Solicitors still operate in Lockerbie today.

The spirit that drove the people in those days is embodied in a proverb of Mr Henderson's liking:."Whatsoever thy hand findeth to do, do it with all thy might." He says it was cheap to live but money was scarce.

I have paraphrased to a minimum from Mr Henderson's memories.

Disasters

The Quintinshill Rail Disaster at Gretna occurred on 22 May 1915, killing 227 and injuring 246. A signalman's error allowed the the 7TH battalion Royal Scots train to collide with the stationary Euston to Glsagow midnight express.

"The disaster caused a big sensation in the town, was remembered and talked about for a long time afterwards." [p.1]

He remembers a huge gail in December 1883 which decimated many trees in the Murrayfield wood and blew glass, slates and chimney cans about the streets. There was a prolonged effect on forestry trading due to glut of timber that resulted from the storm.

Transport and Roads

Transport was by horse. At the Bluebell Inn on the High Street, there were 40 horses available for hire and same at Kings Arms. On market day, there would be 200 horses in the town.

The roads were primitive and very bad. Carters repaired the roads with stones from ploughed fields which was employment for men and horses. Stone gatherers were called stone knappers – they broke up the stones and used them to fill in the pot holes. Stone knappers would build the gathered stones into a square heap, which was then measured by the surveyor and the men were paid by the yard. Broken stones were spread onto declining parts of the road so roads were rough and travelling was slow.

During the Winter, the mud on the High Street was a problem:

"[T]he scavenger used a broad two-handled clat mounted on two wheels. By dropping the handle, the clat was raised and rolled to one side of the street, then lowered and the mud dragged to the other side. Before it was carted away, woe betide the unsuspecting innocent who stepped into a mud heap on a dark night. One lady from a castle in the district ... once remarked that she would require to stop shopping in Lockerbie as the mud on the street was so deep, it was almost impossible to cross to the other side." [p.4]

In the Summer, prior to tarring, clouds of dust blew in the dry weather, so shopkeepers and residents had to keep windows shut.

When cycling, Mr Henderson had to dismount and carry his bike over the road. He had a penny farthing as a child; "It took considerable courage to ride these high bicycles as spills had to be expected. Mounting and dismounting were by means of a step on the back of the frame. It was quite common to mount with the aid of a wall ..." [p.3]

Safety bicycles "... had wheels of the same size with solid tyres which were fixed to the rim with shellac." [*ibid*] The tyres kept falling off. It was a revelation to ride to Dumfries and back on the same day with the safety bicycle, with cushioned tyres on a cross-frame. Then the pneumatic tyre was invented but easy to puncture until the road roller was invented and smoothed out the roads.[*ibid*]

Horses were frightened by bikes because they cyclists used to ring their bells to indicate overtaking of carts and carriages. Cyclists could be prosecuted for not doing so, as could the owners of threshing mills, should a man not outside the mill with a red flag, to assist drivers with frightened horses.

The layout of the town

Merchants lived beside their premises, with bells on shop doors alerting to customers entering the shop, for example, Mr Hall, the shoemaker, and Mr Frank Carruthers, the architect. The streets were poorly-lit, and Jimmy Patterson was the burgh's scavenger who lit the gas lamps. He carried a ladder with hooks attached which rested on the crossbars of the short lamp posts. Jimmy had to light each lamp separately and must have gone through a lot of matches on windy lights Pavements, where they existed, were cobbled with bulletstones and rough to walk on. Candles were still used and made locally. Several large fires altered the look of High Street as cottages burnt down.

The tannery at Netherplace Loaning gave off an offensive smell. There had been a brewery in the Crown Court area of town but it hadceased to operate.

The market was one of the most prominent in Scotland, operating constantly from 10.30 in the morning, till 4 or 5 in the evening. Mr Watret had the market in Crown court. The auctioneer was Mr Smith and his nephew, Mr Smith-Dalgleish.. William Kirpatrick-Annan and Mr Hsylop-Stapleton bought the market in 1901 when Mr Watret passed away.

Mr Harrison had plans for field market in Sydney Place but not enough trade for two markets in the town so MrKirkpatrick-Annan sold to Mr Harrison for 6,800 pounds. There was a proposal to have two market days, fat stock market on Saturdays and butter,eggs and general business on Thursdays. This was a contentious decision and town meetings were held, with the ultimate decision to retain Thursday as market day.

The General market was in the market hall of the town hall. Post wagonettes ran to outreaching areas, fetching people into the town and returning them back in the evening. Trains from Beattock, Carlisle and Dumfries arrived in Lockerbie about 10am on Thursdays and there was a great number of people to market.

There were lots of drunks on market day as whisky was strong and cheap.

There were five blacksmiths, 3 saddlers and 3/4 cloggers in the town, all very busy with trade. Harness was only for hunting horses. Shops sold fishing tackle and grain at 20/26 High Street. There were mechanical looms at Ecclefechan and a weaving mill at Sibbalbie, Duncan Campbell was the proprietor. There was no hnad-weaving then and individuals sent wool and yarn there to be woven into material.

Cheese factory employed lots of people, as did the bacon curing factory and coach building. Mr Thomsons coachworks manufactured laundauns, broughams, phaetons and dog carts. [Note: the original features and outbuildings at our old premises of 42 Mains Street catered for passing coaches and stabled the accompanying horses]

It was a small town when he was boy. There was no Leanard Terrace or Sherwood Park. The Cow Company field was used for grazing the stock of individual households. Kintail Park was a grazing park.. Hay was grown on each side of Dumfries Road, and carried in forkfuls onto the street, for the cows and horses.

There was a public water well with a railing round, half way up Bridge Street. Most houses had a private well in the garden connected by a pump in the back kitchen. The filter beds were opened in 1886 to introduce public supply of water to the town. The sewage drain took waste water from streets and houses, and when flooding occurred, it contaminated the water of Duke of Buccleugh's tenants and stock. The Duke won an action over the town council, to force the laying of another drain for fresh water past the sewage works.

The Town Hall was built in 1888/89, at a cost of 10 thousand, two hundred pounds, in the Scottish Baronial Style. The foundation stone was laid by Sir Robert Buchanan-Jardine, laird on the Castlemilk Estate. It was opened in 1891 as a celebration of the jubilee of Queen Victoria in 1887. The town was in debt for two thousand pounds when it was complete so a bazzar, opened by Princess Louise, was organised to raise money and clear the debt. One thousands pounds was left over so the town bought the Lambhill area of the town for development.

Social Life

The Curling Club on the Quaas Loch was well patronised and convenient to the west of the town – it was used by curlers and skaters alike. An ice house stood near Quaas Loaning: "during frosty weather when hewers could not hew stones, they were out of work and other tradesmen were thrown of out work also." [Henderson, 1937: P.7] Curlers and paddock owners fell out and privilege of flooding the paddock at the Quaas was rescinded. Skating and curling continued at Lochside in Lochmaben, but the Curling Club as never the same after leaving the Quaas Meadows.

Sledging and tandem riding was outlawed in the town, on Bridge Street and at top of Lambhill because it made the streets slippery for horses.

There was lots of coal. The slogan ran *Burn Coal and Help the Miners.* Miners worked in squads with a weekly gaffer and lots of money. The ash pits attacted a lot of flies and carters were employed to take ashes to the dump once a year.

As a source of amusement, boys would hide in a close by the shop, to play tricks on the merchants shutting up shop. There were shutters across the doors with cross iron bar, bolts and pin. The boys would withdraw the bolts and merchant had to come back out of the premises and draw the bolt again. Similarly, boys inserted stone or wood between snib and cottage handle, then knock and bolt. When the householder exited the house, the door would slam shut and lock out the individual.

Nutmeg was used to flavour tea and as a cure for rheumatism.

Fresh-air time from lessons at school allowed the children to run to the fields and put pins on the railway, which were then flattened by the passing train into small swords. During the break, they might run to Muirhead Farm, and slide on the duckpond in the Winter.

The Lamb Fair and the annual hiring market was the largest event on Lockerbie's calendar. There were stalls selling pies, gingerbread, sweets, cheap watches, jewellery, toys and skipping ropes, and other produce. Young children expected a 'fairing' or a present from the fair. Crockery merchants entertained the crowd by throwing plates and catching them. By afternoon, the market square would be dense with people hoping to be hired for work. A man looking for employment kept a straw in themouth and women wore one in the bonnet. There was visiting friends, and a fair at top of the town. Mr Henderson remembers such a dense crowd that horses and cart couldn't get through.

Lockerbie didn't attract knife and scissor grinders in the streets or concertina players with monkeys or dancing bears. There were no German bands of musicians peddling at this time [the 1880s] because foreigners raised suspicion: " When they appeared it was said to be as sure sign of forthcoming rain. In later years, many, on looking back, were quite satisfied in their own minds, that they were composed of spies." [p.15]

There is a story as documented by Helen S Mc Arthur, in *A Historical Walk through Lockerbie* [1989, p. 1] that supports this view:

"One day, long ago, when charity to the poor was held to be one of the duties of every Christian, an old beggar man came walking down the dusty road towards a struggling line of cottages. He was hungry and thirsty and hoped for relief, not in the from of money, for that was very scarce commodity, but, perhaps a bannock or some oatcake and a cup of buttermilk. He passed down the rows od houses, knocking on every door, and at every door, he was sent away without even a cup of water from the well. When he reached the last house, he received the same answer, as the housewife was closing the door in his face, he cried out, "What kind of place is this?" Are there nae Christians in it?" The lady paused for a moment, then replied, "Na', there are nae Christians in Lockerbie, just Johnstones and Jardines", then closed the door.

Daily Life

It was a long day of work, with the town hall bell ringing at 6am and 6pm, respectively, to mark the start and the end of the day's toil.

The lower part of the butchers doors kept dogs out. Postmen walked or used gigs and there was a delivery of letters on Sunday mornings. Warning the toon of a death by the gravedigger was superseded by funeral notices or letters. The church bell tolled as funeral procession went to church, and the toll number differed for men and women. Females wore full mourning dress while males wore a band round the arm.

The County was divided into districts, with district councils electing representatives to act on the County council. Lockerbie District Council Committee had representatives from 11 parishes; "Local matters received much more personal attention than they do now. The schools were inspected by one of the local ministers before the school holidays." [p.11/12]

Peter Hills and Hannah Hills *née* Gass

These are memories of Peter Hills and Hannah Hills, nee Gass, on 22 March 2008. Mrs Hills is a Lockardian and Mr Hills is originally from London. This is their story of Lockerbie life.

Hannah was a member of the Gass family. Her mother was Martha Gardener, born in 1884 in Dornach near Glasgow, and her Father was the first gravedigger in Lockerbie. They lived in Dryfe Lodge, the gravediggers cottage, now the site of the Lockerbie Visitors Centre. Hannah was one of 12 children. Her grandfather was bitten by a rabid dog on the way to church and died.

Hannah was born in Well Street in 1927. She remembers the market behind the Kings Arms, at Victoria Court. When it was wet, her mother sent the children to the market, to get out the house. There were tiered seats at the back and they used to go to the back and watch the cattle.

On Sundays, the family walked to the duck pond, and around the cemetery. After 10 years of perfect attendance at Sunday school, her siblings got a bible, but she had only 8 years perfect attendance because she had a broken shoulder for 6 months. She got six pence every Saturday for cleaning her Father's boots and her three brothers' boots too. One of her brothers was an electrician and the other two were plumbers.

She remembers being in the parade for the Gala, sitting on an ice-cream barrow when she was 4 years old. Hannah recalls sliding down the ice during the winter on

Well Street, which is on a steep hill. One friend would stand at the bottom as lookout for the police, shouting A.B.C - *A Bobby Coming* -at the sight of a copper.

Peter Hills comes from London originally but came to Lockerbie with the Black Watch battalion during the war. He was based down at Kettleholm as a holding battalion going abroad. Each Saturday afternoon, the Pipe band played for the locals and there were dances three times a week. Peter and Hannah met at one of the dances and were married in 1946, aged 19 years old. The Black Watch was disbanded in 1946 and Peter was demobbed in 1947.

The town gifted a mace to the sergeant major of the Pipe Band for all the free Saturday concerts but the mace remained in his possession. When he died, it was returned to the people of Lockerbie and put on display in the Legion Club rooms.

Peter went on a rehabilitation bakery course after he was demobbed and worked for Wilson's Bakery for 20 years until the dual carriageway was built, at which time Peter feared less trade to the town and changed his career to the I C I factory from which he finally retired only 4 years ago.

Peter was the founding chairman of the Mid Annandale FC, 50 years ago. The *Mids* won the Dumfries Football League in the 1970s. Peter is still active in the club and he donated surplus soccer tops to a football team in Sierra Leone, where his niece worked for the V S O.

The couple were in the Friendship Group after the disaster, and befriended the relatives of a victim of the disaster, whose body is marked by the cross at the top of the Golf Course. They went to visit the family in America in 1991, visiting Boston and Nashville, and they routinely send e-mails and Christmas cards.

Their family still lives in Lockerbie.

To the east of the town, the distinctively flat hilltop of Burnswark fills the horizon.

The old sandstone school building, now used as council premises.
(© James Haldane, 2008)

Alternative energy regeneration in the form of wind turbines, in the hills to the north-east of the town. (© James Haldane, 2008)

The new school, that will combine both primary and secondary, is under construction this year, 2008.

The High Street in Lockerbie serves the community.

The old cheese factory on Park Place. Express Foods opened the current cheese factory in 1975, between Lockerbie and Lochmaben.

The much-used ice rink in Lockerbie.

Princess Alexandra, Queen Victoria's duaghter, opened the Lockerbie Bazaar, to raise funds for the financial overspend accrued in building the Town Hall in 1889.
©Dumfries and Galloway Regional Council, 2008

The duckpond at Muirhead has given generations of pleasure to Lockardians.

The ubiquitous coffee morning, in aid of the Riding of the Marches (ROM) with an example of run-down premises in the background.

Tesco Town is the pseudonym awarded to Lockerbie by some citizens.
It certainly dominates the landscape's vista.

Chronology

Many readers, owing to age or geographical location at the time in 1988, may not be aware of the background to the crash. These are the events and data that preceded the downing of the Pan Am Boeing 747, *Clipper Maid of the Seas*, at 7.03pm on 21st December 1988.

The aeroplane originally flew from San Francisco to Heathrow Airport in London on the 21st December and parked at the terminal, in readiness for Pan Am Flight 103 to Detroit later that evening. This also included 47 of the 89 passengers flying in from Frankfurt in Germany to London, then transferring to 103 for the flight to JFK Airport in New York.

On board were 243 passengers and 16 crews. It was supposed to depart at 18.00 from Heathrow but a rush hour delay meant a departure time of 18.25. The flight pattern for American flights from London follows north then takes a right turn over the Irish Sea, then over the Atlantic Ocean.

At 17.00, Flight 103 entered Scottish airspace, and was cleared to begin the Atlantic leg of the journey. At approximately 17.03, the aircraft disappeared from the Scottish Area Control Centre radar screen at Prestwick, 25 miles from Glasgow.

Up in the sky, the explosion from the bomb punched a half metre hole in the left side of the fuselage. The bomb was made of Semtex and concealed within a radio cassette player. Part of a timer's circuit board was also recovered as charred material.

After three seconds, the nose of the aeroplane separated from the body section. The flight control system in the fuselage was shaken by initial shock waves from the blast, and met Mach stem shock waves - impulses from the first explosion – which intensify the original force and its effect. The front section of the fuselage began to pitch and roll.

The roof peeled away and the resulting change in air pressure caused the lungs of the passengers to swell by four times the breathable pressure and then collapse. If not fixed down, people and objects were blown out of the aircraft into the atmosphere. Some passengers were still strapped in their seats on impact with houses in Lockerbie.

The cockpit, the fuselage and the No. 3 engine continued, propelling forward and down; from 6000 metres, it plummeted straight to the ground. Whilst falling, the fuselage broke up, with the wings full of aviation fuel falling on Sherwood Crescent. The resulting fire completely obliterated several houses with everything and everyone in them, consumed the plane itself, and caused a huge impact crater, 47 metres long and a volume of $560m^3$. 21 houses in the crescent had to be demolished. The passenger section fell on the Rosebank area of the town. The cockpit fell in the countryside, at the Tundergarth hamlet a few miles out of Lockerbie. One engine fell in the road of a housing estate in the north east of the town, one fell in the yard of the farm opposite the petrol station to the south of the town, and the other engine fell in the field behind my granny's house.

In early December, the Federal Aviation Administration [FAA] had issued a security warning on all Pan Am flights from Frankfurt to America for the following two weeks, after a call to US Embassy in Helsinki in Finland, detailing that associates of the Abu Nidal organisation would plant a bomb on a Finnish female passenger.

It was an anonymous call, yet it was taken seriously enough by American officials to warn US embassies throughout the world of the threat. The FAA sent the warning to US airline carriers and to Pan Am. In Moscow, the US embassy, journalists and businessmen all knew of the warning, and cancelled their flights on 103, leaving empty seats that were sold cheaply at standby rates.

The day after the bombing, a hard copy of the AAI security warning was found at the Frankfurt Pan Am office the day, under a pile of papers [Cox and Foster, 1992].

A Flavour of the Narratives

Thematic tasters allow the reader to sample salient quotes and get the flavour of the narratives and their stylistic content, while providing a type of theme index. It allows the reader to pre-profile the participants based on their narrative strengths. This is by way of a signpost, where the reader decides which direction to take in the book.

The one unifying action and thought of all participants, and their family and friends caught up in the disaster, was to go to their loved ones, or attempt to communicate with them, to ensure their safety. Similarly, after the event, the over-arching feeling of all the narrators was relief for their family's well-being. In light of the narrow escape from the devastation of the Pan Am airliner, there was a resultant understanding as well as empathy by the townspeople for the bereaved families.

Ella Ramsden

We were all — we're a very happy family. My dad was a very, very loving man and he loved us and — we used to go and meet him, the three of us nearly every night from work ... my Mother didnae show her feelings just so much but she was a hard working woman and we were well brought up in a loving family.

She was so kind-hearted, my grandmother. I mean, it was — she was — when I was very small we had people come round the town, regularly, singing, you know, my granny called them the Gaan people, because they were always goin'. The Gaan people, and my granny went out and spoke to them as if they were bosom pals and if she had soup on the go they got this — she fed them. She just was so kind that that was the type of thing she did

Oh, most important thing in my life, I just love them to bits, and I never stop telling— you know that was what I never told ye; when the place was falling down about me and I said I, all I could see were my three children in my mind, they were as plain as can be, and you know I said out loud, "I never tell them I love them."

Jane Crawford

Obviously it said that the plane had crashed and blah blah blah, but I think what — you were more — I was more concerned with was obviously whether my family were hurt. I mean, if the whole town was on fire, how could they possibly be alive, if that really was the case.

Mary Smith

"I think we just sat, and I roamed about near a telephone...No phones in Lockerbie... Long night....Phoning Jane was just awful; we could hardly speak to each other some of the times.... I think it was about 11.45pm when Jane phoned to say you were all safe."

Of the 12 participants featured in the book, only 2 of them have considered Faith to be an aspect of coping with the disaster. The majority of interviewees, rather than having a change of belief as a result of the disaster, were not inherently religious as a matter of routine behaviour.

Helen Fraser

It's a very difficult thing, because your questioning, questioning all the time, why the hell did this happen? you know, but then good things happen to bad people all the time, and faith has absolutely nothing to do with belief and understanding, faith is just about, Faith, its not something you can see or touch or prove

Alan Thomson

No, never found no religion, never found [Alan chuckles] nothing. Jist get on wi' it! Jist get on wi' it, that's it

Yvonne and James Haldane

We didn't really go very much to church because of having the shop, six days a week, and on the seventh day, we didn't rest [Yvonne laughs] ,we laboured.

John Gair

I think I have become more and more [pause] agnostic, I suppose ...it's been a cumulative effect

The transience of human existence was brought home to us that night. Faced with the circumstances, the difference between living and dying appears to be random and laiden with happenstance. The participants have variously dealt with this notion.

Helen Fraser

Much later on when it came to things like that kids 21st's and things, I did think we had big parties for both of them, big dressy parties, and I, my thinking was, we very nearly weren't here, so let's have things to remember.

Marjory McQueen

You realise that a nanosecond, you might not have been here and that's got to make a difference and yeah I do; you know, life's for living, enjoy everyday as if it's your last because one of these days you'll be right.

Alan Thomson

A've made ma' philosophy from it happen'd, Well, A've jist gotta get on wi it and that's my philosophy in life; whatever—ye don't see gold medallists runnin; backwards, know what A' mean, so ye jist keep getting' on wi' it.

One of the media angles on Lockerbie was the collective response by the townspeople to the disaster clean-up and effort to host the town's visitors. Look behind the headlines and see that not everyone was comfortable mucking in.

Alan Thomson

I think the council have made a good job, whoever was involved in the memorial part of Dryfesdale cemetery have done a really good job; that has been one o' the pluses to it … Some o' the stuff they huvnae got right; I think that's one o' the things they have got right.

Ella Ramsden

I think it all started very voluntary, there's people can do certain things and there's people can do other things and you know there was a squadron of ladies — I don't know how long after — went into the library and replied to every letter that came in.

John Carpenter

As far as the community was concerned, the other aspect of it was, they should be given a lot of credit for it and they are in certain respects, they *did* want to do their piece and they did it by working in the centre, in the school, by photocopying and providing tea and biscuits and cooking.

Marjory McQueen

The local council and the regional council at that time, there was a double layer, and I think they had to be congratulated in the manner in which they dealt with the situation; a very small council, a very small police force; I think they were absolutely magnificent; and I; and I wouldn't hear a word said against them.

Less than 50% of the participants had a negative reaction to air travel. Personally, my fears about flying get worse as I get older. But 100% of us are philosophical about it. If it goes wrong in the air, you are History!

Dave Wilson

I didnae step intae one till aboot two years ago. I would not get on.
I would not get on the plane!

John Carpenter

I mean to say, you've just as much chance getting involved in an accident with a car as you have with a plane you know. I think, relatively, airline safety is pretty good.

Yvonne and James Haldane

Yvonne: I think the attitude, my attitude is, if that's the way you're gonna go, you'll go quickly.

James: Yes, yes, and that's the way it is.

Yvonne: That's it.

There is a lot to be gained from public expressions of grief – they communicate respect and share a great individual burden amongst the collective. There was political representation at Lockerbie commemorations that didn't suit us all, and Time has mellowed the need to memorialise. The prevailing ethos about the twentieth anniversary is unanimous amongst the narrators – simple, understated and final.

Alan Thomson

Went tae the memorials, went up the street tae the, tae the—because I actually ended up in the picture house one wi' a' the people ... and we did oor bit coz that's the only way o' payin' respects really at the end o' the day.

James Haldane

I think something for the children [pause] something for the children [pause] that involves the school: all the, all the, all the things that are organised nowadays never seems to involve the school ... and I think that's wrong because that's losing the community spirit.

Adam Brooks

What I really like was done by Professor Larry Mason and he made a mural, photographic mural of Lockerbie ...I thought was really nice as well, but that commemorates sort of the links between Syracuse and Lockerbie ...is highlighting that from bad things can come good things, and the links to the town are a good thing, and having the pictures sort of shows happier times at Lockerbie. That's something I like

John Carpenter

I think the facility should be there for the people closely connected if they wish in, whether it's a commemorative service or something like that. I don't think there should be any obligation on individuals.

John Gair

But last year or the year before we commissioned Solway quilters to produce a symbolic quilt to be used to mark the twentieth anniversary. And all being well, we should get it for display in October.

The prevalent culture of fear takes many forms – political, ethnic, financial, consumer, pharmaceutical, biological. Some of the narrators had viewpoints on current terrorist policies and activities. But again, it's been a factor for us since way before 9/11, with the Lockerbie bombing and the IRA. The participants acknowledge it's bigger than them and Life most assuredly goes on.

Adam Brooks

Terrorism is going to be here probably for a long time, perhaps the entirety of my life, so you can't really restrict yourself because of it.

Dave Wilson

I cannae get inside the heads o' people who get involved in that kindae thing and I wish I could, you know, but I just don't understand where they're coming from; it seems so random and so on

John Gair

Well the thought of a bomb doesn't bother me, because, well, for a long time we lived with the nuclear balance...I suppose it induced a certain sense of fatalism

The issue of the look of the town was a hot topic when I was in Scotland, conducting interviews. The buildings in the town may not appear at their best but criticism from afar and comments from the outside are not constructive or welcome. The interviewees all agree that it's a national problem for provincial towns in the UK. But unlike other small towns, the glare of international will be focused on Lockerbie in December this year, and what impression will people get?

Dave Wilson

Shifts in commercial and retail operations have put Lockerbie in the same position as every other small and medium-sized town; its not by any stretch of the imagination specific to Lockerbie, and [pause] as far as I can see, its actually thriving.

Marjory McQueen

I don't see anything different from Lockerbie than any small town I go to. They've *all* got their good and bad sides; but invariably I think the people who live here are fairly *happy*; about living in this area.

Ella Ramsden

I remember Lockerbie when it was a beautiful town and, I mean, I could sit here now and tell ye every shop that was in Lockerbie, I mean, the grocer's shops and things like that. I mean, it's true what people say – big supermarkets take over the wee shops

Jill Haldane

Lockerbie is the same as it *ever* was, but on the other hand, it's the same as it *never* was because fellow Lockardians; well, some lost a lot – everything - and some had cause to gain a considerable amount.

Despite the heartless reputation of news media, the testimonies show that there was room for individual integrity amongst some, but by no means all, of the reporters. There is feeling that the media were doing their job, and there are feelings of upset and betrayal. One participant developed a flair for journalism during the disaster that carries on today.

Mary Smith

I still feel it's wrong to have TV footage … so quickly, before anyone knew what was happening to the people at the scene. And afterwards I feel anger and revulsion at the intrusive TV coverage when compassion was what was needed.

James Haldane

I wasn't [laugh] very keen to talk to them, no, especially when one camera crew tried to take photographs from the inside of the shop out the way, through the broken windows and what-have-you.

Alan Thomson

They jist ta'en over – ye' know, you'd come out, they'd be sittin' down the yard phonin' or they'd be doin' whatever and they were jist—huvnae got a lo' o' respect for them really because I think they were only lookin' for what they could get

Dave Wilson

If you picked up *The Annandale Herald* and read the comment there, ye'd be pretty close to the way people were feelin' coz it was—the vox pox were definitely local and so on. I thought they did well,

John Carpenter

They weren't too bad, it was self-regulatory in a lot of respects, in that, you gave them limited access to certain areas so they could take a few pictures [..] and they circulated that amongst themselves and it worked pretty well.

After the coverage by international media, the world and its wife knew about our wee toon. That can be difficult to square in your head, or in some cases, the conscious awareness of tiny-cog-in-gigantic-wheel was forever the levelling factor. Being on the big screen didn't change anything for some of us because, by 1989, Lockerbie was yesterday's news to all but those closely connected with ongoing affairs. Now, generational change allows The Lockerbie Disaster to slip, not into ambiguity, but onto the History shelves.

Dave Wilson

It used to be—people's faces used to change, and you used to think, Och, no, don't have a collection for us [both chuckle] but its okay now, its never a—but its just one of the things that never *bothered* me.

Jane Crawford

They say, "Were you there?" They always usually know where they were and what they were doing, so you probably don't always want to get into that conversation with everyone ...it makes them think of you differently, I think. They think of you as — they associate you with that place rather than look at you as an individual person in your own right.

Adam Brooks

[In Australia] , [t] hey said, Oh, where are you from? I said, "From Lockerbie". They said, Good place for planes! Because they want to ask questions. At Syracuse obviously every time you say you are from Lockerbie, because as I say, you are there to broadcast it. So, you must say you're from Lockerbie and you don't get that sort of – perhaps, ill-considered response.

Jill Haldane

I think I have since then—since the disaster, I have been quite reticence to tell people where I come from, because of the stigma that it now has.

People arrive on this Earth with all manner of inherited ethnic and cultural baggage. Belonging and identity can be contentment in feeling 'at home' rather than inherited lineage. A quarter of the participants are at least third generation Lockardians, and a further quarter were born in Lockerbie. The remaining half of the narrators came to live in the town from outlying townships or the central belt of Scotland. They all have Scottish ancestry.

John Gair

I haven't really let it bother me. I'm very happy to live in Lockerbie, but I have obvious connections with Dumfries, and I like being able to go to Carlisle or Edinburgh, Glasgow or occasionally further afield. So as I say I'm perfectly happy to live in Lockerbie.

Marjory McQueen

Oh I wouldn't be allowed to presume; no no; having been here about thirty six years; no I don't think I could presume to call myself a Lockardian; no I think you have to be about seventeen generations really before you get that title. I'm a lover of Lockerbie [laughs] but I couldn't call myself a true Lockardian.

Jill Haldane

Whilst I always identify myself as being Scottish, and definitely proud to be *that*, I don't generally consider my identify as a Lockardian and I don't feel any sense of pride, or *otherwise*

Helen Fraser

I never wanted to leave Lockerbie, *ever*, and all my friends did, all my friends couldn't *wait* to get away; oh they hated it and they didn't want to be there, but I never wanted to leave, *ever*, no. I would never have left if I had had my own choice

Jane Crawford

I was always quite proud of the fact, I suppose, that I had had a kind of local comprehensive education and it had been fine for me. I'd got on well with it ... I always felt quite proud that ...I was just as good as everyone else.

The characteristics of Lockardians

Dave Wilson

I was surprised at the difference, which was not based, so far as I could see, on any merit, and I just found that— it made me uneasy. And I knew that people could be very, very kindly to people who worked for them and fallen on hard times. ...But the assumption that [Dave chuckles] that because maybe somebody'd inherited something, they were therefore entitled to deference?...; I met any number of, for example, titled people, say, many were [inaudible] people, but it was the automatic deference, I though', What's going on here? So it took a wee while.

John Gair

I mean, Lockerbie is fairly well noted for apathy. Have you ever read the Reverend J.C. Steem's Third Statistical Account? Well it's worth it. Because he wrote that somewhere about 1950, probably early fifties, and he described it as a sleepy hollow, where all sorts of things are started, but usually local interest doesn't last very long.

Helen Fraser

I don't know, cause Lockerbie's a funny place: I mean, I can never get past the fact that people were stepping over bodies to go to the bingo, you know, that was kind of the stories at the time, and I could believe it; I mean there was some people I know who would not indeed give up the bingo for anything, and[pause] you know, there would be folk, oh, what a lot of fuss, they want to forget about it

Marjory McQueen

I wouldn't imagine; and I may be terribly wrong; but I wouldn't imagine that this wouldn't be the sort of place where somebody would die and nobody would noticed. You know, you hear horrible things about a body has lain for so long; I would hope that's not the type of place Lockerbie is.

Jill Haldane

Homogeneity, I think, makes Lockerbie what it is: its strength lies in its internal machinations, and the way it works internally.

All the participants felt disgust and disbelieve at the images of the airliners careering into the World Trade Centre: not because they came from Lockerbie, but due to the indiscriminate nature of the ensuing carnage and loss of Life. One participant mourns the needlessness of such actions and, despite post 9/11 rhetoric, the feeling is still ever thus.

Marjory McQueen

I had the television on and then this news flash came up; and of course it; it interested me because my son and daughter were in New York and where due to fly home that very day; and we watched it unfold and when the other members of the committee arrived we all just gathered around the television and looked at it; and of the nine people, two of us had relatives in New York that day

Adam Brooks

I didn't know where the World Trade Centre was, so I didn't think it was — I didn't appreciate it was a huge deal until I got into this room. My mum was sitting in a chair with the — watching the TV and I came in and said, "What's this about something happening?" She said, "Shhh, shhh". I thought, "Right, that's important then" so I just sat down and listened. When your mother tells you to be quiet and she's staring at the TV. She didn't like sport, so it's not a penalty shoot-out or anything.

Alan Thomson

The 9/11 one was a very hard one to watch, it jist fetched a lot back and ye jist— every time ye see a disaster now, in the past ye' would look at it, and ye'd mibby think, God and ye'd mibby spend five minutes seein' it on the news, or reading it or whatever whereas now, ye' do a lot more reflectin' on disasters because ye; know the bigger picture ... a think ye've got more o' a, more o' a perspective on what's happenin'

Yvonne Haldane

Couldn't believe it ..... You can't belief the depravity of anybody who would even think of *doing* that; I mean, the Lockerbie Disaster was bad in that somebody made a bomb and put it on a plane, but that, the Twin Towers, was just *absolute* slaughter, wasn't it? Absolute slaughter and indiscriminate slaughter

Access to communcation systems is taken for granted now, as people have personal electronic devices and appliances. Yet twenty short years ago, the telecommuncations system was paralysed during the Lockerbie Disaster. It was a stressful time for directly affected and extended family members, and scrambled information in the shock of aftermath reflects the uncertainty in people's consciousness.

James Haldane

And there was no phone lines; tried phoning, you know, phoning Jane and Mary and Granny Haldane, but no phone lines. Eilidh was up, Christeen's daughter, and they decided to go home about two, half past two mibby, and we gave them Jane's phone number coz they said, Well the lines might be alright from down there from Middlebie. So right enough, Eilidh had got through to Jane, to tell her where we were and that we were all alright.

Helen Fraser

My sister-in-law from Perth phoned on the evening of the disaster, you know, the emergency lines, to ask, you know, to find out if we were alive or dead, and they asked for our names, and address, and she gave them the address, and when she said Sherwood Crescent, there was a silence,; Cause everybody thought that everybody in Sherwood Crescent was dead. That was the initial—that was the information that all these people had, and it wasn't until we phoned her, you know, the following day that they found out that we weren't.

John Carpenter

When you have a big enquiry like this in the town, there's not the telephones available, even landlines but we were fortunate in that we were able to get the telephone system that was up in Troon [west coast town] for the Scottish Open Golf Championship, and that was brought into the town, and they obviously had to, sort of, bribe communications for relatives because, in no time at all, you had the relatives from America arrived in the town. So to you had to, obviously, provide them with some means of communication so you needed extra call boxes because, as I say, mobiles were in their infancy at that time

Positivity may not be an obvious result of the Lockerbie disaster but I always believed strongly in the power of positive thought to overcome stress. The response by the townspeople to the horrendous event is an attempt to create good from something awful, an attempt to be

productive in a time of destruction, and an overarching sense of tenacity and continuity in each new day – strengthening of the community in crisis, opening its doors to needy visitors, showing compassion and love for the bereaved, and sustaining relationships with fellow sufferers in the world demonstrates the good that has come out of the disaster.

Marjory McQueen

There's certainly been, as far as the town's concerned, the links with Syracuse, the university that had thirty five students on that flight; there's been a big link between Lockerbie and... so I'm very pleased that out of something awful that has; that has grown and flourished and I hope that continues for a long time

Dave Wilson

I'm a great believer that a wee success, even if you're a big fish in a wee pond, if ye win the local monthly medal at the gold club; if ye win a prize at the Sunday school; if ye just do something well and people recognise it, I think ye stay up there, and I think that a lot o' people, who had just been goin' about their daily business, doin' the messages at the weekend, suddenly found, within themselves, that the felt themselves to be more worthwhile human beings and that stayed with them;

Adam Brooks

People come over here and we go out there, but it's the sort of the symbol it says; it's out of terrorism and atrocity and total despair of people, you've now got friendship.

Superintendent John Carpenter on the job in the Incident Room, in the old Lockerbie Primary. This photo was taken on an F.B.I. digital camera in 1989. (© John Carpenter 2008)

John in police uniform, on the A74 looking South, and Sherwood Crescent in the left background. Nowadays, screens would be erected in similar situation to prevent rubber-necking. (© John Carpenter 2008)

Geoffrey John Carpenter, March 2008.

A Policeman's Lot

The operational side of the enquiry

The following narrator has had connections with Lockerbie for more than 40 years. His family antecedents were born locally and he returned with his Mother to the area from England. He came to live the Lockerbie in the early 1960s, and has remained as a resident of the town, despite working in the regional capital, Dumfries. He has lived in various parts of the town – although a wee place, Lockerbie has districts and streets that comprise micro-communities in themselves – and he has understanding of these communities, as a citizen of 45 years standing and a senior member of a government service. He was heavily involved with the disaster and its aftermath.

He chose to be involved with the Lockerbie project because he put his name on a list of townspeople associated with the disaster who were willing to talk about their experiences and what had logistically happened. I didn't know this when I contacted him about involvement in the project - I only knew he had directly participated in the disaster at ground level. He says he offered to be a liaison person because he has been a member of the Media Group since 1988.

We spoke for 2 hours and 17 minutes on Monday 25 March 2008, in the front lounge of his beautiful Georgian sandstone house in Lockerbie. We agreed to sit at the table: being Easter, there was a delicate tree ornament on it. [I saw several of these decorations during my trip, in stores, and at my sister's house - a denuded, pale wooden branch, about half a metre high, dangling colourful little ribboned eggs . There's nothing like this in New Zealand!] Our situation at the table in the bay window overlooked the front garden, with a raised vista of the hedge and Carlisle Road beyond, with my parents' house beyond. He removed the Easter tree and the lace doily from the table. We sat down at the table.

I didn't know the narrator as a child or when growing up in Lockerbie – certainly not professionally – despite his sons being either side of my age. My family knew his wife's Mother, who farmed just outside of Lockerbie – my Dad used to deliver grocery orders to the farm and we got two kittens from there too We had a white, and then a blue, Renault van; one of my sister's first driving experiences was down that grassy farm lane. I sat on a makeshift box in the back while she careered over the uneven farm road – luckily the grass in the centre served as a second brake before we reached the fence! Now, she is an excellent driver.

The narrator has an extensive collection of local and regional postcards which he proudly showed me. He is very keen on genealogy and is presently involved in tracing a relative's family tree. At one time in the past, he also came very close to being mistaken for Sean Connery and, in the watery light of that spring morning, I can see why!! I suppose it's the golfing connection.

Throughout his life and his career, he had cause to visit many towns, villages, hamlets and farms within Dumfries and Galloway and to cover the outlying areas too. He makes reference to various places names significant to his story.

He talks about a place called Brydekirk, a small village in a farming community about 15 miles south of Lockerbie. He also mentioned Beattock, a village approximately 10 miles north of Lockerbie, on the M74. Interestingly, the village of Beattock celebrates Halloween one day early, on 30ᵗʰ October – I recall a story, and it is just that, of Beattockites being so superstitious that they celebrated a false custom and stayed firmly locked up on the night of the real All Hallows Eve. Maybe there was a curse befell them back in history. 16 miles north of the village is Beattock Summit, a bleak undulating moorland and forested area, where the weather whips round unsuspecting traffic on the M74.

Moffat is also mentioned – it is a charming wee town at the foot of the Beef Tub and the route of the Tourist Trail up through Tweedsmuir and Broughton, and on into Edinburgh. Moffat has The Star Hotel, the narrowest hotel in Scotland, as well as being the home of the celebrated Moffat Toffee. My son, while still a toddler, lost his ball on the frozen boating lake in Moffat's municipal park, to the south of the town, and he cried all the way home to Lockerbie. The Grey Mare's Tail refers to the site of a huge waterfall northeast of Moffat, and close to Loch Skeen – it plunges 200 feet down.

Eastriggs, Powfoot and Annan are all localities south of Lockerbie; the latter is a large town 10 miles south on the River Annan, which drains into the Solway Firth The latter two are villages – Powfoot is coastal village on the estuary of the Solway Firth, where the sea goes out for miles, and Eastriggs is a farming hamlet

Johnstonebridge is about 6 miles north on Lockerbie. The A74 dissected it into North bound and Southbound, in the days when there was a collection of cottages and houses nestling there. Now, the necessity to fuel the thousands of road users and their vehicles has turned the hamlet of Johnstonebridge into a service centre, north and south bound.

Gretna is a town situated just over the English border and it is most famous for the weddings performed over the blacksmith's anvil. The legal age of marriage without parental consent is 16 years in Scotland compared to 18 in England and Wales. So the historical tradition of eloping to Gretna to be wed continues today, with a booming tourist market for all things tartan, and a retail outlet centre.

Dumfries is the regional capital situated 12 miles west of Lockerbie. It is culturally distinct from Lockerbie as regards dialect, connections with the Galloway folk, access to facilities, sports and entertainment, jobs, and shopping. With the hospital, the seat of the regional council and the mighty Nith River running through, Dumfries is the big brother to Lockerbie. But the wee brother has a catapult in the pocket – the proximity to the two main arterial transport links north and south: the railway and the M74.

This narrator really appeared to enjoy our interview and we both laughed a lot. His name is Geoffrey John Carpenter – know as John – and he is 64 years old.

John's narrative starts with memories of his family's historical connections with Lockerbie and school days in the south of England.

JC: Yes, well it goes back a few years now obviously, but my Mother's father belonged Brydekirk in Annan and he met my granny in Newcastle and they became resident in Newcastle for a number of years, where my mother was as born in North Shields. Because my granny was an asthmatic, in those days the medical profession sent you, sort of, to *dry*er grounds and hence they headed south and took up residence in a village called Yately in Hampshire and that's where my mother eventually up met my father and got married during the second world war and I was born in Yately on the date given to you. My father was a farmer and he farmed in a village called Finchamstead in Berkshire. The Hampshire Berkshire Surrey borders come very close together on the river Blackwater and our farm joined the river Blackwater in Berkshire. My schooling was at a prep school called Yately Grammar in Yately and thereafter I went to a private school called Reading Collegiate in Reading.

One thing about — I must say about — it occurred to me, when I was a boy and lived in the south, everything seemed to be a distance away — for instance, when I was at school, I had, what I thought was miles to walk to catch the bus coz we had the farm lane and then down the road which I thought was miles. When you go back an look at it now, you'd be lucky if it was half a mile [laugher] Everything looks that larger or nearer at hand now than it did in the past.

JH: I wonder if that's the way the mind mythologises things. You know, they talk about rose-tinted glasses when you look back. Often, when I'm in NZ, I get a bit misty-eyed then I have to pull myself together and think, Oh God, it's not that good, you know [JC laughs] With distance, comes the ability to turn things into this myth where in fact it probably wasn't.

JC: I think it's just a process of growing up. [laughter]

JH: They say, the summers were always —my sister was saying that the other day, "It was always sunny when we were kids".

JC: It's true, I can remember when I was a school, there wasn't a summer that went by when you didn't have classes sitting outside in the school playground.

JH: Well, but was it really that sunny or was it just as you like to remember. You don't remember the rainy days.

JC: No, you don't.

Nostalgic memories are types of memories described by Georg Stauth and Bryan Turner [Rossington, Whitehead: 2007, p.151], as the positive contradiction between the authentic reality of the present and perceived associations connecting to the past through actual physicalities – a leafy lane, the smell of peaches, a favourite song. These physicalities act like a portal into a lost temporal existence. Nostalgic memories, by definition, are not inherently negative: they can be pleasantly painful as a presence in our consciousness that evokes an immediacy of and proximity to this lost temporal world that still exists spatially.[Frow, 1997] Of course, John can return to the farm road, as a 64 year old, any time he likes. But he can only return to the farm road as a boy, and, most importantly, to his boyhood, in his nostalgic memory. That portal, is, therefore, very precious.

Nostalgic feelings are like pop ups or viewfinders in the consciousness, as online, a pop-up image appears on the scene to distract you from work or the old public viewfinder - put in the coin and direct the telescope to an area of interest for a detailed view or private, little black box with slit at top and framed still photo goes in and lights up from pressure exerted on the top– a street in Edinburgh, driving along a frequently-travelled road, the split-second vision of a building. Most of my pop-ups are outside. Nostalgia can also be a feeling evoked through associated thought. In NZ, I have a parallel life full of physicalities and systems that compare and contrast to the factors of my past life in Scotland. Time being 1 dimensional, I can't experience both lives at once but nostalgic thought is as close as I can come to a dual consciousness.

John has a memory of his farm road from the reality of his childhood. His childhood was real and the farm road was real. He has experienced the reality of the farm road's distance as an adult and he has a memory of that distance. It contradicts his boyhood memory - a contradiction of the two temporal realities.

John on being Scottish

JC: By reason of the fact that I've live here longer than I do in England and of course my young family are all Scots [laughter]

JH: And you sound Scottish.

JC: They say you get like the folk you live with, don't they.

JH: Mmm, but, you know, your identity—do you sort of identify the very internal soul of yourself as being Scottish or...

JC: I think I probably do now. I mean to say, I've been away from—it was in my, sort of, schooling days, it was all in the south—I never ever worked down there so I've always worked in Scotland and I feel I've become very much as part of the set-up—I wouldn't care to move south again, its nice to go back and revisit your roots but it's never the same when you go back.

John recounts his return to the Lockerbie area from England, and his first job:

Unfortunately my father died when I was just 15 years old and my mother decided to sell up and move back north to Brydekirk. Now even at the tender age of 15 years old, my ambition at that time was to join the fleet air arm and I had gone so far to doing various interviews and examinations and was on the point of being accepted when my father just passed away as a cadet in the services. However, on moving back up to Brydekirk, I eventually got a job at the tender age of, I would be 17 there, with the Ministry of Defence at Eastriggs which is now famous for the Devils Porridge exhibition. It's to do with the founding of the factory away back prior to the First World War – it was the biggest manufacturing plant for explosives including nitro-glycerine; it had the largest nitro-glycerine plant in the country, I'm led to believe, and it also led to the foundings of the Gretna township, Eastriggs, and the munitions depot at that time stretched from literally Powfoot right through to Longtown, right along the shoreline – an interesting facet of it is, at that time, it never appeared on any ordinance survey maps because it was of the utmost secrecy, you know.

John's decision to join the police.

So as I say, I spent 18 months there and I was in a quandary as to where my life was going and a family friend of my mother's, who was in the police at the time, said, Did I fancy joining the police? So I said, Och, I'll give it a go, and, as a consequence, in 1963, I ended up joining Dumfries and Galloway Constabulary which, at that time, had a uniform total of about 160 odd officers, a very small force in unitary terms but, I'd like to think, and I'm not just saying because I was in it, a very efficient one. My first posting, having completed my junior training at the Scottish Police College, was to Lockerbie, and I can remember at what was the old police station at Lockerbie which was quite a substantial sandstone building at the location of the current police station which was eventually knocked down in the '60s, mid '60s, and replaced by the new station. I can remember arriving and finding myself locked out but by that time the Sergeant and one of the cops stayed in the house adjacent to the police station and I was able to gain access but I think it must have been one of the only jobs you come to, as a raw recruit, and you find yourself working on your own [laughs]

His 1960s experiences as a young cop in Lockerbie.

At that time there was only three police authority-owned accommodations in 1963, there was the inspector's house which was up the Dryfe Road by the secondary house, and the sergeant and a constable had accommodated which was more or less just a flat adjacent to the police station – the rest of the staff—there was only an inspector, a sergeant and 6 constables, well 5 of those constables were in accommodation and I was in accommodation with Mrs Adamson in the Metal House. [...] In Sydney place, it was opposite the Catholic chapel – the Metal House as it was known and I had a happy time there; I was in with a colleague, we shared a room and we were well catered for and looked after.

JH: And did you tend to go back down to Brydekirk way?

JC: During my time off I tended to, quite often, used to nip on the bus those days and down to Brydekirk.

JH: And what was it like, you know, police constable in those days, what was it like, your schedule?

JC: Well in those days, you often reflect back on it because the main trunk road ran through the centre of the town and I think I'd be right in saying any day you came through Lockerbie, you'd always see police office on the street at that time, invariably standing at the war memorial in the centre of the town and you saw everything that went on, you knew most people and Lockerbie folk I always found very very friendly and you soon became accepted in at part of the community and involved in various things- I mean to say I remember very well used to go round to some of the outlying communities to the local dances and in those days it wasn't unknown for if you were on a back shift and that, you threw a civvie jacket in the back of the car and joined in [laughs] and it was all part of the [laughs] social scene and I think in those days it paid dividends because obviously the folk respected you for what you were and accepted you for what you were.

JH: […] in the '60s when you were a cop, what type of misdemeanours were you dealing with, generally?

JC: Och, you still got your boys who had a little bit of devilment in them but you gave them a ticking off and I think in those days it was fair to say that if you spoke to somebody and said, I'm going to have a word with your father, that was sufficient and it didn't go any further. I suspect these days it's somewhat different [laughs].

John details his promotion and return to Lockerbie from Dumfries. He recounts his conversation with the inspector in traffic in the historical present – the time is past but the tense is present.

Recounting reported speech is layering first-person narrative – here are John's words in the past being told by John in the present. Actual speech filtered through time.

I moved into Dumfries in 1966 and had a short period on the beat in Dumfries before I went into the traffic and that was when— probably reflected a lot back to Lockerbie—in those days, as station, it also had a traffic patrol car and so you also had a big rural area, I mean to say, the Moffat subdivision extended up to the Lanarkshire boundary beyond Moffat and Beattock, it went halfway to Langholm and the boundary to the south took in Ecclefechan and across to the West, the far side of Lochmaben, almost to Parkgate even, so it was a big rural area as well. We still had bicycle patrols in those days although they were few and far between because motorised transport was coming into being and it gave us a little bit more flexibility but we also had to patrol the main routes and of course the A74, being one of the main arteries between Scotland and England – there was a considerable number of accidents and it wasn't very long before I attended my first in this area near Eaglesfield one nightshift and that was it, you were conditioned to expect literally anything and everything after that and I think, because of that experience on the roadside, it stood me in good stead and I was fortunate one day, I can remember this inspector in traffic came down on the beat and said, "Have you got somebody who could come down on a trip to Gretna", you see, and he says, "You used to drive one of these cars in Lockerbie", and I says, "Yes", and so he says, "Drive me to Gretna and back", and I found the next week I was in traffic, which was quite unusual because at that time I would have had about 3 and half years service and they reckon, before you can specialise, you had to have about 5 years. So I went into the traffic and from that time up until about 1974, I was in the traffic department which covered the whole of Dumfries and Galloway and then I was promoted back to Lockerbie as sergeant in 1974 and so I had another stint here, which I thoroughly enjoyed, it was in the new station. There was still one cop, Willie Irvine, who you probably remember, who was here when I joined—he was actually in the old police station house. When I came back here I had a house round the corner in, the Quaas Loaning here, the corner house, until at that time, we officer were getting the authority to purchase their own houses and I purchased a house in West Acres shortly afterwards, towards the end of 1974, [...]

[On the Lockerbie force] every one knew everyone else and, on promotion, I mean say, I went back, I was promoted back into the traffic as Inspector in 1979 and then I had two further promotions within the traffic in a very short from 79, I think it was about 1981 that I became Chief Inspector and after that, they upgraded the position to Superintendent that I fortunately inherited as well, as head of the traffic section and I found that not only within the force was it a close-knit community because, let's face it, even at the time of the Lockerbie Disaster, I think our establishment it would be lucky if it was 350 which is a relatively small force; if you go to Glasgow, that's half the size of a division in Glasgow. But on top of that, because you were what you were, you had close contact with a lot of the agencies you dealt with, particularly the local authority, the ambulance, fire, and you knew all the hierarchy and, I think that in its own way had a lot of benefits particularly when it came to the disaster and emergencies planning.

Developments to Lockerbie's infrastructure in the 1960s necessitated a significant traffic patrol in the local force.

Well I came here in '63 and, as I say, there were stretches of carriageway in existence at Johstonebridge, south towards Ecclefechan and, that was more or less it. And they were in the process of building the Lockerbie bypass in the mid '60s and it would probably open just after I left here in '66, '67 – that was the original dual carriageway bypass of Lockerbie which was in existence from then until after the disaster coz the motorway was only built after the disaster.

JH: So when you came back from Dumfries to Lockerbie, did you see a big difference in the amount of traffic coming through the town as well as going round it?

JC: Yes, because the bypass was in operation then and I know it was a bone of contention with a lot of business people in Lockerbie, they thought it was taking trade away from L but I hate to imagine what it woulda been like if the traffic still had to come through the centre of the town. It would just be gridlock coz obviously, you had dual carriageways either side of the town and two into one just don't go.

John talks about the mucking-in mentality required by a cop in a rural force, and its positive contribution to the job of policing a small community.

I suppose the only difference was the fact that Dumfries was larger and you operated—if you were a policeman within Dumfries burgh, you didn't have any concerns about the rural areas round about you. I mean to say Lockerbie was totally different, not only did you have the town to deal with you had the farming community to deal with as well. I mean to say, in those days, it wasn't unknown for police officer to have to dig holes to cremate anthrax cattle which one never hears about nowadays, I don't know if anthrax has vanished from the scene [laughter] But in those days, you had to dig holes and you had to cremate them and it was the police's responsibility […] because we were responsible for diseases of animals and control of it, you know, its; the same even with Foot and Mouth. I was pretty fortunate—there was an outbreak of Foot and Mouth when I was in traffic in the '60s but it never came into Scotland then, if I remember rightly, it was down in the south although they had the disinfecting mats out at Gretna, this that and that other. I can always remember one dutiful officer who was a household name wherever he went in the rural stations. He was stationed at Ecclefechan for a while and said he was going to sweep the streets clean and, when he got up in the morning, there was a pile of brushes on his doorstep [laughter]. This is an amusing side to it but he'd actually got a cattle float that had come from south and he'd shoved it into a field and was piling straw bales and that up against it—he was going to set fire to it [laughter] But, no, I was fortunate—we didn't have that disease in the area and the crisis that we had recently, you know. I dare say your mother and father would remember the pit they had at their back door, you know. But we still had a responsibility and control over diseases of animals and transportation of such, although, in my young days, the access to the community was one of the—we used to sign stock books regarding removal of animals, you had to go to the farms periodically to check the stock book and possibly you'd to check the stock book against some of the stock that were on the farm. It gave you an input into the community but that has been take away from police control, I wouldn't say it eroded control - it was time-consuming in many respects but, on the other hand, it gave you the opportunity to get to know your community as well, by doing these wee jobs, albeit you could say it had little to do with policing.

Prior to 1988, John had already dealt with incidents of vehicle and aircraft fatalities.

I worked in Lockerbie on various things, I mean to say, one of the things we had—we had a plan crash up at Moffat, up above the Grey Mare's Tail and I think there was about 8 or 9 people killed. We also had at that time some sad things happening; there was a police car involved in a fatal accident at Johnstonebridge and, of course, having been in traffic before I came back, I knew the individuals very well – all four were killed when their car was side-swiped by an articulated lorry and went over the crash barrier and head on to a wagon coming the other way, you know.

It [the crashed aeroplane near Moffat] was a light aircraft but having said that, I think there was about 8 or 9 people on board and it came down at, was it, Loch Skene up on the top of the Grey Mare's Tail ? coz I remember vividly we flew up in a helicopter from the football park at Moffat and it's quite an experience because you don't release it until you get up and you hit the hills and you go over the first range of hills at Moffat and they fall completely away and if you're looking, or hanging, out the side of a helicopter they have you strapped in of course and you see this happen it takes you breath away and that was my first experience of plane crashes but it's quite ironic and I made the point to somebody not so long ago—when I stayed down south during my schooling, we were very close to Farnborough and Farnborough was famous for the air show and my father as a great one for going to Farnborough and I used to go with him as a young boy, and we were actually there the day before the Hawker Hunter crashed on the crowd - at that time in these air shows the aircraft flew at low levels over the crowds, you know, and that's what actually stopped it, you know, and it's quite ironic we were there the day before this happened and then you … you subsequently get a crash in Lockerbie.

Reconciling scenes of death and destruction.

I think the training they gave you, even junior training at the college was such, that they tried to show you, either graphically, by picture or by film, the hazards that you may come across in the course of your work and that went some way towards it but I think it's something that in some ways, a lot of people don't come to terms with. And it's alright it you're quite used to seeing blood and, obviously, if you go to an accident, you see some horrific sights. It's a case of you get used to it in, a certain extent, but there are side issues in that—something that I never got used to was if children were involved and I think that's acceptable if you're a family person or you've a family of your own, you don't like to see children involved in anything but it's something that you come to terms with and you have to get on with. And you see some horrific sights from time to time. I wouldn't care to repeat what I've seen. But I think during my time in the services, I've seen them all, both from the drowning to bodies that have lain undiscovered for some time, and also the horrific injuries you can get a result of road traffic accidents. And a further issue to that was—round about the same time or not long afterwards, we had a coach crash at Beattock and it was one of the—at the time it was one of the worst in the country—I'm just trying to think, there as 12—either 12 or 13 people killed in a bus crash at Grisgin, up above Coatsgate quarry and—as I say, it wasn't a quiet posting, Lockerbie – you had to deal with anything and everything, as well as you major crimes as well.

John remembers a high-profile antiques robberies in our area.

Well, there was a number of break-ins at big houses in and around Lockerbie and antiques were being stolen and one of the items taken was the George III carriage clock which had the coronation procession. A very valuable clock and it disappeared without trace. Now, we did a lot of *local* enquiries and, at that time, there was a gentleman who had retired to L, whose hobby was clocks, and he used to travel all over the country and he'd been in—I think it was Bonhams in London and he'd overheard a conversation about a George III carriage clock with a coronation procession going round the top. And [pause] he felt there was a local connection and described a young lady and, as a result of enquiries, we established who the lady was. And [pause] we also learnt that the clock was in the process of being sold and it as one its way to the Arab States for quite a substantial sum. However, we progressed - the lady was traced, established and contacted and we she as responsible, along with others and the clock was dutifully recovered. And Bonhams asked if they could keep the clock, restore it and put in on show and of course, the laird at Castlemilk agreed to this. Lo and behold, it was stolen again from the showroom in London [laughter] But eventually it was tracked down in Germany. But it's quite interesting - the lady concerned ended up getting two years and I can remember a lot of the silverware wasn't recovered but some of it was actually recovered out of the river Annan, down at Dornmont, which we managed to get back in bits and pieces like that but it's quite an interesting—in itself and, you know, on the periphery of it, there was quite a few personalities involved in it as well. And it was all to do with funding of drugs.

The area has a history connected with disasters.

The major disasters that have happened in Dumfries and Galloway are quite unbelievable over the years. You had the Quintinshill train disaster at Gretna, when the military train, it came off and there was 200 odd casualties. It was one of the worse train crashes— well, it still *is* the worst train crashes ion the country and it was dealt with, but I don't know I don't know what they did about recovery or where the bodies went to because, in those days, they wouldn't have anything *like* the resources. And then, of course, we had the Antrim Princess Ferry Disaster at Stranraer so we laid claim to—[cell phone rang] Yes, so as I say, we had the air, rail, sea disasters – worst ones in Britain and the smallest force in the UK mainland has dealt with them all [pause] over the years.

John talks about the lead up to Christmas 1988.

Well, normal practise at Christmas was we tried to [pause] all staff either had Christmas or New Year, one or the other of the public holidays off and as it so happened, personally, I think it was the first year in all my service that I had actually managed to get both Christmas and New Year off which didn't materialise [laughs] But yes, generally, every sub-division used to be as a matter of consequence, have their own sort of Christmas dance or sub-divisional dance and some of them were before Christmas and some of them were after. They used to involve themselves in Christmas parties for the children in the sub-divisions and so on.

JH: Had you had a dance or anything like that ?

JC: Not that I can think of, no, no, no [pause] I suppose I was getting, at that stage, a bit on it, you know [laughs] having served the best part of 25 years in the police at that time—I did used to go to some of the social things—we used to have a senior officers dinner which we did have—I think it was the week before in Dumfries where the senior officers or the senior management team, as they called it, and their wives went for a dinner at one of the local hotels and I'd been to it but [pause] no, that, that was it, you know.

Yeah, the whole family would've been around because we have an extended family and ... , the eldest son, was actually in Australia at that time with this girlfriend and he got, I don't know how it came about but they found in Australia that he belonged Lockerbie, and he ended up on telly out there, you know [laughs] And, of course, he was the only one who as going to be absent over the Christmas holiday period and [pause] we were gonna have a houseful, as we always did, coz ... used to cater for Christmas dinner and, well, she said last year was the last year and we had 28 or29 for Christmas dinner. Well, her sister's got 7, 8 children so it mounts up and of course, grandchildren are coming on the scene now as well so—we have about 7 grandchildren now and…

John's personal experiences on the evening of the Lockerbie Disaster are intrinsically bound up with his professional role of Chief Inspector. Given the intervening 20 years, John recounts with great clarity how the events of that night unfolded from his perspective. He mentions various streets and roads in Lockerbie which can be traced on the map of the township

Well, at that time, I stayed in Leonard Crescent in Lockerbie, and my usual day was—I usually worked, generally, day shift and there was always a superintendent on call and you knew that, periodically, it used to work about one week in five but, like I say, on that particular year, I was finishing work on the 21st which, if I remember rightly, was a Wednesday.

And my normal working day was, I used to leave home about 8 o'clock in the morning, to go to Dumfries, and I would arrive back home somewhere in the region of about 6 o'clock at night and it was a perfectly normal day, I don't think there was any undue problems and, I arrived home and had our evening meal, as we normally did. I sat down in the chair after I'd done the usual chore of washing and drying the dishes. I know Elaine, that particular night, she'd gone along—a couple of doors along to, was it Mrs Scott? I think they lived on the corner house, to deliver a Christmas present and a card to her and, she wouldn't be away that long when, I was sitting by the television, and Terry Wogan had a programme on, you always remember Terry Wogan and [pause] I heard this loud noise. To be quite honest, I thought nothing about it because Lockerbie was a low flying—an area for low-flying aircraft because, I know the military used to have targets and the castle was one of them and—never thought any more about it but it went on and on and on and then you think, something not right, but you still tend to ignore it and then the whole house vibrated and the china vibrated on the mantelpiece, bits and pieces start to shake, and [pause] then all of a sudden, I heard a whistle and it's best described, if you watch a war film on the television, you know how you hear bombs dropping, and you hear this whistle, and there's this almighty thump [pause] I don't think the door could've been on its catch right because it actually blew open [pause] so it took me a while—I got outta the chair [laughs] to have a look and see what's happening so I went down to the front garden [coughs], and I looked south and I saw this earth and debris and I also saw a silver object which, I'm reasonably certain would be one of the engine pods, sort of, slightly sort of southeast of where the eruption was. And, I mean to say, there was flames and sparks and everything. I thought, Good grief, and I think, within my own mind, I was almost certain that a plane had crashed. I went back into the house and the phone was dead. Well, I utilised my car because I had fluorescent jackets and torches that I used to carry with me coz I used to use my own car anyway, and I also had a blue light—didn't fix on the roof, it actually just flipped over on the back of the sun visor. So [pause] I think ... and ... were in, the youngsters were in, and Elaine came back and I says, Well, I'd better go, and I threw a fluorescent jacket on and jumped into the car, not knowing what I was going to meet and that first—I got no further than Douglas Terrace and Victoria Road. And here's people in their droves, some even pushing pushchairs, heading towards the Dumfries Road, you know. So I got to the Dumfries Road and there as people milling around and I actually got across the junction, only about 50 or 60 yards, and there was debris and bits of wire lying in the road, this was in [pause] heading towards Sherwood, which was Douglas Terrace.[ ] However, I parked up the car and somebody—I can't remember for the life of me who it was, came up to me and said, Can I give you a hand? So I gave him a yellow jacket and a torch and I says, Well, stand at the junction and letting nothing in other than the emergency services but, having said that, I said, Just do your best, but on no account let in members of the public, and I knew there and then it was just about an impossibility because they would just walk past that individual. However, I walked further along, towards Sherwood, and there was thick smoke, it was quite a windy night. There was rubble and debris all over the place. There was pools of oil burning in people's front gardens, on the roves of some of the houses and, when you got to the junction of Sherwood with the crescent, the smoke was even thicker and thicker, I could see a fire at the back of the petrol station on Carlisle Road, which turned out to be a tyre store and your immediate thought, of course, is how close is that to the fuel pumps? However, there was certain individuals who I knew came up to me and said, What can we do? So it was a case of—I knew it was difficult for me to go and have a look round because somebody had to take control so [pause] we have a policy of setting up a control point so I set up a forward control point, possibly no more than about 50 or 60 yards from the Crescent and I directed—there was one or two off-duty officers, one or two retired police officers came along and said, Can we help?. So the other thing was to seal off the Carlisle Road junction to Sherwood. The other one was to sort of survey the area, trying to establish just what the problem was. That was done very quickly because someone came and said, There's houses disappeared pause] in the crescent, there's vehicles burning on the dual carriageway on the bypass and [pause]

Casualties at Sherwood Crescent. There were only 6 people admitted to hospital that evening.

You got individuals, I'd say, because being part of the community, and you knew—one woman came up to me and said, "Have you seen my mother, John?" And I says, No, we're trying to establish what the situation is - I well knew, at that time, that the house her mother stayed in what no longer there, you know. And [pause] the [pause] other prime thing was to see if there was any casualties. Well, the only casualties that there were the Smiths who stayed in the crescent. You know, ex Army and Navy stores [inaudible] They were brought out.

[…] the Town Hall was always earmarked as the place for the mortuary [pause] but the sheer weigh of casualties made that a nonsense, you know [pause] Latterly, they utilised the ice-rink you know [pause] We had a mortuary set up that worked along with the pathologists, dealt with the bodies and [pause] it would be a harassing time for them but, at the same time, it's an off-shoot again with the community,

I mean to say, ambulances! There must've been the best part of 100 ambulances arrived. I think they only utilised one! I mean to say, there was no casualties as such, there was just bodies at the end of the day. You had, I can remember, there was a whole line of ambulances in the Main Street in Lockerbie but nothing for them to do

The crime scene procedure:

[…] organise people to check the houses as far as they could. One of the things we do with houses is mark them to say that they've been searched, that isn't to say that somebody after you've searched them, might go back in, you know, and they might be done again – the tendency is to tie something to the door and that allows he police or the emergency officers to say that house had been searched and it' clear, you know. So that was the idea, to sterilise the area, allow the emergency services—allow the ambulance service and the fire service in. And, eventually, well, the fire service *did* arrive on the scene pretty quickly because, fortunately that was the area where there was any fire. [...] round at Sherwood [...], when the fire service appeared on the scene, [...] that was one of the problems with the fires, I wouldn't say the fires were that bad to begin with but because they had no access to water, they got worse. And it's quite ironic – three of the engines came down in Netherplace Farm and severed the main water main

Despite inadequate communications that evening, John coordinated traffic measures and access for emergency service vehicles into the town, as well as dealing with first-hand witness accounts.

And also, when this is happening, you get folk coming with other things, you know - someone else said two planes have collided and someone else came up and said there's another plane down in Rosebank, then somebody else says, There's a plane crashed at Tundergarth, So what you had to do was, and I didn't have any communications. Eventually, a police car turned up with a —what was a mobile phone and it those days they were the size of a big suitcase but the problem was, it was useless and it took a while before it could get through to headquarters and when we did, we just had to keep the line open because the airwaves were such that they were taken up by other agencies, you know. You couldn't isolated them for the emergency services which you can now, you know.

[...]people were coming along and, fortunately, they were coming to me and I had to direct them – I was directing them across to Rosebank, I'd to direct them up to Tundergrath, to see what the situation was. And at the same time, ensure that everything was taken care of and one of the big concerns was the petrol station so we extended the area—I mean to say, immediately, when I got though to Dumfries and it was an emergency, we put a diversion on from Beattock and Gretna round by Dumfries, to take all the main road traffic away. Internally, we had to try and inhibit traffic from coming anywhere near Lockerbie so they tried to do that via Dumfries as well, to stop folk coming across other than the emergency services traffic, emergency vehicles.

[...] on top of that [...], you had people coming to you in Sherwood saying, We've found body parts in gardens, and things like that [pause] can also remember somebody coming—there was a body [pause] on the grass in front of the window at the ambulance station, just along the road here [long pause] You had to take a note of these things and see that they were attended to in due course but [pause]

I mean to say, it's a nightmare, and, I would say, a lot of what you did was spontaneous reaction [long pause]

John uses his local topographical knowledge to ascertain the scale of the wreckage.

I reckon I must've been there [at the control point in Sherwood Crescent] a couple of hours, then there was people appearing and I was able to put on another responsible [inaudible] because, when we did get a phone link, I *did* manage to speak to both the chief constable and the deputy chief constable, they were coming across to Lockerbie and my remit was to meet up with them at Lockerbie police station and, obviously, they wanted to see the lie of the land - by that time there was information coming in about these other places and I later—because of my knowledge of the area, did a reconnoitre with Paul Newell, who was the Deputy Chief at the time, to show him round the area, you know, we did circumnavigate as far as we could, the whole of the crater area onto the road, round by Sherwood, we had a walk around, we went up to Tundergarth and he became familiar with the area albeit was during the hours of darkness. And things happened very very quickly because, in no time at all, you had press agencies from all over the world, arrived

The longest night of his professional career.

Not really, if I can put it this way, I went out at 7 o'clock that night and I didn't get home till midnight the following day [pause] and in that time, initially our centres of operations was the police station, obviously and we had to sort of formalise things but we were fortunate that the school—it was the start of the school holidays, so we were able to take over the Academy and also the primary school. When we were at the police station, things started to happen quickly – coastguard appeared on the scene; helicopter pilots at the office, they arrived, landed down at Blackford down here, asked what they could do, and in no time at all, we had about 14 helicopters and troops started to arrive. Officers from other forces, particularly Strathclyde, Lothian, even from Cumbria, appeared on the scene and [pause] the town probably doubled its population overnight, just about, because .the briefing at the school the following morning, and things started off at the school the following morning, you had about two thousand plus police officers appeared from Strathclyde and that, and, I mean to say, a lot of work went on overnight, we all had our specific jobs to do, my responsibility then being traffic was to ensure all the routes and that were open, there was sufficient transport to get the officers from A to B and we were fortunate in that respect — we had helicopters.

John's feelings when daylight came on 22ⁿᵈ December 1988. He contemplates the potential enormity of the disaster if the aircraft had not broken up at altitude

Couldn't believe it. Well, you'll have seen the pictures of it yourself and I think for an area and —-I suppose, on reflection, it could've been an awful worse, and it was brought home to us because a lot of people said the plane was coming from different directions and, a couple of weeks after it, I got the opportunity of going up with one of the helicopters. The helicopters were utilised well through the exercise for the search sectors, flying men out - they were also used for recovering, lifting bodies off the hillside and also the recovery of the debris of the plane itself. But they were also doing radar checks the day I went up to Prestwick and they were doing radar checks above Lockerbie and they were asked to go up to certain height. And when you're up 10,000 feet above Lockerbie and people in Hightae say it was coming from that direction, Bankshill, that direction - if you look down on it, you've got Lockerbie and Hightae and Bankshill almost side by side so you can appreciate that and the scenario is such that the explosion took place about 3 or 4 miles south of Lockerbie and the momentum of the plane kept it going towards Lockerbie because of the wind on the nigh and then it stopped and it just floated down. You quite often see with aircraft crashed that they keep—the momentum, if they're coming into land or take off, scythes from one end of a place to the other. So it's frightening to think, if that had happened at a lower level, that plane may well have travelled from one end of Lockerbie to the other, taking everything with it. And it's a thought, having seen that, I can remember in my boyhood, [pause] an airfield between ourselves and Farnborough which was, where I stayed, Farnborough was maybe, as the crow flies, about 14 or 15 mile away. In between there was an airfield called Black Bush, on the main A30, London Southampton road, and there was a plane came down in forestry plantation near what was, well still is, the police college down there, Bramshill. And it must've gone the best part of a mile and a half through this forestry plantation and taken everything with it and I hazard to think if something like that had happened here, you know.

The world's media descending on Lockerbie that night: how did John and the constabulary handle the press

Within a matter of hours, yes, and you're talking not just half a dozen but hundreds, you know [pause] and, with the best will in the world, you've got to try and keep them at bay.

But, I mentioned the press, we actually put them up in the Masonic Hall, next to the police station; we got access to there and Strathclyde send down their Press Officer with a team of men and, to my mind, they did a very good job I that they regulated them. The important thing with the press is, nowadays, you have to keep them briefed. For that reason there was always a press conference, usually in the morning, to begin with, and one at night, to update them on the day's proceedings and to keep them advised at to what was happening.

[...] one of the bonuses we found was the way we were able to exercise control over the media, because we had a team in place, albeit came from one of the larger forces, who obviously has a certain amount of expertise in this, and they knew how to deal with them and, you know, I was certainly in briefings with the Chief Constable that he had on a daily basis, and the press officer would quite often say, "You could do with doing something for the sake of the press" because I think he realised, if they got nothing, that was when your problems are gonna start, so you had to point them in a certain direction and say, Look, if you want, you can have access to this and do a wee piece on this—

[…] They weren't too bad, it was self-regulatory in a lot of respects, in that, you gave them limited access to certain areas so they could take a few pictures but you based it on one photographer and somebody else to do the scripting for them, and they circulated that amongst themselves and it worked pretty well. They were asked not to print certain types of photographs and things like that. Did happen once with one of the papers and they self-regulated it themselves; the individuals involved with the picture and the reporting of it were…..

Ostracised!

John remembers his preparations for VIPs to the town, and dealing with all kind of interested parties.

I mean to say, within 24 hours, you had your politicians - Hector, who was the local one, Hector Munro; Malcolm Rifkind, who was Secretary of State; you had Margaret Thatcher appeared on the scene and she arrived at the same time as the Duke of York and neither the two had to meet. How do you keep them apart in Lockerbie? […]

You have all this programming and planning to do. And then it's endless after that, you know – it's said, Why did the Duke of York come? Surely someone else should've come. Well, after that Charlie arrives, you see, and all they seemed to be interested in was, he had a whisky in the *Black Bull* [pub in Lockerbie] [laugh]

But, no, as I say, you have all these people to deal with in the middle of it and they want *answers*, you know. In any disaster, of any type, you will get that – there's always someone of prominence who wants to be on the scene and, of course, when you had the memorial service, you had all the political leaders of the day, arriving on the scene.

[…] its quite amusing – the press officer at the time—I was speaking to him coz I knew him before—when we heard that Margaret Thatcher was coming, I was in on the briefing he was giving the Chief because we had to do routes and that, to keep them apart, and he says, "You'll find that with Margaret Thatcher, when she speaks to you, she goes right up to you and puts the shoulder in", and, you know, she'd right in front of you and, you know, she is! [uproarious laughter] [..] I can remember when Margaret Thatcher came to the police station, I'm standing and she made a bee-line for me but she went past me and the guy I was standing next to was Michael Burke, you know, who does the television, and she obviously [pause] has individuals who she gets on with and made a bee-line for him.

The FBI was here, the CIA were here, Mossad were here. [...]You know, [pause] I don't think anyone really knows who all were here. But, I may say, they appear at these disasters coz they have an interest, as obviously they do. Let's face it, it was an American plane, you'd *expect* them to be here . I don't think that—as far as the FBI was concerned, to my mind, from the very outset, they would only have one or two individuals as a liaison. [pause] They—you know, the bit I know about on the identification side, provided the facility by way of digital camera and computer technology, satellite technology, of relaying bits and pieces whereby Americans were identified.

[...]Well, there you are! Never in the world did I think I would have to, or would be, involved with anything like that [...]

John on what the random nature of the crash means to him.

Well, in truth, if the plane had been to time, it would've happened over the Atlantic.

[...] I mean to say, I quite often say, there but for the grace of God go I because from the crater, my own home, as the crow flies, would've been no more than 5, 6 hundred yards from the crater, on the same path. So I might not have been here today either. And I s'pose, in a lot of respects, is it luck?

JH: What do you think?

JC: Being in [pause] the wrong place at the wrong time. [long pause]

JH: Yes, that [pause] that's quite an enormous concept, isn't it?

JC: It is, you know and [pause] och, you *do* reflect on it.

John talks about his religious faith and his mantra on life.

I'm afraid I'm not a church-goer. But I do *go* to church on occasions like that and, as I say, don't find fault with it at all. Whether it helps at the end of the day, I don't know.

JH: Have those *intervening* 20 years made any difference to the strength of your faith, or it's not impacted on it whatsoever?

JC: Not really, no.[...] I have been to some services but principally, the main ones I go to are funerals and weddings, you know, maybe a Christmas service but that's totally different. People go to a carol concert at Christmas but, as for a regular Sunday basis, you know, I personally feel conceited in some respects because I'd prefer to go for a game of golf than go to the church or maybe that a bit to do with my background – I was forced to go Sunday school as a kid and maybe that had something to do with it, but I've never really been a church-goer.

JC: I s'pose you always, from time to time, reflect on what's ahead of you and how far you're gonna go in life, you know. I s'pose it's something I never really thought about a great deal. You *do* reflect on it sometimes, you know – I'm getting to the stage now where and somebody'll say to us, Oh, I'll see you next year, and I say, well, if I'm around, you know [laugh]

No, as I say, it doesn't pay to think what might have been, you've just gotta get on with it as long as you're here. Let's face it, you can walk across that road and get mown down. And you see it all too often.

In the light of this happenstance, John directs his attention to the job in hand; his associations with relatives allowed him a rationalising perspective.

It could've been an awful lot worse that what it was.[…] You need a—I mean to say, from my own perspective, I worked [pause] on the operational side of the enquiry for, oh, it would be up till the end of April so at least 3 months, just over three months, resourcing the enquiry, and you saw all sorts of things, I mean to say, as far as the enquiry itself was concerned, I had nothing to do with the investigation side. But you met with relatives occasionally, you dealt with phone calls as best you could and, it wasn't always easy because it was a 24 hour job because, one remembers, I think it was 20 nationalities on board that plane [pause] The bulk of them were Americans of course, and then you're got to appreciate the social backgrounds of the people from all these different countries and they're a different makeup

[…] But, I mean to say, other agencies as well that parted their part in it, you've got the Salvation Army, The Red Cross and people like this - you know, we had soup kitchens out in the country.. I mean to say, the school meals service were a boom because they played—because we worked in the [inaudible], and all the research teams operated out of the primary school, they were flown into the rural areas and I mean to say, that saved a great deal of time as well because, as far as transportation was concerned as well, there was times when we had to operate one way systems, and they certainly were a boom,.

On strategies for coping professionally

I'm gonna say something here which you may find strange but I think, and it was said by somebody who was involved with the police at the time of the disaster, that I don't know how you do it and, it was a female that actually said this, and she said, "I don't know how you do this but in the times that I've seen you working, and I've seen you doing the things that you have to do, you never loose your sense of humour. Now that's a strange thing to say but I think there is a sense of humour but we still respect the job we're doing. And I think it's the ability to work with the two that carries you through at the end of the day.

JH: Do you think that's a control, you know—it's something that you can fall back on? Constantly maintaining professionalism, being aware, doing your job - in the face of all that, do you think that's a control mechanism possibly?

JC: It probably is and it's, it's, it's—don't get me wrong, there are certainly officers that find problems with this and will admit to it and, it's like everything else – you'll get others that you can see it in them and they don't admit to it and I think that's where you come in, particularly when you reach a rank, that you have to identify with this, and try and exercise some control over it and that's part of becoming a supervisor in the police service.

John's memories of the psychological assistance and trauma therapy offered to Lockerbie police and their families out with the agencies in the town; this foreshadows a dark side to the collective mentality on coping.

As far as that was concerned, John Boyd, very early on, made it clear to the local police, the local officers under George Stubbs at the time, that they go out into the community and make contact – go out into the pubs and clubs and speak to them. I know personally, I still went about the town and there were still individuals, as you'd find anywhere, I'd imagine, were prepared to talk about it and others that just didn't want to. It's difficult to know how you overcome that. I think you; probably need to be in the professional sphere and that is where the health board came in.

The services for these people was available but it was the same—the same even with police officers, I mean to say, we had ten police houses round the back here. There were actually police lodgings in Sherwood Crescent, one of the houses that disappeared, and he happened to be *working* that night. You had to cater for their needs as well. We have our own welfare system.. Because we were a relatively small force, we were on the back of Strathclyde in that respect but, it's like everything else, we recognised early on that even the officers, or even their wives of families, didn't like to be seen to be speaking to these people. [...]because of the nature of the community here, it's very small and everybody knows what everybody else is doing, we recognised the need and it was agreed that it was available, if anybody wanted it, and they could go outwith the region and speak to the people that were gonna help them

So the way we actually got that, and I think it was even reflected in the community side, we got around it by saying, if there's an officer—they didn't come through the force, direct to the officers from Strathclyde, and the arrangement was they could meet with them outwith the area altogether. That way, there was no comeback by, 'Och, they're needin' some help, we didn't need any', you know. You'll always get that...[...]

JH: Do you think there was a stigma attached to people who were looking for help?

JC: I think there probably is in some respects because, even in the community, for example [pause] you hear of individuals and, it's always a sore point, always a very difficult point—a lot of money comes into the town as a result of disasters from various things and you always hear the people, "och, why did they get that', you know, and yet there's some perfectly logistical reason for it but when you hear of people that weren't directly involved and, it's even be suggested to be, weren't even in the town yet they managed to get money out of the disaster, this is what breeds a bit of acrimony as well. I would say it's a very small minority and whether there is any truth in that or whether it's just rumour, it's difficult to say but—[…]

John's involvement with disaster preparedness and emergency planning, prior to and during the disaster; the lessons learnt from that incident at that time are shared with others today.

Well, I think we're always conscious of the need to update anything we do within the service in keeping with changes that are happening along the line. It's important that now and again you look at your plan on a regular basis, to see whether there is anything that needs modification and quite often they are based on things that've happened elsewhere. It might well be as a result of new technology that's coming in and so on. So it's an important facts of life nowadays, you should keep your finger on the pulse, you should keep looking at it and, to follow that up, ensure there's adequate training for the officers who are gonna take the relevant positions in any emergency that's gonna develop.

JH: Did the Piper Alpha disaster inform the decisions to become more prepared for any type of large scale emergency?

JC: Probably was, I mean to say, every disaster that occurs, there's something crops up that nobody has ever thought of before – I suppose Piper Alpha, in some ways, is similar, but on the other hand, it's somewhat different in that it's [pause[based in the middle of the North Sea somewhere and you possibly don't have, other than the individuals that were involved on, and the relatives who are on land for the likes of those who are working on a ship like that or an oil rig, you don't have to [pause] secure it the same or cordon it off and you don't have the problem of trying to keep people out of it whereas here or on homeland, that it one of the prime—you're gotta preserve the crime in case it becomes contaminated that this is a very very difficult [inaudible[

[…] You know, I, for my sins, was involved with Emergencies Planning and it's quite— I often reflect on this, a week before the actual disaster, we had a pre-planning meeting of the local authorities where all the local agencies involved to discuss further developments for the agencies plan for Dumfries and Galloway yet that was hit on the head when and I often wonder—I can always remember John Boyd [Chief Constable for Dumfries and Galloway] saying, when he came across to Lockerbie on the night of the disaster, we had quite a substantial Emergencies Plan as far as the police as concerned and it was in a file but I don't think it was opened because you just get on with the job at hand and, although you'll probably have the basics of a plan appear, everybody knew what job they had in the case of such and you got on with it. And you had the beauty of knowing the other agencies and who was involved in the other agencies. The other things I would say with some of the other agencies, they did possibly jobs that were completely foreign to them, but they got on and did it. […]

You know, it's the same with any disaster in that it's the Chief Constable that takes the ultimate role but, nowadays, he is directly responsible then to the PM. You'll hear about COBRA being set up in London which is for major incidents now and it's the same with Lockerbie, the Chief Constable, from time to time, had to go and brief the PM at the COBRA offices in London

JH: But would it be fair to say that no plan could have prepared Lockerbie for what happened on the 21st.

JC: That's right, I mean to say, no-one in their wildest thoughts would ever think something like that would happen. [...]I would say that emergency planning, and of course, you got into the concept of forces and training establishments all over the country were interested in how we coped so it meant that a lot of us when round various areas, giving talks on how it happened and the pitfalls in how things were organised. But, it's like everything else, you know, in groups like the emergency services, you just—I would say, although there is a primary template for dealing with emergencies, we have the ability to cope with any problem that arises.

Communications in the aftermath of the disaster were a previously untested conditional in emergency planning.

In those days, out wireless systems were such that, there were a lot of hills round us and you didn't have communications everywhere, so we actually had to back that up with an organisation called Raynet – an amateur set-up who used low band radios and we utilised them in certain areas as well [...] The helicopters communications, they had their own but we also used the coastguard for that as well although we did have an antiquated system with sort of command and control point that could access those frequencies.

[...] Nowadays, they've come on tenfold since then. I mean to say, an example was, when you have a big enquiry like this in the town, there's not the telephones available, even landlines but we were fortunate in that we were able to get the telephone system that was up in Troon [a west coast town] for the Scottish Open Golf Championship, and that was brought into the town, and they obviously had to, sort of, bribe communications for relatives because, in no time at all, you had the relatives from America arrived in the town. So to you had to, obviously, provide them with some means of communication so you needed extra call boxes because, as I say, mobiles were in their infancy at that time and, I mean to say—lessons were learnt in that respect, and shortly after that, when mobiles came in, the facility now is there for the emergency services so they can isolate them, so they have them specifically for their own use in the case of an emergency. It would've been a boon, you know.

John explains the legal slipknot in the Scottish criminal system, as a result of the disaster, and the reason for this exception to the law.

Well, basically, at that time, the Scottish legal system was such that we have the *sub judice* law, whereby, if it's a criminal act or a criminal case, nothing [pause] no evidence in that case can be published until after it's come to trial [pause] and it even comes down to pictures and photographs, etc, *but,* and don't ask me what they were, but I do know that the Lord Advocate at the time *did* give certain dispensations in certain areas, to allow certain things about the case to be mentioned and I suspect one of them would be, when the AIB Mick Charles made the famous broadcast saying that it was an explosion on board the aeroplane that could, in some areas as far as Scottish law at the time, have been regarded as *sub judice.*

[Other nationalities'] legal systems are somewhat different [pause] They're used to everything being laid out in the public domain, openly, whereas we have our own laws. There are aspects of criminal enquiry that do *not* go into the public domain for the principal reason they could affect the outcome of the trial at the end of the day. That's maybe not the case - the agencies that you're involved with as well, because of the nature of the beast, you're involved with forces all over the world, principally, we were involved with the American agencies, certainly the German ones, Maltese, and so on, that [pause] you had to keep an open mind and realise that their legal system was somewhat different to ours and what we did in this country, they may well make public in another country, you know.

John remembers the positive community reaction to the practicalities of the disaster.

I mean to say, as far as the community was concerned, the other aspect of it was, they should be given a lot of credit for it and they are in certain respects, they *did* want to do their piece and they did it by working in the centre, in the school, by photocopying and providing tea and biscuits and cooking. The school meal service, they provided the canteen because all these people had to be fed, and then, because the local authority wanted to get the town back to normal, we decanted into the old school so that the academy would be up and running for the start of the Spring term.[…] But, I mean to say, other agencies as well that parted their part in it, you've got the Salvation Army, The Red Cross and people like this - you know, we had soup kitchens out in the country.. I mean to say, the school meals service were a boom because they played—because we worked in the [inaudible], and all the research teams operated out of the primary school, they were flown into the rural areas and I mean to say, that saved a great deal of time as well because, as far as transportation was concerned as well, there was times when we had to operate one way systems, and they certainly were a boom,

A lot of people became involved with the laundry—we set up a laundry for laundering all the belongings of the individuals on the plane and there was a full scale laundering service. Some amusing side issues, you know, I can remember John Boyd – somebody came to him and said, the community are wondering what they can do. He says, "Tell them to bake some cakes". Well, we got that many cakes, we didn't know what to do with them, you know.

John narrates how, in the months proceeding the disaster, Lockerbie citizens came together in support; they forged new communal relationships. All but one group has folded over the years.

[...] I've always found the Lockerbie people to be friendly *but*, like any community, you got communities that—individuals literally didn't know their next door neighbours, and I know some of the community groups that were set up, although I wasn't directly involved with them, I knew people that were there and they said, do you know, we've met people we didn't even know existed in our area.

Some of them were street by street groups, some were area groups, you know, and they, as I say—in that way, it probably brought the community closer together in many respects

And those community groups continued for quite a considerable time afterwards; I don't think there's many left now, I think there's one left up in the scheme who are heavily involved with providing a playground there up in King Eddie's Park, you know.

JH: So were they coming together to provide moral support and see what they could do as street for the baking, tea making or was it to do with helping people write letters - multi-functional?

JC: It was multifunctional and I think also the local authority were involved; they wanted to glean from the community what way the community wanted to go in the way that they restored the areas that were damaged, you know, and that possibly has some bearing on it as well. They were very, very, very conscious at that time—it was the advent of what was then Community Councils, which are the in thing, where politicians try to float things in the community before they do things. I don't know if that's par for the course, whether they do in every avenue, you know, but they certainly try to float things in the areas they're prepared to do, just to see what the reaction is. Whether they go ahead and do it or not is down to them at the end of the day.

John shares his memories of the stone-laying ceremony in January 1989, and we talk about the feelings evoked by the memorials at Dryfesdale Cemetery and Tundergarth Church

[...] a couple of months afterwards, they had a big service in the cemetery. That's when they laid the [long pause] the remnants of a lot of the bodies, you know, were buried in the cemetery, that weren't physically identified.

JH: Was that quite a stressful time?

JC: It would be for the guys who were involved with the, sort of mortuary side of things, you know. I mean to say, it was a [and] those that were actually involved with them and involved with the relatives, they made long-standing contacts with the States as a result of it, and continue to this day. Some of them in the police as well, because they worked—particularly those ones that were involved with the set up to deal with relatives, became friendly with the people from America and continue to be.

JH: Do you think that may have been the start of the healing process, the stone laying at the cemetery?

JC: I'm sure it did. Undoubtedly and I think I said at the outset, when you're dealing with people from different countries, and I'm sure you'll recognise this, their whole set up and background is such that they react to these things in a totally different way than we do, for some reason.

JH: They bring different cultural expectations to the piece.

JC: They do, and you just need to go to Tundergarth or to the cemetery and read the book where there's a little piece on everybody who was killed in the crash and that's reflected in it I think, you know.

JH: And it's a startling metaphor, I personally feel, down there that Lockerbie being the small tiny town that it is, opening up itself to the world in that respect. It's almost like a micro –world down there, isn't it.

JC: It is, very much so.

John's feelings about flying and airline safety.

I have no reservations. I mean to say, we've been abroad since the disaster and.…

JH: Can you remember the way you felt the first time you went on an aeroplane after the disaster.

JC: Well, I think what helped was, certainly I had the opportunity of going up with the military at the time of the disaster, for a trip round Lockerbie. It [pause] probably helped in many respects but, like I say, the disaster [inaudible] thought anything about it. It's just like driving a car. I mean to say, you've just as much chance getting involved in an accident with a car as you have with a plane you know. I think, relatively, airline safety is pretty good [pause]

I s'pose, some would say, I've seen in the way on mutilation on the roads more than I did in the disaster to be quite honest with you because, although there were bits and pieces—I didn't see a lot, I saw some of the bodies [pause] no, as I say, I think I've seen worse as a result of ordinary everyday accidents on the road.

John narrates his experience at Camp Zeist in the Netherlands, for the murder trial of the two accused Libyans in 2003. John remains

understated about giving evidence at a mass murder trial.

I mean to say, it was a secure courtroom, and it was fairly large as courtroom go, you know.[…] it was a military camp and I'm trying to think of the town it was close to but we actually flew into [inaudible] airport and we would be about an hour's drive from there I was trying to think of the name of the *town* - was there not a town, Zeist and we stayed in a hotel there. […]

Because I flew out with one or two local residents [pause] what do you call, the drainer [long pause] Gosh, there's a guy, he stayed up at Bankshill [pause] My memory's gone haywire, I tell you, put it down to senility, it's age coming into it. Oh, the guy who does the drains, in fact, […], next door to your Mum and Dad, used to work with him—[…]! Went out with [..] and 3 or 4 others, you know, and, fairly straight forward. All I was doing was laying the scene basically on the evening and sort of my role in resourcing the people that were involved – anything! Recovery, even the enquiry officers, if they required vehicles, if they required flights abroad. I don't think there were many countries abroad that we didn't visit during the course of the enquiry.

JH   And was it kind of a large gathering in the courtroom or an intimidating array of people?

JC: Well, there was two pieces to it, I mean to say, the public aspect – I would imagine would take up to a hundred people – was completely glazed off or partitioned, obviously for security reasons, I think, although there was security for everyone going into the place, and I can remember arriving there and the first thing you came to notice, and we were pre-warned about it, was the press, and they had a big grandstand of their own where all the press folk were, you know, clicking away everybody that was going in, this, that and the other. And you were searched, went in and they gave you—I mean to say, I maybe gave evidence for about an hour or so, and that was basically it and there were literally no questions coz a lot of the evidence—I mean to say, mine could have been accepted—I mean to say, it's like a lot of things, evidence can be accepted in Scottish court if the prosecution supplies the defence with a witness statement, and they accept that witness statement, there's no need for that person to give evidence. And when I reflect on it, for what I said, and there's a couple of things that I was cross-examined on, or asked questions by the defence. I'm led to believe I was the first person, and I was by no means the first witness in coz there was lots of civilians in that'd been accepted, like I mean, maybe they just needed that grounding for the sake of the people there spectating or what, I don't know, but it could just as easily been accepted, because it wasn't as if there was a jury, the judges were there anyway. It was an unusual courtroom in that respect – it was no jury, it was three high court judges that were…

JH   Had you been in any murder trials prior to that?

JC: Yes but you don't have a mass murder like this every time.

JH: So were you quite pleased to get on the plane and get home again.

JC: I think you always are with these, you know.

John and I discuss the media today compared to 1988.

JH: That's quite a startling contrast for me, looking at the media *now* and how they respond and portray Bush and so on, compared to Lockerbie, because there was a huge opportunity for the media to behave in a completely dishonourable and disrespectful way, but they *didn't*

JC: […] and I experience this a lot, prior to Lockerbie, when you were dealing with the press, they were getting very *close* to the stage of saying something totally outrageous, to get a reaction. *Now*, you could probably say to something that was totally outrageous to get a reaction and my response is reported out of context, yeah! And, I mean to say, that seems to happen a lot and, I mean to say, that's down to investigative journalism in a lot of ways. Yes, there's some areas where, I don't know, you could say they do a good *job* but there are a lot of areas where everything that is done nowadays is based on what comes out of the television.

John's thoughts on the 20th anniversary commemorations for December this year, 2008.

That's a difficult one! You'd have to ask the community, I think.

JH: Well, you're *part* of the community [JC laughs] What do you think?

JC: Well [sighs] how far do you go with these things? [pause] To be personally honest, I think the facility should be there for the people closely connected if they wish in, whether it's a commemorative service or something like that. I don't think there should be any obligation on individuals. I think if it came to the churches or some other to say, we will be having a service to commemorate the 20th anniversary; it will be held in such-and-such a place, [pause] free to anyone who wishes to go along. […] I dare say you'll get a large press coverage for the 20th anniversary, there's no doubt that people will come into the town, willy-nilly, television and so on, to see what's happened to the town

With regard to Lockerbie's current image, John tells me about the widely publicised comments, valid but misplaced, made by an MSP on a fleeting trip through Lockerbie.

JC: What had happened, he'd stopped in Lockerbie, got off the train and I think he'd walked up towards the statue and, of course, if anything, Station Road would be the worse part of Lockerbie to see and he says it was Tesco Town, and things like this, you know. It's all very well and there's probably an element of truth in there *are* a number of shops that are unoccupied and there are one or two of them that are a bit tatty and could do with some refurbishment *but* you don't degrade a community to that extent, particularly if you've no involvement in the community; there are other ways of doing it. I think he just got his wording wrong but he certainly made a bit of a [inaudible] about it. [...]Well, I recently walked down [...] in Dumfries and that is horrific [pause] so you could say that about most towns, I think.

JH: Although, would it be widely accepted that it might need a bit of a spruce up for the 20th anniversary or generally?

JC: I think it probably would benefit from that but, it's like anything, with the state of the economy and the way things are going, it there money there?

John verbalises his feelings about use of money from the Lockerbie Community Trust Fund, established during the time of the disaster. He details what a sustainable approach to spending could have meant for the town.

[...] the trust fund was set up for the benefit of the people in Lockerbie. Now, I would like to suggest—a lot of these properties that are derelict, why should that money be used to upgrade them when they probably, the properties themselves, could, to a certain extent—the likes of the old Co-op [pause] belong a national organisation? Is it fair for the community to have to fork out and do that? Well, your family were in business in Lockerbie but, surely, [pause] business folk in Lockerbie, if they're in business, should be able to look after their own premises. Now, fair enough, you could probably turn around and say to me, a lot of them are probably leased from somebody else. Well, surely, it is the owner's responsibility to ensure they—it's a difficult one, that. I mean to say, you could do a derelict property up and it could lay derelict for another ten years, and you're back where you started. And the other aspect of dealing with—I know there was a lot of money—oh, I don't know what's in the fund, it is not dedicated towards a swimming pool or something? I think they were trying to get a swimming pool in Lockerbie but I don't know how it's developing but, it's a very very difficult one, when you have money to dispense through—I mean to say, we experienced it in Rotary, and [pause] it went on for a long long time; we didn't have the money that they have but we had a sum of money that came from other Rotary clubs, for the good of people and those in Lockerbie. But it's a very demanding job, trying to identify who should get and who should not.

[...] I have my own thoughts on it, and it's not an easy one. I mean to say, another way of looking at it would be for the local authority to say, well, for this year, we'll not charge you rates; do something like spend it on your property. I would've thought that might be a better exercise than putting money from the funding—you know, surely, one has to ask, all that money that came in [pause] what has Lockerbie got to show for it? [pause] There's nothing of any, sort of, long-standing nature, other than probably the windows that were put in the town hall. Now, possibly some of the money,—I don't know how they funded the Lodge or the Tundergarth church, whether some of that was done through local authority or what, I don't know, or whether that came out of the funding.

But, to my mind—I mean to say, Lockerbie hasn't got a *community* resource. Prior to the disaster, there was a community resource in the old school and even *that* —I mean to say, I was up there the other day – I was taking { }kids up to the school and somebody had mentioned half the wall was down and they've put up this monstrosity of a six foot wire netting fence. Looks *terrible!* But, I just think there should've been something more longstanding done for the town. [...] Surely there could've been resource put into the community that would've benefited the community for *years.*

John and I compare the reactions of others outside Lockerbie and the area, to the hometown question.

JH: When you *do* go overseas, go away, and get chatting to people, do you feel reticent about telling them that you come from Lockerbie

JC: No, not at all people do ask where you come from. Lockerbie! Oh, right, and....

JH: How do they respond?

JC: That's as far as it goes, I think, you know.

JH: That's interesting I have different experience all together.

JC: I don't think I've had many, what I would call, reactions or wanting to know anything about it or you know, Well, where were you when it happened, you know – it's just an acknowledgement – whether it's because the people I've spoken to [pause] know the score or what, I don't know, but I've had very little in the way of reaction.

John retired from a long-standing career with Dumfries and Galloway Constabulary in 1993. He had already done 25 years service by the time the disaster occurred.

It was – 30 years to the year. I think I did about 3 months over my time. As I say, I quite enjoyed my time and I'm often asked if I would've served—I don't think I would've been in the police anywhere. I never fancied the city life. I like the rural community down here.

[...] when I was Head of Traffic, I became involved with a lot of other things that took me away from the force quite a bit, I was involved. I was actually the Chairman of what we call the Central Traffic Officers Conference which the head of traffic departments from all over Scotland and we also had a lot of representation on a lot of national bodies – for instance, we had speed detection devices, motorway patrols and so on which took you all over the UK and even abroad sometimes because at that time, I can remember speed cameras were coming into being, you know – they're ten a penny now, and of course the first countries in Europe to have them were Germany and Italy and it was as a result of that, the obvious thing to do was to go and see how they operated and—I never went but you used to get somebody from one of the larger forces to go across and report on what the issues and problems and what-have-you were, before making decisions and things like that.

I was also involved with the Superintendent's Association National Body and held representative post on that – in fact, I was responsible for Public Order Training, was on the interview panel for accelerated promotion of the police college, various other things over the years [laughs] but also you had to do with your own work back at the house but it's art and part of having—I was lucky in a lot of respects; I had a good team round about me, they were able to cope when I was away and they knew the way the things were. Made a lot of [inaudible] within the job and outside the job since, you know and I [hesitate] quite enjoy my lifestyle; I enjoy my golf and other bits and pieces that I've done in the community.

What you *do* find when you retire is, folk have great expectations from you, that you're available to assist with this, that and the other, you know, but it's not always the case. My observation on that is you can do too much. It got to the stage that I was out of the house more after I retired than I was working for a period because of my commitments to various things, you know. I became involved, this'll make you laugh, with the WRVS; they asked me to give them a hand with the hospital; runs and I said, As long as you don't asked me to wear a skirt. [laughs] But, I mean to say, they're one of the agencies there were involved with the disaster, the WRVS, because their facility for reception centres they utilised and are very good at it […]

John gives his view of the ultimate positivity of the disaster.

[I] think the community as a whole, as such, came out of it very well, and I'm sure it's similar to a lot of other communities, in times of disaster, they come together and they want to, and they're prepared to, get involved in any way they can and, they certainly did that in the town. And did for an awful long time, when you of the incident centre must've been in situ there of 18 months, 2 years, and the laundry was there for the best part of a year, and there would be local people involved in the recovery aspects, not a great deal of the recovery aspects, from the likes of materials and parts of the plane, etc, off the land. They did their utmost to their credit.

At the corner of Sherwood Park and Sherwood Crescent, observing the Smith's burnt-out home. The occupants survived. (© John Carpenter 2008)

John with Air Accident Investigators from Farnham at Ella Ramsden's house in Rosebank, just after the crash. Extra-tough rubber boots were provided due to the coverage of nails and tacks in the area.(© John Carpenter 2008)

Elizabeth Jane Crawford, 2008
(©James Crawford, 2008)

Relative Distress: Suffering from the Outside

This narrator's story is unique within this collection of oral transmissions about Lockerbie and the disaster – she has a spatially distinct perspective on thoughts, feelings, meanings and emotions borne out of the immediate circumstances of the catastrophe - yet it will surely resonate with the rest of the world, who came to know of the events in that wee place as they trickled then poured out of the channelled lens of world media that evening, that night and beyond..

Indeed, this narrator's account can be shared by all who had family or friends in or around the town and the outlying villages, or who knew of the place and had a passing acquaintance with it. Indeed, this narrative could be identified by anyone who has suffered stress over the welfare of a loved one. Lockerbie sits on the main route North and South and I have met dozens of people who have had a meal, spent a night or stopped for the loo in Lockerbie over the years. The first news reports, however, mentions the general impact area as Dumfries and Galloway, without specifying Lockerbie as the site of the crash. As the map of southern Scotland came up on the television screen, add ten or so thousand other similar experiences to the proceeding interview: that is a measure of the commonality of this narrator's story.

She was not in Lockerbie on the night of the disaster yet her family were.

The narrator was not born in Edinburgh, but moved to Lockerbie with family who still reside there She moved away to university in Edinburgh, now resides in Port Seton in East Lothian, and has never returned to live in the town.

She was schooled at the old primary and then at the academy. She was very involved with local community groups and sports clubs such as Girls Guides, Young Farmers Club and the Curling Club at Lockerbie.

We performed the interview in my parent's back room late in the afternoon on Saturday 5 April 2007. She had just returned from a curling match in Stranraer and we spoke for 37 minutes and 7 seconds. I was due to fly back to New Zealand the following day and we had talked about doing the interview ever since I had arrived in Scotland. So this was a long-awaited interview, longer than I realised as it turned out.

She told her story because I asked her to participate.

This narrator is my elder sister and, as such, we shared a frank and open interview. Implicit in the easy of our nature of relationship is a non-requirement of formality . This takes the form of a de-regulation of language and an informal attitude to content of questions and answers. no icebreaking, overcoming barriers, miscomprehended inference of meaning. There was a free flowing meander through consciousness although observing the parameters of the subject which was a pleasant experience.

There was a duality of understanding between us when conversing about her past and present experience of Lockerbie; siblings that share childhood can create a jigsaw of events with interlinking, overlapping memories - differently-shaped contours but the scene selection is the same. – I could anticipate her answers about that time on our common past.

I couldn't do likewise about her experience of 21st December 1988. Strange to say but her experience of that evening was news to me; heard for the first time; as if it was going in fresh to my consciousness: in short, I didn't have a semantic memory of that information. I can't say I'd never heard her narrative prior to this year because that seems impossible – families and sisters share many stories and these experiences were life-altering. Surely I had heard it sometime before but I don't recall it.

Consequently, three outcomes present themselves, all of which are revealing in the myriad complexity of this study of memory, community, and relationships. Possibly, I had never heard it because I had never asked - when assembled in a family or social group, the focus was on my family's story - stories of immediacy and urgency, proximity and drama, and happenstance. The second possibility could be that she had never wanted to tell it, the reasons for which I could only guess. The third explanation could be that I have forgotten it which is highly likely given that I have retained for recall all but a few vague memories and my sister's narrative doesn't feature in that archive.

Upon reading her transcription of the interview, my sister reflected on the text and contemplated on her memories there written. She realised that some of the recollections were "not correct"; that she had misremembered. This misremembering was only evident to her when she read the words in context. Words are easy to recall but the context – words that come before and after or the reason for uttering those words – is nebulous and consciously indistinct

Herein in the issue of veracity of memory – how true are memories and is their falsity a problem? How does my sister now remember that part of her evening then? And what is truth? This asks the question – do our memories only exist if we verbalise them or textualise them and then examine them by substantiation from actors in the memories? She'd been telling herself the same story for 20 years, as have I with mine. She would never have learnt of this rogue memory had she not verbalised her experience in detail this year, nor, and this is the salient point, if it had not been textualised. She would have forgotten she's said it. What is interesting is why she remembers it that way.

My family have talked about the disaster more this year than in the past twenty years, because we were all too busy coping with it and then we wanted to forget it and the distance from the event lengthened and it was no longer the defining incident in our life. People's lives continue - births, deaths, new jobs, retirement, holidays, new houses, opportunities, regrets – the event of the Lockerbie disaster is just another stitch in the textured tapestry that people weave from their lives.

Truth about events, the type that can quantified and proved otherwise, is based on evidence. Hard evidence is paper and documents which, we assume, don't lie. Evidence based on first-person narratives - recollections of events or memorised versions of others' recollections - are third-person narratives open to interpretation and the imagination.

The narrator discusses the importance of the media that evening. It was a mixed blessing to view scenes and images of initial devastation around the clock with wall-to-wall coverage. - glad of some link in the absence of the telephone - but the scenes on the television and the scant information presented the worst news If the early reports were correct and the images were genuine, how could any parts of the town escape significant destruction?

It should be remembered that this was 20 years ago, when there were four channels in the UK and live television was rare enough, but 24 hour broadcasting with satellite feeds were practically unheard of, except for news items of global significance like the space orbit in 1972 or the Royal Wedding. 20 years ago, people switched their TV off when TV stopped transmitting, between about 1am and 7am, because 24 hour broadcasting didn't exist.. The cancellation of evening programming so close to Christmas, for continuous news footage, would indicate a big event . This must have been alarming for the viewing public because it was unknown to happen except for pre-organised national occasions. What were they to make of this ? BBC Scotland elevated their international media profile in 1988 with the global broadcasting of two major disaster on Scottish homeland, the Lockerbie disaster and The Piper Alpha oil rig disaster - from a parochial and small budget nephew of Aunty Beeb to a recognised media organisation

The narrator's name is Elizabeth Jane Crawford. She is 43 years old. She currently works for the Scottish Childminding Association.

Jane talks about her cultural identity and pride in her rural background

I suppose when I was younger I'd always wanted to get away from Lockerbie but I don't think that — that was nothing about Lockerbie. I think that's quite normal for, you know, teenagers, young people growing up in a small, rural sort of village thinking, "There must be a bigger life out there" and wanting to go and experience that and find out what it is. And also, I suppose, wanting to get on and, you know, I left Lockerbie and I went to Edinburgh University and I think I saw that as a passport or a gateway into a different sort of life.[…]

I was never embarrassed to come from Lockerbie. I was always quite proud of the fact, I suppose, that I had had a kind of local comprehensive education and it had been fine for me. I'd got on well with it. I didn't feel bad about that when you would be mixing with people who had come from private schools. I always felt quite proud that I'd not had that kind of background but felt I was just as good as everyone else.

I don't know — I think now — no one would have known before, you see. You would say to people before, I had come from Lockerbie but they wouldn't know where that was, but I think that was okay. I mean, that anonymity of where that was, was fine. I didn't mind that at all but now when you tell people that you come from Lockerbie, it's famous, infamous, really.

Jane remembers first hearing about the disaster: She was working in a busy department store on Princes Street in Edinburgh, in the run-up to Christmas.

Usually if you were working of an evening, you wouldn't start until about 11.30 am. The shop would be open late because it was late night shopping and we had got it was Christmas, so probably the shop was open until about 9.00 pm but I would be — I don't know if I started the whole day but normally that would be kind of 11.30 am or 12.30 pm till 9.00 pm.

[…] I don't know exactly what I was *doing* but I was on the shop floor somewhere and the phone rang and I got — it was a phone call from one of the security guards. They had a kind of office downstairs in the shop and they sort of said that they thought I should come down and — because they had heard something on the radio about Lockerbie. So, I went down to the security guards' office and they said that they had heard — they didn't say that it was a bomb or whatever but they said they heard something on the radio about a plane crash near Lockerbie and they thought I should go home because they knew that I came from Lockerbie.

[...] I think afterwards I thought that they were being deliberately vague- they probably knew more than they were saying but they were deliberately not saying a lot so that they didn't panic me. But I do remember thinking, "Oh my goodness, what's happened?"

JH: So, did you just get your coat and say to somebody, "Well, I'm off, see you"?

EJC: Oh, yes, I think I did. I think I probably phoned up to tell the deputy manager, you know, "I'm having to go home, there's something happened about Lockerbie; can you do whatever it was to finish up that night?" There'd be someone else I could ask to finish up. I didn't just abandon it but I did just go home quite quickly, The Store manager gave me a lift in his car.[...] .It was dark. Maybe it would be evening. I left the shop before it properly shut, so[—]

JH: Did you feel a bit panicky or a bit concerned or wondering, mysterious kind of event?

EJC: [long pause] I don't really remember that bit now, I think because then once you got home to see, actually what it was became apparent, so I don't really remember what I feared about it before that. . I remember thinking it was something serious but not really understanding the enormity of it until I got home

When Jane returned home, one thing dominated her attention all night – the television.

I remember when I got in that [...] was watching the television; he was watching the news. He'd heard and when it was reported it was on the new just constantly all night.

JH: Can you remember what he said to you or vice versa?

EJC: No.[...] But I remember sitting in front of the television because the television was just a small wee kinda portable one sittin' over in the corner and normally you would sit in the armchair sort of further away watching it, but I remember sitting on the *arm* of the sofa, so that I was right — it was right in front of me, the screen, because you were trying your best to make out in all the flames and all the fire engines and all the stuff where things were. Where exactly was that, you know? What street was it? What houses were round about? So, [laughs] I was sitting as close to it as possible in order that you might be able to work that out.

Alarming news and disbelief.

What they [the media] said, you know, to begin with, often with these things that the information isn't particularly right or[—] I mean I remember saying that the whole town was on fire. It was quite[—] sensational. And you thought, "Oh, my goodness, the whole town's on fire" and then they kinda pinpointed it down to the fact that it was this petrol station, which obviously was the petrol station on the same street between where mum and dad lived and granny lived, so, you know, really close to my family; not far away really. Right in between it all. And you could see that, you could see the flames and whatever but you didn't really understand how that — how what you saw, what that meant to damage to people's individual houses, if you know what I mean. Obviously it said that the plane had crashed and blah blah blah, but I think what you were more [—] *I* was more concerned with was obviously whether my family were hurt or injured or[—. I mean, if the whole town was on fire, how could they possibly be alive, if that really was the case. But it just seemed that they showed the same clips over and over again when we turned over to another channel to see if we saw something different or heard something different but it kind of got to the point where they just showed the same thing over and over again. They didn't really have any kind of different news ...

Telecommunication problems brought anxiety for Lockerbie relatives.

... you couldn't phone anyone to find out. I remember, obviously, trying to phone mum and day and granny or whatever and then phoning other people; I remember Aunty Mary, she phoned me to see as well if I'd heard anything, because obviously she was worried.

JH: Where does she live?

EJC: She lives at Cloverhill Farm, near Broughton - in Broughton - and she's a really good friend of my mum's. She's not really my aunty, she's a good friend of my mum's and of course she's worried, so she's phoning me. I probably spoke to her on the phone a couple of *times* that night, actually.

JH: What did you say to her and what did she say to you?

EJC: Just, "Have you heard anything?". I can't remember the detail of it but neither of us knew anything, so anything that we would have spoken would have just been — I suppose what our interpretation of the news was. You know, it would have been TV news.

I got a phone call, eventually, from dad, I think, about 1.30 am, which confirmed that they were okay. We didn't go to bed until after that and I remember getting a call to say that they were okay and that — it wasn't a very long call, but they were fine, and that mum and dad and Jill were fine and that granny was as well, and I think then I phoned Aunty Mary to tell her, from what I remember.

JH: Was your other grandmother still around at that time? Would she call you?

EJC: She was still around at that time[—] Can't imagine I didn't hear from her. I must have because — I mean, I can't imagine she wouldn't be ...But I don't remember that at all.

The person referred to in Jane's narrative is Mrs Mary Smith from Broughton in Peebleshire, about 25 miles south of Edinburgh. Mary and our Mother became friends when teaching together at Broughton Primary school many years ago; growing up, our two families had annual New Year gatherings at Mary's farm and annual summer holidays near Ayr, on the west coast on Scotland.

Mary wrote to me at the end of April this year with her experience of the evening of 21/12/88. It illustrates the helpless distress from outside the disaster zone.

"*I'm a control freak and I wasn't in control that night – anything; accidents, terrible as they were, I was there and doing something whereas being at Cloverhill Farm with a TV switched on, the screen showing black and red, was dreadful.*"

"*I think we just sat, and I roamed about near a telephone[...] No phones in Lockerbie[...] Long night.[...] Phoning Jane was just awful; we could hardly speak to each other some of the times.[...] I think it was about 11.45pm when Jane phoned to say you were all safe.*"

"*[...] went up the hill with his short wave radio, spoke to his cousin who was in a lorry on A74, talking about debris, melting tyres. Didn't help us![...] We thought it was just a low-flying jet but the extent of the carnage in the air didn't sink till next day.[...] That was it – we read the papers, watched TV ad the horror emerged.*"

"*I still feel it's wrong to have TV footage[...] so quickly, before anyone knew what was happening to the people at the scene. And afterwards I feel anger and revulsion at the intrusive TV coverage when compassion was what was needed.*"

"*It really was the worst time of my life – in spite of[...] accident, my heart attack, etc.[...] Looking up my diary it says, "terrible disaster US plane at Lockerbie" and I didn't write in the diary for days after that.*". *[personal letter, n.d.]*

Jane talks about how she coped with the uncertainty of her family's safety as the TV coverage

I remember I hadn't had any tea obviously, and James was saying, "Do you want some tea?" and I said, "No, no", and I don't remember doing anything else except sitting in front of the TV, watching it. I don't think I even took my coat off for a while, because you are just kind of sort of staring in disbelief at what had happened, thinking — and then at one point, I think when you probably heard the same news story over and over again, you kind of thought — I don't know, it was almost like you convinced yourself. You just couldn't — you couldn't let yourself believe that really something that awful would have happened to them. You couldn't let yourself believe that they would all be dead, so at that point I said, "James, I'll have some soup then". And I remember going and making soup and I remember James saying, "How can you eat soup?" and I said, "No, because they will be okay. I know they will be okay" and I didn't know but you just, I suppose, can't — when you didn't know you can't dwell on the fact that they're not there. I just couldn't — I got to the point that I had to think, "I can't think that", you know.

JH: What was James — what was James saying to you during this, apart from, "You can't eat soup"? Did he seem to be —

EJC: I don't know. I don't remember anything about what he said. He was there all the time but we didn't — stupid thing to say, but we didn't, I don't know, console one another. Do you know what I mean? I don't remember him giving me a hug or saying, "It will be okay" or you know, anything like that. I don't remember that. I'm sure we didn't do that. We just stared. We just sat and stared and it in a kind of complete disbelief really. Complete. I think because it was such an unlikely thing to happen anywhere but particularly to happen, you know, in the town that you were born — grew up in when you knew that you had, you know, your family there. You just couldn't believe that one day, that morning you got up, everything's fine and it was all just normal, preparing for Christmas and blah, blah, blah, shop's heaving and then that night, gosh, something like that. You couldn't possibly believe that that would ever have happened.

Overnight, Lockerbie hit the headlines: from a distance, Jane found that hard to deal with.

There was a bit of you that didn't really want to see the devastation or whatever. You wanted to be there to see your family in person and check that they were okay. You didn't really want to see any other horrific stuff, so I went to work.[…] the thing I really remember most vividly was the time on the bus going to work, next to these people who were reading newspapers and there it was all over the newspapers, "Lockerbie" in great big words and that was really weird because these strangers were reading all this stuff about the place that I come from, you know. On the day before if you'd said to somebody, "You came from Lockerbie", they wouldn't even know where that was and then here today they're all reading this stuff about my town and that was really — I still am angry about that because it's like violated all my — the memories that you had of Lockerbie being a nice place to live when you were a child and because now it's not that quiet, little, anonymous place that I grew up with. It's not like that any more and right from that day it wasn't like that because all these people were reading about it. It suddenly wasn't about what the village was like any more, it was about the fact that this plane had crashed there and that was just really, I suppose, unbelievable as well, but annoying. I remember being angry about that.

Struggling with her normal routine, in the face of the tragedy.

But the thing I do remember though is about people's problems or dealing with customer complaints and things that day. They just didn't really seem important any more. You know, people moaning about the price of something or "Can you take money off because there's a chink in this?" Somebody brought back a pair of jeans, I remember, and they didn't have a receipt and they said they'd had them for so long and the zip had broken and normally you would have not really relented on that. You would have said, "Well, that's just wear and tear" but I just remember thinking, "I just can't be bothered arguing with this woman". It's not important in the scheme of things - whether that pair of jeans is neither here nor there, so she just got a replacement pair of jeans and that was that, because it kind of put things in life into perspective. All the fuss about, "Is the sale ready?" and "Have you marked down all these things and does everything have a ticket on it?" and all the trivia of retailing anyway just wasn't important, I suppose, for me, in the bigger scheme of things.

Lockerbie as Jane's hometown: how do people on the outside of her experience categorise her?

[…] people always then speak about the disaster. They say, "Were you there?" They always usually know where they were and what they were doing, so you probably don't always want to get into that conversation with everyone or certain other people who maybe didn't know you very much beforehand. So, if you say where you come from, that gets them — it makes them think of you differently, I think. They think of you as — they associate you with that place rather than look at you as an individual person in your own right.

Jane reveals how she feels about commemorating the anniversaries and why.

I have a friend[…] and she did speak to me about her feelings about what it was like that night and she said she thought that the end of the world had come, because you used to hear that on the TV then. […] The sound, the smell and the way she spoke about it really made me think that there's no way you could really appreciate how — what that was like unless you'd been there.

[…] I think I would feel like I'm an outsider.[…] I remember feeling a bit like that at the time but I really think unless you were there, unless you were there and experienced it, I suppose I would feel that me, as someone who hadn't been though that, had no right to be involved in the grieving with others who had been there, because I think that experience a kind of — whats the word? Like a — not just a common bond but it's something that you just can't possibly understand unless you were there and so if that is the case then why would you want other outside people who are standing there feeling upset as well. It's like crying at the funeral of someone you don't know. Why are you to be there? I suppose I've felt like that.. I feel more of an outsider now because I wasn't there than I ever did before, but also because I have been away for a long time now — what, 43 now, so I was 17 when I left. It's a long time, so I don't really feel part of that. I don't feel the right to be as annoyed about it or grieve about it at that time, you know, because I wasn't — I know I probably was affected but not directly affected like the people who lived here.

JH: So, do you plan to return for any commemoration of the 20th anniversary?

EJC: No. No. I think — I think I don't want a part of that really. I don't know why. I think it's just as that I've said, that I don't think it's my right to be there and I wouldn't –

I can understand why people in other parts of the world, even other parts of Britain, Scotland, would think it was an important event that was worthy of commemorating but that's different from them having a right to know what the people of Lockerbie are doing now and I think the people of Lockerbie have got a right to just be left to get on with their lives in private, without the rest of the country or the world always wanting to harp back to, you know, this event that happened and tar them with that brush for the rest of their lives, because it was 20 years ago now and people's lives have moved on and none of it was the doing or the instigation of anyone in Lockerbie anyway. It was something that happened to them and so it doesn't really help the people getting on with their normal lives while the media or the rest of the world to be constantly going on about it and saying, you know, "What's life like now?"

The importance of the history to the children of Lockerbie post-disaster:

I think if you come from here now then what happened is part of the history of the town you are now growing up in[…] I mean there's children growing up here now who don't know anything about that at all.

So, it is important to know about what happened and probably to know and understand as much as anyone about the bigger picture of why it happened and whose fault it was and all the rest of it, because those children kind of need to — they weren't born at the time but they are then born now in a place which has had that event and whose reputation is — whose identity is now more about the disaster than it was about just being a small farming town[…] So, the identity of the place they've been born into has changed and so they need to know about the history of that, but that's different from me who grew up in it as it was before, before it became changed and altered by this event.

Jane remembers that she had never spoken frankly or in detail with her family about the events of that night.

Yes, yes, we must have. I mean, they [the family] would have said — I know that they've said that what happened — well, maybe not everything that happened on the night, to be honest, but you know the basics about going up — they had to go and marshal in the town hall or something. Dad had a shop — a grocers shop and the window was all blown in, so they had to make that good but I don't suppose I really know the detail of that, you know, exactly how they did that. I know that that happened.

JH: Did they talk about their feelings to you, about how we felt about that experience?

EJC: No, I don't think so. I remember things like mum not liking Christmas after that and the sort of really good memories she'd had about Christmas and the lovely Christmas when she was like a child were, she said, had gone because of that, the fact that the sight of decorations now brought bad memories not the good ones and so I felt that I had kind of tried to overcome that I suppose by doing more things with her that Christmas,. But never really have they said to me or have we had a discussion about how — whether they felt scared on the night or whether they thought they were going to die, or whatever. Never

Jane remember the town of her childhood with surprisingly few changes.

[…] we always come in off the bypass, past the school, where I went to school and now the primary school isn't anymore because they used it as the sort of centre for the investigations and things like that at the time and I think that changed its purpose for ever and they then built a new primary school[…] But the secondary school is still just as it was […] Actually it looks exactly the same as it did all those years ago when I went there. They're doing some building work in the car park or whatever but the actual —

JH: They're building a brand new school, apparently.

EJC: Oh, are they. Well, it's about time because the actual outside of the classrooms that you can see, with the blue chipboard around the bottom and then the windows, looks exactly the same. I've never been in it since then –[…] the road has made a big difference, I suppose. When I was here there was no motorway. There was no M74, so that's cut through a lot of the fields and the places that I remember going as a child with my pony and stuff like that. That's changed. Cut down a lot of trees but basically it doesn't look any different.

The Mace shop, with windows decorated for Gala Day. 42 Mains Street, my family home was semi-detached, to the side and above the shop. (© James Haldane 2008)

Haldane's bakers van outside the bake house in West Linton, 1950s. (© James Haldane 2008)

Yvonne & Jimmy Haldane in 2006.
(© James Haldane 2008)

Mrs and Mrs Mace: Retailers Retell

These narratives belong to a Lockerbie couple, husband and wife. They were interviewed together and share a common experience although not identical memories because they are individuals with a separate consciousness of the past.

They have been married for 47 years. They had a business and family home at the foot of the town at the time of the disaster. His shop on Mains Street was a regular central point of contact but with the disaster, it became a forum for interchange between customers who had common perceptions on the events but different experiences and circumstances. They were witness to many situations which mark these narrators as agents in multiple stories of the disaster and the aftermath, not to mention a gauge of the affect of the events on the collective: their customers. He retired in 2006, sold the business to a hardware retailer, and they moved to his wife's parents' home further south of the town, on Carlisle Road.

They have been resident in Lockerbie for around forty years, and are well-established identities in the town, and we have no other relatives living in close proximity . They have two daughters – my sister and I; this pair of narrators is my parents.

I hadn't planned on interviewing them for unspecified reasons, until the publisher came and they were chatting with him about the stories from the shop and their first-hand accounts. I realised when listening that they had great descriptions to inform the body of narratives, and I would be remiss to leave Lockerbie without recording their voices. They agreed without hesitation to be interviewed, as they had been very involved in the project prior to this.

So we left it, like all good things, until my last day in Scotland. The grandchildren were quiet and peaceful in the lounge for a couple of hours. On 5 April, Jimmy, Yvonne and I sat in the bay windows of the back bedroom, where the diluted late afternoon sun highlighted our reflections.

I asked Jimmy and Yvonne about our heritage. This is not an oft-discussed topic: a name is missing and I learnt my grandmother's profession.

EYH: My parents were David Wardlaw and Isobel Wardlaw. He was the headmaster at New Galloway public school and [pause] Mother was just [pause] Mother!. Isobel McLoughlin, she was, before she was married.

JH: She was a homemaker, was she?

EYH: All her married life, yes. Before that, she made hats.

JH: She was a milliner? In New Galloway?

EYH: No, no, no; in Dumbarton, I think

JH: And so their parents?

EYH: Their parents? David Wardlaw's parents, my Father's parents, lived in Clydebank. The father was a head plumber with Singers sewing machine factory, and the Mother—well, they didnae work in those days, did they. Just at home.

JH: Well, my parents came from—well, they stayed in West Linton. James Haldane – he was a baker and he ran the baker's business. My Mother, Isabella Haldane, she helped; she was also—she was a teacher before she was married, and then she worked—Ministry of Agriculture and Fisheries in Edinburgh, paying the grants to the fishermen. So she was very much involved in the fishing trade. When she was young, she stayed in Aberdeen so she knew all about the fishing trade.

JH: My grandparents came from East Lothian: Bonnyrigg and that area [pause] Don't know what they did. [pause] My grandmother's name was Lawson. Ma Mother's parents [pause] were in Aberdeenshire and James Cobban was an architect at Haddo House.

JH: What about James' wife? What was her name?

JH: Don't know! Margaret rings a bell.

EYH: Don't know either. No. I don't know *what* she as called? [both speaking at once] She died fairly—you would never know her? Coz he married again, you see.

JH: No, no. Coz my Nan— well, her correct name would be Agnes and she's the one that *I* knew.

JH: So we don't know—Oh, dear! Well, we'll need to investigate that!

Jimmy's skills training was in the family trade: Yvonne was a Domestic Science trainee, graduating in 1959

JH: I went to school in West Linton, until I was fifteen, then I left and I went to bakery college in Edinburgh in 1957,8 I finished that when ma Father took ill and I had to work fulltime in the bakery [in West Linton]

Yvonne and Jimmy met and eventually married in Dad's wee village, West Linton, in 1961.They describe the circumstances that brought them to Lockerbie.

Came in Nineteen sixty five, November. We came because the family business was getting [pause] what can I say? Too big for the family?

JH: The number in the family were too big for the business—

EYH: That's right.

JH: —so we felt we had to branch out on our own and we decided to come here because Yvonne's Mother and Father had just retired here, so we decided to come and set up this business in a shop that was very much run-down.

EYH: And Dad knew the man that owned it.

JH: And we—we had quite a bit of hard work but—

JH: And was it a bakery business?

JH: It was a licensed grocer. I'd finished with bakery..There would be six or eight; six to eight [grocers in the town then] ; something like that.

JH: And when you retired [28.09.06] , how many grocers were there in Lockerbie?

JH: One—private and one other. During ma time in West Linton, we were bakers abut then we developed the grocery, so it was half and half; bakers, grocers; so therefore, I knew about the grocery trade before we came.

JH: So, Yvonne, did you keep on teaching when you got back down to Lockerbie?

EYH: Just part-time because Jane was just nine months old when we came here, in the local school in Lockerbie: Lockerbie Academy, and I also did supply primary teaching, in the country schools.

What attracted them to Lockerbie as a place to settle with young children?

It was quite a pleasant country market town; nice place to live, nice place to bring up the kids. They could about, you know; they'd quite a good school in those days.

JH: That was on the main things about it; the fact that you were able to go to a good primary school, then go to a good secondary school without leaving the town.

The population at that time was about 3,000 whereas those small places like West Linton and New Galloway—oh, they were less than a thousand. So it was a bigger place—

EYH: Much bigger.

JH: —and in those days, in seemed as if there was more development.

EYH: They dual carriageway had just opened. When Mum and Dad came here, it still went through the town because we had a terrible time getting out the gateway and, by the time we came here, the carriageway was open, which people sort of said, Oh, it'll kill the town, but, in fact, it didn't because more people could come through and stop and get out whereas, before, you didn't have a chance of stopping, in was just nonstop. In fact, to get out the gateway, we'd to go and hold up the traffic—that's true, isn't it?

JH: Now this property we're talking about is not the property we're in now! Where was your shop and house then?

JH: It was at 40/42 Mains Street; it stood [long pause]

EYH: Detached!

JH: Detached. Had a large pavement in front and it just looked as if it was on its own. We built an extension a few years after, to double the size of the shop.

EYH: And when we came here at first actually, they had just—they were knocking down the houses across the road and up from us, to built new flats; so that contributed quite a bit to new trade.

Jimmy's shop, The Mace, was a licensed grocers on the main route through the town: he employed some help and it was getting busier until the supermarket arrived

We employed, what would be then a school girl leaving school then at fifteen, and we employed them until they left to get married; three of them? And then we gradually had other part-timers, coming filling in. We also had a message boy [pause]

EYH: With a bike!

JH: We had country trade as well. Later, I delivered to the country trade. In those days, everybody didn't have cars so you had to deliver—maybe [to] a radius of five miles about the town

Christmas and New Year of course were busy, real busy, but we had some good summer trade as well. But the whole point is we had an all round business trade; it wasn't up and down like a holiday place would be. Lockerbie's just on the main road, its not a holiday town.

EYH: We'd quite a lot of passing trade [coughs] —'cuse me—from lorry drivers and commercial travellers and all these who would regularly have a run up and down and they always stopped in to us because they stop at the door, pop in and get rolls, biscuits whatever, and pop out again, so it was easy to park and—we'd a lot of that trade, hadn't we? And it wasn't so busy at Christmas after the supermarkets opened.

I can't remember when the first one was [pause] can't remember, Jill, but it began to get that it wasn't so busy. In the olden days, you were shut two days at Christmas so people stocked up but, you see, after the supermarkets opened, you didn't coz they were only—well, if they were shut *at all,* that people didn't need to stock up the same so your Christmas Eve and your Hogmanay weren't really so busy.

JH;   The first supermarket would be Templetons, it opened as Templetons. It's much bigger now, that same area, and is now Somerfields.

EYH: We had the Coperative [both speaking at once]   but, I mean, it shut, it closed.

JH: But the Cooperative had always been there, hadn't it? Coz I read that it paid to knock down the Mains Farm that was on that site

EYH: Yes, it was always there.

JH: But it got bigger.

Jimmy and Yvonne established the Sugarcraft Guild in the town, with national success.

There was a girl came and asked if we could like to help her start up the Sugarcraft Guild, you see, so we thought, Yes, we would, so Dad helped her, to set it up, and we had quite a lot of *members* at the start and, I mean, I joined too – not really my hobby but I joined just to make up the numbers [laughs], and eventually learnt to do sugar flowers and things. Dad was sort of the royal icing expert and through that, he got a lot of orders for cakes, you know: wedding cakes and birthday cakes, so he was really quite busy, as a sideline, doing that.

JH: And how many members did you have in the club?

EYH: Oh, Gosh, I can't remember. What, about twenty mibby?

JH: Yes, twenty at least

[All speaking at once]

EYH: We actually won the Scottish Sugarcraft Champion in—I can't remember where it was; Edinburgh, was it?

JH: Ingelston, in the early 90s.

EYH: No, it must've been in the late eighties because we were doing it when Jane got married in 1990, coz we'd just started the sugar flowers then: so it must've been eighty— must've been after the disaster right enough. I would say about eighty nine.

JH: And does the club still function?

EYH: Yes, its still going, its still going on. I'm not sure how many members now; we stopped going because it got away from royal icing and flowers, it got really very—doing flowers on slate and that—you know, as pictures and things; not really—No, so got a bit disillusioned.

Changes to Lockerbie in the twenty three years on Mains Street, prior to the disaster

JH: We'd quite a few grocers shops had closed. Not just grocers shops but [pause] grocers were the ones you noticed that weren't there anymore.

EYH: Well, more new houses built over the road and of course the motorway had come into being.

JH: Not at the time of the disaster, though, eh?

[Both speaking at once]

       No, the motorway was built—

JH: It started after the disaster coz they were still using the dual when the plane came down.

How Jimmy and Yvonne recall that night in December, twenty years ago. Their memories are clear and vivid after this time.

EYH: Well we were at home and daughter Jill was there, and we were going up the stairs to watch Terry Wogan and his Christmas show.

JH: And I was sitting downstairs. We'd just had our meal and I was downstairs and was gonna go back round to the shop because we were really busy because it was coming up to Christmas. So I was going back round to the shop, to do some work The shop was closed but I was going to do some work in the back way.

EYH: And then, when we were up the stairs, my daughter said, "What's that awful noise?", and I said, "What noise?" ""That noise?" "What noise?" [EYH laughs] This went on until I actually *did* hear the noise and it got bigger and bigger, and louder and louder. My daughter was dancing about from sofa to sofa shouting, "What on earth is it?" And we hear the bang and looked out the window – foolishly looked out the window - and we saw the flame just across the way, and we thought, we thought at first that it was a low-flying jet come down because we were apt to get them over the town, and then all the debris flew out and the noise – it was awful – so we rushed down the stairs.

JH: I was sittin beside the fire and I heard the noise coming down the chimney [pause] After the first shock of it, I ran and shouted to Yvonne and Jill to come downstairs, come down coz I felt that the thing was above us and was gonnae come down into us. Then we made our way, not out the front door, out the back door.

EYH: And the cat shot in [laughs]
JH: As we were about to go out the back door, I closed the door again because I realised the glass was broken in it but then we *did* go out and we could *smell* the fuel, the aeroplane fuel, soon as we stepped out, and the mud and the stones and the rubble and the burning on the roof.
JH: On your roof?
JH: No, on the roof of the garage next door because we didn't realise that our sheds were burning as well; we didn't go that far [round to the back yard], we went towards the street, and then we saw other people.
EYH: All coming out, wondering what was happening. And the big shop window was smashed.
JH: Yes, this shop window is immediately one storey below the window that Yvonne and Jill looked out of, as it was about to happen.
JH: I don't think I looked out of it [Jill and JH laugh] . She did! [lJill laughs]
JH: Yes, so—Very lucky escape. But then after we were out, and you saw other people out, some sittin' about, dazed and shocked: not dazed; shocked.
      And they evacuated and by this time, the police had arrived and fire brigade, and running down the street; by this time, we realised it wasn't just us, it was over Sherwood Crescent and the police ushered us up the street, to get up and clear the area, clear the area because they were frightened the petrol station would explode. about two hundred yards, mibby, down the road from us.
JH: It's halfway between the shop that we had and the house we now stay in.
JH: But the police were also stopping the cars from going past our shop and either making them park or making them turn so it really seemed an awful lot seemed to be happening because the police obviously didn't want them to do down near the garage, the filling station.
JH: So what did you do then, Jimmy?
EYH: Just hung about and our friends from across the road came across.
JH: But, just as we were coming out, Granny from The Lea—she telephoned to say there was something going on.
EYH: A fireworks party [laughs] [imitating Granny] "There's a fireworks party going on out there, Jimmy, there's an awful lot of banging and lights."
JH: And how old would she be at the time?
EYH: Oh, gosh, 92, 91.
JH: Well into the stages of her senile—
EYH: No, she'd be eighty eight minus three; she was born in 03 so she'd be—
EYH: Yes, she'd be eighty five then—she was just a bit vague then; aye, she was a

bit vague, and Jimmy said, "Where are you?

JH: When I asked her where she was, she said she was gong to her bed so I told her to go to her bed and stay there, and we'd be along later. Then I tried to go along to see her, coz I knew all the short cuts and the back ways, but unfortunately, I couldn't get the back way and I came out onto the street again and he police ushered me back. So we were then avacuated, with everybody else from Mains Street, to the Town Hall. Granny was evacuated to the Somerton Hotel, that's to the south of the petrol station, and her neighbours helped her along.

JH: Gosh, that must've been really upsetting for her.

EYH: She didn't realise the significance of it, did she? And she said to me afterwards, "Do you know, they were all having a drink!" Yes, this man that she knew from round there, won't mention names, was having a drink; in fact, "I think he had one or two!" I said, "Well, so would you if you'd just been bombed out your house, wouldn't you." [laughs] She was quite shocked. Doug and Famie saw her back [to her house]. Aye, that's right.

They remember the devastating news delivered to friends in the street: rumours filter through the stories

JH: And we hung about the street, spoke to various people and everybody had their own stories to tell.

EYH: Spoke to Doreen and Vera.

JH: Who are they?

EYH: Doreen was the niece of Dora whose house was demolished in the crater but at that time, we didn't *know* that it was it; we had heard *rumours* that it was Dora's house but it wasn't confirmed. And we were standing there, talking to them, when the priest came up who lives about—the other end of the crescent from Dora and Maurice, and he said, "Yes, it was—" and one of them collapsed in the street, and we sorta left them with the priest and went on up but,; by this time, there was word they were going to be using it as a mortuary and it was a passenger jet [pause] that had come down but nobody knew anymore about it, so.

At the Town Hall:

EYH: Daughter Jill didn't want to go into the Town Hall [but] we were s'posed to go in and sign our names: register that we were alive.

JH: Because we were in the area of the disaster: we were also in the area of filling station and that was the big trouble, that the filling station would explode.

EYH: And you did that, didn't you? You did that? [asking JH]

JH: No.

EYH: Did you not?

JH: You didn't put names down [laughs] on the list?

EYH: I thought we had.

JH: No!

JH: Okay well.

The evening progressed until they were eventually allowed home: a call from Canada was a surprise

EYH: We went to the Blue Bell Hotel. Jimmy being the only one who had any money in his pocket. So that was handy [chuckles] and various other people started coming in there and we were all sitting chatting and one thing and another and then we went out to West Acres, to stay with friends out there for the evening, you know, they were—asked us out to stay there. So we went along with Christeen and Howard and various other people and—I went back to the shop to make sure it was secure. [pause] Did we board up the window then?

EYH: I think we boarded up the window *before* we went up the street to—Howard across the road, came with a big sheet of plywood.

JH: Aye, that's the only way that anybody couldae got into the shop so I was anxious about the fact that people could just go in. In hindsight, I know it wouldae been quite *safe now* ; at the time I didn't. So we boarded it up with a piece of wood. An A. A. man, who appeared, he came and helped us. He had obviously volunteered himself to do what was needed. But we did—we hammered it up. So I went to the shop then back up to the meeting place, and then we went to West Acres.

JH: We still hadn't seen the telly, the television: we didn't see all the pictures that everybody outside Lockerbie saw.

EYH: And we never have done; haven't seen them: to this *day*, haven't see them.

JH: You see snippets, but, we didn't see that—

EYH: And there was no phone lines; tried phoning, you know, phoning Jane and Mary and Granny Haldane, but no phone lines. Eilidh was up, Christeen's daughter, and they decided to go home about two, half past two mibby, and we gave them Jane's phone number coz they said, Well they're lines might be alright from down there from Middlebie. So right enough, Eilidh had got through to Jane, to tell her where we were and that we were all alright. But Jane, of course, couldn't phone back [pause] and we went back home—we decided about four o'clock, to go back, and it was only because we had no gas in the house that we were allowed back.

EYH: They said, Have ye gas? We said, No! Oh, ye can go back in then.

JH: So, when you walked round from West Acres at four, were there policemen standing in the roads?

EYH: Oh, all over. And reporters.

JH: Aye, yes, all over the place.

EYH: And cameramen; just everywhere.

JH: An awful lot of activity.

EYH: Still fire engines

JH: But we didn't go home; we decided to come along, to see that Granny was alright. And there was even more police, standing at the roadways and the entries.

EYH: And there was army searching her garden

JH: And there was big cranes out in the roadway here, that had obviously come south, ready to lift—

EYH: Debris!

JH: Things that were needed to be lifted.

EYH: And so, what were they looking for, in Granny's garden?

EYH: Body parts, anything—

JH: Anything they could find

EYH: Not that we know of, we were never told. But I don't think they did. She had a hole in the roof, with flying debris .

JH: They *did* find an engine in the field that's behind—

EYH: The house.

JH: *The Lea* house, which is probably why the police were about, and I couldn't get that way the first time I tried to get.

EYH: There was also a body found, just down [pause] there, the way Dad would've come. It was a girl.

So we went home [pause] we came in here and we saw Mother. She was in her bed and we said, That's fine, you just stay here, we'll be up in the morning, you know; she didn't quite grasp the enormity of the whole thing and never ever did, actually, but anyway, we went back down home and the phone rang [pause] and it was my sister-in-law from Canada! [pause] And *how* she got through, I don't know!

JH: Coz we didn't have another phone call for days and we weren't able to use the phone for days after

EYH: Days and days. Well, we did—we must've done coz we must've called *Jane* or maybe Jane did the phoning; she phoned Mary and your Mother and all these kinda folk, eh.

The following day, a Thursday, The Mace shop opened but it was hardly business as usual

JH: And the first customers I had were reporters, cameras [pause] and I wasn't—

EYH: You wernae polite to them [laughs], put it that way.

JH: I wasn't [laugh] very keen to talk to them, no, especially when one camera crew tried to take photographs from the inside of the shop out the way, through the broken windows and what-have-you. And they got worse as the days went on.

EYH: I remember I got one of these reporters at the till and he said something about—asked me a question, and I said, "You know, we do *not* want to speak to you, we've got friends who've been involved in this." And he said, " Do you know that for sure?" and I said, "Yes, we know that for sure." So I said, "If you don't mind!" I was more polite that Jimmy.

JH: So did they respond to your anger?

EYH: Yes, they did.

JH: They left, yes.

EYH: They went out; they didn't bother. I think the word must've gone round amongst them, Don't go to that shop, he's rude. [EYH laughs]

JH: So obviously people were coming in the next day and were they talking about their experiences? Did they come in to buy things or did they come in to talk?

JH: They came in to talk, they came in obviously to buy things, but they talked more and more, and you could tell the ones that were more affected by the way they spoke and the agitation in their voice.

EYH: Quite a lot of them came in to buy something and then couldn't remember what it was.

JH: Yes!

EYH: A lot of that

JH: All symptoms of shock.

EYH: And sort of said, A' cannae remember what A' came for!" So they would go away and come back again when they did remember, you know. But, no they were—they talked and talked and better talked, and I mean that went on for *weeks* after the disaster.

Jimmy's Christmas sales were obviously disrupted but the produce didn't go to waste.

It was—most definitely was affected; in fact, it was affected so much that everything we had left at Christmas weekend, because the Saturday night was Christmas Eve and Old Year's night was Saturday, so for both weeks, everything that was left, we took up to the school, the Academy, because that's where they were feeding *all* the volunteers and the police and everything. So we just took everything like bread, cakes all perishables, anything that was perishable, and we also took all the veg, everything like that.

Jimmy and Yvonne see the disaster as a distinct reference point: Yvonne remembers the Kennedy assassination

EYH: I mean, even now, any date in Lockerbie, was it before the disaster or after? You know, its a point in Lockerbie's calendar that, Aye, that was before the disaster, wasn't it?, or –

JH: Like where were you—what were you doing when President Kennedy was shot.

EYH: You know, this kinda thing; its the same thing. I remember exactly what I was doing when President Kennedy was shot. I was in the house with Lillian Stevens and you were on night shift in the bakery. Lillian used to come and clean my cooker on a Friday night—because she needed pocket money so I used to let her come; she used to quite like cleaning the cooker, and Lillian and I were sitting talking when it came through on the—must've been television I those days too, and we went round to the bakehouse and here was Jimmy had it on the radio, and that's where we were, that's what I was doing.

Loved ones outside of Lockerbie had the worst experience of anxiety: Jimmy explains

JH: And we certainly know where we were when the Lockerbie disaster—in fact that's the whole *point* about the Lockerbie disaster, and our feelings: we knew fine that we were alright within 10 minutes twenty minutes of the incident – we were fine, we were alright, we were just looking after ourselves so we knew we didn't have any worries. We didn't have to worry the fact that it was coming coz we knew it had happened; it had come and passed, we were alright.

Christmas and New Year 1988 – fragmented recollections from my parents: Yvonne connected with a distant relative

EYH: I can only remember Christmas dinner' I can't remember opening presents or anything like that; can't remember that bit. I can remember being at Christmas dinner and we had Granny down, and we were having Christmas dinner when the bell rang and it was a Salvation Army officer, looking for my Mother; some relative of his secretary was my Mother's nephew [John] and wanted to know the situation. So he came in and spoke to Mother, and I explained things but, even at that, she didn't quite fully understand the whole thing.

And of course, since then, John and I have met up and do Christmas cards and all that which before then, I didn't even know—well, I knew he existed but I didn't know anything about him but since then, John and his wife have visited two or three times, and she decorates cakes so we gave her quite lot of Dad's books away the last time she was here and [pause] yes, aye, yes; we've got to know John through that, otherwise we wouldn't have done. And that's all remember about Christmas day.

Boxing Day, I remember; we went up the road. We went to Mary's, my friends, and or course, they were overjoyed to see us coz they thought they wouldn't ever see us again, and we had to spiel off the whole story there and then we went to Jimmy's Mother, and we had it all to say again there, and then we went to Jane's, and we had it all to say again there. So we were all talked out by the time—

JH: Part of the reason we went was because they wanted to see us but also because of the telephones, it had been difficult to speak to them so we felt that that's what we should do; get away up there, just out the way.

EYH: Coz even when the phones did start working, you could get cut off anytime, you know.

JH: Now, that would be the Sunday after New Year

EYH: After Christmas! Was it not after Christmas?

JH: Oh mibby Christmas.

EYH: I think it was after Christmas.

JH: And what did you do for New Year? Did you stay in Lockerbie?

EYH: I can't remember.

JH: We stayed in Lockerbie and—

EYH: Did we? We didn't go up to Mary's?

JH: So you can't remember it being eventful in any way?

JH: No, not at all, because everything was still happening in the town. Compensation and repairs occupied the town post-disaster: Jimmy and Yvonne sustained damages.

EYH: Yes; we had community meetings; street—oh, that's right, street meetings, street meetings. If anybody in the street had a kind of grievance or decided they wanted to claim something, then would come to you and say, Look would you bring it up with the committee, that I need a new chimney pot, or something, you know, and so we met, quite often, didn't we? Can't remember how often, to be honest, but [pause] it was fairly regular.

JH: So each street had representatives—

EYH: Two representatives.

JH: And you then met with the council.

EYH: Eh, was it, was it the council? No, I don't think so. It was a disaster committee, made up of, presumably, some members of the council and some other [pause] heed-bummers [laughs], you know what I mean? Eh, It went on for quite a while after; yes quite a while after and there was quite a talk about insurance: everybody wanted their—What if I have a crack in ma' house in three years time, can I put it down to the disaster?, you know, this sort of thing, but, it began to get a bit petty.

JH: There was a firm employed to assess damage all over the town, and came and visited every premises in the area; the area that was damaged. The name *Pan Am* was—everything got lumped under the name, *Pan Am*, if it was insurance companies or if it was lawyers or it was—it was all *Pan Am*, that was *the* one that everybody seemed to be against.

JH: And did Pan Am give out any other compensation to the people in Lockerbie?

JH: Oh, well, we did received a hundred pounds because we were E—Evacuated, so there as an 'e' against our name in the register so we got a hundred pounds from Pan Am or from the company that worked for Pan Am.

JH: And of course, Pan Am has since gone out of business—

EYH: Yes

JH: The fact that they were sued—

EYH: So many times. After the disaster, there was groups of workmen going round—any workmen who could, would go round—there'd mibby be one chap who was a roofer but he'd mibby had ten people helping him who wernae roofers; they'd be painters or plumbers or something else, you know, and they would—they tried to repair all the holes in the rooves as soon as they could ...

Well, outside, we'd small damage to the car – quite a dent in the back of the car. We had various garden pots and things smashed, but then it got more serious—oh, we'd the roof of one shed and it was the firemen that come and covered it with the big tarpaulin; just hung the tarpaulin over it, weighted down, until it was repaired, it was a shed that we kept things in—shop goods. But, then, we had the back door of the house was damaged, the porch; but we had the flat roof, we had one hole in the flat roof, quite a big hole too, and a flat roof—there's a lot of repairs to be done it you've got a hole in the roof. Then the plate glass windows and we had another small window above the shop door was broken. So someone came frae Carlilse and just repaired it [...] so it was all done and I was quite satisfied with all the work that was done

During 1989, there were events to normalise the catastrophic effects of the disaster

JH: It took a long time. It took six months; it did. There was so much happening in the town, for the first month at least. Well, there was the funerals and all the church services.

JH: Did you go to them?

EYH
 & JH: Yes, we did.

JH: Then there was the *Cheer Up Lockerbie*, with things held in the town hall, bands,—

EYH: The pop concert! Capercaillie, Fish! What else? What other groups were there? I can't remember; terrible noise, it was. It was in the cinema.

JH: Marillion. Did you go to it?

EYH
 & JH: [Both speaking at once] Yes, we did, aye [both laugh]

JH: All free tickets do all you had to do was go and get ticket.

EYH: Quite well-known Scottish pop groups anyway that were—was Runrig there? Were they, Runrig?

JH: Aha, aha. Then there was Ed's Party. Ed was a young American boy who suggested, Wouldn't it be nice to give all the people in Lockerbie a party! So.

EYH: Because they missed out on Christmas.

JH: Yes, so, soon as the weather got a bit better, we had Ed's Party. Ed came and visited, and he was in the shop once or twice with his folks—

EYH: Buying his sweeties!

JH: Yes, and we did get a letter from him, after he went back to America. It was more for the children but there was a huge turnout.

EYH: Stalls and races and funfairs and things like that, yes, it was.

My parents attended occasions to respect the bereaved and the victims of the crash

EYH: Just, just standing listening. Out to show their respects. And there was also—when the bodies were taken down, fro the mortuaries in the town down South, we were all asked if we'd like to go out and stand by the pavement to show our respect so a lot of people did that. We did that; we went and stood at the police station there actually, and it was very strange; very quiet and eerie – coz it was the dark when they came down – and there was all these hearses with coffins in, going slowly down the street.

I think these were the bodies that had been recovered and were going to be sent back abroad; going to be flown back to the countries where they were going to be buried: that was them, it was these bodies that were going down the street in the coffins, very—there was, yes, yes, a lot of people standing.

JH: We also went to the cemetery; to a service at the cemetery and the American relatives were here, it would be after that, that it was officially a garden. Yes, we went to—aye

After ten years, Jimmy and Yvonne reflected on deaths in the community: were they causally linked?

JH: [It was then] history for us. We had worked through it [pause]

EYH: Yes, lived through it.

JH: Seen quite a few changes because of it [pause]

EYH: A lot of people died which you wouldn't have expected.

JH: Any unexpected death, you felt that people put it down to the disaster

EYH: And some of them were. I think quite a lot was inhalation of the fumes. One youngish person we knew who taught at the school [pause] died [pause] of lung cancer actually and she never—I men she would never have smoked in all her *life*, and she died of lung cancer and she'd been round in a Red Cross capacity, helping, round at the houses so whether that was contributable to it, it coulda been, it coulda been. But, there was a lot of, a lot of deaths that, as I say, wouldn't be in the statistics but would have happened indirectly [inaudible]

JH: And so [pause] and what about your own health and well-being? Would you say that you got through the disaster without any adverse affects to health and well-being?

JH: Yes, yes, I would say we did. Oh, yes, there's no doubt about that; we did, we did. [pause] I'm quite sure of it.

Church-going for the Haldanes was inhibited by work and family commitments

EYH: We didn't really go very much to church – intermittently - because of having the shop, six days a week, and on the seventh day, we didn't rest [laughs], we laboured—

JH: In the shop?

EYH: Well, no, all over. We did Granny's painting and decorating; we helped with her garden, we did all sorts of things on a Sunday because that was the only day that we had; so we didn't—we weren't *really* regular church attenders, no. No, we weren't, I must admit, but—

JH: And did anything change after the disaster?

EYH: No, not really. We still had only one day in the week [chuckles] to do—I always feel I had special dispensation from Mr Annand - a minister and he lived across the road from Mother. Lovely man. Because I remember him saying to me once, "You were busy doing your Mother's lounge. I could see the ladder and Jimmy up it." I said, "Yes, we were." I said, "And hopefully we'll finish it this Sunday!" And then, oops! [Jill laughs] And he says, "It's quite alright, I do realise you only have one day to do all these things, and you are doing things to help other people." So I really felt we had special dispensation not to go after that.

JH: When did Mr Annand finish up his parish duties?

EYH: Mr Annand finished the year Mother died, which would have been 1997, because the new Minister—hers was the first funeral—the new minister buried her and she was the first one that he buried, so that would be when Mr Annan left.

Yvonne shares her feelings about the Trade Centre and the Lockerbie bombing

EYH: Disbelief, just couldnae [inaudible]

JH: Unbelievable, just unbelievable.

EYH: Couldn't believe it. Saw it on the telly and these planes going [inaudible whispers] Couldn't believe it. You can't belief the depravity of anybody who would even think of *doing* that; I mean, the Lockerbie Disaster was bad in that somebody made a bomb and put it on a plane, but that, the Twin Towers, was just *absolute* slaughter, wasn't it? Absolute slaughter and indiscriminate slaughter- the bomb was put on that Pan Am plane for a reason. It wasn't to kill the poor people; it was for another reason, I think. Diplomatic reasons, I think.

Because there were people who had been warned not to go on that flight, and the common Joe Soap just went, unfortunately. And, ye see, if the plan hadn't been late in leaving Heathrow, or wherever it went - Heathrow, wasn't it? - it would've been over the sea and not a *thing* would've been found of it; no trace or no evidence or anything, and that was what was *meant* to happen. Wasn;t *meant* to blow up over Lockerbie. [long pause]

Jimmy and Yvonne found a closer affinity with people who shared their experience while outsiders didn't ask the hard questions. A few lights went out in my parents' lives after those events

EYH: Well, certainly we didn't go into detail like we have with you here. You know, I think [pause] no, I don't think—I don't really think they *asked* the ins and outs; I mean, the general goings-ons were recorded on the radio and the television – Mary saw Jimmy out on the pavement, sweeping the glass up the next day on the television, things like that – but they never *asked* about it, didn't they not?

JH: No, and most of the, most of the horror stories and what had really—the things that'd happened to people, you always spoke to the people that you knew were involved. The people that were in the same position as you, especially in the town, because there was lots of the town not affected at all: probably affected because they knew some of the eleven people – affected that way – but not affected by the plane [pause] goin' over the top.

Jill And was that because you didn't want to bother people who hadn't experienced it with the facts and the details?

JH: Either that or you felt you were closer to the people that you knew something similar had happened to.

EYH: Who had been in the vicinity; A' mean, for instance, really we used to have rare parties before the disaster – round at Helen's [Fraser], Mossbank, you know, the [inaudible] one, you know, an' all this; and we've never had one *since*.

JH: Nope.

EYH: And we used to write funny poems and things, you know, about Howard and myself, and people wrote funny poems and songs and things, but that stopped as well. Ye didn't seem—they've said, Oh Yvonne, write a funny poem for Howard's birthday, 70th birthday, but do you know, you couldn't [pause] you couldn't somehow or other, because I think the disaster loomed and you couldn't really think of anything funny to say *after* it.

Remembering on 21st December

JH: You *certainly* always remembered it [pause] You *certainly* always remembered it, but I don't think that after the first year after the first year, Christmas got back to normal [pause]

JH: So did you go down and visit the [memorial] garden on the day or the night or?

JH: Yes, yes. By then, the cemetery was upgraded and it was all lit up and I'm quite sure that it's the busiest cemetery in Scotland because the number of people that even used to—the signposts are all up, but the number of people that came into the shop, to ask where the cemetery was, where the garden of remembrance was! [pause] I was always very careful, even if it was busy to take time and tell them where it was, just in case they were relatives because we had some many relatives, and still *do* have, come to the town – American relatives, other nationalities as well, of course – so you always felt that you had to very careful how you approached the, how you replied to what they asked you.

The profile of the town today: Jimmy and Yvonne's suggestions for improvement

EYH: I think they're trying to, they are trying to rejuvenate it, I think, but I mean the supermarket's got a lot to answer for; that's really what's wrong with the shops closing, in all the towns, not just Lockerbie, but—that's what's wrong, its taken away the little country [pause] attitude, you know, with a drapers and a newsagents and all this kinda thing, that, that—but they are trying to rejuvenate the place.

JH: But they tried to rejuvenate it after the disaster but there were so many ideas and you would get half the money to do up your shop outside – outside only – and, to me, it was a complete waste of money because they were gonna employ outside professional tradesmen. Everything came from outwith the town. That, for a start, was the wrong thing to do to a town that needed to be brought together and boosted, was to bring in tradesmen from outside. So it didn't happen.

EYH: And there was a lot of money donated to Lockerbie by people, disaster fund and things, and what happened to it? No-one knows, and to be quite honest, I would never ever give to a fund like that for any disaster. On saying that, I did give to the [Indonesian] tsunami coz I thought that was dreadful—

JH: But no-one seems to be accountable for it. There's nothing written down; they do not have to *tell* you where the funds have gone.

EYH: There are a bunch of trustees who, presumably, know something about it, but nobody else is ever told anything about it; so how much money there is in it?

JH: So there certainly wasn't any money spent on the outside of any of the buildings in the town, and to me, they don't look any worse now that they did then.

EYH: The Town Hall is falling into disrepair so to me, the money should be used for that.

JH: But it does seem quite busy in the town

JH: It does appear to be.

EYH: It does appear to be yes, I think it is.

JH: Mind you, if there weren't so many yellow lines: sleeping policemen. Traffic calming measures.

EYH: It'd be even busier.

EYH: As Dr McQueen says, I don't know why they're called traffic calming measures coz they just raise your blood pressure. [chuckles]

JH: The town might even be busier.

Suggestions for the coming commemoration of the events this year

JH: I think not too much. I think a church service; I think something for the children [pause] something for the children [pause] that involves the school: all the, all the, all the signs that are organised nowadays never seems to involve the school; it had to be organised by someone outwith, and I think that's wrong because that's losing the community spirit. I think it should be something in the school, and that they should be—the children that are growing up *now* should be taught about the disaster because, well, loads of them weren't born so therefore they should be taught but—we shouldn't go over the top either.

Jill"   And what do you think would be a nice way to commemorate the disaster, Mum? Appropriate, maybe, if not nice.

EYH: I think maybe Doreen's suggestion of a church service would be quite nice. I think quite a lot of people would go, so that might be a good idea. What else, I don't really know; you don't want a whole group of people trailing down to the cemetery or anything like that, and what else would be fitting? I don't know what else would be fitting. You don't want to put up another plaque somewhere coz there's plenty of them. I really think Doreen's probably right to say a church service would be ideal, I would think.

Jimmy Mace, the grocer. (© James Haldane 2008)

Jimmy and Yvonne with Ed Blaus, outside the Mace shop, June 1989. Ed was the boy who had an idea to give the kids of Lockerbie a party – Ed's Party. (© James Haldane 2008)

The premises of A. Thomson & Sons, 16 Mains Street, and the Masonic Hall next door, looking north up the High Street.

Forged in Pragmatism: Mains Street Memories

The profile of this third generation Lockardian is straight-forward, with no frills. He is a weel-kent face, and not just on Mains Street, the location of his business premises and family home. His professional skill and trade as blacksmith welder extends back further than his Lockerbie heritage; back to his great-grandfather who came down from Glasgow to fashion gates for the kirk on the hill and stayed on in the town. Horses have been the life-blood of Lockerbie for those ensuing generations – first as transport and work horses; then hunting stock and now a strong recreational horse culture in the rural community keeps the smiddy busy although the narrator specialises in welding and fabrication. He is developing his commercial and domestic contract opportunities locally and internationally – he recently went to America with a business concept in wrought-iron memorial headstone design.

The narrator lives a few hundred yards up the road from where I was brought up on Mains Street, between the St Mungo pub and the Masonic Hall: a one time coach-building business. My family home at 42 Mains Street was also a stabling establishment for coaches and horses. Our mothers were close friends until Margaret's untimely passing. I have some lovely memories of Margaret: I remember the day my sister got knocked down in a road traffic accident on Mains Street – I was seven and home for lunch at the time. Margaret heated up some mince and sat with me at the table, amidst the panic and uncertainty of the ambulance that had just departed. My sister subsequently had a toy cat that was christened Mrs T. Margaret worked in the shop for a spell, too. And of course, there is my family's idiomatic phrase, levelled at those who always leave something on their dinner plate: "You're just like Margaret's policeman!" after a boarder at the Smiddy who was a consistently picky eater.

Eckie, the narrator's father, shod our ponies and horses – the smell of the hot metal shoe, sizzling at the hoof, is particularly vivid after 30 years. Not to mention the wee Jack Russell, Suzie, that used to love chewing the hoof pairings.

Then there was the day on the back lane, when I stuck my tongue out at the narrator's grandfather, Bobby! I was in so much trouble, and the shame embedded in that misdemeanour still makes me squirm today.

The narrator patronised my Father's shop on a daily basis: he maintains life is not the same on Mains Street, now Dad has retired.

So my family has had close links with the narrator and his family for as many years as we have been resident there. He is 49 years old.

This Lockardian was disinclined to participate in the book project, revealing that he involved himself only because we had close familial links and for that, I thank him. He is a quiet and humble individual, who understands the small town inside out. He has few strong opinions on the affects of the disaster of himself, the town or the people, and does not regard himself as a voice piece. I have attempted to demonstrate my respect for his reluctance to air his thoughts by channelling his story through the events of the night, and using his voice as authentically as possible.

He is responsible for the subtitle of the book, summing up in a phrase what I regard as the revolving axis of shock; reactive feeling, then comtemplative feeling; corresponding attitude, and final response to the catalysts of the disaster: the penetration of Lockerbie town and life, firstly by the physical catastrophe and then by the associated mêlée of sheer number and scale of outside interest.

There were two abortive interview appointments before we finally pinned down a mutually suitable time. This demonstrates the busy schedule of this individual's working environment. We spoke for around an hour in total, in the front room I had visited many times before as a child. The narrator's father produced a sweet photograph of my sister and I when we were small, a memento of almost 35 years ago. As I walked home from Alan Thomson's smiddy, I recalled that, as a child, my family received a much-anticipated and gigantic tin of sweeties from his parents each Christmas – Quality Street!

Family details

Ma' great grandad's name was Sandy Thomson, ma' grandad's name was Bobby Thomson. Ma' father's name is actually Alexander, in brackets, Eckie, and that's what the state o' play is.

On ma' Mother's side, her Mother and Father lived in Lockerbie and obviously, ma' Father has lived in Lockerbie for—he's never moved actually off Mains Street in his life and he's now 76; he's moved from one side of the street to the other side of the street, and that's it: so that's basically as much [inaudible]

[My father has] never lived anywhere else: he's never lived off this street which, in seventy six years, which is really unbelievable.

Ma' Mother was born in the other side of Dumfries, in a small village called Kirkbean: so that's where my Mum was born and obviously, she met wi' my Dad coz she worked in Lockerbie. She worked in a place called Cossars, up the street and she altered suits and dresses and did all that, so—

The smithy tradition

Well, basically, yeah. I'm fourth generation of the family business. Ma' great-grandfather moved down here from Glasgow in 1896, to work at the Dryfesdale Church, which is well documented. His son, ma grandfather, was in the business in which I've served my time, along with my father, and my grandfather, in the family business, and I'm basically fourth generation so that's the state of play.

Alan's early years: school, sport and smiddy, but not in that order.

School was school! No; prison! No my thing, really. I think I've learnt more since I left school than I ever would at school.

JH: So when you were at school, did you do sports, did you do footie and all that?

AT: Yes, sports champion at Lockerbie Academy, eh, Lockerbie Primary and yeah, was quite good at sports, yeah yeah. Shoulda mibby persevered wi' it, was actually okay at it. It was maistly athle'ics; played most sports, enjoy that. Most sports, pretty all round coverage.

AT: I had ma' time served before I started to serve my time. Started to weld about twelve or thirteen, and literally, by the time I got to the stage of being—coz of living on the doorstep, you just went down at night and you worked away and that was it, really.

Alan's preference in the blacksmithing trade was not for horseshoeing

Ma Dad—it would be at the time, I'd a thought, fifty, fifty: whereas I did serve my time for to show horses, I never was fair keen on it, and yet, having worked with horses, ye'd have thought I'd have been certain to go down that route but never did. Never picked up on it; never ever really fair liked it, and I just went more on the fabricating and everything else, and then, when I ta'en over—ma Dad's still shoeing the horses, and it's still quite a good tradition but the rules o' changed where ye' had tae be registered an ye' had tae go tae college and ye' had tae do this, unless it was the grandfather rights which I could of got, but I thought, Well, A'm no' doin' it anyway which probably was a mistake in hindsight because I could jist o' walked into; it's very lucrative now, very scarce: so.

Knew it anyway, know what I mean, especially workin' wi' horses and everything but—Dad still does the shoein', still does everthing, yeah.

JH : Prior to motorisation, was blacksmithing a booming business in Lockerbie?

AT: Was, yeah, definitely was, but on sayin' that, at that particular time, there'd probably be, mibby another three blacksmiths on the town so, as it's evolved now, it's very limited, in fact I think, well, within our radius, it's very limited now like so. But every village had its own blacksmith's shop but now they even seem tae—we have got no farmers on our books and ye'd think that it would be them but I think because imes have changed so much, that when farmer's son's go tae college now, instead o' sowing seeds in the ground, the first thing they teach them is how tae weld. So it really just—ye' know what I mean, so we went more industrial than what we did goin' the other way, y'know.

Greyhounds and race-horse are a passion for Eckie

A' star'ed [the greyhounds] off and ma' dad picked up the mantle and he's had them for a long time: he really has—he's been very successful to be honest, yeah. Just as a hobby but very successful at it.

JH: And where do they race round here?

AT: Gretna and [pause] can go tae Glasgow or whatever: a lot o' the independent tracks are now closin' because [inaudible] financially and a lot of them've been taken over in the bigger places for buildin' now coz buildin' seems to be the way that everything's going' : if there's a piece o' land that's flat, they wanna build on it. So, that's it.

We had horses, aye, but they just turned very expensive, really, tae be honest, and it the environment wasnae right in the town, we needed the space for more workshops and we just actually they just fazed out; I know that sounds very strange but it's always a case o' We'll get them, We'll get them, We'll get them, mibby in time but as ye' get older and I think if ye' mibby can got the right premises, I don't think it's fair, tae a degree that—I think ye gotta have the land, really, tae be honest, tae do it right, or rent a farm that takes a lot o' money.

They were mostly racin' and they were a' jumpers; A' dinnae really like anything else except the racin', that's just the way that it was.

JH: And do ye' still actually go to the races?

AT: A' huv tendencies tae go up tae Len's on a regular enough occasion, jist tae see what's happen'n but not always.

Alan recalls the initial downing of the aeroplane and the aftermath of the crash

First of all, it just seemed such a very ordinary night wi' ma' wife was gettin' ready tae go out tae a Christmas party: she was getting' changed; I was stayin' in a flat at the top o' Bridge Street which looked down on the whole o' the town. It jist seemed an ordinary night, everything was happen'n: I jist said tae her, "A'm jist gonnae go and fill the car up at Townhead garage wi' fuel tae take her across co I was droppin' her off at her works night out. Then all o' a sudden the noise and the windows started tae shake, stuff started to fall off the walls, and it jist— basically, I thought it was an earthquake was my first reaction; we kinda threw ourselves to the ground and obviously it eased off and I opened up the curtains, come outside and I heard the noise was absolutely phenomenal: it's one o' the one things that probably does stay fresh in your mind; I don't think anybody could ever imagine the noise levels: the noise level was something— no, ye' jist would never really hear, and I seen this massive explosion, then it goin'—the flames goin' up in the air, then it mushroomin', very like what the Hiroshima bomb was like, in fact that would be your only description for it.

My immediate reaction was—we'd been smellin' gas from the Masonic Hall and a' thought, That's that gas blowin' up, and that's what I thought because, if ye' looked in a line of vision frae where I was, I knew where our place was, and if ye' looked at the line, it was actually beyond the line by about, ye' could say, mibby, no' even quarter o' a mile, the meterage, ye' could work out: I thought, Ma' Mother and Father's dead, I got out and we both jumped in the car, come down here and there was rubble all over the town, it was rainin'—it was literally rainin' fire and it was jist—and obviously ma' dad come out; somedae was runnin' down the back road holdin' their head tryin' tae escape, that was Jack Green runnin' up – he'd been out walkin' his dog. When I saw that they were okay, obviously there was all this debris and all the stone and all this fire, I jist couldn't work out what it was, really, to be honest. My Mother and Father were safe, really, which was the first priority.

We've come from there and obviously everyone was startin' tae gather When I opened the front door, there was cars drivin' up the pavement because there was that much debris, that I nearly got knocked over by a car when I opened he front door coz they were drivin' up the pavement coz there was that much rubble and debris lyin' around. We went from there and we decided that was wasnae—that this was somethin' quite major but we couldn't understand wit it was: we were tryin' tae put it together. They said that mibby a jet fighter had crashed into the Townfoot garage and by this time, a lot o' people had amassed tae go down to the Townfoot garage Walks down the street—a crowd o' people started to go down the street and, when I got down to Scott and Rafferties the plumber, Andy Burgess was lyin' on the road wi' his head cut and people were attendin' tae 'im. A' asked him if he was okay. A' seen that he as reasonably okay and walked on down to the fillin' station; don't know what a' coulda done or wit it was, it wasnae a sightseein' trip, it was jist a case o' Let's see what can be done here. And we went from there—somedae said that it's gonna explode again and everybody started tae run up so ye had the people comin' down the street and the people comin' back up the street which were meetin' and people were runnin' back up the street—was all the debris—come back up and jist basically stunned. There is a bit of void where I don't know what happen'd: a' wondered, Well, if people need cut out or there is rescue stuff, I knew o' oor boys ended up meetin' here, comin' down tae here coz obviously this is, no central point, but it was near where the initial explosion was: so we done was, we had to say, Was there anything?—coz they could all work like, cuttin' gear and stuff like that which was a logical enough thing that we could put a team th'gether that could go in and work cutters or do whatever to get people—but [pause] that was, that was, that was it; then what we found out, obviously later on was that it still had been—it went to two jet fighters had crashed into each other and that how it's happened.

It was in complete darkness; it was very very –and at the point initially when I did look out it was thought it was rainin' fire. The description of rainin' fire is that obviously aviation fuel is kerosene: I couldn't understand, when I looked out – ye' mibby need tae put this back in the statement a wee bit but – when I looked out the window how, as much was on fire and yet in the morning, how little was damaged but I believe aviation fuel burns on the vapour which is like a foot above wherever it is. That's how in times, when they used to say this suit, when conmen were sellin' suits, covered it in kerosene and say this material won't burn and they would chuck a match and it would burn like a foot above that it doesnae damage but they were usin' kerosene – ye mibby need o' research that a wee bit but that's what A've heard anyway so that's what that was.

And then obviously the police came round an' they said they had to be evacuated – ma' Mum and Dad had to be evacuated up to the Town Hall. We went from there, we went across, everybody seemed tae be mullin' around; we went tae the flyover; we obviously kinda worked out that that's where it was, and fur quarter o' a mile along the motoway, it was basically still on fire. There was cars burned out, there was pure carnage; its looked like something like middle o' Beirut: like a like a road down the middle o' Beirut – cars burned out and everythin' – and we come back and the night jist—we had no power, we had no phone, we had no way o' tryin' to get to people to tell them we were okay and a whole load o' things.

After time long went by, they were allowed back but they were fetching people into the Town Hall [pause] My wife was a nurse and she organised—she got blanket and—she was really quite good through it all, you know what I mean she got blankets and she got whatever and she tried tae—but they was jist nobdae tae attend tae, nobody left: ye' either survived r ye' died, really that's as simple as what it was, there was no, what ye' would call, injuries as such: very minor: I don't know what the listin' would be at the end o' it but—it was jista, sorta daze; and then everything wi' the carnage and then, when I went back up Bridge Street, there were hosepipes seemed to be running everywhere for the Fire Brigades. I believe that there was an exercise on – I don't know if this mibby be true, mibby you can [inaudible] research but there was an exercise on and that's how o' the army and everything was as quick here, I don't know, mibby, something on those lines; and then there was the rescue, fire brigades and o' the ambulances seemed tae be queuin' but there was nobdae realty tae take; ye' either survived it or ye' died: simple as.

I saw what was an engine down our back road and o' went down, A'd a look at it and A' thought, That's no' a jet! This is big [Alan clicks fingers] – major league here. Embedded in the road, yeah.

And then obviously—one o' the strangest things is, there really shoulda been nothin' left o' Lockerbie but the signposts when ye' see the size o' the jumbo jet, but [pause] it was very sporadic: there was like one bit's here, bits there, bits here, ye' know, ye' know what A' mean; I don't know, it jist seems very strange that it should be as—and I never realised for one minute that obviously I drove down past the entrance to—coz everything was in darkness and it wasnae till the mornin' that ye' realised and ye' started lookin' round and bodies were on the rooves and there was total carnage [inaudible] the extent of —ye' were basically in a daze: if ye were tellin' the truth ye' were jist stunned by it, and then a' the media came in, and then everything else, and the Fire brigade – it was jist utter chaos: ye' couldnae get tae people tae tell people that you were okay: folk were tryin' tae phone you, there was jist no phone lines, jist— then we realised that it obviously was a priority to try and tell friends and family that ye' were okay because [both speaking at once] we managed to do it and for the life o' me I tried to work out how I done it and for the life o' me, I cannae remember. I really—I think they set up, like, phone boxes if I remember rightly— It was up Townhead Street they were! They put up the temporary phone lines.

Damage was sustained to the Mains Street premises

We were very very lucky – there was damage here: we had tae get a wall rebuilt and a roof done and everything else, and the insurance people, in all fairness, were no problem whatsoever: they jist come, said whatever ye' needed, jist get it sorted. Was never abused but we jist put back like for like, know what A' mean [speaking at the same time] they were really quite good in the aftermath and that's [hesitant] it really. We were very very lucky – there was damage here: we had tae get a wall rebuilt and a roof done and everything else, and the insurance people, in all fairness, were no problem whatsoever: they jist come, said whatever ye' needed, jist get it sorted. Was never abused but we jist put back like for like, know what A' mean [speaking at the same time] they were really quite good in the aftermath and that's [hesitant] it really.

The impact of media coverage on Lockerbie's collective response to the event

We ended up havin' the media next door [in the Masonic Hall] ; they were climbin; over everything, a' the vans, a' the media vans were parked down the back road: they were usin' our yard as jist walkin' up and down through frae the bottom, ye know, they jist basically ta'en over, they jist ta'en over – ye' know, you'd come out, they'd be sittin' down the yard phonin' or they'd be doin' whatever and they were jist—huvnae got a lo' o' respect for them really because I think they were only lookin' for what they could get but really and truly, that night, at the end o' the day, the world came tae oor door and for a sleepy market town that had absolutely nothing; at all tae world exposure and everything else, and no' the stigma to it but the after affects to it all is that ye' say ye're frae Lockerbie, that's the first thing they associate with [speaking at the same time] which makes it hard really.

Alan's feelings on coping

I don't as bad now as what I wouldae been in the early days o' it. I think that everybidae, everybidae has tae, has tae, come to terms wi' it: think everbidae, in their own mind, handles it different. Ma' sorta philosophy was, and has always been, they're no' gonna beat me, sorta thing, much as they wannae take up on: like ye'd expect it.

A' think ye' actually end up wi' a wee bit—my philosophy is well what's for ye would go past ye, and I think that's what probably kept me—ye never forget it: but I jist think ye've jist got tae put—life goes on.

Ach, yeah; at the end o' the day, we could all o' been gone; we should all o' been after it, A' think: we've jist been lucky, we've jist been very lucky: ye' cannae have a disaster the scale o' that, on your doorstep, and survive it and not be lucky. That's my philosophy mind.

Aviation security: getting home from Africa

Think ye're more aware o' the terrorism threat noo, when ye're travelling'; when ye're in airports, I think ye; do be more aware, o' think ye would be more aware in general: the fact that we have seen the aftermath o' what it can do, and be part of it, jist makes ye more aware. If I go on a plane, I look round the plane tae see who's there, in the airport I do ma' own security checks and I've got, no' a system, but tae make sure A' check what A' need tae check; never complain at them checking bag, never complain, whereas before A'd o' said, ye know, pain the backside sorta thing: never do that again and like A' say, my first flight out since, I was fortunate enough to go to the Gambia. And so we went out and we went across and we went down the tunnel onto the plane and it was [inaudible]

Like a' say, we were very very fortunate that we went down a tunnel onto the first plane, but when we were comin' back, we'd tae walk out the airport under the plane and go up which ta'en a bit o' getting' yer head round coz it flashed it back. The whole was [inaudible] when ye got n, the made everyone come off and put the baggage o the runway coz they said they couldn't account luggage to the amount o' people that were on the thing and I must admit, Well, I gotta get home so I gottae get through this, but it was not the best o' journeys but a've jist said a've travelled a lot since, been all round and jist go with the philosophy, Well, I managed tae survive it once, it couldnae o' been meant.

A no-fly zone exists around Lockerbie but not further to the south of the town

I don't like low-flyin' jets—I wis at Len's doin' a job yesterday, would ye' believe, this bloody jet came o'er, I nearly fell off the thing, I got such a fright. [JH chuckles]

Fond memories of a Sherwood Crescent couple

Maurice and Dora Henry lived in Sherwood Crescent; they were victims of the crash which obliterated their home when the wing section fell and created the crater

I was very friendly with Maurice and his wife, and I'd jist finished a job round there and Maurice used to live with us, when he first come across, Maurice live wi' us for a couple of years so I was very friendly w' Maurice and A' had jist finished a job for them coz Maurice had been ill and there were red brick pavings, quite a—no a unique thing, but Maurice used to work on the roads and he had flagged out o' his back and A'd jist finished his railing, and it was quite weird that we actually [pause] our yard there was all the debris and that—I'd recognised some of the flags lyin' in the middle o' the yard which was quite, no, in the cold light o' day, was quite upsetting coz they were nice people: ye' dinnae grow up in a town and know no' people, but like A' say, A' wis friendly wi' Maurice and his wife because they were nice people.

Community involvement: Alan's ethos

That's no' really my thing; it's jist never been my thing: I jist sorta deal with myself and whatever and ye' jist get on wi' it

A've got tae be honest wi ye' here, its never something a've fair voiced an opinion on coz my opinion is, A' do ma' own piece: like, even on the time or whatever, ye can have yir own thoughts; as long as A' do what A' huv ate do for tae square it in ma' head, A' let others got on wi' what they've got tae do. Dae really fair get involved wi' it. Its mibby no' fair what ye' want tae hear

Alan reflects on the current appearance of the town and the positive aspects of community management

I thought it might be a major—I thought, Well this might help the town tae grow, get itsel' established, not back on its feet but, there was a lot o' empty shops and I thought that it might jist work tae regenerate it. Don't know that it has.

I think a lot o' people in the town have got a slight lethargic attitude tae certain things: they want it tae happen but if they're the same as me, they don't so nothin' about makin' it happen, which, A'm as guilty as what everybody else it But in the same instance, I thought that w as mibby a chance tae regenerate it and then obviously that guy sayin' what he said about Lockerbie in the paper, everybody – this could be a wee bit—everbody said, to a degree, *to-a-degree*, not entirely, mibby 20% of what he said was probably truth. When you do go out of here, the first thing ye see is that old Quiksave buildin', which is boarded up, ye' know what a ' mean. I jist thought it would be a good chance to regenerate;

I think the council have made a good job, whoever was involved in the memorial part of Dryfesdale cemetery have done a really good job; that has been one o' the pluses to it, I think the people on memorial side of that was done quite well I think it's quite sympathetic, I think it was okay: I often go down because my Mother is buried jist further along so A' walk past it quite often and I often think, Well, yea, that's okay. Some o' the stuff they huvnae got right; I think that's one o' the things they have got right. Tundergarth [both speaking at once] they've made a really good job.

I think that it—I jist hope they've learnt lessons from it. If there was mistakes, there was stuff done, I jist hope they've learned by them, ye' know? That's it! But, no, I think they've got it [pause] certain part o' t right.

The significance of remembrance

Went tae the memorials, went up the street tae the, tae the—because I actually ended up in the picture house one wi' o' the people, they turned the picture house into—when they were doin' it: 'member o' the big one that happen'd, we went' tae that and we did oor bit coz that's the only way o' payin' respects really at the end o' the day.

The other thing as well is the timing o' the year o' the unfortunate tragedy is that it is round about Christmas; it had got a particular date sittin' round it as well, it is—I would never like it tae be forgotten: I think that people that died deserve that it isnae forgotten, it should always be remembered,

An internal perspective on televised disasters

The 9/11 one was a very hard one to watch, it jist fetched a lot back and ye jist—every time ye see a disaster now, in the past ye' would look at it, and ye'd mibby think, God and ye'd mibby spend five minutes seein' it on the news, or reading it or whatever: mibby no five minutes but ye know, ye'd read about it or ye'd look at it, and even before the disaster, ye would say whereas now, ye' do a lot more reflectin' on disasters because ye; know the bigger picture, for every one person there's another five or ten that's been affected by it: so when ye' multiply that up through mibby, if there's a hundred people lost, that's affectin' five hundred people, ye' know what A' mean, a think ye've got more o' a, more o' a perspective on what's happenin' because I think jist through life, I think ye jist, won't happen tae you. Jist disnae happen, ye' jist cannot get in into yer head that it's gonnae happen. If ye're goin' in a volatile situation, i.e. the troops that go into Iraq, they know that they really are takin' a chance but tae be honest wi' you, when people are goin' to go on holiday or they're gonnae visit relatives and they're jumpin' on a plane, they don't expect, know what A' mean?

The tsumani, ye're lyin' on a beach and ye see this comin' in and everything else. It seems tae be ye're more aware o' disasters, that disasters seem to be happen'n more and more frequently.

The futility of premeditated disaster

The one thing that was hard to believe out o' the Lockerbie one was that it was man-made. That's the hard bit, that it was man-made – the whole thing couldae been so easy avoided and it didn't need tae happen ye know, it was, it was planned it was executed by the evilest o' people tae think that they can sit on and when ye' do read reports, that the timing was wrong, it should've gone off when it was over the sea but it was delayed or whatever, A' believe, I don't know: delayed and that—tae think [inaudible] , but as well, I think with it being a plane, the carnage was so spread

Lockerbie town turned upside down

It was all over the Langholm direction, it was all over Newcastleton, it was all over the place, and [...] they didn't move the people right away because they needed to know where they sites were, and they turned, likes o' the ice rink, they turned likes o' the Town Hall into mortuaries which was right in the town, and A' had finished cleaning out a factory in Lockerbie which was Dexstar which we'd jist finished cleanin' it out and obviously, they used that as a part of a—for tae store the coffins and they made it into like a mortuary or a funeral parlour, if ye like, and we had cleaned out the factory; he planes were landin' on King Edwards Park, the helicopters were landin' on King Edwards Park

An eternal memory for Alan: his ethos prevails

We had jist finished cleaning out the Dexstar factory and A' got a phone call to go up and do work, they wernae happy wi' the security on one o' the big roller doors and they asked me tae go in and the one thing that A've really got stuck in my mind really—they ta'en me through and the plane luggage and the wreckage was kept in one part o' that building and the other part was turned into a funeral parlour, if ye like, I don't know what your classification o' that would be, and they asked me tae weld on this catch and they had it nicely set out but they had like rows o' white coffins and at the end of the white coffins there was 3 or 2 or 3, I cannae remember how many kids, there was either two or there was three or whatever small kids and it jist didnae seem right that I hammerin' and workin': I wouldnae let none o' the boys go coz A' said that A' would go and do it and I went up there and it jist didnae seem right. That's the one image, lookin' round there and seein' a' these rows that has always stuck wi' me. Never had no nightmares after it coz I never allowed it tae happen: A'm sayin' Never allowed it tae happen, I jist didnae go down that route: A've made ma' philosophy from it happen'd, Well, A've jist gotta get o wi it and that's my philosophy in life; whatever—ye don't see gold medallists runnin; backwards, know what A' mean, so ye jist keep getting' on wi' it.

What is Christmas like now?

I always sorta go on holiday now at Christmas and A've jist done that, that's jist ma' thing, o' jist go, a jist get away, slightly through work commitments coz that's a good time fur me o' go and the other thing is jist tae get away out of it really tae be honest I've jist never been mixin' that way and it's no' somethin' A'm gonna start now, but, that's it.

Saying where you come from: Alan doesn't relish talking about it

They never—some people did, it's like when ye; travel, if ye say where ye're from, some people'll either ask you or they won't: it a' depends on the individual – some o' them would, some o' them wouldnae, and if ye' decide tae mention somethin'—I'm no' a believer—this is the first time A've really talked about it coz, at the end of the day, it's a private thing really, it's yer own emotions yer dealin' wi' here and what ye' say, it can affect other people as well, and tae be honest, it's jist the fact that if it hadnae been you, without been funny, A'd o' never o' got intae this, like, and jist as simple as what it is coz, at the end ' the day, it *is* your own thoughts, it *is* your own thing and that's it.

On the issue of financial compensation to townspeople:

A've heard a' the stories, which ye' always do, but a've never picked up on them, not really *interested* in them: that's *their* lives. A' deal with my life and the people surroundin' me and A' know fur a fact that that was the only thing.

Alan recalls an inverse effect on the dogs' racing performance

We went to the greyhounds on the Friday night, just tae get outta the town, and there was a collection and a minutes silence down there. Ma dad was gonnae run two dogs. The dogs were down the yard when it happened and their was a lotae debris on the dog' roof and everything, and we had one dog that was really really nervous, and we'd one dog, any more laid back and he'd be in a coma. And we went down there and the first one went down, that was the really nervous dog. Naw, sorry, the one that was the laid-back dog; wait till A' get this right! I was the one that ye' wouldane o' thought it wouldae affected which was the nervous one that was always jumpin' that went in and it just stood there, it was an absolute mile behind them and ye' o' thought, Well, wi' it knowin' it wouldae jumped at anything, it wouldae been the one that wouldae been *okay* but it was the opposite; jist was strange tae see.

The state of Lockerbie in 2008

It's gettin' there; A' think as ye' drive in, ye' see the KwikSave building [inaudible] it boarded up does *not* reflect very good [...] A' think that industry-wise, its on the up coz there's a lot o' industry startin' up which is good for us. A' think they jist need tae get some o' the other stuff squared up; A' think they need a good community centre: A' think they do need [inaudible] it would be nice tae think they would jist bounce it into gear, really know?

Alan does feel strongly about one aspect of the twentieth anniversary planning

A' don't know what's planned. It jist would be quite a good time for the whole community tae pull the'gether really, and try and make that the second step tae movin' forward. A' read a wee article in the paper that they havnae been involvin' families, which *that* upset me because they deserve *that*, they deserve their say; like the only thing A' *would* voice an opinion on is A' would *not* like them *not* tae be involved, A' think that's outa order, know what A' mean, because A' think they deserve that.

They'll have what they want to do and, at the end o' the day, they havnae really made a bad job up tae now.

Bobby (on the left) and Sandi Thomson (the narrator's grandfather and great-grandfather) with their award-winning gates for Dryfesdale Church, Lockerbie. (© A. Thomson)

Ella Ramsden, with her grandchildren, outside her house in Kintail Park, 2000.
(© Ella Ramsden 2008)

The House is a Shell but the Home is the Heart.

This narrator has a richly compelling story to tell. She is unique to the participants of the oral history project in that she suffered extreme destruction to her property – possessions within the family home - and huge upheaval as a result. The story of how she coped with this has been inspirational to many, as she explains, and her selflessness is symptomatic of a wider Lockardian characteristic.

She has deep ancestral roots with Lockerbie and she talks at length about her kith and kin and about the filial experiences of her own past: she is an honest citizen of long-standing in Lockerbie. The family is the strongest aspect of her life experience: the strong bond with her children and descendants in the family unit. The narrator discusses the various jobs she held; descriptions of war-time; the town's festivities; her enduring relationship with the media since the disaster, and the development of her status in the community as a result.

She has lived in two distinct parts of the town during her life – to the east of the railway, on the hill as it slopes up to the top road to Tundergarth and beyond, and in a quiet park area near the school, heading north. She recounts her memories of both streets and the community bond existing there, amongst her family, and fostered there by her and like-minded householders.

She has lived away from Lockerbie and she had travelled extensively: She has balance and an open perspective on the human spirit, and a guileless attitude to her horrific experience.

I hadn't met the narrator before the interview although she knew my family in relation to my father's grocery shop at the bottom of the town. Her children are a generation above me.

I suspect the narrator involved herself in this project for the same reason she has told her story to many over the intervening 20 years – firstly, she has a garrulous disposition and secondly to allow perspective, not on the frailty of the human spirit under duress, but rather the tenacity of the human will to endure an attack on one's mortality that was completely random and without precedent.

This narrator's story will illustrate the extreme end of the theme of the introduction: the indiscriminate nature of this particular disaster, as it falls through the sky without warning into the heart of Christmas homes.

I went to her place in the evening of March 24. It was cold and crisp in Lockerbie. Her livingroom was cosy and light. She took a big armchair and I positioned the mic. The dog was snoozing in its basket. I think she was a little nervous – she reminded me to stop her if she started rambling because Ella Ramsden, on her own admission, does like to blether.

Ella Ramsden is almost eighty years old but she looks twenty years younger. She had just come back from a holiday in Malta with her friends. She had seen Dr Swires and his wife there, by accident, one evening in a restaurant. Ella was bothered they had done the wrong thing, by approaching them while on holiday, and I guess that epitomises Ella – ever concerned with others' feelings and self-effacing.

Ella's Lockerbie lineage

Well, it's from my Mother's side that it goes really back quite a long way. My Mother's name was Varrie, V—a—r—r—i—e and there was quite a lot of them when I was small. My grandmother lived here. My greatgran — no, sorry about that. It's my Grandfather that lived in Lockerbie. His Father — I think my great, great, great. I think there's three can go into, that all lived in Lockerbie.. Varrie, Varrie. It was always Varrie we said but it's V—A—R—R—I—E, so it really is Varrie.

Well, my own Grandfather was a tailor. And my granny—her brother had a tailors shop up at the top of Bridge Street and my Grandfather — my earliest, earliest memory was seeing my grandpa was in a shop window, cross—legged, sewing.

My Father worked on, at Hart Hill, on the roads repairs. He drove a steamroller and things like that, up until the start of the war and then he went away early in 1940. He volunteered and went away to the RAF, so he was away for 6½ years and then he came out and got a job in the post office, which — he was a postman until he had to retire through ill health at 59 but he lived until he was about 82.

Mum worked during the war because, well, you know there isn't much money coming in for a family, three of us to look after, and the RAF forces didnae pay a great lot of money in these — at the start of the war, but she went and helped out quite a lot of people in the town. Great worker, my Mother. I'm not a bit like her [chuckle].

Ella remembers her Grandmother's generosity to travelling folk

My granny, I don't think, would ever work. My granny brought up seven of a family, so she hadnae time to work I don't think.

But she was so kind-hearted, my grandmother. I mean, it was — she was — when I was very small we had people come round the town, regularly, singing, you know, my granny called them the Gaan people, because they were always goin'. The Gaan people, and my granny went out and spoke to them as if they were bosom palls and if she had soup on the go they got this — she fed them. She just was so kind that that was the type of thing she did.

Anecdotes about Grandma Varrie

She had some good sayings as well.. Always if you had a long face she would say, "What's the long face for?" She said, "I've told you, it just takes as many muscles to turn your lips up and you look an awfae lot bonnier, as wi' them curled down."

I never seen granny withoot an all-over pinny on. She had one in the morning and then she had a dark one — and a lighter one she changed into in the afternoon. But my Mother wore an apron, a T—apron, high up on — she wouldn't have her good clothes — yes, I hate aprons

Ella's family bond has been strong since childhood.

We were all — we're a very happy family. My dad was a very, very loving man and he loved us and — we used to go and meet him, the three of us nearly every night from work. He'd come down on his bicycle and one of us went on the seat of the bicycle, one of them were on the bar and one stood on the pedal and he wheeled us home. And — my Mother didnae show her feelings *just* so much but she was a hard working woman and we were well brought up in a loving family.

I had my Granny in Kintail, we lived in Kintail Park, I had an uncle at the top of Kintail Park and I had an uncle across from my Granny and an uncle in the street there, and an uncle just round in Victoria Park.

Schooldays for Ella were anticipated and happy

Went to school five year old. I can remember it as if it was yesterday.. A new waterproof I had to go, because it was raining as usual, and my friend and I went together, and we couldn't understand why all these bairns were crying and there was an awful lot of Mothers crying as well, because we couldn't *wait* to get into the school. Mind you, many a time afterwards I wished I was away from it, like.

No, no problem going to school and got to hang our coats up and Miss McConnell — have you heard Miss McConnell that used to be at — she was the infant teacher for years and years? She just says, "Just go home, they'll be all right now" to my Mother and Mrs. Richardson. We were taken it in class, and that was it.

It was infant's school down at the bottom. I don't know whether you'll remember it; there was a—you know, secondary school up a wee hill that you could go down and down there was this solid— there would be 1, 2, 3, 4, 5, 6 classrooms in it – everybody wonder't why they did away wi' it when the built the new part o' the school which has never last't, but no, it was a *lovely* wee school. It was a long time ago, you know.

Memories of Lockerbie in the early years before the war

It was just the freedom of the place, I mean the whole of the street was covered in beds [pause] frae top to bottom. I mean, every different household had their own beds in the middle of the street because there were no cars. I've got a photograph taken of my brother and me when, och, I mibby was 11 or 12, he would be, two years younger he was than me, and it's right in the middle of Kintail Park and there's only one car in the Park. Now ye cannae move, like. We used to play skipping in the middle of the street, and my Mother used to come out and skip – we used to get Mothers to come out and skip with us, and things like that. We used to go away with baskets and gather rasps and brambles and things like that, and go round the neighbours, to see if anybody wanted to buy them, and if ye got a penny, ye were really on cloud nine, like – ye could get ten caramels for a penny. So this was really good until my Mother put a stop to that, like. I mean, we're not allowed to ask for—well, we didnae *ask* for money but we shouldnae have taken it [chuckle

War time is a vivid recollection for Ella

Never forget it because, in a way—I was 10 when war broke out and, it was like an excitement to me because I didnae understand, and I couldn't understand why my Mother was crying and my Granny had come up, and she was crying, and next—door neighbour was crying. And I always went to church in these days and, could wait for my cousins to come up to get me, like. And, to me it was—I can still feel the feelin' of excitement that I was goin' to live during a war, but I was only *ten* . I mean, it changed drastically as time went on. But.

Troops at Lockerbie: local casualties and saying goodbye

It was war time when I got to teenage and there was things to do – start't workin' before I was fourteen

They built a YMCA where the Legion is, and my Mother and another neighbour volunteered to go and work in the YMCA, mibby one night a week –got my Mother out as well, like; and I start't goin' to the YMCA with her, and I had a great time, with all the young troops that were here – met in with a lot o' nice people. I wrote to about 6 o' them, I think, all during the war but then, I think, things ease off after that.

JH: So, there was troops stationed at Lockerbie.

ER: They were at Castlemilk [estate castle] – the 10th battalion Black Watch with their own pipe band and Lockerbie actually presented them with beautiful silver mace and when it was disbanded—the *mace* is in the town hall, I think they returned it. No, there's no 10th battalion now. We had great times with the pipe band and that. We had troops.

We had troops come here—they were here for 6, mibby 8 weeks, then there were on fortnights embarkation leave. You've no idea the amount of folk in Lockerbie that knew when the train was going away with all these troops, and Mothers and us all collected at the station, and took cookin' and sweeties from our rations, and never ever—always got to me – when the train start't pullin' out, the Pipe Band always played, Will Ye No Come Back Again. It just was so *sad* and that was the start of goin' over to France, like. Oh, no, quite a few troops got killed withoot bein' in action because they got tested out on the hills with live ammunition.

Oh no, we had the Black Watch; we had the Argyles at Kettleholm and we had the Remes at Hallheaths, it was a big army camp; we had troops stationed in a big house down the Carlisle Road. Lockerbie was quite full o' army personnel. We had the what—dae—ye—call—ems, no the paratroopers, the people that went in on parachutes – Blue Caps, they were, not the red—hatted ones; they were special troops that went in because I had an aunt and one stayed with her: they came and asked private people: one stayed wi' her and one stayed further up the park.

68 years on, Ella still recalls the stress of the air raid procedures

Well, you know, the sirens went quite a few times and my Mother was a nervous wreck, she lived on her nerves, and she worked at the Kings Arms [local hotel] at this time. And I remember goin' down to meet her one light Saturday night and just went straight to meet her and as I got to the Kings Arms, the siren went off and they wanted us to stay – bright daylight like – and my Mother says, "No, I can't stay, the boys are at home, I'll have to get home for them"; and goin' up the street, from the Kings Arms to Kintail Park, we watched German bombers goin over, we could see them *so* clearly in the sky, a kinda shuddery sound in the sky, and we watched them and that was them on the way to bomb Glasgow and Clydebank and that night; and we got brought into the house and my Mother's house was just exactly the same as this, and we were gather't togther and we pushed in under the stairs, and we'd to sit there till the all—clear went; it was hoors later. They bombed Gretna that night as well because, well, there has been a meeting on in one of the halls and it was maintained that somedae came out to have a look. And they saw a light and had bombs left on, and— they were Masons –quite a few men killed: was it Gretna or was it Annan? I cannae remember now.

JH: So were you scared, sitting under the stairs with your brothers, or was it quite exciting?

ER: No, I hated it, hated it because my Mother was just *so* nervous, like. She was doin' the best she could, like. Must've been *terrible* with no man to do it. But we've had laughs about things since, like. I mean if I heard the siren, I just want't to go out and watch the sky and I wasnae allowed to do it. But, no, I suppose it was frightening, to a certain extent, but [pause] quite exciting as well.

Ella's family greatly contributed to the war effort

I had an uncle that was called up on the third of September; he as in barracks in Glasgow by the Sunday night. And he was away already, he was in World War One, you see – must've been in the territorials or whatever you call them, — and all my Mother's brothers went to the war; one of them too young to go but he went. But luckily, they all came back.

Ma dad, you know, they were calling out for people to build air fields, you know, for planes to land, and that was his job was doin' roads—and, I mean, they called out for them right away, and a few of the young men that worked did go away right at the start and they weren't away about, 6 weeks, I think, until them were into Egypt, I think it was – building things in the desert. Dad

– my Mother made him very conscious that he had three children – 10, 8 and 6 – but I think the feeling got tae him that he had to try and do something, and unfortunately, he volunteered on April first and my Mother called all the biggest April Fools [chuckle] But he was away for seven years; he spent half of them in the Shetland Islands and half of them in Northern Ireland so he only was home every six months. It was like an overseas postin'.

An anecdote about her Father en route to a posting

Letters came all the time – there was no phoning or anything like that. He had written to my Mother to say that he was being posted to Scotland and just keep your fingers crossed that it might be close. And somedae arrived up from the station with a letter for my Mother and, it had a cigarette lighter in it, and he'd thrown it out, as the train had gone through Lockerbie, to say he was makin' for the Shetland Islands. He *threw* it out the train as he was goin' through Lockerbie, and I've still got the lighter.

Ella's family circumstances altered when the war ended

There was changes all over because [pause] he was demobbed on the Friday, and I had a wee sister born on the Sunday, my sister, Elan Do you not know Elan? Och, no, it's more my family that you would mibby know! She's too old for you to know. I'm being insulting, here. Yeah, she's 16 and half years younger than me and she had Elan on the Sunday and my Dad had come home on the Friday. And, I mean, let's face it, Elan kept them young and it was just after that—I can't remember—Elan wasn't very old, when my brother next to me had decid't her was goin' to go to the Navy

A first job and moving away from Lockerbie

I had started working two or three weeks before I was 14, because I went to the Rector and said I need't to leave to get a job to help my Mother out wi' money and I brought one pound, 2 and 6 home in my first pay, as if that was goin'a help a great lot but it did. [chuckle] It was a pound she got.

Went to the Cooperative – was there for two years, then went to Coopers – it was in the—you know where the clothes shop is just in the middle of the town, just at the cross? Well, that used to be a Coopers away back then.

And this lady came into the shop and her daughter was looking for a baby minder – somebody to help with a newborn baby, she wasn't very well after having this baby, and I said to my Dad, "I think I would like to go, just for a wee—", and I went away to Edinburgh, was there for 6 and a half years.

And my brother went away to the Navy on the Monday, and I went to Edinburgh on the Tuesday. So 6 and a half years.

Ella fondly remembers the Craiglockhart family: a room of her own!

I had a room to myself for the first time. I mean, I slept with my two *brothers*: I was still sleeping with my two brothers when I was ten. And, by that time, they'd given us the house in Kintail Park but it was still only a two *bed roomed* house and it wasn't till after my uncle went away to the war and I was sent to sleep with my Granny and Grandpa, still in Kintail Park

I really was—I was very very lucky; I was like one of the family, and she called me her Mother's Help. One of the boys, the older boy, who's the same age as my sister,, called me a maid one day: he never called me the maid again because his Mother fairly gave him a telling off. She was really a nice person.

He had his own solicitors. W.S.! I always thought the W.S sound't really important. Writer to the Signet! He always signed himself, McLaren, W.S.

Edinburgh Life with Alice

I didnae go out a great—I had to two half days a week and I did pluck up courage to go in the tram down into town, and I would have wander, but it was awful difficult I found, to go into a café and have a meal on my own, I'd never been used to goin' to the pictures on my own and I used to just come home and listen to the wireless. Then I met my friend. That's my friend there. [indicates a photograph]. She had her golden wedding last year and I was up at her golden wedding and, we met each other and she did exactly the same as I did, pushed a pram around, and she just lived down the road from me at a doctors house so, what a difference it made! We got our half days made the same, or if there was a night she wasnae doing anything, she'd come round to me or if there as nothing happening and the kids were in their beds, Mrs McLaren would say, "Are ye' wantin' to go down to Alice's for a wee while?" It wasn't far to walk like. And so, it was lovely.

Heartache for Ella at the MacLaren's

Mrs McLaren, she had a daughter just before I was leaving. Two boys she had, and unfortunately, one of the boys got killed when I was there. It doesnae sound nice saying I wasn't with him, he was with his Mother, and he run right into the street, like. But that was a heartbreak to me, it was kinda the first time I had met up with anything like this. And she sent me straight home and, I was home for about three weeks before she actually came down and picked me up and, then she had another child but, by that time, I had met my husband

Harry Ramsden – not of fish and chip shop fame!

Harry Ramsden. He didn't own the fish and chips shops, unfortunately But then— Dad and him got on awfae well together. He came frae Dumfries. He's still got a brother lives in Dumfries

He worked on the railway, and he came to work in Lockerbie. He was a great football player and he started playing with the Legion, and my Dad had something to do with the Legion Football Club, and occasionally, he felt a bit sorry for Harry being in digs, and he would bring him up for his supper. But I wasnae there at the time, like. .

Well, he just didnae work on the railway; he was a technician, class one technician on the railway with electrical signals, etc, etc, All he had wished for himself, my husband, was an education; he'd loved to have gone to college or university and that's all he want't for his family, to have an education. And they would have an education is he had anything to do with it, he said. And he had a good way of—he didnae exactly *tell* them what to do, he was gearing them up for it.

Well if ye' asked all my friends, they all maintained I had the best one o' the lot. [laughter] He was so easy goin' 'E didnae, like—'e wasnae a house worker, but 'e did all the painting and decorating things like that. He would, in the winter time, 'e would, in the colder weather, he would set the fire in the mornin before he went to work and, if it was winter weather, he would light it, so that we had a – there were no other heating then, and 'e did an awfae lot more I think than, some husbands did.

My husband really keen gardener like, he loved getting this house, great big garden at the side because he used to grow chrysanths for showing and I mean, and ye' have to have them covered so part of the garden was taken up with chrysanths, and the other was vegetables and fruit, I had blackcurrants, strawberries, raspberries, everything we had in the garden but it—one of the, my neighbours frae up the road after Harry died used to come doon and keep it tidy like but we didnae put the same things in but there was always fruit, I made—ah, when I think o' all the things I used to do that I don't do now, I made jam and— gooseberries, we had gooseberries as well and all our own vegetables Harry grew. 'e loved his garden.

He loved his kids, loved a Sa'urday when he wasnae workin' cause he'd just get the three of them ready and take them way down the street to get some messages, and always was quite happy to be seen with his family, he just loved his family.

Ella's pride in her children

The two girls went to university.

Katherine was the first to go when she went to University, in the October. Two years later, in the October, Jimmy went to the RAF and finished up at RAF Halton, which is the RAF college for nine months, and did all his City and Guilds. and two year later, in the October, Louise went to university.

1981, my Harry died, and it wasn't 1980 so it must've been 1979, I mean, he took ill the year Louise went to university, and he died in '81, January. So I was on my own, by that time. [pause] No, very proud of my family

Family holidays

We went in a tent, camping. And then it kinda' got better, we borrowed a caravan from his brother and we had to borrow his car as well because our car wasn't heavy enough to pull this great big heavy caravan; and then, Bert, he was inspector with the A.A . [Automobile Association] and he bought this Bedford van and he did it all out with bunk beds and I think we put a wee stove in, one thing another like that, and we had that latterly, and we *always* made North, we did most in Scotland but then we started to go down to seaside places for the kids, you know. But— and we, we just come home when we run outae money. [chuckle]

And one of the things he always did, car or whatever, he used to take a bit of panel off the front of the car— when we first start't goin' away this was, an''e put a ten shilling note— hid it away so it was there for us to come home with if everything else we wernae well off but we we wernae the poorest.

The kids on Gala Day: dressing up

I've got some gala memories as well. My kids *never* wanted to go out –"I *don't want* to go out!" – until about eight o'clock the night before, and then they want't to go out. It was my Kathrine was the one that— I always look for something funny to dress them up in, like, and I can always remember getting' a pair of right old—fashioned knickers from a great big stout Auntie that I had, and Harry dressed up the bicycle all wi' Daz packets and bits, and ae' roon' the wheels, and one thing or another, and then put a couple of bits o' wood and a bit o' wire across and this great big long, enormous pair of bloomers, like, hanging [laughter]. And on that bike was "Wash your Ma's" — M—A apostrophe S — "in Daz" [laughter] and somedae sent a photo o' it to Daz, and we actually got a letter back; I don't know, I think I got an amount o' money, [laughter] a cheque or something, because I remember Katherine sayin "It's *me* that should've got, it was a Daz theme that got Daz for; they should've sent *me* somethin." [laughter] We bought chocolates, Roses chocolates, one time and stitched a' the papers ontae a dress, and she went out as Roses chocolates. She just went—she went out in a turban and an old long peeny and just like a char woman you know and, Oh god, it was quite funny.

Oh yes, but they had such a big crowd of children, which they don't do now-a-days. It gets done in the afternoon. We all met down at the— I remember Louise going as 'Mary, Mary, Quite Contrary', wi' a lovely dress and a watering can and a pokey bonnet, and that's all she had, like, but quite happy, quite happy.

JH: Did they have a gala queen and that kind of thing, have they always had a gala queen?

ER: Oh *yes*, oh they've always had the gala queen, my Katherine was the Tina Deluca's big attendant. You know when Tina was the Queen, Katherine was one o' her attendants. And then [pause] Louise was a small attendant. Katherine was a wee attendant, as well as a big attendant.

Well, you know I still go down to the gala every— I worked to help with the gala for years and years over the time the kids were wee, and I feels there's such—can hardly get a committee now; and younger people arnae interested in doin', doin' things, and I mean we used to do things. No I don't do things *now* for the gala, like, but I usually go *down*.

Flitting house to Rosebank from Park Place

Well my Louise, [counting] 51, 59, 50—she's fifty seven come September. And she was the first baby born in Rose Bank Crescent. And we were the fifth house to go in.

There was no houses across the street when we moved in. They were just gonnae build. We were, you know those—if ye' go right along the top of Rosebank Crescent and down the middle hill, my house was the last, on the right hand side.

Park Place was still round the corner. We moved to Park Place when we put in for a bigger house and we got the one—we were there in Rose Bank Crescent and we come right around there and in there to Park Place. And wha' a laugh that must ay been to the people because we did most o' oor flittin', Harry pushing a barrow [chuckles] and me runnin' behind: you know it was so easy, we just needed a lorry for the heavier things.

JH: That's a bit like, "My old man says follow the van" just like that.

ER: But it was nice. I liked it when we—I liked Rosebank Crescent like, I've been happy forever, I was, to be quite honest.

The day of the disaster: Ella felt low

I had my son and his wife and the two children here from Germany, they're stationed in Germany, and he couldn't come at Christmas, so he came the week before Christmas, well, he was here for a week, and, I mean, we actually had Christmas day on the Sunday 'fore the disaster. We made Christmas dinner, Louise came down from Aberdeen— was she in Aberdeen at that time? oh yeah I think she was just in Aberdeen I think; and we had Christmas dinner on the Sunday, a week early, open't presents and everything like that, so that we were together; and on the Wednesday Jimmy was going back to Yorkshire because the next morning they were travelling down to Hull to get the ferry back over. Right, because he had his car.

And they went away about lunch time and I just— well really, I'm always the same when everybody goes away and you're left on your own, I was lost and I was fed up and— my cousin's husband, I used to help out a wee bit after she died, I used to go to her when she was ill, and I continued goin' — made them a meal sometimes and tidied up for them — and I went to Billy's, just for something to do, I wanted out the house

The end of the world?

I was sitting just, at night, television was on, because 'This is Your Life' came on, and I got some Christmas cards and I was opening them and, I kept looking at her [indicating the dog] , I mean she was lying—I was sittin' on the floor with my back to the chair I was sittin' sideways when she started that low belly grumble that a dog can do, it's a way down here, and I said, "What on earth's wrong with you" but she heard this noise long before I did like. She heard it comin, nothing surer. She kept this really low belly growl, it's no' a growl here.

And then all of a sudden, it was terrible, it was like a 'wooo wooo', and it was coming closer, closer to my house, like. And I thought, What on earth's goin' on here? and the sofa was sittin' at the window because the door had been spread open for a' the family to make the room as big as possible, and I remember goin t' the sofa and onto my knees, and I mean, there's this bright red glow outside, orange or red — couldn't see where it was coming from – and I was sayin', What's going on, and I had often heard when I was young folk talkin' about the end of the world is night, [inaudible] you know just, I was thinkn', What's happen'n here, is this the end of the world? And, the explosion went up, you know— where I was in Park Place I had a clear line right down to Sherwood where the crater—I had ma knees on the sofa lookin' out the window and this—really went up high, this dark red and black and I'm sayin, That's a, that's a atom bomb, I wonder if it's one of these wee jet fighters, you know the jets that were flying over at all times. And I looked for a wee while and I'm saying, What ma goin' tae do?' I'm sayin, If that's an atom bomb, you know, you think stupid thing, I need to be in company, I'm no goin' tae stay here maself, something has happened.

Well I very rarely use the front door and I just automatically made for the back door. And, by this time I had picked up her [indicates the dog] in this arm, leanin on me — no hand bag, nothing else like, just her — and I went to the back door and it wouldn't open, it just was jammed; now it musta been jammed wi' the explosion, because I got down tae see if a mat that I had at the door had got caught in it and that is when my house stared comin' in on top.

Ella's home caves in

The lights had gone out before I got to the door. I mean, for the life of me— sometimes I hate having to relate this story because I think—you know how people say when you make up a story it's right every time they say it, but it's so imprinted in my mind I think I say the same things each time; I cannae remember *noise*! I can't remember noise but this—I could feel it fallin' in on my head; the plaster and things like that, and then— oh God, things went through your head, like!

And you know I actually got my eyes shut tight— you'll didnae understand this but mibby you will, you know I'm, I'm sayin, Harry, what's happ'nin, what's happ'nin here. And you know I think I was expectin' to see him in some way because I, I thought everything was comin' in and all I could see was my kids' three faces, no' Harry's, just the kids like. And then things must of [pause] went because, I mean I dared to move but I cannae remember; nobody could understand how I cannae remember. Must'v made a noise. And [pause] I was frightened to move. And then I thought, well I've got 't get out o' here, what' ma goin' tae do?

The beginning of a calm escape

But you know, I'm thinkin, I cannae break that window because I've got fablon on it and I— things, quite honestly, I thought them all out so calm and cool and collected, and one dog in this arm, ye see, wi' only one hand, I'd two marks in there like, her feet had clawed into me; and my cupboard, my pan cupboard was there and I remember goin' in and fallin' because I was lookin' for my stew pan that had a heavy bottom, and I fumbl't till I got this stew pan and then— folk laugh like when I tell 'em I had it I the han' like this and you know I actually swung [chuckles] like that at the window and it did, it went through the very first time and I kept knockin" till I kindae got a bigga hole and then I look'd out—there wasn't a soul and there wasn't a sound there.

Yeah, well I can remember being cool, calm and collected when I decided that I was goin' ay knock the window oot. And then when I looked out I was amazed that there wasn't a sound 'a anybody shoutin' or doin' anything because—I finished up shouting so politely, "Is anybody there, can anybody hear me? Can somebody please come and help me an' my wee dog."

Couldnae see. But I'll tell ye what had happn't but what I did do, I was standin' right at the door and I looked up like that and my ceilin' had moved back while the front had moved forward. I could see the sky through that much there.

Friends at the scene fear the worst

I mean my friend had been up at her daughter's and they came really runnin' right round — she lives in Park Place as well — and when they came to go to my house— I mean they just talked—Mary and Caroline and Jimmy and Niven and said, "Go back to the house!", and she said, Oh, we've got to go... "Go back to the house.!" and they walked forward, and I mean they actually shook their heads because they thought— I mean, I had no front o' the house. If I'd gone to the front door I'd had it; I mean, you've seen the side of the house, I'd no bedrooms, so the whole side had gone. The only place that I could've been was where I was or even mibby in the toilet I would mibby 'ave got away with it. But you see, my kitchen was there, the toilet was next to it, there, that distance away.

Ella is rescued

Well I'm still standin there when I suddenly hears this voice shouts, "Alive. Come— come on you chaps, come and help us get 'er oot o'here" and, "We're comin' Ella", they're shoutin' like. And, still got a dog like, and it was a big chap got in first. And he says, "Stand back Ella, I'm gon'ae see if I can knock the door in" and he hung up somewhere and he swung on the door, and, oh!, the whole hoose shook and I remember—,"Oh dinnae dae that again, I think I mibby could get through the hole I'll see if A' can get a chair", and I seen a boy that I knew fraw up and I says,"Look", I says, "Will you take my dog?"— because I knew he had a dog — and I was frightn'– stupid, like! — frightn'd to let the dog down in the hoose in case she took off, frightn' to put her down outside; so she went quite calmly to this laddie like; and then I went over to find a, a chair, and I found a chair. I came to the door, climbed up in the door. And you see, the hole was about this size. I didnae know exactly how jagged it was and I says, "I'll stand in the door, ye' know, I'll put my foot up on the door and I'll try 'n hop through and you pull me through— and that was how—I don't know—I managed to get my feet kindae away through the winda and ontae the hole so that my body was through.

He pulled me through and, I remember l was the one that heard the shoutin' and he was coming to get me and A' says tae Niven,, "It's a gied job you wernae getting' me through the door, son", because I mean, I nearly took the big fella flat on 'is back the way that I really practically jumped through like.

Once out the house, Ella recalls her perspective on the scene

I went up onto the gard'n—up the steps up onto where the garden starts, and then there was a path up tae the fence but Harry had already built steps up there, and I just used to climb over the wall because it was quicker to go roun' tae Moira and George's that way, as a way round that road; so I made fur there, like.I stood on the grass and watched. No idea.

I still didnae know what had happen't I could see— the one thing I did notice, and I'm glad I didnae notice anything else, was clean cutlery. You know the white plastic cutlery seemed to be everywhere on my grass. And I'm glad I didnae see what else was in ma garden because it was, it was dark by that time; although it a light, a moonlight night and [pause] I decid't to move and get myself the chappie. I said "You go over first, I'll get the dog", and I go over the fence quite matter of fact again. And then there was a [pause] [whisper] body lyin' and somedae had covered him up like; and I'd the nerve to go an' say,"Has anybody sent for an ambulance and the police here?". Shock kindae works in an' awfae lota different ways, like. A guy came over and said, "We can't do anything and the doctor and police cannae do anything".

But by then, it was one of ma neighbours, [whispering] who's no' here now, like, and he says, "Wha' a mess Ella! You're no gon'ae be leevin' in tha' hoose fur a long time." And I think that's when I suddenly— I've go' tae get in touch with Aberdeen. [clicks fingers] Got to get in touch with Aberdeen! I mean, there's something drastic is happened here and my Katherine was eight months pregnant.

Ella's friend is overjoyed at her survival: a funny story about Mary

I heard my friend comin, hollarin, screaming her head off up the road from her son in law's again and she's screamin' my name and one thing another, and when we— "Oh Ella, we didnae think you would get ootta there", and I says, " Well, I'm *here*, now calm doon".[laughter].

I'll tell ye' what happen to her; I was taken to Niven and Caroline's house — no light, the candles goin — and Niven came— two or three people and they come roon wi' a packet o' cigarettes, and I took a cigarette, like, and, I can remember it quite clearly what it was like. I was outside it, looking in. I can remember taking the cigarette, and then he came round again with a lighter, and I put the cigarette in my mouth, just this hand. [laughs] came doon past my nose and she took the cigarette away and says, "Niven, she stopped smoking years ago". I don't know what would have happened if I'd smoked that cigarette like. But that was Mary, my friend.

The indirect victims of the disaster

I mean she—I still blame, I really do— I dinnae blame the disaster for anything else as far as I'm concerned, but I blame it for my Mother havin a stroke because the lassie— the woman next door had heard this and had look't oot the window an' she came in to my Mother and went to the doors and they actually had seen the flaming wings coming; well they didnae know they were wings, it was this—like a great big ball of flat fire, my Mother said, going across, it wasn't fair high: well you can understand where they're situated and it's lookin' more or less right onto where it came down. And that was alright; she couldnae fully understand I think, my Mother, but it was the next day listenin' tae the news... I mean she took this stroke, no long after the disaster like, and she was out in a night and then she was taken back to hospital in April [1992]

Ella's thoughts in the aftermath: people's generosity.

I couldnae, I couldnae [whispers] turn the news off. I, I,I had the news— I couldnae go to bed, couldnae go up the stairs; I just lay on the sofa: I wouldn't even go up the stairs—I don't know how I could go because I needed to go for a loo, but. "I can't have a bath tonight", I'm sayin' to Moira, "I'll get up in the morning, have a bath, wash me hair". I don't know what came over me.

I needed to talk to [my family]; and—well, I got in touch with Louise, and she was a nurse at that time in the Intensive Care Ward, and I says, "If you get word to Louise, just tell her I'm alright and that she doesnae need to come home because she'll probably be busy tonight.': and it was well through the night when I spoke to Jimmy like. I did get— Ian got though to me, and Katherine was at a Christmas dinner wi" "er staff.

The next day at Kintail, I had so many clothes, I'd nothin' but what I was standing up in; and it was a skirt I had on — I've never worn skirts for years, — and a blouse and a jumper. And you know it was thick [inaudible] and plaster, but [pause] ; and Moira had given me another skirt and a jumper like: and there were people arrived wi' underwear still in its wrappers and all kinds of underwear, jumpers, nighties: you know, you've no idea the amount of people: the only thing that people nobody ever brought me was a bra. [Jill laughs] And it seems strange— I never got any of my clothes out of the house at all; and then Moira and George took me away the next week which was just like— I was in a daze like

Visiting the ruins of her Rosebank house, Ella is self-effacing about her loss

Well, it was only a house, this is the first thing I said. I says it's only a house. I says to this chappie that says you're no goinnae be back in that house for a long time, I will say," It's only a house, ma family are away and I'm here". And, this is wha' I used to say afterwards. I mean, when folk came to see me, I don' know what yer seein' me fur I only lost a house, you know, how many time: there's no comparison.

You see as I told you, I've never been able to get it in here that it was my—say, it no house, home! It was my home and I just—it's like I've cut that piece out.

It's just, you have that awful feelin'. It seems kind of stupid again, what's goin a happin wi' Harry? You know, you see, you never leave them behind where-ever you go. It seems strange that—see I had a wee cupboard at the top of the stairs, even after he died when I was havin' some decorating done, never had that done, I had to leave it because Harry had paper't—I had to keep that room where he had—one wee room you know—

I don't— if I'd lost a member of my family I probably wouldnae be alive the day — it would have got to me — but, I'm sayin' that, I don't know whether it would've or not […]

Ella's margin of escape was the narrowest in the town that night

I was classed as the wee miracle in Lockerbie because o' the carnage at my place anyway. That's what I found difficult to live with. As I say, my house doesn't seem to ring a bell here but I was so—I felt so guilty, had this terrible guilt feeling that I walks out of here and all these—.

All I kept sayin was, " Thank goodness my family were away because there's nothing surer, if there had been five of us in that house there was somebody going to be caught somewhere because we couldn't — I mean, we wouldn't just all've been, we'd have run for something and we would've been in the wrong place..

The comfort and joy of family

But, no, I'm very lucky as far as my family are concerned like. But that day I was rushed home was because Katherine had come down and, I mean Louise knew she was at my sister's and there she was all, eight months of her pregnancy and she says, "I was desperate to see you, to see that you were alright" and she says, " think that you've been desperate to see me so here we are"—.

JH: So when did the baby come?

ER: On the last day of January. My third grandson. Well, as I say to people, its—you know the sad thing is happening and years go on and I remember sayin, "Well, I've got another grandson since the disaster", and then I remember saying, "I've got"—was it Alison next? [pause] Well I finished up— I'd two grandchildren when the disaster started and now I've got six, and the youngest is goin' on fifteen, so I mean it happens.

Ella was assigned her present house in Kintail Park in the new year of 1989

Well, they actually gave me this house quite early on. It had been emptied for, there were having houses done up down in Queens Crescent and they had this house for people to come out of the house to see it while it was being modernised. It just so happened nobody was in it at the time, and I could have this house if I want't to stay in it. Now, in a way it might sound terrible but, I wasnae doing my Mother any good and she certainly wasnae doing me any good. She didnae want me oot o her sight and you know, being older and that as she was, and I didnae know in a way what to do but I got some bits of carpet and laid it down at the fireplace and I brought a chair down and I thought well, at least if I need to get away on my own for a wee while I can come down here, and this is what I did. I took it and I just kinda come down when I felt like I just needed to be on my own. And then they asked if I would, if I would take it if they offered it to me, because the only thing I had said to them— I mean, I tried no' to be picky and choosy, but my house had been modernised in Park Place, my Mother's house had been modernised here. I mean I had the—I kept my mum and Dad while theirs was modernised, and then I'd had mine modernised. I said I couldn't go through it again, not on my own, so I wanted a house that had been modernised, and this had been done like, so they offered it to me.

One of the reasons that I think made me take the house was the closeness to my Mother, withoot being on her doorstep; and I mean I knew my Mother was goina be needin' a bit o a helpin' hand so it was handy for her

I miss my Park Place house, it was a lovely house, it was a three bedroomed house, a decent sized house, it was, now in a way, it woulda been far too big fur melike, but, as I say, I got this and that was it.

The Ramsden soup kitchen

My brother was a cook in the army when he was in his National Service, and I mean, right frae day one, when we knew what had happen't, they were bringing in young troops from all over, there was young airforce me, young army men, must've been terrible for them, but there was hunting in the hills, you know, there were pieces of plane and people, and he went down the street you know to the shops and which vegetables and one thing and another that e could get from them and he come up and he had a couple of pans of soup for him goin on his stove and within five minutes 'e had a couple of pans goin on my Mother's stove and 'e took them— the school was down, you see. At that time school was closed — Christmas holidays —and—but, very soon there was a staff arrived at the school and they came frae two or three different places, volunteers, and I think they took a week each to do it, but George was there wi' his soup [inaudible] [Ella laughs] and I went up to see what I could do — I needed to get out — and I went up to see what I could do. And then of course they built the dining room, what you call it, one o' these things ye build easy like a—Prefab actually. And they were callin out fur— actually I got paid fur workin'; then, the police advertised fur people, and I'd been up helpin' to dish up soup, in other places I've washed dishes, what ever, just in the school kitchen

Keeping busy was the key to coping

Well workin up at the— cannae remember how many days I went up there, two or three or more, three days I week I think I worked up there at the kitchen, and I got to know such a lot of people [cough]. And then the policeman that everybody got to know because they built another place next door to the dining room and that is where they brought the possessions of the people that were found and, you know they were all washed and cleaned up and put into here

Families would arrive, and mibby the police woman was away somewhere else and Harvey just would came out into the kitchen and say, " Ella we need ye", and you know I would have to say, " Is it alright?" Well, half an hour, just so that I think there was a woman wi' the person that was coming to see the things so I got to know so many of the families if you're able to help at all it takes the stress away, I think, I think: I need't be involved, if I sat in the house mibby things would've just—

Unity in purpose and a cheese sandwich

I met an awful lot of people when I worked, when I worked at the school, because after I worked at the, in the dining room for a while, and then somedae left the centre, inside the centre for the snack bar and they came and asked me if I would like to take over in there, just the lunch time, mornin' till lunch time, and I thought, "That's quite nice", and I mean it definite was a place that I'd to wear my name which I didnae in the other place, you had tae sign a book to go in and sign to get out, was where they were doin the investigation, and I thoroughly enjoyed that and Procutator Fiscal became a great friend believe it or not because he likes cheese sandwich so, I mean, I always had his cheese sandwich wrapped and ready

Help came in all styles: Ella recalls striking up a conversation

And—did I tell you that I was scraping a pot one day, mucky, dirty pot beside this woman and this great big—the water was so hot that we were scrubbin' away and she was scrubbin away a custard pot and I had this pot that I was cleanin' and we just got on to talkin about one thing and another and it turned out she was the Lord Lieutenant's wife I was standing next to at this hot water sink scrubbing pots and that's what Lockerbie was about fur quite a while

Ella elaborates on the mucking-in mentality that pervaded Lockerbie

Everybody want't to help and everybody— people baked and it was taken into the library and the library took this bakin' round. They actually brought me home baking at my Mother's, a bag of home bakin' and a cake that people had put into the library, Could you please get these to the people that are out of their homes.

I think it all started very voluntary, there's people can do certain things and there's people can do other things and you know there was a squadron of ladies — I don't know how long after — went into the library and replied to every letter that came in ...

Ella shared her big heart with victims from other cultures

... and I helped with a friendship group as well, like when families came, they always had somebody that would see to them and tell them anything they wanted to tell and I went with this other— I mean I don't drive or anything, but I went with this other lady. We went for miles up in the country one day, to plant a tree. And we planted a tree in part of the cemetery at Tundergarth but this was, we were quite a way up in the hills but she had a map to show us exactly where to go like.

One of the family that I kindae helped in the anniversary was a kid from, they were, what's the main town in Iraq? Baghdad!

Things—there's so many things have happened, I met so many people that

I've kinda forgotten but she definitely came from there and it was her husband she had lost.

The generosity of strangers

I mean, somedae arrived up at my Mother's one day with this parcel, 'To the lady who lost her house in Lockerbie but got out with her wee dog'. So that's what was on it. Wait an' a'll show ye what was in it plus dog food. [Ella gets up] I huv a notion that this would be an old person sent me two of them [Ella shows JH china ornaments]

I just feel an old person that had had them sittin on 'er mantle piece— but that, stupit things like that, I mean, I got letters sent me with [inaudible] postal orders. You know it's so hard to believe [Ella goes into the kitchen] walks away and how [inaudible] , money fur dog food: Please buy the dog food, I love my dog too.

I thought, Such a lot of people,—but it got to a point that I just hadnae— I just couldn't keep on doin' it. But I still phone one lady at Christmas time, we always have a chat at Christmas time, and she sent me money for dogs, and she has two or three dogs.

Her religious faith had been strong but declined before the disaster

One of the first things I did in Edinburgh was to find— there was a church right across the road fur where I lived wi' the McClarens – Criaglockhart church, just right across the road. But McClarens didnae use that, they went to, you know where Holy Corner is It's all churches isn't it. And they went to one up there.

But Alice and I, when we started goin' one another, when we finished goin to one just next to the theatre down Leith Walk way, just start to go down Leith Walk, and you know the, is it the Empire Theatre that's near it? Yes, well there was a church there, the front is still there but the church has gone but they forget the front. And we had been a way a walk this Sunday and the lads were standin' at the door were sayin' Would you not like to come in for the service, and then the Minister, Mr Goldie, I remember his name, came to the door and said, "Would you not like to came in to our service girls?" He says, "What church do you go to?" and he said, "Oh, I think you'll quite enjoy our church", and of course what did we do, we wernae dressed fur— you know how you got dressed fur church. "As long as you've got clothes on you're welcome in my church". And he was— oh, he was so good. And of course Alice and I slipped into the back pew but during 'is sermon he asked everybody in the church to welcome the two of us [Ella laughs] So we started to go, we went nearly every Sunday, it was lovely, we went trips with them and we went to different things, and ...

No, I lost a lot of faith when Harry was ill; you need somedae tae believes in these things and I'm still of a mind that there's more trouble in this world wi' religion: well, who's is the right religion?

What words of comfort meant to Ella on the first anniversary, 1989

First year, I remember being down the street and I've always been meanin to ask Father Keegan to write out the words he used because I can't remember them now but, oh they settl't me. I was in a state, I was in a worst state on the first anniversary as I was on the night it happened and I don't know what it was aboot. I think there was an awful lot of people on a high, there was an awful lot of people out in the street like because I was a wee gathering, I don't know but Father Keegan had said all the right things just calmed me down; he was the one that helped me the most.

He was up addressing the crowd and, I mean he was well loved in Lockerbie by a lot o' non Catholics like as well. I mean I'm no' Catholic, like. [inaudible]

Grief and stress affected many but Ella applied her determination to get through.

There's bound to be a lot of grief there. I mean I didnae even know the families, I knew them, when I seen them like, but I didnae know the ones that were killed in Lockerbie but [pause] oh it was a sad town, there was no getting away from it. And [pause] of course I mean, I'm Lockerbie born and bred so everybody—all the local ones knew me, and that was [pause]

We had to go and see a stress professor or something at—us that had been involved; I was classed as having been involved. I got this notice to say that an appointment had been made for me at seven o'clock with a Professor so and so at Henderson Mackay's office and would I please come and see them. I never forgot this really—well it was a professor, he looked the part like, a big tall chap, he stood up when I went in and he said, "Oh, I'm so pleased to meet you Mrs Ramsden", and I says, "It's nice to meet you too. And I haven't got stress" [pause] He said, "I'm very pleased to hear that, we'll just have a little chat." There were so many people wanting to have stress I think at that time— but I never heard any more aboot it. It was very nice. He went through quite a lot with me [..] No, no, he didnae tell me I had stress he just want to check me to see if I had it.

But that's the kind of person, if I make up my mind about something, whether I've got it or no like. My Doctor McQueen used to say to me, he says, "It's all in here Ella, what you" [inaudible] It's quite right tae a certain extent. [inaudible] dinnae try tae tell people their work but I didnae wantae' have this stress that was botherin such a lot o' people'.

I don't live in the disaster at all. I think about it periodically. I mean, I believe that there's some people have never recovered from it.

You've got to move forward whatever, I mean some would say it's the worst thing in the world that could happen but I'm afraid it wasn't to me but losing Harry was the worst thing in the world that happened to so far, so I mean, I got through that and I knew that I was goin' tae get through this because it's quite different like.

Community efforts to help the common effects of trauma

I'll tell you what we started as well— a Social Worker in the town started a group, right, about the week afterwards, she come round and says, "Would ye be interested?" She says, "You know all the people in Lockerbie, would you come? And if I can get some of the other ones, especially some of the ones that had been really involved. I mean I'm not goin t' talk about disaster or anything but just to get together, a cup of tea and a biscuit." And some of the old ones frae Sherwood Park came, Mrs Robertson you know, and her husband died no long after the disaster, they come out the house an'— but they all arrived, we had aboot twenty or twenty four arrived, and you know, we talked about anything *but*, you know things started—and then somebody would say, "You know, that night—," feeling that—and somebody would say something and somebody else say, 'I know exactly what you're sayin' and you know I felt that way, and things just seemed to come away, and before we knew where we were everybody was had a— not all night, just for a wee while, and this happened every night we went, it was talk about anything else but disaster then somedae would bring something in and I think it did us all well to—you cannae bottle things up, but it was a very good thing, it went for a week or two.

Ella's mantra

Ye've always in sadness got tae look to the good side, there always is. You know if you write all the things down that are bothering you, the bad things and then write the good things in your life.

Like many in Lockerbie, Ella has stuck up a lasting friendship with bereaved American family

It was when I met […] the first time and then, she came another time: she was doin' this programme and asked if I would come and do it with her and they actually asked us to walk up the road where my house had been like, and we just stood at the fence and just actually talked, she kinda said one or two things and just the twae o' us walkin' up the road, it was the nicest I feelin'—I don't— I've no real footage and the photos and things.

She was coming and she wanted to meet me because I think she thought that, it was her daughter that was on top of my house and I mean I really—I didnae know how I felt about it at all like because why did people wantae meet me and this had happened at my house like. But you know she was just so un-American, if you can understand wha' I mean, and it was up at Lockerbie Manor and I just— I go' out the car and there she was coming down the steps.

And I went out to America like and spent a holiday with her and— well I spent a fortnight—I spent time with my cousin, and quite a bit of time wi' different members of my family that I could visit in. We still have a night out: there's a couple a' families, […] and they come nearly every year and I've always invited them t' Somerton for a meal with them, and Father Keegan comes and yeah they come over every year like.

JH: And do you talk disaster or do you try and keep it away from that?

ER: No really, it's—some things might just come up but we do it after all these years kinda style.

20 years experience of the media

I was very angry at the beginning with them, at the time of the disaster, because there was a man came to my Mother's door one day and I went to the door and[…] I says, "Not talkin' anymore, excuse me" and he put his foot in the door and I couldn't get it closed. And just by good luck my brother had landed in at my Mother's back door and I heard his voice and I gave 'im a shout, I said, "George, I don't want to speak anymore," and he says, "For goodness sake, leave my sister alone for a wee while" and he kinda man handl't him out the door [chuckles] Well my brother looked after me quite well like.

And other times—the day that I went over when I went over to see my house when I came back on Boxing Day I wanted to go and see it and I went and had a look at it and it did nothing for me at all and then you could—the four houses were there, you could walk up there and get onto the road there, so we walked through that way, when I looked down I could see my back garden and this mount o' dirt and on top of the mount was a crib that Stephen had been in and now *that* got to me and I just dissolved into tears and my daughter Louise was with me and she just put her arms roon aboot me and she says, "Oh come on Mum, it'll no do you any harm to have a good cry" and the photo was in the Sun the next day that Ella Ramsden, comforted by a neighbour; didnae even know—they must've been in somebody's house cause there was nobody there where Louise and I were standing and that really made me mad. I wouldnae have cared so much even if it had said was comforted by her daughter, but comforted by a neighbour

I just about got to the stage that I needed to walk down the street and I mean, they seemed tae get tae know— I don't know whether they've got photos o' me. There was one day I was blimmin, surrounded. Gets to the stage that you'd be betta stayin' in. Och I don't wanna stay in my house, but I didnae wantae be surrounded by them, I like being in the fore—end honestly.

Some of them that were genuine enough, but I suppose but I couldn't—it was, that last time last year! I mean I've never seen cameras like them and that was the history programme, and it was just in here like, and, it was just to do with the disaster like, and I mean they were very, very, very, very nice and my hoose upside doon wi' cameras, I've never seen so many cameras or things like it. Och, so I said that was the end.

Lost and found! A wee bit of china charm in a plastic bag

I just kept sayin', "I only lost the house, what's possessions"— my engagement ring bothered me for a while but it was my own fault an' I had a nice side board and I had a toby, see the toby jug? [Ella indicates the ornament] , I had a toby set with a teapot, the jug and the sugar basin and it was in this glass—and it was the first thing I bought for myself when I went 'tae Edinburgh to work, I loved this toby tea set: I'd seen it in the shop when I went to the library and says well, "What about just bringin'— I'll keep it for you, just bring what you can afford in every week and I'll write it down in the book'", and I don't think I'd ever bought anything like stupit for masel', and one day she comes in and she says to me, "Have you got five shillings Ella?" I says, "'Yes". Says, "Well you give me five shillings", I give her five shillings and she gave me this wrapped box and it was my toby tea service and—see I didnae work with my engagement ring on, used to take it off and Harry used to get mad with me because I forgot to put it back on, and I shoved it into one of the toby dishes.

Frank shouted fur me, he worked up at the centre as well, he says, "There's a bag of stuff just come in from Park Place", and he says, "Some of the things look as if they're mibby yours" so he says, "Are you up to comin' and havin' a bit o' a look?", and I says "Oh well, alright then". He says, "Well, 'I've had a look, there's nothin' untowards, we've just put it—had a look and then we've put it all back in the bag" so they're slidin' things oot o' this bag and there was material things like cushions and [inaudiable whispering] then all of a sudden he appeared. "Oh", I said, "that's my toby tea set! See if the other things are there; my engagement ring and the.."—, that was the only thing I got.

I was taken to one of the rooms one day - the police rooms-one of the classes they'd taken over, and this music was playin, he says "Hear that music?", I says "Yes, it's lovely." He say, "Who does that belong to?", and here it was a wee radio, I says "It's mine!" He got it out the house like and they tried it and it was goin so they cleaned it up and were usin' it and, "Do you want it?" I says, 'Nae, you can keep it" and I spoke to a policeman, oh, about a year or two ago but that long ago, he says, 'still got wireless, still goin', [Ella laughs] so there you are.

Anecdotes about fragile remnants of total destruction

Stupid things we got— you know I had an alcove in my house at one side of the fireplace, it used to be a cupboard and it had the boiler in the bottom cupboard and Harry knocked the door down and he put shelves in it for me and I had a mirror on the back and crystal vases just in the alcove that I'd got as presents from different people and somebody came to see me one day and said 'ella, you know I look right into your living room as you know', it's somebody on the other side and she says, "You know, there's still vases, you know your wee alcove, there's still vases and things sitting there, did you know?" and I didnae so I says to Frank who was a police worker who was there working with me at the time, so he managed to get them all out, they're up in the cupboard now like but crystal we were getting out and yet—but that's one of the things Moira did when she worked there with the washing and thing like that; said there was one day it was so amazing, a bottle o' whisky, not broken.

On flying, Ella adopts the same philosophical approach I heard her apply to many aspects of our conversation

I got on in Glasgow and when it started to rev up it was noisy, I couldn't stand noises, I had to know where noises were coming from, the noises of the plane. And you know when it started to rev up I half stood up and said, "Wha' am I doin' here, I'm stupit", and then I realised, I mean there's no' really a great lot a' difference between nerves and elation, excitement and really being nervous, it's all kind of the same feelin, and I just said, "Oh well, I'm in now, there's nothing I can do about it and I'm goin' tae enjoy it". And I did, I came doon in Birmingham, I didnae know wheather I'd get back on the plane again but I did. So I've flown all over, I mean I dinnae mind flyin'; "There's nothing wrong with the plane"; that was what I kept sayin' t' myself, "There's nothing wrong with the plane".

Ella had wonderful personal memories of visiting the Twin Towers, New York

I had been out that day and I come in and the first thing I do is turn the television on and when I came back here's the twin towers and the middle of the telly and this plane flying into it and I thought it was a horror picture. You know, how they make up these scenes in American pictures, and then they started to talk and I says, "What's going on?" and it was—had just happen't, I mean they were showin' it and I couldn't believe, I couldn't believe it because it was the— when we were in America — one of the times I was at my cousin's — they took us— 'The place ye' want to go is up the Twin Towers", my cousin's husband says, "not up the other", what you call it, "Empire State building" — a bit of it was closed because it was being repaired. "Ye're not high enough there", he says, "we'll go into town and I'm goin' t' take ye up the Twin Tower'" and that is the tower that we went up, the one with the flag pole. And, oh, it was absolutely wonderful up there, like and I've got photos and I mean you can see [inaudible] and a' the rest o' it.

And we took photos of it, we were in over it, the Statue of Liberty and ye could see the Twin Towers, I mean there were a view frae everywhere, we were— nearly in all my photos were the Twin Towers like— it was dreadful.

I mean I still feel dreadful aboot it but no, I'm no— it doesnae make me— this is today, that was— it was dreadful and my cousin's daughter worked in a bank in that area and 'er boyfriend at that time actually worked in an office in the tower, that tower, and that day e'd got off 'is train at one of the stations to go and get something, and by the time he got back on the train to come, the train was stopped before they got there. So he lives with a lot of guilt now, believe it or not and— oh, no it was—this was bad enough what happened, with somedae puttin' the bomb in the plane, I mean it really is, it's awful; but to think that somebody actually took over a plane full 'o people now, they're crazy, crazy people. They're fanatics and its turned their minds. They're not sane to do things like that.

War is good for nothing; the threat of bombings is a reality.

I don't agree wi' it, I mean my son was at the first, he was down in Iraq at the very first to-do [back in '91] and I didnae really like it very much and I mean I remember when he come home, he says there's goina be nothin' but trouble over there, it should have been finished there and then, should never have all been taken out before it was finished, and he was back again like; so no, I hated it when he was—he's been away in lots of different places.

I mean not, he's not a frontliner cause I mean he keeps the helicoptors flyin, I mean he's chief mechanic because that's what he was, so that was their job, to keep them goin' and, it's terrible, they used to, first time they used to lie watchin' the skud things goin' over and he says, "They wernae a' that high above us like".

I hate all the wars in the world, I don't know whether it was right or wrong in doin' it I don't think they're much better off withoot, what dae ye' call him, that horrible man, Hussein.

Saddam. Don't think their country's—a little bit—they were talking the other day on the news that they're definitely better off some of the people said than they were before, but I don't think it's that much better, but there's fanatics there an' ae, ye see.

JH: Well we've had the London bombings since then haven't we?
ER: That was terrible.
JH: So keeps on going.
ER: It could happen anytime; we had the one in Glasgow. I mean that was another miracle, if you believe in miracles, that that could've done an awfae lot more damage than it was allowed to do, and the only people that died were the people that were settin' it—a lot o' heroes there as well.

Reflecting at Christmas times

Christmas' always been the same. I don't dwell, honestly I don't, I mean, lots of happy things have happened, I mean, I must confess on the twenty first, a few thoughts goes through my mind but, it's no inclined to go through my mind on the date, it's the Wednesday, kind a style, Wednesday night seems to be in my mind, you know and it used—it happened on a Wednesday night, so it's the Wednesday nearest the date that I'm inclined to think about it rather—it doesnae seem right in my mind if the twenty first is a Friday, you understand, I've a stupit mind; I mean it works strange ways.

Has Ella been reluctant to divulge the name of her hometown?

Not now. I did at the time, I remember the first time when I was taken the trip to Germany, when Frank and Louise took me up to the plane, and the last words Louise said, she says to me, she says, "If you get talkin' to anybody don't tell them ye come from Lockerbie", and I remember when we got back on the plane at Birmingham, it was a girl from Ireland that sat down, she was a teacher in Germany, and we got talkin', and she says, "You're from Scotland", I said, "Yeah"; she says, "Where abouts in Scotland?", "Oh", I says, "down in the South West", and she thought for a minute when she says, "You were no where near that terrible plane disaster" and I don't know whether I turn't white or whether I turn't red or what I did, I says, "I'm not supposed to tell anybody where I come from" [Ella laughs] you know just so quickly; well, she was askin a few details and one thing and another and—it was strange [pause] just nobody knew you when you said you come from Lockerbie: you find that?

Ella remembers commemorations as a time to come together as friends

Everybody was just so nice to me. And then, as I say we had this night, it must've been an anniversary because I had—the town hall was open for snacks and drinks and things like that and Moira came with me and she said, "I've never seen anything like it" so many police inspectors comin to give me cuddles and kisses [Ella laughs] because they'd all kind a gone through the ranks and some of them had made inspector and the ones I had worked with, well I didnae work with them but they came and got their sandwiches and their rolls from me. And then a voice says, 'ella', and here's this man comin like this to me : Procurator Fiscal but I can't remember his name; he was retired by then like: "Ye made the best cheese sandwiches in the world". [Jill laughs] and it just was so nice that everybody seemed to remember, not just with the disaster but workin' there as well like.

Ella wonders about voluntary support for the ageing population in Lockerbie

We do this lunch club tomorrow — it's down at the Salvation Army Hall now — because we just couldnae get helpers to do it and the ones that were doing it, it was getting too much for us, and we couldn't get more helpers [...] ye' know, we're all gettin past doin it but there's people come that are ne'er as lucky as we are because they don't get out as much as us. The bus goes and collects them and we now have a ramp on the bus that lifts them into the bus, we now have a chair that takes them up the stairs to the place up stairs; now it's no place—, if I stop goin workin there, I wouldn' go, I don't feel I'm old enough to have folk waitin on me [Ella laughs] but other folk arnae near as lucky as me and thoroughly enjoy their one afternoon, one day a week, we come up at about twelve o'clock, half past twelve, and I mean, they dinnae even have a lunch, it's soup, they have soup and bread with butter and then have a filled roll with a cup o' tea an' then a biscuit.

Ella's feelings about latter day Lockerbie

I just seem to remember it goin' downhill. Because, I mean, I remember Lockerbie when it was a beautiful town and, I mean, I could sit here now and tell ye every shop that was in Lockerbie, I mean, the grocer's shops and things like that. I mean, it's true what people say – big supermarkets take over the wee shops. Do *you* not *see* it, being here just now?

JH: I think it's changed a bit since I was a kid – yeah, definitely.

ER: The way they carry on in the middle of the town on a Saturday night; you just have a look at the pavements to see just how rundown this place is at the present moment. Surely tae' goodness they can afford to get someone to burn the chewing gum off at the cross and the black angel's green

I don't know, I thought there'd be money left for the good of the town and, I don't know; it's like years ago we all started going to different things to put money into things for a swimming pool. Where's the swimming pool? We all put money towards that. I don't say I gave donations and things like that but I brought raffle tickets, I went to quiz shows with people and things like that and we still huvnae got it; we got nothing. We havenae got a Day Centre for senior citizens here: Ecclefechan's got a Day Centre. [...] They've got a day centre at Lochmaben, a day centre at Langholm: what have we in Lockerbie?. We havenae got a Youth Club for kids, wonder why kids haven't go' tae: it's alright sayin there's the skating, [inaudible] got money, mibby doesnae want a skate, the, there's nothing in Lockerbie. No film, no picture house and, just nothing. I mean it's just so sad.

JH: So there's a growing population, it's growing in size.

ER: Of course there is, it's such a big place. But it's run now wi' two supermarkets an' that, and all the wee shops are closing, I cannae see Whiteman's lasting much longer and now because there's clothing at the big supermarket an, I mean, a' the wee shops are— I mean my kids, when they were wee, used to love for me to— they'd say one night, Go on, tell us what Lockerbie used to be like when you were a wee girl, and I would start at the top of the town and give all the shops all the way down the street, I mean, no' in just in the middle of the street there was something—I mean, comin from Townhead Street there was MacKenzie's, the Grocer shop, one that's all boarded up now, and MacKenzie's the Bakers, and then come down there was a Tad Hetheringtons that sold motorbikes and things like that and had petrol pumps and then ye' came—there was the [inaiudible] , one of them did a fruit and vegetables, and then just further up the street was the Fish Monger's and chickens and things like that, fresh fish, things like that; down the street you had Gardener's, the Grocers; Geordie Irvine's is a clothes shop, there was another; Richardson's the Fish Shop, I forget now [inaudible] we've aye been there; there was Greenleas, the Shoe Shop; Miss Richardson's, the Clothes shop; Cameron's the Fruiterers. I mean there were shops the whole way down the street, and then all the way back up the street, and they all did alright. Cooperative was the only one that was like a, could say, a supermarket, it was never really a supermarket.

It was a lovely wee town. I've always liked Lockerbie and I see it being run down; there's lotsae things I would like to see get done but I'm still no frightened to go out in Lockerbie. Some people are frightened to go out but I don't go down the main street. I think all places are the same now, aren't they?

The primary aspect of Ella's life is the same now as always – her family.

Oh, most important thing in my life, I just love them to bits, and I never stop telling— you know that was what I never told ye; when the place was falling down about me and I said—all I could see were my three children in my mind, they were as plain as can be, and you know I said out loud, "I never tell them I love them"; we just take, you know us Scottish people, we take things a lot for granted; and I've never made that mistake again, never made it again, I tell them I love them now. [They] get embarrassed but I don't care [laughter] I mean [they] actually tells me back; but no, it's a silly,—you know we're dour, us Scottish people, at showin' our feelings sometimes.

We're always in touch with each other as a family, although we're apart; *you* know what it's like? Inevitably, you dinnae stop lovin, just because you're away.

Outside the family home at 7 Town head Street: Ella, aged 5 and a half, with her Mother, Mrs Shearer, brothers Archie, aged 3 and George in the pram, aged 1. (© Ella Ramsden 2008)

Dressing up for the parade on Gala Day.(©Dumfries and Galloway Regional Council, 2008)

Ella's Rosebank home after the crash. Her front door is the red one on the left of the demolished building. (© Ella Ramsden 2008)

The gable end of Ella's house, with near complete destruction of the upper storey. (© Ella Ramsden 2008)

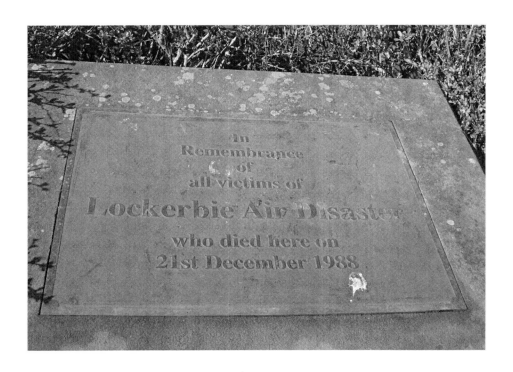

Memorial plaque at the approximate crash site at Rosebank housing estate. Ella's house was rebuilt.

John Henry Davidson Gair, March 28, 2008.

Lockerbie Historian: His Story

The background to this participant covers the key sectors of communal life in Lockerbie – education and volunteering. He was a teacher at the Academy for 40 years, and he has been involved with the establishment and development of the Lockerbie Visitors Lodge, located at the cemetery on Dumfries Road. The common theme of these two functions is history. He taught History at the secondary school and he compiled the exhibition boards for the visitors' facility.

He is not a Lockardian by birth, yet he knows the region well, having taught in towns to the West and East of Lockerbie. He has been retired for the intervening twenty years yet still remains active in exam administration and historical projects.

I knew this narrator solely in his capacity as a teacher, from my schooldays. Some of his children were the same age as my sister., The participant chose to be interviewed because he is interested in recording recent history, and he believes that personal memories can add to the "generally admirable official records" of historical enquiry.

I first met him at the Visitors' Lodge: he showed me the historical panels on Lockerbie and its topographical, social and architectural heritage; the visitors book, the dedication memorial on the wall to a young local woman who was killed in the London Tube Bombings in July 2005, and the couches from the premises at Camp van Zeist, which was the location of the trial of the Lockerbie Bombing in the Netherlands.

John Henry Davidson Gair, whose name denotes his male lineage, is 73 years of age. He has lived in the same comfortable house on the approach road into Lockerbie from Dumfries for 33 years His garden harbours rabbits and, on the day of the interview, 28th March 2008, green banks of Spring daffs.

A pleasantly secure childhood in rural war-time

Well, I was brought up at Amisfield near Dumfries; my father was a photographer; my mother was a schoolteacher. Grandparents: maternal grandparent was a chief signalman and at Dunbar, paternal grandparent was master grocer in Edinburgh but he was a native of Shetland.

Very, very pleasant and in the middle of the Second World War and in many ways I think our childhood was more secure than children seem to be today. I know there were occasional intervals with German bombers overhead at times, but generally speaking it was a very happy and secure childhood.

Memories. Two very hard winters: one in the middle of the war, well, early in the war, actually, and one in 1947. In 1947 when we were cut off for *days* except for the railway which was then open. My father actually phoned the bakers in Lochmaben and got bread delivered by train, which we then sledged from the station: the roads were completely blocked because of this very heavy snowfall. The war years of course were, in a strange sort of way, rather exciting, because Dumfries was the base for a major Norwegian unit for a while. The town was full of men in uniform, but actually at times more Norwegians even than our own services. The airfield at Heathhall of course was very busy; it was a maintenance and training unit and because of that it had occasional accidents. I remember the tail end of a Whitley bomber was visible at the edge of the Lochermoss near Locharbriggs. For quite a number of days if not weeks, I found out later that two aircrew were killed on a training flight when it crashed and burst into flames.

Obviously there was a black out, and the army convoys which came past fairly frequently. A massive amount of damage done locally to property by Churchill tanks on exercise, and as far as the children in the village were concerned, when the Americans first appeared, it was absolutely memorable because their convoy stopped just on the Locharbriggs side of Amisfield I remember. They were dishing out sweets and sugar and all sorts of things that we only saw very occasionally. The other wartime memories— the strange things like the hedges along the sides of the road in the countryside were left uncut, so they grew up to six, seven or eight feet. Everything of course was in blackout, and the cars and pushbikes even had very very heavily hooded lights. I remember being on a visit to an aunt and uncle's in Dunbar, and hearing an air raid going on all round about, and being grabbed when I made for the window to look out and see what was happening. [laughs] What else can I think of?

Travelling by train in those days involved very often sitting in the corridor if there was one, on a piece of luggage, because the trains of course were just absolutely packed a lot of the time, mainly with servicemen, obviously. Another memorable feature of course was the arrival of the prisoners of war. It must have been about 1943 that the Italian prisoners arrived, obviously when the war in North Africa was going against them. A lot of them in, oh sort of middy, almost reddy-brown uniforms mainly worked on the farms, mainly, and then some time later, it must have been at the end of the war in North Africa, the Germans started to appear, mainly of course in the field grey uniforms, and they all had patches on of course. to indicate that they were prisoners of war. And again, they of course went into the fields, *mainly*, but a lot of them were extremely ingenious at making toys and all sorts of things out of near rubbish. And obviously, as the war moved towards its end, it emerged that quite a lot of the German prisoners for instance were Ukrainians or various others, who had been, willingly or unwillingly, in the Weimar. Remember of course that a lot of these eastern European people were caught between Stalin on one side and Hitler on the other. And of course a lot of them remained after the war as what were called European voluntary workers. I remember attending a Christmas gathering of Ukrainians at the Barony, which at that time— Barony of course was one of many camps, mainly made up of nissan huts or the type of hut that you see still at Hallmuir. And it was quite interest— quite sad to see some of them near to tears. They were eating— there's Ukrainian type food, they were playing Ukrainian type music, and a lot of them, of course, knew because they'd been in the German army, if they went back they would be eliminated. What else can I remember of the war?

I remember of course, more than once, sitting in the dark in front of the fire, blackout of course and all the rest, and hearing German— big numbers of German planes going overhead: probably, I suspect, going to Belfast, because of course the big shipyards and other industrial plant at Belfast were targets for heavy raids. There were some of them of course that had this very distinctive engine note, quite different from ours, and I discovered many years later it was a particular type of BMW engine that these planes had. And so on, there was— the memories can keep coming. [laughs]

Teaching was a natural choice for John

It was [pause] almost accidental in a way, my mother had been a teacher. It's difficult to pin down a precise reason but in certain respects it had been almost a natural thing to do. There were various other things I had a notion to do at different times. I remember one—it seems so strange now to look back on it. When we were still—before we'd graduated, we, some of us attended Colonial Office interviews for what was then northern Rhodesia. And had one gone on with it and been accepted and so on and then been a district officer in Africa but I decided against it, and in actual fact one or two who did came back quite quickly for the simple reason that the pace of Africanisation had speeded up and what might have been a tour of duty of ten years probably boiled down to 3, or at the most 4.

John's first two teaching positions back in the region, after Edinburgh: Langholm and then Lockerbie

Well it was just a job that was available locally, really, that was the start of it. And I suppose Langholm was where one tended to learn. [laughs] Sometimes— sometimes there was difficulty in the job, I had a—to begin with a lot of very, what are called less able classes, well they used to be called less able classes. I can't remember the latest jargon. So, it was a learning process to begin with.

Oh very, yes, [Lockerbie Academy] was a very pleasant school to work in. And a very very well-run school at that time. I'm not suggesting it hasn't been since, but it seemed to be a particularly happy school, and it was run most effectively by a headmaster, a depute director who was Head of Chemistry, and a lady advisor who taught English and Latin. And that was *all*. Now, of course, the schools have a whole host of, you know, the depute head director who's not— doesn't have a department and the same applies to a number of assistant head teachers. And again, guidance of course has grown into all the [inaudible]. So it was a simpler world in some ways then, I think. And— but we didn't perhaps— well in those days there was the fairly new O Grade Highers and when I came, the very new sixth year studies. No standard grade of Intermediate 1 or Intermediate 2 or Access or all the various things that have emerged in the last twenty years.

John's Lockerbie connections then and now

Well I'd known Lockerbie, of course, from childhood, so I was perfectly happy to live here. The reason why we moved to Lockerbie was because the family— well one, I was working here, two, the family were growing up and needed a bigger house, and three, it seemed to be a good school and if they'd stayed on in Dumfries they'd have gone through the two-tier system at that time. So it worked out perfectly well that we—

So the summer tended to be very busy coping with the garden a lot this place requires a lot of work of the time or coping with the family, the kids, as they grew up the— 2 of the girls joined the pony club, I remember, the Dumfries Hunt Pony Club, but I had quite a lot of connections in Dumfries because I'd been a member of the Antiquarian Society since childhood, and various other things like that. I was *president* at the beginning of the eighties. I have been convenor of various committees; I have for many years been in the council; I was convenor of the committee that handled or is still handling the annual project at Kirkpatrick Fleming. And so on. For a while I was in charge of excursions. That has just gone on and on over the years. Of course, there was a fairly heavy workload, fairly heavy correction requirements, so— and the family was very demanding; there seemed to be a lot of *need* to drive the family around to different places, so I don't think I became, at that stage, especially involved in community matters. I was, for a while, secretary of the Parents and Friends Association for the schools. At a later stage, I became a Justice of the Peace, so obviously that had various connections.

Memories of extra-curricular responsibilities

Oh yes, regularly, to do Hadrian's Wall with first year, of course. History and Modern Studies used to do day trips to London, for, what you may remember—

Usually, it was Friday and we'd go to House of Commons for question time, and various other places after that. And we used to go to Edinburgh of course. New Lanark occasionally. Can't think of any others. These are the main ones I think, but they varied a little in time and content, but that was the gist of it.

[Lockerbie Academy had a] very, very pleasant staff; extraordinarily pleasant staff, I thought, when I came. There was the staff curling of course which were very enjoyable. I remember one trip up to Edinburgh, third year, and—well, we got them all on the bus, and we offered to stop at Broughton for the toilet facilities: now none of them wanted to go; when we got to just above the Beef Tub, two or three of the boys had admitted that they were absolutely bursting, and at that time, the area above the Beef Tub was planted with, had just been planted with softwood trees. [laughs] So the trees were about this height, and these boys had to [inaudible] and had to, head first at least, try to find cover amongst trees that were about a third of their height, if that. [both laugh] Oh

144

it was just a very, a very happy school, I'd say. Yes they were the main memories, I think.

Arriving home from Langholm that Wednesday, John and his wife hear the thunder-like rumbling reported by all participants

We had just come back from Langholm, which— where mother-in-law lived, lives actually still, and we had two dogs or three dogs in the house, I can't remember how many at the time. So I brought some presents, I suppose, in from the car and let the dogs out. My wife was busy emptying the car in the back yard. I remember I walked into the bedroom with the presents; the dogs I think were outside by this time, and just as I double back through the hall, there was a most extraordinary noise like peals of thunder. But instead of tailing off, they seemed to get closer and they ran together, more and more together, it was this most peculiar noise, and it rose to considerable intensity, and then the whole hall sort of lit up with the— with a red, reddish light, and I remember the carpet at the end there lifted slightly and some small pieces of plaster fell off the ceiling, so I don't know what on Earth had happened; I rushed out to the back door, where I think the dogs were getting excited, and wife was out with them, and just managed to look over towards the area where the wings came down, Sherwood area. And saw the second explosion and there was just a— an enormous column of, you know, almost yellow to white flame, with incandescent fragments in it. And that, of course, was the fuel going in the wings.

And we all assumed for a while, of course, that it was a military plane that had crashed, because in the years previously, a lot of military planes flew over here and we discovered later they seemed to use this house as a turning marker, it must have, you know, been fairly visible from the air, so that you come over here and then turn off like that. And I remember once seeing a Hercules transfer plane flying incredibly low over the field at the back, and felt as if it must just've cleared the house. And of course there were Tornados and various others quite commonly flying around. So the first assumption was that for some reason or other they'd been flying at night, that it was probably a Tornado fighter bomber and that the second explosion may have been bombs. And I went out to see what was happening and it was obvious Sherwood was on fire. It was amazing how quickly the police and others got control of the streets where the damage was.

Well I walked— I remember we walked down the what was then the main road, past the crater, and, of course, there were these rather— as well as Sherwood being in flames, and this huge crater, there were various burnt out vehicles on the road. Fortunately there was nobody inside them. But, you know, by that time, after we sort of wandered round, there was nothing much one could do.

As I say, access to the worst-hit areas was sealed off very quickly by the police. We were obviously concerned about what had happened to people in

Lockerbie, and it looked horrific, the number of houses that were obliterated or burning, but discovered of course there was no way that one could do anything to help at that stage. And obviously I'd realised that in view of— we obviously we watched the television to get the— that people would be concerned. So—So I came back I think later on to the house - I can't remember how far I wandered round - but came back to the house and tried to find out what had happened. And it only emerged very much later, of course, that it was the unthinkable. You know, the big Boeing airliner coming down; I remember when they came out, and hearing the passenger numbers, if one of these ever comes down when it's full, the death rate will be huge. We were never expecting it would happen here. Fortunately it wasn't completely full but it was full enough.

The other thing that became important was that, as the news filtered out that this plane had blown up over Lockerbie - come down over Lockerbie - various members of the family were frantically trying to make contact, and my son, at that time, was working as a dentist in Thirsk or Ripon, and that particular day he had seen an old lady being knocked down by a car in the main street in Rippon. He had just, you know, looked out— happened to go outside of the practice window and saw this happening, so he was in a somewhat upset frame of mind, and then the news came through, when the news came through. And Gillian was working as a vet in Orkney, which was out up country somewhere, when the news came through - it must have been a night call or late evening call - so the head of the practice radioed her and said, "Gillian, I think you'd better come back, there's been an accident at Lockerbie." So she was wondering what on Earth was happening.

My brother, who at that time was chief met officer in Shetland, obviously was worrying, and, of course, as you would probably remember, all the phone lines were down, or occupied. How much do you remember of the night? There was no— there was no way of getting communication out in any way whatsoever. And eventually, shortly after midnight, the phone rang. My brother in Shetland, using a Ministry of Defence phone, found we were still alive, found that, you know, we had obviously been fairly close to some of the things that had happened but had not been seriously affected. And then he was able to phone round the other members of family to see what the state of affairs was.

For the next few days, John researched for a fundraising project: he recounts the sadness surrounding the Lockerbie victims

Well I'd just retired. It was *incredible*. I'd just retired that— a few— well two or three weeks— a couple of weeks or so before. Was trying to catch up on a lot of things that, you know, needed to be seen to. [pause] Just trying to remember the exact sequence of events. I can't remember exactly. So there wasn't any question of going back to school as it happened.

I remember being interviewed by a journalist: a young lady from somewhere in the north of England, for information about the history of Lockerbie, basically, and what I could tell her about it, so on, and again, as one wandered round to see what was happening. And then, fairly quickly, I suppose when you begin to think if there's anything you could particularly do, the— I got this phone call from a lady called Anne Pitcher, and she was a nurse I think, somewhere south of England, or— I can't remember where she's from, I think it was the south of England, and she proposed to produce this book, Lockerbie Remembered, I think they called it, I can't remember now, I saw a copy down at the Lodge, on the same lines as the Hungerford one that she'd done, and what she wanted to do was to produce this book as quickly as possible, and make it available for sale, for what was bound to be a disaster fund, and I think somebody at the school had said well contact me because she wanted to collect pictures, she got a lot from Ian Henderson and various other sources, but she wanted somebody to write an account of the time and so on. So that quite oddly— It seemed a slightly oblique diversion from what one might have been doing, but it did occupy quite a number of days; reading things and checking up on things and then drafting it so that it could be sent off to her, and so that she could get the thing printed and then sent up. I never found out whether it really made that much money for the disaster— I suppose it probably did because— quite a lot—That was the whole idea; that it should be sold in fairly large quantities. *Lockerbie Remembered*: that's what they called it.

Oh yes, it was specifically aimed at the disaster fund. But obviously, one couldn't tell anything like the whole story of the disaster. I mean, I obviously mentioned the disaster and wrote about what Pan Am had done or had said they would do, and wrote about a lot of aspects of it, but it wasn't— it was a history with that, and then a section in looking to the future.

And quite early on there was a sense of looking to the future, in the town, I think. I mean, a lot of people were doing volunteer work, very admirable volunteer work. A relatively small number of people were grieving for their own losses. Molly next door, for instance, lost her mother, Mary Lancaster, whose remains I think were only recognised when they found her metal knee joints. So in other words she was very badly burned by the disaster and obviously she was very upset.

The tragedy of the Somervilles of course was that they were simply wiped out and I never— I didn't know the daughter or the wife but I'd known the father slightly, and the son had been a very, very good pupil. So I remember being particularly upset to think that they were gone just in a flash. And the Flannigans: there was a horrible story about the irony of the Flannigans. One: the fact that the elder brother, who'd been estranged from the family – David, I think, wasn't it – was planning to come back to Lockerbie that Christmas for a reconciliation. And of course his mother and father and sister were killed, the only survivor being Steven, because he'd gone next-door to help the neighbour's daughter with her bicycle. So I think that was a horrible business. But the irony, of course, of the Flannigans was that David later died. I think it was in Thailand,

and Steven was killed by a train after an evening out, somewhere in England.

And funnily enough when I did I got Anne Pitcher's work out of the way; I then went into the library to see if there were any particular volunteer work done, needed, but by that time, the only thing that they could suggest off-hand was to go round and pick up bits of the aeroplane. And most of that had been done. They did it very quickly.

And the other thing that—so extremely quickly the police and police from all over the place, I mean the Dumfries force wasn't anything like big enough to cope with the situation. And the local authority acted very, very quickly, and I think they all emerged with— the local authority I think emerged with particular credit. But then Neil McIntosh was the chief executive then and he was a very, very capable person. And it was full of voluntary organisations - the Salvation Army, Red Cross, and so on and so forth. Some of the council people— a cousin of mine who worked for the council, for instance, was sent out to pick up bodies, along with a lot of others, obviously, so it was *incredible* how quickly, you know, the operations got going.

The thing that particularly stuck in mind though was the endless noise of Chinook helicopters. Now you'll be familiar with the Chinook, are you? It's the twin engine one, and it has an extraordinarily distinctive sound, and there were other helicopters obviously, but the Chinooks seemed to go round and round and round, all day long and beyond. And, I remember people at the night of the disaster, or just after, offering blankets, and, of course, it very quickly emerged that there was hardly *anybody* who was directly involved in the disaster who was still alive, only a handful of people on the ground and nobody, of course, from the plane, so that, you know, offering blankets was in fact unnecessary and, of course, a lot of doctors and nurses and others poured into the town, and found very quickly that there was nothing to do.

A minor incident on a walk with his daughter when they encounter some personal articles from the crash.

I have vivid memories of going up the Quaas Loaning. Gillian I think, had come down on holiday from Orkney for a few days, can't remember the exact . Anyway, we walked up the Quaas Loaning, where I was in the habit of taking the dogs for walks and— No, that was later, that was another occasion. When I was taking the dogs out regularly I remember noticing in the field to the right hand side of the loaning - I think the field that's now partly covered by the motorway - and it was absolutely covered with tiny fragments of aluminium, metal, which were sticking in the ground like little arrows, just an astonishing sight. Later I remember going down there with Gillian and we wandered up onto the side of the road and noticed there was something rather, rather sad, appalling— not appalling in the sense that it was a dead body or anything like that, but just at the side of the road there was a sort of trail of soil, burnt cloth, all sorts of different things, and in the midst of it two pieces of— it was either a silver or an EPNS tea set. I thought, Dear goodness, that's been from the house that's, you know, been blown up by the explosion. And shortly after that we were wandering back down on the road, and a Strathclyde policeman and policewoman - the policeman I think was a police sergeant - became slightly officious and said, "What are you doing here?" And I said, "Well in actual fact I used— I come here every day." So he backed down somewhat after that. And then I said, "In any case, I think it would be worth your while to have a look up there; there are personal effects that clearly belong to some of the victims: perhaps you should do something about that." So that was that minor episode, I suppose.

John's opinion of the media reporting

Well the paper— at times I think I looked at the other papers, but the paper I normally take is *The Scotsman* and, by and large, I would have said their reporting was *very* accurate. And the local papers seemed to be, by and large, very accurate.

The effect of that media presence: getting back to normal

I think, very rapidly, almost frighteningly rapidly, people in the town got— I'm not saying this in a nasty sense, but they were *overwhelmed* by the media. Obviously, I remember— I mean the— in the period when the early aftermath was taking place, there was the service in the Dryfesdale church, and I was able to hear it from in front of what's now the library or I think a bit further up: sorry, further up in the street, because it was really quite a loud speaker, and obviously you saw Mrs Thatcher and Neil Kinnock and all sorts of others going in. It was at that time that the term, *ambulance chaser*, was bandied about, which was rather unfair, but you know—

And I can't remember who all else was there, there was— these were two that stuck in my mind. And if you remember the Duke of Buccleuch arrived in his adapted Volvo because of his wheelchair. But you see when that happened, the media was everywhere, and my impression was that quite quickly, people wanted to see things back to as normal as they could be. I think that was easier. I don't want to sound too callous, but because the number of people killed on the ground was limited and therefore you had, as I say, one, well, several families that were wiped out in the end, but the numbers were small in normal terms. There was the wonderful escape, of course, of — Mrs Ramsden, Ella Ramsden, and there's a lovely story told there, of course; you've probably come across, have you?

But as I say, I think fairly quickly there was a movement, a desire to get back to normal. I've no— I picked up no feeling of people wanting to dwell on it for an indefinite period of time. I think there was the hope that it would be, you know, the guilty would be found. But it was something that had happened, that had been horrible. The deaths on the plane, obviously, particularly I think the students and Flora Swires and so on, ghastly tragedies, and they were sort of wiped out in the town, obviously likewise, but somehow or other I think people wanted to move on.

John's observations of visitors at the Lodge

And I think that— my feeling is that [a desire to move one] has persisted, as I said to you, down at the Lodge, when we went, people from various organisations, I was one of the two representing the visitors' centre, went to this meeting in the town hall, I think I actually mentioned that we felt we wanted things to be low-key for the twentieth anniversary. Everybody agreed. So there was definitely a feeling that it's not— it's something to be marked with respect, and some people no doubt still feel a sense of grief about it, but not high-key. It's twenty years ago now.

Americans, particularly, who come to the Lodge, and some of them are still very emotional— I think the Americans tend to be, some of them, more emotional than, or more open with their emotions than we are. I think there's a certain reserve, perhaps, about a lot of the people here, a stoicism

Those of us of my age remember the war, when loss of life was colossal: HMS Hood blew up fourteen hundred-odd men, killed in a few minutes. Huge losses of life in aeroplanes and in battles and so on. So on that sort of scale, it's, you know, a lesser event, however dreadful, and however tragic for the number of people who lost their lives— and obviously we find we get

John's work on the Visitors' Lodge in Lockerbie preceded Adult Education duties and the Lockerbie Book Festival

But I think the first thing that happened was that I got involved with the - what do you call it - the type of educ—[laughs] The service that has now disappeared almost— Community education.

Well it was adults— well I did a bit of that, but it was also community education in a wider sense, and for a wee while I remember I'd edited a wee newsletter for the adult education and so on of the school, that was our attempt to develop an integrated system, which just faded out eventually. And through community education, I was approached by one of the community education officers, who said, We'd like to start something in Lockerbie to help the community after the disaster. And they came up with the idea of a book festival. So I was asked to get involved in the community there and actually it was— it lasted ten years, and I was secretary for the first part and chairman for the rest, and we actually had some very, very enjoyable events in September usually, working mainly with the Scottish Arts Council, and that brought in— we were able to bring in all sorts of writers and some performers, but in a fairly modest way. We never set out to fundraise separately; we got not very much anyway, we got some help, but a fairly modest amount, and ran it, I think, very enjoyably for ten years, without going out for the sort of huge-scale sponsorship that well, Wigtown has done since they became the book town, and Langholm is doing with their festival. It helps of course that there are three or four millionaires with connections with Langholm. So we had a lot of interesting writers down, mainly using the little theatre. So that lasted ten years.

Some were, but a lot were, you know, of either national importance in Scotland, or in some cases more than that. One of the last we had was Jordan McDonald Fraser, who was extremely good. But we had people like A.L.Kennedy, and we had the fellow who lived in Hightae for a while, a poet and writer whose name has escaped me for the while. I remember we tried to get Jessie Kesson, and I still have somewhere her letter, regretting that she couldn't manage this time, and referring to Lockerbie as a sad little town.

She wrote two or three very successful novels, one of which at least was made into a film, set in the northeast of Scotland. She had actually— it was an interesting character, she'd been the illegitimate daughter of a prostitute in Elgin, but had discovered, or had been discovered for her an extraordinary literary gift, and was a very highly regarded local novelist. So she had implied in the letter that she would come again, but in fact she died later that year.

We had a faithful clientele who liked it very much but it didn't have the mass appeal to allow us to accumulate enormous funds to, you know, pay for the sort of people who wanted, you know, huge fees and all the rest of it. And then in the end, we had to decide either to try to go much bigger, or wind it up, and we had got— The Scottish Arts Council at that time, used to publish a writer's list of people who would come to events like that and they partly subsidised it and we had to partly subsidise it. We had Hamish Henderson, for instance, on one occasion, which was very— We had him actually in the Bluebell : we had a really big crowd there. And another time we'd had Anne Lorne Gillies, and she got quite a large attendance. So it was good, but it had run its course at the size that we were able to provide, and I'm not sure quite how—how did I get involved in the Lodge? I probably— I think a meeting was held partly through, I think, a community council, I can't remember exactly how it happened, and a steering committee of eight was formed and I was appointed secretary. Basically, the idea was to convert the very run-down semi-derelict cemetery; the gravedigger's lodge; into the visitors' centre. And there were times when it looked as if it wouldn't happen, but in the end it did.

So we've been very pleased with it, actually, and I think it has become quite an asset.

The popularity of the Visitors' Lodge: the present nature of recreational past-times

Last year we had four thousand— between 4200 and 4300, I think. It was quite a bit over four thousand, anyway. And that was opening five days a week, or four days a week— Four or five days a week, and from Easter till just before Christmas, so it wasn't— But we get Americans, of course. Last year I don't think there were all that many.

[A] lot of people thought, well, this is just for the disaster And some other people were not keen on it from that point of view. But it *was* aimed essentially at visitors who would want to know, or *might* want to know about Lockerbie, might want to look at various exhibitions, but also some of them would want to know about the disaster. And in fact we provide a key, for instance, to Ving, the undertaker, so that if the weather is appalling in a funeral then people can shelter in there. And on one occasion when I was on duty, he actually conducted a funeral service in the Lodge because the weather was so appalling.

[A] lot of the community are not particularly aware of it. But then, if you go to Dumfries, you'll find that a large number of people, many of whom you'd thought would know better, don't know about Gracefield.* [Arts Centre] So it's like a lot of other things, people— I think this is probably particularly true nowadays because of television and computers and the internet and so on: people tend to be perhaps less *aware* of what is going on in the community. I mean, you can spend your whole day watching television if you choose to do so, and I know some people who seem to be almost organically attached to their *computers*. So, you know, it's perhaps not surprising that not everyone is aware of it. I would have said all through recent centuries, only a minority tend to be very keenly interesting in these things, and that minority may have been shrunk a little because of the, as I say, television— I mean, I remember when I was a boy, my father used to produce The Blaze for general rheumatic club at Amisfield and between 1946 and somewhere about 1952, the whole village wall was packed to overflowing with people. It was— I think we used to run for two nights, then it was extended to three and then it was extended to four. Border television came on stream, somewhere about, oh maybe '54, '55, '55, and the audiences started to taper off. So that we started off with two nights a week, we went up to maybe four, and then drifted down to two. Now that is fifty years ago, more than fifty years ago now, but again it's a reflection of how a small country parish community could come *hugely* together for a thing like that, before, you know, television became more conquering. And I'm sure this is worldwide.

We don't advertise it particularly, but we get a steady stream of visitors, particularly in the summer, and very large numbers sometimes. And what is striking is the huge range of countries from which the visitors come. Quite extraordinary how big the range is.

Disaster experience at home and away

I remember, when was it? January eighty-nine or January ninety, I can't remember which; my son and I decided to go out to Shetland for Up Helly Aa [Viking Fire Festival each January] in January, and on the plane back I was sitting beside a girl who I think it was a community education worker or something, young woman, and, you know, when you mention Lockerbie the whole face changed. Previously, well you must have encountered this, you've told people that you come from Lockerbie: "Where's that" or "Oh I think I've gone past that in A '74," and that's it. And then you mention Lockerbie and they say, "Oh, oh!"

Development of Lockerbie may be hampered by pervasive inactivitiy of the community?

I remember it being quite striking, son and daughter-in-law and my daughter and I visited Devon, oh, a few summers ago, and we called in at Lynmouth, and Lynmouth of course was where the appalling flash floods were in, probably 1951 or fifty-two, before your time. But basically, there'd been an absolute storm of rain on Exmoor or Dartmoor, Exmoor I think it was, and the water just come tumbling down two deeply indented river channels, which meet just at the top end of Lynmouth, and a huge wall of water just swept away houses and cars and, quite a considerable loss of life. So we visited a room, which was dedicated to the disaster, and we got talking to one of the men in charge, when I just happened to casually mention that we'd come from Lockerbie. He said, "Well you'll know all about this sort of thing," and there was a sort of— almost a fellow feeling emerged, that they had had their tragedy, and this was how they had displayed it, because people wanted to know about it, and we haven't got as far as that, but the Lodge fulfils a little bit of maybe that need. It may be in the future that more will be required [...] but I certainly think the local community, from what one can judge, would not be all that keen. But I don't know.[...]

I mean, Lockerbie is fairly well noted for apathy. Have you ever read the Reverend J.C. Steem's Third S*tatistical Account*? Well it's worth it. Because he wrote that somewhere about 1950, probably early fifties, and he described it as a sleepy hollow, where all sorts of things are started, but usually local interest doesn't last very long. So I'm not worried about that aspect of it, but if you consider who is among the trustees at the moment, Joe Meechan's a native of Edinburgh, I'm a native of the Dumfries area; Marjory McQueen's from Collin, I don't know where Lavinia Vaughan originates, but certainly not in Lockerbie; I don't know where Tom McInnes comes from, he may have been Lockerbie; the Rews are both from Ayrshire, Ayrshire and Yorkshire, and Frank Ritchie is from a long way away, I don't know where. There's at most one native of Lockerbie on that group of trustees. And you will find, repeatedly, that the same people tend to run similar things, till they get fed up.

Reflections on the Trade Centre bombing in 2001: John shares his feelings on blame and the quest for truth

Oddly enough, that day we were having a steering group meeting at Marjory McQueen's house, and the meeting was to start at two. I was here at lunchtime: I think it was the radio news was on, and there was a reference to a plane having crashed into one of the twin towers. So I thought, Well that's a bit of a tragedy, but it must have been a very, very stupid pilot. Walked along the road, arrived at Marjory's, and those who were already there were in a sort of back room, glued to the television. And the whole thing sort of unfolded in front of us, like a bad horror movie almost. It was so utterly, unbelievable, and what in a sense made it even more so was that Marjory McQueen's daughter was in New York City that day, and one of the other members of the committee, I think had a next-door neighbour whose son or daughter was in New York that very day. So it was just something that was so utterly unexpected and unprecedented and horrible that you could hardly believe it was happening. And to have two people in the room who knew young Lockerbie people who were in the city at the time made it even more striking, in a way. More memorable.

Can't remember how soon we realised they were suicide bombers. Must have been fairly quickly because obviously there were mobile phone messages. I suppose there was a connection *realised*, because— but the difference in dimension arose from the fact that the pilots were suicide [pause] bombers, if you like, they are the equivalent of the kamikaze. And that added a different dimension to it. I mean, now suicide bombers are unfortunately commonplace. But they weren't so much then. And it certainly pointed obviously very quickly to the Middle East situation, and in that respect there was a connection.

The Lockerbie disaster connects back to the Iranian airliner that was shot down by the Vincennes [which] was obviously a mistake on the part of the Americans. The Americans are sometimes rather dangerous allies, because they seem to have a particular skill in friendly fire, shall we say, and in that case I think it was just a sheer mistake, but a horribly tragic one. And ironically, the Iranian airliner crashed in the sea, which of course— They Maid of the, whatever it was, the Pan Am airliner was supposed to do here. If it hadn't left half an hour late then it would have been well over the Atlantic before the bombs blew up.

The temptation was to think early on that the Iran would be involved as a reply to the Vincennes tragedy, but I have no— I just don't know. I have heard one of the fiscals describing the trail; the evidence trail pretty convincingly, but then doubt has been cast on the worth of the Maltese shopkeeper, at the worth of his evidence. I mean Gaddafi was daft enough to do anything, but I don't know; I think the honest answer is I don't know.

People like Jim Swires had their lives absolutely, you know, turned over totally because of the death of a fine and obviously very, very much-loved daughter, and it may give people like that some sort of relief from a sort of agony of continuing grief. But [the quest for truth is] relevant from the point of view of justice, but I don't think there's any point now in getting excessively hung up over it, on the basis that we may never find out. Maybe the only people who really know are those who were guilty.

Security has been enhanced but not the flying conditions

Well the thought of a bomb doesn't bother me, because, well, for a long time we lived with the nuclear balance, and I remember I was actually in a classroom teaching in Langholm at the time of the Cuban crisis and at a certain stage there was a very loud explosion, I sort of looked out the window and couldn't see anything, and thought, Well, if that's *it*, you know, we could be dead within minutes and there's nothing we can do about it. You know, there's a— I suppose it induced a certain sense of fatalism. So I don't think that would bother me about air travel.

What does bother me about air travel is the cramped seating and a certain sense of not exactly claustrophobia because I'm not prone— particularly prone to claustrophobia, but I find the modern airliner, unless you can afford the really expensive seats, a bit trying. I remember I made one flight back from Tobago, which— My son was a dentist in Trinidad at the time, and we'd a nice flight from Trinidad to Tobago, we arrived at Crown Point airport to pick up the plane. We were onboard in plenty time; the plane left substantially late because of baggage handling problems at Tobago, and we were supposed to have one scheduled stop I think at Antigua, but in actual fact we touched down at Antigua as planned. We then touched down at Grenada for so long that we landed in the transit lounge, and Trinidad and Tobagan dollar, they didn't know, want to know in Grenada. [laughs] And then we finally got away from Grenada *hours* after we should have left Tobago, and they started serving what should have been the evening meal at about eleven o'clock West Indian Time. Three hours later, if we had managed to sleep, we were wakened up for breakfast, British Time. And I thought, That really is ghastly! They're wonderful things, aeroplanes but they are not the most comfortable air travel.

If you go to any airport, big airport, there are so many planes going in and out all the time— They have been for fifty years or more. I remember when my uncle worked with BOAC at Heathrow, about fifty years ago, you know, standing—there's a village called Cranford I remember, and you could actually stand practically underneath the landing light and there was just a continuous flow of airliners then. Now with more runways, more terminals and so on, it's just—I mean, statistically, the chances of being killed in an airliner are very low. If anything goes wrong, then you've had it, but—

John has never relied on a strong faith

I think I have become more and more [pause] agnostic, I suppose. Well it's been a cumulative effect. I know at least one person in Lockerbie who *lost* his religious faith because of it. But I find— I always had a slight tendency to scepticism; I remember this occasion with the minister when I was a tiny tot in Sunday school, I think he was talking rubbish, which he was, as it happened, and I think the scepticism has grown over the years, rather than the other way round.

On identity and the Borders characteristics

I haven't really let it bother me. I'm very happy to live in Lockerbie, but I have obvious connections with Dumfries, and I like being able to go to Carlisle or Edinburgh, Glasgow or occasionally further afield. So as I say I'm perfectly happy to live in Lockerbie.

JH: Do you think people in Lockerbie have a certain characteristic because of their closeness to the border?

JG: Yes. This is true in most border communities. In certain respects, they're sort of ambivalent, in the sense that they like going to Carlisle or— but they also sometimes tend to have a stronger Scottish identity, I think. I'm not sure that's true now, but it certainly used to be one time. It's very obvious in Langholm, that they were very Scottish, but going to *Carel* [Carlisle] as they called it was a frequent occurrence. And they still do as far as I know. So the rest is— And there are of course extraordinary differences that are beginning to iron out now, but between Langholm and Canonbie the accent and language, to some extent, differ— used to differ. And certainly fifty years ago in Canonbie, people still used to talk about thee and thy and thou and so on. But in actual fact, their particular dialect is probably, slightly, related to Chaucer's middle English. But it's very different, or somewhat different, from how the Cumbrians speak.

The scourge of the small UK town – housing policy and centralised shopping areas

The usual mixture I suppose; it's become more and more of a dormitory because there's been so much house building. I think it has probably got an increased elderly population, it always had. There are quite a number of social problems, but that's because of local, well, housing policy you know how they— I mean, the— what do you call the place in the middle? The new houses—oh it's gone, that's ridiculous. Anyway, it became a sort of—almost a hot bed of trouble for a bit: I think they have to rethink it, you know, how these housing associations have to take in so many people who are homeless and have problems and so on, they've put them all into the one place, in the middle of a town, you're asking for trouble. What Chris Harvey said was grossly exaggerated but partly true. Obviously he came off the train at the station, and saw about three boarded-up shops, looking incredibly scruffy, and the Chinese place which looks very scruffy was boarded up and thought the rest of the town was like that, which it isn't.

Obviously Tesco's is a big change; the disappearance of the Co-op / Quicksave was a big change but I gather that's going to change again. Crown Motor Works: I was rather sorry to see them go, but it had become derelict. There's [pause] an odd mixture of what seem to be quite successful new businesses, I mean I can remember when Protect started and it seems to have survived very successfully. When Cossars went, which was a great pity, the land really has become a great asset, huge improvement there. I would say Lockerbie's like a lot of other small towns; pleasanter than most, or many, but it has certain problems, most in terms of trade and socially, but they're not unique in any sort of way whatsoever. I remember, oh many, many years ago now, when younger daughter was working in Stoke-on-Trent area, my wife was interested in Brother Cadfael, you know the stories?

And these stories were set in Shrewsbury, so we thought one day we'd set out from Stoke to Shrewsbury, and on the way through, I think we'd stopped in—oh dear, my memory— it'd been obviously a lovely wee place at one time, the place where Robert Clive [Major General, 1st Baron Clive of Plassey, 1725-74] was brought up. It's gone at the moment, double-barrelled name, and it had been a lovely little country town, market town and so on, and it was dying on its feet. There was a—you know, half-timber inn, that was closed: a hotel; there were empty shops; there was a general air of decline in it. Market Drayton! And, good heavens! What's happened to this place? Then we came to the outskirts of to Shrewsbury. Oh, probably Tesco, MFI, Homebase; the whole bloomin' lot of them, and that was obviously what had partly done for the grocery chains and so on; had done for Market Drayton. Now Lockerbie was nothing like as bad as that. But it would be a very optimistic person that would say that all the shops are going to open again and be profitable.

John details the economic climate which affects present-day Lockerbie.

The other thing, of course, that's happened to farming and forestry: they have— farming has gone through some pretty hard times lately. I think there's a revival at the moment because milk prices have improved. An awful lot of dairy farmers were going out of business in the last year or so, but the supermarkets and the like of Wiseman and so on are now paying more for milk, which is helping. Pigs in Scotland are very bad at the moment: they're not profitable at all, so a lot of that could disappear if there isn't an improvement. And the foot and mouth of course hit very badly in 2002. Beef, I think, as far as I know is a bit better, just now; but the farms, you know, the prosperity and otherwise tends to go in cycles, and I don't think the Common Agricultural Policy helps. But don't ask me to explain it. [Jill chuckles] And of course the— because the returns have been sort of poor at times in farming, then what were once many-men operations have become one- or two-man operations. So the whole farming community has shrunk, if you include farm workers. I mean, the farm worker I think is slowly becoming an endangered species like the coalminer, and forestry; I used to work in Ae Forest as a student sometimes, and it's very labour-intensive then, and felling was done by a big man with an axe. Nowadays an awful lot of forestry work is done by contractors and of course they use those chainsaws and all sorts of things. So the amount of employment there has shrunk.

[The new power station] be helpful to the economy here in the short term at least, because obviously there's a huge market for either waste timber or, you know, small section timber that's no use for much else, *or* for willow but of course there's a huge controversy on about biofuels at the moment, as you'd probably noticed: they're arguing that the biofuels in the United States are simply putting up the price of corn and other foodstuffs, and the same argument is being used here.

Now if my memory's correct, Inverkip, up in the, you know, up the west coast towards Greenock, was rather an attractive little power station actually, was built as an oil-powered station, oh maybe twenty, thirty years ago, and I think it has produced very little power, because while it was being built, the price of oil soared. So that what *would* have been an economic power generator was priced out o' the market. So this great plant has done relatively little of what it was planned to do. Now I don't know if this will happen with Stephen's Croft [Eon Power Station]; I don't think so in the short term, but anything could happen in the long term.

Well I think there is a much wider question because we're in the throes of globalisation, and I have a suspicion that as wage rates begin to rise in India and in China, that the reverse process will come in to some extent. I believe it's already happening with the call centres, that because the Indian economy is booming, you know, you can buy {inaudible] and Jaguar and Land Rover, then their wage rates will rise, it'll take a while and they won't necessarily rise to the same levels as here, certainly not in my lifetime but possibly not even in yours. The same process is happening inside the EU, which has been extended so far to the east that you've got basket-cases like Romania, where wages are very low, and Poland where wages are probably higher but obviously it's paying a lot of Poles to come over here. Now it depends how far these processes go and whether they reverse. If they don't reverse then we're going to have to live by our wits more and more, but then that's been true for the last fifty years.

But the only thing is that the manufacturing industry has been very substantially lost and an awful lot of our income nationally is coming from financial services. On the other hand, I suspect that if the world population continues to increase; if standards of living continue to rise in China and in India in particular, then the farmers may come into their own, because the demand for food will rise. But it's when these things all happen. *If* farming becomes very prosperous here again then Lockerbie will boom, but not in the same way. Because the process has become so mechanised.

The tragedy of it is at the moment because house prices are so hopelessly unrealistic then the average person in their twenties can't afford to get in the property market. So, I'm not in the least bit surprised. I think what is tragic in this country is that the taxpayer is gonna be fleeced for Northern Rock when it probably should have been rescued instantly, or allowed to go bankrupt, and what I find inexcusable is that the manager; managing director or whoever he was - chief executive-, what a shame to have a local name so traduced. I think he was able to walk away with 380,000. Now he should have been jailed, or at any rate thrown into the middle of a shareholders' meeting and manhandled. And that—if the bankers keep doing that, then it's dreadful.

But it depends on the economy in general, only the farmers. I mean, one thing that emerged out of the foot and mouth, the last - the 2001 episode - was that farming is actually less economically important— was less economically important then than tourism. But obviously because of its market town connections, then farming is really important here. But I mean, the service industries of all sorts are big employers.

But I think the tendency is for the pressures to come from outside. Mainly, I think the churches would have felt obliged out of decency to do something, and obviously they were very involved in the disaster itself. One of the memorable statements of the first service, of course, was that the Moderator saying, you know, having thought it was an accident, we then discovered it was an act of wickedness. An act of wickedness - the bombing […] the sabotaging of the airline, which it was I thought was rather a good way of putting it.

The collective efforts of bereaved parents will take a commemorative form.

Well what's down in the lodge at the moment is only a picture of the quilt, which was prepared by, I presume, the mothers of the students from Syracuse University, who were killed. But last year or the year before we commissioned Solway quilters to produce a symbolic quilt to be used to mark the twentieth anniversary. And all being well, we should get it for display in October, down at the lodge, yes.

John and his wife, Sheena and family, late 1960s.
(© John C. Gair, Dumfries, 2008)

John in 2007
(© Arthur Johnstone 2008)

Dryfesdale Lodge Visitors' Centre at the cemetery in Lockerbie, with which John has been very involved.
The interior of the Visitors' Centre, features the couches from the Camp Van Zeist facility in the Netherlands, and disaster memorabilia in a glass case

Adam Peter Brooks, March 25, 2008

The Last Born Lockerbie Scholar

The following narrative differs in focus from the other oral transmissions in that this narrative does not feature any experience of the events leading up to, or in the aftermath of, the disaster. The narrator is a true Lockardian, born and brought up in the town; resident in Lockerbie on the evening in 1988, but has no experience to recount of that night because he was 4 months old.

The narrator has an experience of a different nature to share – the thoughts, feelings, meaning and memories as a representative of the town in one of the positive inter-cultural community initiatives that developed from the disaster. This was my primary reason for asking him to participate and I suggest his reason for agreeing will be clearly obvious from his narrative. The two motives are explicitly linked.

He spent his childhood and school years in Lockerbie with his family and he has recently gone away to university in the north of Scotland. His maternal family has a strong link with the town and the surrounding area; he plays the bagpipes in the town pipe band and curls at the local ice-rink .

He spoke to me on Tuesday 26 March 2008, in the front room of the family home in West Acres, a sub-division of Dumfries Road. His family was preparing for his sister's forthcoming 21st birthday celebrations that week, and he had returned home to Lockerbie for the Easter break, having completed his first semester at Aberdeen University.

I was at his family home on the evening of the disaster – we had been evacuated from Mains Street and some of us went visiting. My parents were friendly with his parents. The narrator must have been there – as a baby, he was probably asleep - but I don't have a memory of him that evening. Whilst I had heard about him in the intervening years, I had never met him prior to the interview. I hadn't been in that house since the 21 December 1988 and I had only a vague and unsubstantial recollection of the interior from that evening 20 years prior. I do remember the television images of my town on fire that evening although not the setting or surroundings in which I saw them –surely, it would have been that very front room where the narrator and I now sat.

He mentions two towns in the locality in connection with his family history. Ecclefechan is about 7 miles straight down the M74 from Lockerbie. It is famous as the birthplace of Thomas Carlyle, the 19th century writer and poet. It is affectionately know as 'the 'Fechan'! Lochmaben is 4 miles west, on the road to Dumfries, and it is positioned on the Bruce Loch, with Bruce Castle, now ruined, on the northwest side of the water. Lochmaben has a close affinity with Lockerbie, as its closest neighbour geographically and culturally.

During our interview, which lasted for 1 hour and 8 minutes, he was personable, eloquent and forthright to be with. He is Adam Peter Brooks and he is 19 years old.

Adam's family connections with Lockerbie and an anecdote about Grandpa.

Well, my grandpa on my mum's side is from Lockerbie. I believe my grandmother on that side is from Ecclefechan. They were living in the town as well at the time and my mum has lived in Lockerbie all of her life. An interesting story about my grandfather now, they're talking About him as on the night of the disaster — my grandfather's got a great memory, he's dead now. He died in 1995, but he had a really good memory of the roads and where things are in the town. He's big into the hunting and things and he's was obviously — he drove milk tankers, so he also went to all the farms so he knew where everything was. He had these great old maps that we've got map, that told you every little road, every little farmhouse and things like that, but on the night — of course when all the power lines went down, no telephone, no nothing - he tried to go to Lochmaben to phone my other grandparents to tell them that we were still alive, obviously, and somehow he managed to get lost [Jill laughs], going to Lochmaben, which is a straight road and he's probably travelled that road — he's probably travelled in his lifetime thousands of times but he got lost.

Like as I say, my mum's always lived her, so you always find her when she's out and about in the town she knows most — a lot of the older people as well, through her parents.

There is a scholarship initiative called the Syracuse Programme, an opportunity for 6th Year students from Lockerbie Academy to study at Syracuse University in USA 35 students from the university were killed in the disaster. It is as an intercultural experience, prior to their chosen studies at their chosen university, but, as Adam explains in detail, representatives from Lockerbie perform a very important function in linking the collective consciousness at Syracuse University with Lockerbie Academy on the disaster and the wider process of remembrance and commemoration.

The idea is you continue the link between Syracuse and Lockerbie, by telling fellow students what happens to them when they get into sort of their final year, they become a Remembrance Scholar, which is the sort of Syracuse equivalent of a Lockerbie Scholar and they are the ones that run the ceremonies every year. So, part of the job is to educate them so that they can then [inaudible] and actually a few of my friends this year are now Remembrance Scholars. My RA, my residence advisor in one of the dorms last year, she's now Resident Advisor and of course I've told all my friends who are in first year now into second year that they've gotta be one to but I think they're keen.

After successful exam results, Adam remembers a change of heart about the scholarship programme

Well, the main way you hear about Syracuse is obviously through the students who have gone before. I was always aware of it at school but — and especially — in first year as well, when you get your introductory speech by the head master, Graham Herbert, he does talk about Syracuse; one of the things you can achieve in sixth year, but at the time when I really started thinking about it was in 2004. I was in the pipe band with […], who was the scholar who had just come back, probably a matter of weeks before the Gala, and he said, "Are you thinking of applying?" I said, "Not for me". I wasn't really the kind of person at the time that probably would have gone in for it. He said, "It was the best year of my life, you should really think about it", and that sort of stuck with me […] he was wearing his Syracuse ties around at the time. He's not just talking about how great it is but he's also trying to represent it in the pipe band. We have — you know, pipe band, it's uniform, we didn't have official ties at the time, but also picked that tie out. He thought it was fine. He was wanting to bring it home with him as well. So, that — just wanted to really consider and then obviously, when I got into sixth year, the talk really started to get moving about it. "We are going to have to go with this".

[…] a lot of my friends actually went to Syracuse, some of my older friends, because living in West Acres, most of the people are older anyway […] So, you found that you just all hung out together, didn't matter how old you were. Most of my friends were four years older than me, when I was about ten, so you got to know a lot of their friends and those were the ones that were going in the years preceeding and I thought, "Well, there was […] and […], who lives down the road, friends of mine. […], again, and I thought, "You know, all these people that go that I know, none of them have ever complained. They've all said it was great. I thought, "There's something in that, you know. If they're all enjoying it and I like them, then I'm thinking probably some similar minded, then surely I would enjoy it as well.

JH: What was making you think that it wasn't for you, initially?

AB: I don't think it — I just perhaps — I was only in the fourth year I think at the time. I was quite study-conscious then, so I wasn't really thinking extra-curricular — gap years and things like that. It really wasn't — it was sort of more after fifth year that I started to really think about what I could do with exams, because up to the Highers and fifth year I was just thinking, "Get that, get into uni". Once I'd got that thank goodness I thought, "Right, let's really look at other things".

The scholarship application process at Lockerbie Academy.

The way it works is — I think it varies a little bit each year but pretty much. You write your letter of application, which is pretty much the same as what you would write for your head boy or you "off to uni" personal statement. Just sort of outlining why you want to do it, why you think you would be good for and what you think you could bring to the scholarship and then you have your interviews and those were with local town dignitaries, head master included, councillors, people like that. There were about three sets of interviews there and then they would go away and discuss it for about a week and then they'd come back and then they would tell if you had got it. But there was no immediate requirement of, "You must get this grade, you must have done this, you must have done that". It was open to anybody.

[...] They asked you sort of obviously the very general questions. They can't you ask you anything too specific about — what courses would you like to do? They didn't ask you what exact courses have you picked up out but things like, Would you feel homesick? How do you think you would cope with being away, all the responsibility? And of course, one of the things that I think I managed to catch a few people out on, because a lot of the other applicants — in fact I might be right in saying that none of the other applicants, apart from — oh, Janice wasn't born, she was [inaudible]— I might have been the only one who had lived in the town at the time. Obviously Janice would also have family that always lived in the town, but I had a lot — I had more knowledge about what actually happened than they did and that was a big part of this as well, you know. "Can you just tell me something about the disaster?" And I could come out and say, specially on the Lockerbie side, how many people died, where sort of things happened and that was something they were clearly looking for because that's a big part of — when you go up there, you are expected to talk about it.

The inception of the programme.

The first scholars went out in 1990 [...] I believe it was more of an approach from Syracuse to do something for Lockerbie. [...] I think Sam Gorwitz was very high up there; he was very involved. He was head of the Honours Department, who I did meet once or twice. But if you go into the archives at the Syracuse Library, you can find it all. I did look through. I didn't take notes or anything, I was just sort of going through it all and noticed his name was up there at the top. There were massive piles of documents, archives.

What representing Lockerbie meant to Adam: the significance of the scholarship's tradition.

I was going for the experience of being away for a year in another country and also to represent the town. I was keen to do it. Syracuse Scholarship is a big honour, especially if you are from Lockerbie. I can't talk for what people think of it in Loch Leven but to come from Lockerbie, to hear about the disaster, to know the people that have gone before you, you know, it's really important. When you're in for it, you really want it and you want to make a good impression on people. You don't want to let the side down.

JH: Had you stopped to consider if you were proud of that prior to the Syracuse programme coming up.? I mean, had you ever thought about your roots and your identity as being a Lockardian before that?

AB: Perhaps not but I was always in the pipe band for the Gala so maybe that's something. Showed I liked to get involved. There was a lot of pride I think from the school as well. I think we have a good school at Lockerbie. [...]No, I mean, when you come from Lockerbie Academy and you know you've been picked by people who have taught you for perhaps six years, and something says you've been picked over your friends, you know there's sort of pride in there. I want to do well for my school. I want to look good for Scotland *and* Lockerbie, you know, because you represent also your parents, your other members of your family, your friends, you know. So, there is that sort of pride, like, I'm going to make sure they all look good, or try to, anyway.

The nature of remembrance at Syracuse.

The Lockerbie Scholar's job is — you have to give a speech at that. I gave a speech in a poem and played the pipes. Remembrance Scholars from my year didn't actually give as much of a speech. They represent one of the Syracuse Scholars that died, each one. Thirty-five Remembrance Scholars, thirty-five Syracuse students. So, their job is to just give two or three sentences on who that person was, but they really have responsibilities of getting everything in order. — they run it, basically. It's their job.

The Remembrance Reception

[…] The Remembrance Reception is really for Remembrance Scholars, not so much the Lockerbie Scholars. You get recognized but it's their thing […] Yes, so the rose laying ceremony is the big event and that's when you get a lot of the relatives and family members of victims, they come into the university. So, you give your speeches in front of — the other remembrance garden, just at the front of the Hall of Languages, which is their oldest, most grand building on campus, and then came television crews and school dignitaries, the chancellor, the chaplain — the dean of the chapel, rather. There was about 100 people I think there at the time and that's your main thing. There were other things that we did as well. We had a candlelit vigil on the Friday before it and one or two other things. They have discussions, meeting on terrorism and things like that but, as I said, the main thing is definitely the last Friday, because it starts on Friday and goes on to the next Friday. I notice they have their Remembrance Scholars reception, where they get recognized for their achievements.

And it's a really tough scholarship to get into for them. Very, very tough and I think that the year that I was there, they were looking at new applicants, this year, and 160 people applied.

JH: So, it's a great honour for the students from Syracuse to be a Remembrance Advisor?

AB: Oh, Absolutely, yes.

A new generation of Lockerbie scholars began with Adam.

JH: […] this will have been the last year that somebody who was alive when the Lockerbie disaster.

AB: Yes, we were the sort of benchmark, because Janice was the first that wasn't and I was the last.

JH: That was last year and of course next year they won't be —
AB: Same with this year. Neither of them were alive.

Giving back to Lockerbie Academy

[…] Christmas 2006, I gave a short talk to prospective scholars, who were thinking About it, and again I went back — I went back this Christmas as well and again did the same again, and the two scholars from this year were in as well. Generally sort of talking About — saying what it's going to be like.

[…] It's just a way to sort of — advertising it to people back in Lockerbie because you don't get that much advertising out of school. I think they have tried to increase it in the last couple of years […] it's getting to the stage that a lot of people don't know About it;, well, it doesn't — because they're not born, it's not as relevant to them —

JH: I would imagine it should be even better advertised for that reason.
AB: Yes, I think they have now started to think About it; putting more energy into it. Also, in the first few years, it could sell itself.

An untimely security scare: Adam on the age of terrorism.

AB: The week before we had the liquid gel crisis. You couldn't take any fluids on to a plane. They thought they were going to blow them all up.[…] Obviously it was plastered across the news. Mother wasn't too happy that I was going down at that time, to fly out from Heathrow to New York, of all places. But it was a little bit awkward at the time.
JH: How did you feel About that?
AB: I wasn't going to miss out. I was never going to not go. […] Perhaps if both parents had said, "Really, we don't think it's a good idea", I would have really thought About it but my dad was always sort of, "Well, you shouldn't change your way of life". Thinks like me. Terrorism is going to be here probably for a long time, perhaps the entirety of my life, so you can't really restrict yourself because of it.

Adam remembers his surrogate mother at Syracuse.

AB: Syracuse is about 4½ hours upstate New York. You're not really that far from Canada. […] You're not really far from the lakes. You've got to go across Lake Ontario to get to Canada but we got picked up by Judy O'Rourke, who basically looks after every Lockerbie Scholar, when they come out each year. I believe she was heavily involved in creating the Lockerbie Scholarship and, as I say, every year — she becomes sort of, as Mr Herbert would say, "Your surrogate mother" when your out there. She really does because she totally looks after you. You stay with her for a couple of days to recover the jet lag and then you go into your Halls. But I saw her three times a week maybe…into the office. You always sort of — you check in; she's the one that's sort of responsible for you, other than your parents obviously. You've got to sort tell her when your alive. If you travel you've got to tell her where you're going, when you're going to be back. No, she's really good.

First impressions of the campus and adapting to different living arrangements.

Well, it was a nice day. That was a start. Of course it always seems a lot bigger when you first get there than it actually is. It was the same with Aberdeen. When I first walked about and getting kind of lost. "Oh, no, this is not really that big at all". No, I did like it and we got shown around. We got a little tour around as well and I met my roommate, not on the first day there. I actually moved some of my stuff in but was staying with Judy for the next day or two and I met my roommate. He seemed like a nice guy and we actually hit it off quite well. We had a good sort of relationship where we weren't overly friendly but we were definitely good friends. So, we didn't spend the entire time together, which probably would have driven us crazy.

There was a few singles on our dorm in fact but it was largely doubles.[…] That's the way they do it in The States. […] it's open plan […]

Well, I could tell that he was the guy I would probably get on with quite good because he actually — when he first moved in, he put the wardrobes that were against the wall in between the beds and he said, "You know, it's just to give us a bit of privacy", and I thought, "You know, that's a good idea" and a few other people on the dorms copied that.

[..] It was nice to have someone over the other side that was — you know, if you are watching TV, watching a film at night.[…]

Adam explains the expectations of a Lockerbie scholar

I think what they expect is for people — like as I said, to educate your friends in what happened and to maintain links with them and also to get involved when it comes to these services, Remembrance Week for example. You've got to be able — you've got to say your piece. Be an ambassador, because also when you go out to Syracuse you are also representing Syracuse, because they sell this scholarship. So, if you're just messing around, you know, you're making them look bad as well, the people who are going to fault it. So, it is an ambassadorial role. It's not sort of — you're not there as a grade A student. You don't have to be.[…]

It is a non-academic year. The emphasis is on representing Lockerbie, and experiencing Syracuse and America. You are there primarily as an ambassador for the town, but also to have a year which enables you to get a perspective on the world outside of Scotland, to have a year where you meet new people and see and do things you have never seen or done before. You must not abandon your studies though by any means. Classes must be attended and passes attained. But this is not about getting straight A's. B's and C's will suffice […]

His Syracuse study schedule was a diverse range of academic and practical subjects – the bla, bla, bla and the cha, cha, cha!!

I tried to take a mixture of classes that would be interesting and fun and ones that I thought were a little bit more serious but still be interesting. I didn't try and take anything that was going to be necessarily hard and boring, because there is no point because the credits don't transfer over to Aberdeen or to Scotland. You can perhaps try and wrangle a few credits but I didn't think it was worth it because then I would have take courses that were going to be heavy going and it's not why you're out there. They do emphasise that at university and people you meet say, "You're not there to study". By all means do some work; you have got to go your classes. You are going to a university but if you get 'C's, that's all right. You don't have to get 'A's. So, take things that are interesting.

So, I took — first semester I took Introductory Geography, because I had never done geography at school.[…]. I took Astronomy, because I've always liked that. I took Philosophy, which was an Honours course.[…] Well, Philosophy perhaps wasn't the most fun I've ever had. It was quite a difficult …….

[…] I took also Backpacking! Yes. A half-semester class […]Learning About backpacking, then going on a trip.[…] how to make stove out of a Coke can and — things like Country Code. A little bit more complicated than shutting gates but basically that sort of thing. It wasn't even that complicated.[…] No. I think we did compass work once. But we got to go on a trip, out to The Adirondacks, which is the mountain range just outside of Syracuse and that was really good.[…]

[…] I also took International Relations. I took Public Advocacy; that was in first year […] because I thought, "Right, that might actually be useful for law" and that was really good because you got to do presentations and things in front of your class. A lot of it was public speaking. I think we spoke in front of 60 people at one point, arguing About whether we should endorse the government to spend money on going to wars. […] one of the highlights, I think, certain parts of it. I was doing ballroom dancing, which I was all right at, actually. I was quite surprised. Wasn't too bad at that. Again, so a little bit more fun. A little bit social.

Listening to the stories of Lockerbie was Adam's knowledge base.

Well, most of it I already *knew*, to be honest. Most of it I could just — my parents have never *not* talked About it as such. I mean, we don't — people from Lockerbie we don't *talk* About it every day but we don't necessarily *hide* from it. If I asked them About it they would tell me. They just wouldn't bring it up themselves. So, most of the information I had. I sort of knew already […] Perhaps town stories are the best way to learn About terrorism. […] You had to learn more About the Syracuse side of course. But write the speeches, just sort of, whatever you knew and then try and get it in a coherent sort line of thought.

The Rose-laying ceremony; choosing a poem and a piece for the Pipes.

I don't know if … I think it was something that I was definitely … was very concerned About for the Rose-laying Ceremony; the speech I had to write.[…] That's, like as I say, on the last Friday of the week. Big service. I knew that — that that's when most of the big cheeses of the school are going to be out. There's going to be TV crews. Most important there were going to be relatives; parents of victims and they are going to be every word. I really did work quite hard on trying not to — and I basically thought to myself, "Right I don't mind if I sort of make a screw-up of presentation here, presentation there, presentation in class, playing the [28:46] , as long as I get that speech and that point right on that day, I'll be happy". As long as I don't do anything stupid, awful, like fumble, something else. I didn't mind if I talked in class About space travel to Mars and I'd got zero points, as long as I got that one right at that time, I was happy. And of course when I'd done I thought, "Yes, that's okay".

I think I probably spoke for about five or six minutes; nothing really that long. Janice, she had to write a larger speech. Mine was more sort of — obviously you are going to say similar things but the idea was that one would so that took up half of my time. I remember sort of really thinking, okay, got get this to sound right. I've got to learn it. I was quite nervous because I remember when I gave it, I did sort of read from a sheet that I had but at the same time, I thought, "Right, as long as you don't screw it up, who cares?" I wasn't sort of confident enough to just sort of go for it, but I tried to speak up and I think I managed to speak relatively well because most people seemed to hear it.

There was about a hundred, I think, but again all — a lot of my friends they turned up as well, but maybe even more. You mates are there; they are going to talk About it later. I came last. I was the last. I had to play the pipes as well, which isn't quite as nerve-wracking I don't think as giving a speech. The pipes are sort of — I have done it more often and — it didn't help that it was freezing cold and it had been snowing during the day, because I was there in my kilt.

I remember at one point I was playing 'Highland Cathedral' and this massive gust of wind came through at me and just — it sucked every bit of air out of my. I just sort of buckled actually. I thought, "Right, just blow, blow, just keep playing, just don't screw up".

[…]Highland Cathedral' is pretty much a given at an occasion like that, so I knew that would be something that would be fine. I did wonder about the other one and ended up choosing 'Flower of Scotland'. Obviously you want to play something that is appropriate. I wasn't going to play a jig or anything like that.

One of the things I thought was pick something you are comfortable with, because I always get told by the guy who taught me the pipes if you're playing in public, which is probably the biggest occasion I've ever had to play solo […] just pick something you know you can do. Do 'Highland Cathedral' often enough and do 'Flower of Scotland' so I thought, I could have done 'Amazing Grace' or something but I'd actually played 'Amazing Grace' on the Friday before at the candlelit vigil, so I thought I'd play something different.

Adam's memories of a bereaved Mother and some relatives

I'd found [a] poem. That was the idea, that you would — because a lot of friends of written poems about the deceased. So, I went to the archives and thought I am going to find something here. I was also looking for something that would fit in. You just couldn't pick any one and I didn't want something — I did read them. I had a few of them and I thought, "Right, okay, that sort of suits my line of thought more and sort of the way I feel About what happened". Some of them were a little bit different, you know, they talk a little bit more About terrorism. I didn't think I really to talk about must terror — it was more About loss.

But a couple of odd stories, unbeknown to me I had been assigned a seat in Hendricks Chapel afterwards, for the reception, for Remembrance Scholars, and the person that I was sitting next to was the mother of the guy who the poem was written About.[…]That was quite odd. […] I think we just sort of — she said, "Hello, I'm such-and-such". I said, "Oh, your son, the poem was About". Yes. But, she was quite open About it. She wasn't terribly — she was obviously upset but she wasn't in a position where she couldn't talk About it or anything, so we spoke quite freely.

Something else I did was met some of the relatives. They were having a meeting because they are part of the - forget the name - some sort of Pan Am-Lockerbie Trust thing that they've sort of been campaigning for years and things, for more information about it. My role there wasn't really to talk about what they were *doing*, it was just to talk about what I was doing *here*

Adam talks about the pervasive feelings of cultural responsibility and what the solemnity of the commemorations at Syracuse meant to him.

I always sort of felt the emotion every day I was *there* at times. It wasn't just then as such, because you would be walking around and you think, I've got here from Lockerbie, there's sort of 4,000 people there and I'm representing, like I said, my family, my school, my friends, my town and my country. There *is* a lot of pride there and I found myself quite a few times thinking, "Yes, this is pretty big, you know. It's something you'll never forget". That sort of feeling.

It wasn't necessarily *that* day. It was more sort of very often, especially if you walk past the Remembrance Garden by yourself, you think — that was quite a moment as well.

JH: There's a little *wall*, is there?

AB: Yes, they've got a wall with all the names of the people that passed away.[…]

On Liberal America and Terror

People in my dorm - because we were in an Honours dorm - so a lot of them are very, very smart. Far smarter than *I* was, that's for sure, and they'd got great grades and — you find that the more educated Americans, the more *liberal* American. So, they obviously — everybody pretty much has the same idea About terrorism. No one ever condones terrorism but they would perhaps be more opinionated of George Bush, negatively, than other — even within the university than other people would be.[...] Yes. I did sort of see that thing. The more educated you are, the more liberal you are in The States.

JH: Did they ever ask you what you thought? Were you ever asked for your opinion?

AB: Oh, yes, we used to have long debates on what we thought of George Bush and what we thought of Barack Obama and Hillary Clinton as well. So, there was always a lot of discussion going on.

JH: Did you quite enjoy that climate of debating?

AB: Oh, yes. Pretty interesting getting their perspectives and they were quite interested to see the European perspective as well.

JH: What would that be then?

AB: I think the European perspective is very anti-Bush, anti-Blair, which perhaps they weren't quite as aware of. They know a lot of Europeans don't like Bush but I think they felt British people quite *liked* Blair, or perhaps it was just one or two I spoke to perhaps. I said, "Not now, not really". Or I didn't anyway. They were interested as well from Barack Obama, Hillary Clinton, because Europe, as I read it in the papers, is generally more supportive of Barack Obama, probably including myself in that as well.

That was possibly more on the backburner because the race between Hillary and Barack hadn't really started then, it was just Barack as an idea, would he run? It was more sort of Bush/Blair, particularly Bush.

Where's Lockerbie?; Adam spreads the word.

Not everybody knew about it. [...[But that was why you were there, to talk about it. But a lot of people — you were just saying — I remember talking to a security guard when I was downstairs in Burger King, which is right underneath our dorm, so we had a Burger King downstairs — health of the nation there — and he said, "Where are you from? Your accent?" I said, "I'm from Lockerbie". "Gottcha." He knew exactly what I meant by that.

I think sort of obviously the higher members of the faculty were well aware of it. If they had been there all the time they know about Remembrance services and my roommate knew about it, I think actually before I met him, but obviously he got more aware of it. I think students — say, some would, some wouldn't.

Comparison of Syracuse and Aberdeen university; college sports and the fraternal spirit.

Syracuse has a very, very big mall, which is slightly outside of town and that's — if you're not at Syracuse — for example the sports, college sports is so big in The States that you don't support the town teams, you support the college teams. So, when you have got shopping down at the mall, you don't need to go anywhere else and you've got your sport, which is on campus, 50,000-seater in-door stadium for football, basketball and lacrosse, you don't always have the need to perhaps, go into the city. It suffered for that, I think; the city I mean.

The university and the campus has got a lot to do with it. That's the thing as well, that Syracuse University used the campus for extracurricular a lot more than I think in the UK do. At weekends in The States I'd be at a basketball game. Weekends in Aberdeen our people go to the pub. It's just different that way.

JH: Do you find yourself being more critical of— well, it just so happens you're going to Aberdeen but do you find yourself sort of always constantly comparing the two uni's now that you have spent time over in The States?

AB: I do, yes. Also I miss being at Syracuse quite a lot but at the same time you had to compare the education systems and I think — I knew that when I came to Aberdeen I'd be made to work more than I was at Syracuse, and I have been, but that's part of thing when you say, "Oh, you're not enjoying it as much". Well, you're not enjoying it because you have got to work. But that's why you're there. I never had any illusions that it would be as fun as Syracuse. It can't be, because of the nature of the work you are doing. If you're at one university to have an experience and at another one to study, which one is going to be more fun? I think what Syracuse had going for it was that it got a lot of speakers in; very high quality speakers. We had Al Gore on climate change. Jessie Jackson. Jane Goodall was there; she's the woman who first discovered Chimps using tools.[...]

I didn't actually see him, but John Bolton, who was the former US Ambassador to the UN, was also at Syracuse. I would like to see perhaps more of that at Aberdeen. At Glasgow, for example, I think had Gordon Brown. So, it also happens but perhaps I haven't yet.

JH: Yes; and Aberdeen is very traditional, isn't it, you know; it is!

AB: Yes [...] And it's very different. Universities in Scotland don't have the university spirit they do in America, partly because of the sport probably.

Even if you don't like basketball or football - American football I'm talking about here - it is still sort of your team. There's a lot more college spirit. Everybody wears orange in Syracuse. That's their colour and I think I've got seven or eight pieces of orange clothing now. I don't have any Aberdeen clothing. [...] It's not to say we're not proud of being at Aberdeen, but it's just perhaps more subdued.

His 10th Anniversary memories

I remember going down to the cemetery. I don't remember doing anything at the church. I went with Helen Fraser, actually, and [...], I think, and I just remember — I was quite small, so there were just a lot of people. I remember the Duke of Edinburgh was there [pause] But I don't have any major recollections; apart from the most people I'd ever seen at that cemetery at one time, undoubtedly.

Adam has frequent cause to visit the Dryfesdale Cemetery site of the Memorial Garden, but, like me, he has never been to the Tundergarth memorial. He discusses memorial sites appropriate to Lockerbie commemoration.

They have a museum now at the cemetery, which I used to work at, and my mum still works at it now.[...] you get a lot of American visitors coming it. You'd obviously talk to them about it. I think actually we've met a few people now who can work out you've got links with because you know such-and-such who knew such-and-such who they know; 6 degrees of separation. No, I don't find myself necessarily going down to look at the Wall of Remembrance. Obviously, every time we get someone from Syracuse, we take them. We were down at the weekend taking the girl who was up from London. That was actually the first time I had ever been to [Tundergarth] I had always thought about going but ...

JH: That's a good point, because I've never been up there, ever, actually.

AB: Yes. It's just—I don't know. It's not that it doesn't bother you.

JH: Yes, but that's the site up there has got a different significance, doesn't it, I think, in my mind, compared to — but this is quite an acceptable environment or forum here. Not acceptable but you know it's quite safe, whereas up there on the hill, it's kind of quite exposed.

AB: It does have a different atmosphere, doesn't it?

JH: Yes, that's what I'm trying to say.

AB: You might sort of think it's perhaps more — I don't know how many people ever go to see it but there might be more relevance for Lockardians of Sherwood Crescent than there would be at the cemetery, because obviously Sherwood Crescent is a memorial to the people of Lockerbie that died. So, you might just think, well, perhaps that's their friends, that's their family. Down at the cemetery — okay, so there's a memorial to those people too but it's more victims of the plane. I don't know if that's the right thing — it's less relevant to Lockerbie people down there as it would be in other places.

JH: When people from the outside come, they go and visit [...] all the places that you know [...] because they've come from outside, so they found relevance in things that you don't find relevance in because they're on your doorstep.

Adam's experience of townspeople's attitude to perpetual remembrance.

But Lockerbie just doesn't talk about. I mean we don't — I don't want to say, "Go on about it" but it is that sort of, "Well, it happened, yes; we have a memorial, yes; but we keep living". We don't sort of get dragged into the past because this is a living town. People have to keep going. They build new houses. They put new shops in. They just get on with going to work.

I think it is perhaps easier for people who were not there to come to the memorial and have more significance to people that are there.

The response to Adam's hometown

AB: [People in Aberdeen] don't know where it is but they know all about it.[…] Pretty much everybody […]Well, maybe not, but certainly over 80%.

No. I mean, they don't sort of ask for details or anything like that. People *abroad* might. So, you don't tend to say you're from Lockerbie if you're going abroad sometimes, just to sort of avoid the hassle.

JH: What kind of hassle?

AB: Well, you know, you might get somebody asking a stupid question and they say something quite insensitive at times. I remember somebody said that once to me when I was in Australia.

JH: What did they say?

AB: They said, "Oh, where are you from?" I said, "From Lockerbie". They said, "Good place for planes". [pause] because they want to ask questions. At Syracuse obviously every time, you say you are from Lockerbie, because as I say, you are there to broadcast it. So, you must say you're from Lockerbie and you don't get that sort of – perhaps, [pause] ill-considered response. You might get it at places so you just don't want to draw attention to yourself perhaps when, not relevant to them. But obviously being at Aberdeen, there's no point because you say, "I'm from Lockerbie", because if you're in Scotland and you sort of fudge where you are, people will figure it out. If you say you're from Dumfries and Galloway. Right, "Where?" "Oh, I'm from just this little town". "Where; I'll know where it is!" You say that in sort of Australia. You can say I'm from the south and they won't ask you, "Where in the south?" They won't know where in the south.

Adam and his cohort use 9/11 as an historical hook for their generational memories.

I don't think a lot of students were really — obviously they're either the same age as me or possibly younger. We'll mainly talk about then, Where were you on September 11th? […] We can all tell exactly where we there then.

I was on the way home from school. I was being driven home by a neighbour and she told me it had happened. I didn't know where the World Trade Centre was, so I didn't think it was — I didn't appreciate it was a huge deal until I got into this room. My mum was sitting in a chair with the — watching the TV and

I came in and said, "What's this About something happening?" She said, "Shhh, shhh". I thought, "Right, that's important then" so I just sat down and listened. When your mother tells you to be quiet and she's staring at the TV. She didn't like sport, so it's not a penalty shoot-out or anything. It's something important. I just remember watching all day. But everybody can tell you exactly where they were. Lockerbie also — it's not like that because they have no idea.

JH: Yes, that's right[…] can you recall your feelings […] when you watch the Twin Towers and a plane going in, what's your gut reaction? How did you feel?

AB: [pause] From that I think — I think have started to — well, once you — the more you learn About it the more you start to appreciate this was serious. Perhaps I didn't — I'd never quite figured out how serious it had been until say later years. Now, when I've seen sort of — post Iraq perhaps 2004 or 2005, you really start to think, "Well, this is really all happened from that one thing". We've gone through two wars and now we're into the state where, like, where you have to get so many things to get a passport, you know, it's just getting sort of very, very serious in the UK as well, security and things like that, so perhaps I didn't quite appreciate the significance until I started getting a bit older.

JH: That visual of the plane going into the Towers, as a kid were you going, "Oh, wow, look at that?"

AB: No, I wasn't going like that, because besides you didn't know how many people had died but I won't say it was necessarily raw, but it's now you sort of — as you get older you perhaps appreciate the lives of the people who were lost more. Because when I went to Belgium, we took a battlefields trip in fourth year, I was About 16 at the time, perhaps even 15, About 15-16, but suddenly you get to that age now where you can — like if someone that is not related to you, you can still get very emotional About their death. If it's not your family when your younger and it's somebody that dies, it doesn't necessarily mean that much to you. Two thousand people died in another country that I'd only ever visited once. So, it didn't quite have as much significance.

The same perhaps a little bit with Virginia Tech. That happened when I was in The States but part of that I think is the fact that America is so big, we could not relate to something that — and there is much that happened hundred and hundreds of miles away. Everybody in Syracuse was quite upset. For me that would be like something happening in France, you know, from here. Same sort of linear distance, you know, in France. You don't feel as much emotion as they did perhaps — the size of America. Even things that are hundreds of miles away are still close for them; they're not close for us. But you do sort of — that was one of the best trips that I could take at Lockerbie was the Battlefields Trip because then you go and see all the graves, cemeteries out there; the Somme. Once you've learned all about it in class and then you go there, it really opens your eyes. Probably you might attribute that point to the time perhaps you really started to appreciate other people's suffering and things like that.

Adam talks with experience about the style and nature of commemorating the Lockerbie disaster this year, and looking forward

Well, I know that people have got involved with a new quilt I think. You must know the story About the quilt? [...] A patch to commemorate each victim. I think that was just Syracuse as well and I've *seen* that quilt. That's kept in Hendricks Chapel. [...] what I really like was done by Professor Larry Mason and he made a mural, photographic mural of Lockerbie. [...] I thought was really nice as well. But that commemorates sort of the links between Syracuse and Lockerbie. That's kept in a Syracuse building. So, that's something that — so that's perhaps one of the better things that have come out of this disaster. The negatives, of course, which is part of what he scholarship's about, is highlighting that from bad things can come good things and the links to the town are a good thing and having the pictures sort of shows happier times at Lockerbie

That's something I like. I wonder if perhaps the 20 years will be the last major commemorative service for it. [...] I just sort of think it's perhaps — you had the ten years obviously, you could understand that, but 20 years. It might be sort of 30 years a little bit too long ago for a massive remembrance service. But then again, that's sort of us from Lockerbie as well. We will want to perhaps move on from the negatives, perhaps more time to focus on the positives. Obviously when the people that lost relatives, they want to remember them every year. I don't know About in Lockerbie, if there'll be any larger after that.

JH: So, would you welcome Mr Brown with open arms, if he made an appearance on 21 December?

AB: He didn't get my vote. He can come if he wants. He didn't get my vote and I don't think he would get many because our area is the only one to return a Conservative MP. It kind of says it all, doesn't it, to be honest.

JH: So, you don't think the big wigs and the dignitaries should bother travelling —

AB: Well, no, I mean ... it's not perhaps about them. It's about — it would be perhaps nice if people from Syracuse came over or vice versa. It's not about — the Duke of Edinburgh came to the memorial service ten years ago. He's got nothing to do with it.

Positive outcomes for Lockerbie; how people coped

I think that the Syracuse example is not just about the fact that people come over here and we go out there, but it's the sort of the symbol it says; it's out of terrorism and atrocity and total despair of people, you've now got friendship. You've got ties that will last forever. So, I think that sort of — the relationship between the two towns stands for a lot. It's not just About the actual relationship. It's obviously great that we get to go out there and .a lot of people come over here. But it's more than that. [pause] Other than the fact that we've got links with Syracuse, I can't see anything else that has benefited us at all. I don't see how it could be a benefit. A lot of people ... obviously people died.

People's lives were changed forever. A lot of people are still struggling to cope with it. No, I wouldn't say they struggled to cope with it but they've suffered a lot for it. I don't see, other than the fact that we've now — they're going to send two students out from Lockerbie to go p'raps places they never get to go in their life is certainly, at the time p'raps you could not see them going out and I don't see anything else is really good About it, orpositive, other than the fact again we sort say, "Well, look, you know, we can move on". Setting a precedent. Obviously there will other terrorism around the world, similar atrocities, New York for example, and at least you can sort of say, "Well, look, yes, it happened to us but there are ways to move on and get on with life".

JH: So, people might be looking to see how Lockerbie coped, as a model.

AB: I think they do. I think they have. I remember someone came over to Syracuse before I went out. That was the very topic of discussion. They were looking at how Lockerbie has coped with it. How it's moved on. Perhaps getting ideas for other places thought everyone deals with it differently of course.

JH: Because people are saying, since I arrived, that the town is really run down, it's all down on the town. What do you think of that?

AB: I think for a while, when I was younger, it did go down quite a bit. I felt like it's come back in the last few years. We've got the biomass factory now. There's another factory built. The school's still doing — I think the school's pretty good. Whether you like Tesco or not … I sort of feel —

JH: So, from a socio-economic point of view, you mean, it's improving?

AB: I think so, yes. I think it has. It went sort of down quite a bit but it's picking up again. People say, oh there's not much to do, well we've got an ice rink, which is good.

JH: Are you a skater?

AB: I was a curler.

JH: A curler.

AB: I used to curl quite a lot. There's plenty of sports clubs at the schools. Sure, there isn't a swimming pool. There's a golf course, you know. I played golf, do that too. You don't live in a big city. Nobody has that doesn't live in a big city, all these great amenities. We don't have a cinema. There's one at Annan. There's one at Dumfries. There's one at Carlisle. So, you can go to those. It would be nice to a cinema but we're a smaller town, so. I don't know. Perhaps it is maybe better just to make the most of what you've got rather than get loads of things that never really can work. It would be nice to see some of the shops that are empty, get filled. Perhaps spend more money getting better football pitches or upgrading football — putting more money into the Mids would be a better idea.

The first Lockerbie Academy students to go to Syracuse University in 1991. Back row (L – R): Dave Wilson, Drew Blake (Rector), Hugh Young. Front row: two unnamed Syracuse official party flank Katharine Grant (left) and Fiona Griffin (right) (© Lockerbie Academy 2008)

The Memorial Garden at Dryfesdale Cemetery. The younger generation assimilate the collective memory of their culture.

Assembled staff of Lockerbie Academy, December1989. Dave is in third row back, fourth in from the left, wearing white shirt with arms folded. (© Lockerbie Academy 2008)
The brand-new Lockerbie Academy in 1963. This was Dave's working environment for 30 years. (© Dumfries & Galloway Regional Council 2008)

David Thomas Robison Wilson, March 27, 2008

A Community Spokesman at the Heart of the Matter.

The working commitment of this narrator as a council official, and much more besides, has been recognised at a national level, much to the deprecation of this individual.

This individual's contribution to the project consolidates, from a culturally relative distance, the utterances of other interviews. It provides a mould into which the real experiences of the narrators could be poured. Although he has lived in Lockerbie since 1966, his upbringing on the outskirts of Glasgow has informed his perspective of industrial, urban milieu, not to mention his internal comprehension of the workings of social structures and community systems and polity networks. It underlines and highlights the salient issues and themes running through the community of Lockerbie, which other agents have described as their own.

He is a word-smith — on our first meeting, he referred to the recently-demolished power station at Annan, called Chapelcross, as the 'elephant in the corner'. Yet he is plain-speaking. On his motivation to take part in this project, he said he took part because he knew me and because he was a spokesman for the community on the subject of the disaster. This fact coincides with his willingness to participate in the Media Group - the right words came easily.

He was my Social Studies and Economics teacher at Lockerbie Academy in the mid-eighties— I recall his words in class on supply and demand of imaginary tins of beans from my Father's shop. He must have been a great Economics teacher, because I got my Higher in one year, disregarding the natural impairment of my propensity for any figurative computations. The trip to London was uneventful although I remember it being suffocatingly hot in the wee rooms and no-one wanted to drink the tap water. My sister went on the trip with Dave too, but a few years before me. She came home with this anecdote: one of her cohort had rushed into her room, exclaiming, "We can see the Albert Hall from our window! Really, we can see bugger all from ours!" was the retort. I wonder if, on contemplation, this was one of his urban legends, developed on the train journey down from Lockerbie.

Despite being officially retired since 1996, he still "supply teaches [mostly at Moffat Academy] , writes a column for the local paper, makes up exam papers, writes some school text books, and plays in a band."

He is a train enthusiast and a photographer – he admitted to having no shots of the disaster in real time. He is a jovial character, ready with pertinent comments arising out of insightful connections.

The following chapter is taken from the longest interview I performed – three hours, on a chilly Thursday evening, 27 March. And I'm sure I left the narrator's residence with at least twice as many audio hours of narrative left unsaid.

He had tidied some sofa space since my first visit – there was nothing 'spare' about this room, it was put to good uses and was an excellent venue for our trip to the past.

Roots and beginnings on the west of Scotland

Well, I was born in Motherwell which at the time was very much a steel working town. My mother was a single parent so my grandparents played a very big role in my upbringing; he was—having been in the First World War, he worked in the steel works since then till he retired; he was a labourer in the steelworks and I always have a recollection that they were absolutely determined that I was not going anywhere *near* the steelworks whereas the other branch of the family, who were miners, were equally they were going down the *mine*. So, different attitudes. So the upshot was, secondary school, Highers and university; off we went.

Well, yes. They had been there probably since the 19th century at *least*. My grandparents were *all* from Motherwell and, although some members of the family have investigated some family tree stuff, its never really been something that's exercised me. I'm really quite happy to occasionally look back with some nostalgia but I don't a lot of time doing it in a family context, despite being a history teacher. So I have got photocopies of all the birth certificates but I don't spent time looking them all up but I *do* regard Motherwell as my hometown. And even today, when I go to the football by car, I drive through Motherwell in such a way that I pass my grandmothers house and I follow the same streets to the football ground that I did when I was wee. Call it superstition if ye' like! Doesnae make any difference; they don't always win but I *do* follow exactly the same.

You know, I remember a few years ago, there was a particularly important match and I sat in the grandstand and I met a least two people I had not seen for decade; one - a social worker in Hull and he'd come back for this particularly important game; ye' know, the roots, anybody's roots in their community really are quite deep, and I know my sister, when she left college, went straight to Australia to work. She has dragged back both my nephews, to wheel them round Motherwell [Dave chuckles], to let them know where their roots are.

[My kids] are not all even Motherwell supporters! [Jill laughs] I dragged them to the Cup Final in 1991, but for a time when my grandparents were alive and Betty's parents were alive, we were regular visitors so we [inaudible] the place. Coz we *did* have family there; we visited them regularly. If I try to read the local Motherwell newspaper, it just washes over me now because I don't recognise any of the names or whatever, so whatever the dimension is, it's no superficial, it's really quite deep down.

Schooldays in Hamilton

I was in the situation where I didn't actually go to school in Motherwell. I went to secondary school in Hamilton and I'm absolutely sure that all over the world, people hear or read that, they'll guess 'Hamilton Academy' [mocking upper class accent] which was a focus in Lanarkshire. It was a highly selective secondary school for the whole of Lanarkshire and I was actually all talked up in primary – I had the Dalziel High blazor and the Dalziel High shirt and tie, jumpers and everthing like that. Whatever somebody told my Mother, she went and changed and I got carted off to Hamilton. Really, the nature of the school was such and I don't say this with *any* attitude of boorishness or arrogance, but hardly anybody failed anything. Nor should they have, and having had 40 years in the teaching profession now, I think I can safely say that the teachers in that school at that time did no know when they were well-off. [Dave chuckles]

Dave's hometown in recent years

Well, where I go, in some respects it's the same as it was, but there's a lot of clearance and regeneration and so on and there has been a lot of changes and traffic arrangements and all this kindae stuff. The Town Hall is a snooker club now so, even the old buildings are still there, they've found other uses but when you drive down some streets, little has changed. The big local school, Dalziel High, still looks the same as when I was wee; the Duchess of Hamilton park – still a tremendous open space where the flowers and the war memorial and the bandstand and everything; they're all still there but, in other areas, it's really changed beyond all recognition.

Dave's move to Lockerbie Academy, his only post till retirement

The unique characteristic about Glasgow is nearly all the students just go in for the day and go home [Jill & Dave chuckle] They do, so that's what we all did as well and we got through at the other end; and I went from there to Jordanhill Training College, there were no combined degrees which allowed you to train as a teacher while you were—you went to the uni first then went to Jordanhill for a year. And one of the amusing recollections of Jordanhill was, at the end of the year, all of the Directors of Education in Scotland, came to Jordanhill, and went round then, and decided which of them you were going to patronise with your presence [Dave chuckles] That's actually true. Now, a lot of people are scraping around for any employment anywhere.

And I actually—I actually went to Dumfries County Council, as it was at the time, and the Director of Education was a smashing man called Lamont Brown. James Lamont Brown. Absolutely courteous and so on. Because at that time, my auntie and uncle had moved to Moffat and I had visited them a few times and I thought, Here this is a nice place. I was looking for a job in Moffat Academy but he says there aren't any at the moment, what about Lockerbie? At that juncture, I'd only ever visited Lockerbie once in my life, and that was on the occasion when my uncle, who worked on the railway in Beattock, had fixed up a lift on the engine which came down to Lockerbie, to shunt the goods yard so I got a trip down on the footplate, you see, and I went back up on the Blueband bus; that was my sole connection with Lockerbie; the only time, other than passing through on the train. So I said, "Aye, OK." I came down, I got fixed up for a year with digs in Park Place with an absolutely kindly woman, Auntie Vi; Vi Thomson whose nephew is still the local undertaker. So I was there for about a year. Got married in August 1967. We bought this very house but couldn't get into it until the occupant had built her new one out the back. So we were a couple of months in digs and then we moved in here, and we've been in the same house ever since and worked in only one school till the day I retired and that was Lockerbie Academy.

Dave's countrification

What I was not used to at all was the country area. You know, when you go to school across the road from a steel works, and that is not an exaggeration. My wife; the primary school Betty went to – over the wall was Motherwell Engine Sheds, the railway, [pause] and Braidhurst High School in Motherwell shook when a train went back. While I lived in Motherwell, they built the Ravenscraig Steel Works nearby, the traffic awe went past our door and so on. On the other hand, over our back lane, the first thing you came to was a farm – well, somebody had to provide the milk so it was milk-producing farm. So I have an idea about *coos* and so on but there's a whole series of attitude and things that are different. And, I didn't find it difficult, I just got a few surprises every so often; and I *still* get them because I look in the local paper and I listen to the local news and hear people talking and they get very exercised about windfarms and all kinds of things; and I'm thinking to myself, My God, I could show you *pollution* [Dave chuckles] But the imperative was the work so I still maintain the balance, you know, on balance, let's have the factory; until you can show me really why we should not entertain the idea, let's have the factory coz folk can work in it, that let's them spend money in local shops, their children can go to the local school and work, employment keeps things going round. It's also the case that, I don't think anybody— in some ways they weren't as alert and aware as people are now in general terms so I don't think it would have occurred to anybody to write a letter to the local paper saying, We don't want Ravenscraig whereas now, they'd be inundated wi' letters and there are changed attitudes, many of them positive because, you know, 50 years ago, people accepted things that maybe they shouldnae've swallowed, perhaps the pendulum has gone over far but—och, it's no a bad balance now, really. It must be good because neither developers nor objectors think its fair so it cannae be too bad.

The complex composition of Lockerbie is causally linked to its location on the border: Dave's sense of identity in the town

This is not judgemental, not judgemental at all but, I'm still surprised by the number of people who live *in* and *around* Lockerbie who are not *of* Lockerbie.

They do their shopping elsewhere; they don't trouble the local school, they don't—they are Lockardians but you really never meet them; like the medieval knights – the English had more in common with their French counterparts than they had with the people living in the same castle and that's no reflection of their [inaudible] or what good people they are, but I'm still surprised by the number of people who carry weight in Lockerbie but who remain very much in the background. I think there is too—I remember my landlady, Auntie Vi saying she was frae Gillhead down by Cummertrees and at that juncture in Lockerbie, she had been in for 35 years. Oh, I'm an incomer, she said. And I think ye had to work or ye have to be there a long long long time before ye call yourself a Lockardian and expect it to be accepted.

The west coast railway line, for about 160 years now; its on the main railway line and its got a station. The main Anglo-Scottish trunk route – 75% of Scottish traffic goes up the M74. You know, it doesnae go up the east coast, you know, and you've got all this stuff so . I think, art and part of it, there's a *tranche* of professional people who have come here and they, in a funny way, stick together. I was speaking the other night to the local rotary and, just thinking round, I was as near a local as they had in the room and I remember – it's related – I worked for a wee while for the Open University down in Yorkshire, social subjects social science, and one of the tasks sent students round villages to ask about compositions of the parish councils and with few exceptions, all incomers, and I think what happens is you do get motivated people and, you know, hard working people and they come and they don't try to impose their anything but they just participate in ways and at the levels they want to and I think, one of the upshot is, with things like Rotary and so on, if you put it in local terms, it's high incomers and that's about it. And I'm one of them, I'm no saying its terrible coz I'm one of them and I'm sitting here saying my hometown's Motherwell so why would I except to be regarded as a Lockardian and I think in Lockerbie—its no a transient population, we're no running away anywhere, but we do—there is a core, families have been here for generations and they'll be here for more generations and it gets kindae like the Burgess version of City – it gets woollier and you get a different bunch and then you get a different bunch and they don't always have a lot in common.

On the other hand, once that disappears and once other things change, you'll get people looking at Lockerbie differently and thinking, Well, we could live there, and this is to some extent reflected in the new housing areas like West Acres and so on. I suspect there's a leavening of people come in, having retired frae farming or whatever, but I'm pretty sure most of them started their career somewhere else. And you get, Gosh, its not a ghetto but its an area where there'll be no many locals and you'll find other wee enclaves as well.

The post-war educational climate and its on-going legacy

It was the baby boomers with a surge in population after—they were building schools all over the place and 1960 schools are instantly recognisable A lot of them are falling back down again [Dave chuckles] It was a combination of things – there was a cohort of people who were available for educating and wanted to be educated, so there was a clientele there and there were people who—I'm having to couch this carefully because I don't feel in the least better than anybody else in my family but, they were aiming at jobs which previously, their families wouldnae've aimed at – they were getting into the civil service, becoming lawyers and so on, and, that would've been—20 years before my time, that would've been out of the question but it came into the question and of course the educational opportunities which came up, a lot of the people were able to take them; there was a huge demand for it. And of course, when you train people into professional occupations, they're going to make bloomin' sure their children get the same opportunities. So there was a roll-on effect that probably lasted well into the seventies And then, question marks started to arise after that so it was a good time to get started [in teaching]

Placing the dynamics of the Lockerbie population within a wider Scottish consciousness

I do think that the people in Dumfries and Galloway, at the time of the devolution referendum, they equivocated most of all. Yes, the vote was closer here than anywhere else in Scotland, and I do think that for many, the big local centre is *Carlisle*. Not Dumfries at all, its *Carlisle* because you can go straight 18 minutes in the [inaudible] and you're in Carlisle so I think for a lot of people, for example, live in Gretna, work in Carlisle. They're not about, Well, wait a minute, our apple cart could be upset here. And, I mean I [pause] I'm pretty sure they all regard themselves as Scottish but, for some of them, its Murrayfield Scottish – you know, Scottish when the rugby team's playing [Dave & Jill chuckle]. But not Scottish if, for example, it came to an independence vote. Now, wait a minute. Coz people say, Where do my interests lie – particularly financial interests – where do my financial interests lie? If the answer is Carlisle, that's what I'm gonnae do. And it's more pointed here than it is in Glasgow. They don't worry about Carlisle in Glasgow.

Well, the fact is, the border keeps moving. It doesnae move within a generation but if you look back for hundreds of years - you know the Armstrongs and the Elliots and so on – they did perhaps [pause] what some African and Asian—what happens in some Africa and Asian areas. People can draw their political boundary wherever they like. For a particular group of people, every Autumn, they go somewhere else, they just go, and okay, the Sark is there and we've got big signs up and awe the rest of it: I just, you know. I think it was when England won the World Cup in 1966, somebody said, you know [laughs] how can basically the same ethnic group be crying on one side of a burn and cheering on another, you know [laughs]; it's a bit o' a farce really. But I don't have any—I can handle my Scottishness without being anti anyone else [Jill chuckles] you know, I don't, "What nationality are you? They're rubbish" [Dave chuckles] I can get by without that and I think [pause] I think most people—och, there'll always be [pause] thirty, forty years ago, somebody tried to blow up an electricity pylon or something but, no, I don't—I just don't think its significant, I really don't; don't think, don't think it's a massive issue: when you reflect, Lockerbie had a black councillor. Lockerbie had a black councillor. You know, old fashioned, never changes, backward Lockerbie elected a black councillor and wasnae an issue. So, maybe the fact that its always been a market town and really, despite remarks made recently by academics, a dynamic town and it is, it's a working town, keeps moving, people keep coming in, people moving out; maybe that's what, that's what towns like Lockerbie do. Sortae soak up anyone who wants to come and when they've had their time, they wantae; move on, they move on; somebody else comes in: maybe that's what we do.

Lockerbie in '66 — Dave's impressions

I think there were several big transport companies—nearly all I think derived frae agriculture on way or another. In 1966, one of the shops was Boots the Chemist but it was really an agricultural Boots. You found shops like Rogerson and Jamieson, ironmonger – people came in for a new shaft [Jill chuckles] for the axe and so on; and that was, that was really the, the, the professional area really was *family firms:* you know, there was a Stevenson in McJerrow and Stevenson. There was a Henderson in Henderson and McKie, and I think its moved round a bit now, no totally, but that was another characteristic: tae some extent, obviously it had a town council and people would look at it now and say, Och parochial, but that's what they were for: to be parochial [Dave laughs] you know? And the same, the same parochial Lockerbie, many—ye might not admire the design but they did for example respond to changing population trends by really building quite a lot of houses in Lockerbie – Lockerbie town council – and what I can clearly remember is that some of houses in those streets were actually bought up very quickly when the right to buy came in. So, let's say, they couldn't have been *that* bad although people are always turning up their noses at them but, bought up very quickly, and the town council always, I think, gave the impression of not moving anywhere under any circumstances: I don't think they were like that at *all:* maybe did a bit more that they got credit for.

I was surprised at the difference, which was not based, so far as I could see, on any merit, and I just found that— it made me uneasy. And I knew that people could be very, very kindly to people who worked for them and fallen on hard times— I was told that the occasion that one of the big estates had fifty-two former employees living rent-free on the estate. Ye know, you've got tae make sure you've got all the angles. But the assumption that [Dave chuckles] that because maybe somebody'd inherited something, they were therefore entitled to deference? Never mind— I mean I'm okay wi' a fair hearing in court, I say, that's fine, I hope that's what I do, but I was astonished because you did not get that Motherwell till you'd earned it. [chuckles; Jill agrees] Ye had, Oh he's okay. He's a good' yin, and that was fine. Oh he's a no-user, and so on. So when I came here, find people talking in hushed tones aboot folk; I met any number of, for example, titled people, saying, many were [inaudible] people, but it was the automatic deference, I though', What's going on here? [chuckles; Jill agrees] So it took a wee while. And then, of course, eventually, I realised that, basically, there was a stratum of Lockerbie society that wasnae going to bother me. Because they live their own life. It involved ponies and things

The boomerang effect on Lockerbie's youth population

Well the thing is, that, what is it, eighty, eighty-odd percent or something, of school people go to university, but we don't have one, so they're bound to go out— I said this very thing on Radio Scotland but a few weeks ago! [both chuckle] I said, There's nothing for young people. That may be true, but it's also the case that if you wanna be an airline pilot, a doctor, a lawyer, a dentist, an accountant, you're going to have to leave Lockerbie, as you have to, indeed, leave *Falkirk*, you know, [both chuckle] coz they havnae got a uni! So ours scattered to the four winds at various times at Aberdeen, Stirling, Heriot Watt, and Edinburgh universities, and we thought it was great. We thought it was great. Just to— You see, Esther was the first to go, and when she picked Aberdeen [chuckles], it's the furthest away, and not one o' them even thought about Glasgow. [laughs]: But see I wasn't disappointed, I've damn near heard parents, trying to get the kids to go to the same uni as them, and oh na, I don' like tha'.

Oh, they come back, there's no doubt about it. They do come back. I think that the customary— the cliche is about there being nothing in Lockerbie. There might be nothing in their— it might not meet their requirements at a particular time in their life, but if they do go away to Edinburgh, Glasgow, London, wherever— there also comes a point in your life when you've worked out that every disco's pretty much the same, you know, and if you shut your eyes you could be in Wigan, Warrington, wherever, aye, doesnae matter, and I do get the feeling that people start to think, Wasnae that bad back down home after all. But I do know people, I do know people who have come back and this applies not just to Lockerbie but to Moffat and Annan as well, they just look for a, particularly once they can afford it, a different lifestyle. We walk along the shore of a Sunday morning, which frankly you don't get in Glasgow.

Dave's reflection on moving on and out.

I think it's a— really reflects, maybe no' having a full understanding of why some people really have to go doon sooth. You know I've got one relative who went *doon sooth* because that's where the man she married was. [chuckles] You know, what dae you do? Worked in London University.

On the one hand, [pause] there's implied dismissiveness in two directions, and I'm no' sure if it's maybe no' just pantomime dismissiveness and that if people will leave saying, Oh, nothin' here, I'm going to where the lights are brighter. And on the other side of the fence, they're saying, Oh who do they think they are, they've left, and so on. But I think it's maybe, even if there's a grain o' belief in both sides, it's maybe just a wee tiny put-down. [Jill agrees] A wee put down. But I really don't think they mean it.

Ecclestiastical connections with the kirk: Dave compares the Motherwell church experience to Lockerbie, and made the change

So we were never in, I mean, for example, I was never a freemason, I was never— my wife was never in whatever, and one of the connections that did get severed, totally, quickly and inexplicably, was the church. The only church services I go to now, although I would still on my death bed say I was Church of Scotland, the November, the Armistice services. Beyond that I had never— well when I was on the local authority, I needed to go o the kirking of the council and so on, but I just stopped going to the church. And it really would take too long, it's something else I've thought about very hard, because I think, am I Christian, I think I'm Church of Scotland, I just don't go to church. And I think it was [pause] partly [pause] it was a different kind of church.

. Although it was the church of Scotland, and the Reverend James Annand, the minister, was a kindly, articulate, sound man. Somehow or other [pause] it didn't have the, [pause] Gosh I'd better be careful here or I'll get sued [pause] I'm searching for the right way to put this [pause] I thought I almost discerned a feeling that [pause] I must say it's an awful [inaudible] on people, but just [pause] the church in Motherwell was quite hard-edged in the sense that the kirk session was all guys from the steel works. And if the church hall needed painted, set about it, and I better put it in terms o', it was a more genteel approach here. And talking to people and so on— Betty actually learnt a few times to [inaudible], coz whatever the— it wasnae a message wasnae a problem with th' message, but whatever the— it's almost a culture. We just didnae find the same spiritually. It wasnae the same as, you know, they knock about stuff and [pause] we were used to. And I've struggled to put that into words because I don't really have a very good explanation.

I have some very good friends who are elders and all the rest of it, and blow me away, and they would be right because it doesn't apply to them, but there was *something* where, as I say, you're just not gonna get the guys coming in, stopping their lorry, coming in with their overalls on. And, I mean, the church in Motherwell was, you know, snottery wains frae the housing schemes, and everything, I just— That's not what happens here.

They had the men's club, women's guild, embroidery things, [chuckles] they really did a lot, and over Motherwell itself, that's dozens of churches. There was our church, Dalziel Church, Saint Andrew's church was less than half a mile down the road, Brandon Church was half a mile up the road, the EU congregational church, Chalmers church, never mind the half dozen subsections of brethren, Roman Catholic cathedral, and so on, and this is maybe a one-mile radius. S'all these churches. And no danger at that time o' any of them closing down. I think there's a struggle now, a struggle for the church everywhere.

Lockerbie Academy days, 1966-96: anecdotes and past students

It was completed for of use, maybe about 1965. Just the year before I—it was more or less new. Yes, it was more or less new.

I would get into a fight if anybody suggested, who interpreted what I'm going to say as not interested in Lockerbie Academy, I hope it does nothing but good for as long as it's there. But, I found myself, I find in general, that I do better, if I cut the cord, and I still have a very great deal of interest in the school, I go to school shows, Betty still works there, an' so-on. So I would not like anybody to think that in any sense it's lack of interest. But in the same way, although I've got my golf handicap down t' three, I stopped. I never think about it, don't dwell on what I used to be able to do because it's not relevant. And the fact that I was in Lockerbie for thirty years. Most of the— None of the pupils will have the least idea who I am, so that's the context you have to work in. So I'm very interested in them, I hope it's tremendously successful, but I've never, since the day I left, lurked around the place, you know, but I still know loads o' the teachers there.

I think [pause] wherever you start, that's where you do— where you some of the first things, some of the things you do for the first time, you know, you go on a school trip up the road, and everything, and you take a football team and so on, and it's really a series— There were no earth-shattering events—

A series of anecdotes, most of them are quite personal. I remember, when I sat my driving test [chuckles] one of the sixth year sat beside me so I could drive across it, coz he'd already passed his. [both chuckle] William Anderson, the headmaster, let a chap called Kenny Anderson so that I could take the car over to Dumfries so I could take my drivin' test. So one of the pupils is sittin' next to me, coz I'm a learner an' he's not. [both chuckle] That's the kind of thing you never forget. And I have the awful feeling it's the kind of thing that could not possibly happen now. Could not possibly happen now. I remember my digs at Park Place, they didnae have a shower or anything, so Harry Reid, the principle teacher of P.E. used to let me shower in his room, because he had a shower, you see, so at the end of the school day, I'd go in and there was a hockey practice going one night, and the lassies in the hockey team were complaining about, you know, lack of space and lack of facilities [both chuckle] so Harry comes around the corner, and *suddenly* I hear this voice says, "You think you've got no room, look at the size of that!" [Jill chuckles] and he throws open the door and I'm— [both laugh] Now that's true, that's true. That's the kind of thing that you remember.

You remember— Och, I say, you remember individual pupils. One I remember was Bill Howitson, who's now Provost of Aberdeenshire Bill took Modern Studies, Higher, did very well. One of my recollections of Bill is that - forgive me Bill - in order to get into Edinburgh University, he had to get I think it was an O grade Botany. [Jill chuckles] He was an Arts man, you know, and I remember one o' my colleagues saying, "Well, he really shouldn't be going to university if he has to— if they have to impose that kind of requirement on him; I'm not sure that's a good idea." Well, a first-class honours, a degree and a PhD later, I think Bill [both chuckle] I think Bill has proved the point. [both chuckle] And that's sometimes it's these massive mis-judgments, you know, and in the staff room I remember the Mens staff room, as it was again in those days, one of my colleagues not realising that the headmaster was sitting there. [Dave chuckles] And it was the winter, and people were talking about lagging in the pipes and this chap, who later became the Director of Education, he starts going on about how, "Oh it's okay for headmasters, they can lag their pipes for five-pound notes!" [both laugh] and the headmaster's sitting there. So these are—

Och and there's piles of them, but they're not sequential, they're not coherent, they're just wee stories. But I don' remember any of, you know, those sorta cataclysmic changes when we stopped doing O grades and they became Standard, that just wash over, they just passed over, you know, coz the lead-up is so long, the debriefing is so long, it just sorta washes over you. So it's not things like that that I remember.

The headmaster at that time, Drew Blake, who was quite astute, very astute— I've got a theory that as time goes on, Drew Blake will look a better and better headmaster, I do think tha'll happen. But he was ne'er afraid to take people on, and so on, an' I think he realised that I had reservations about school uniform, so he sent me to survey the parents. [both chuckle] And of course it came out, oh eighty-odd percent in favour of uniform, so we did the black, it used to be a red and yellow tie, or a black tie with red and yellow stripes and the school crest on it, that's with the white shirts— That was the early one, but it got slacker and slacker, and we decided to bring it back— And I remember, Pat Cairns, who is a head teacher now at Edinburgh, she was in the Home Economics department, she had a look at a range of clothing, that might be, that might have been brought in, y'know, t-shirts, sweatshirts and all the rest of it. But I think it was going to be economics, really, many people couldn't afford it, so it was actually taken seriously. But the easy way around it is jus' to wear the black jumper and the white shirt an' of course the nature of tie-wearing has totally subverted [both chuckle], the intention, because the ties sorta dangle above the knees, an'—

A view from the South – Dave and his wife saw the town aglow on the southern approach road

This is what happened to us. We had been at Carlisle, for tea, we'd been at, I think an Italian restaurant, and we were on the way back in the car, and as we came over the hill, south of Lockerbie, the farm called Cowdens, we became conscious of a very, very red glow in the sky over Lockerbie, and I could see a helicopter, smoke rising, so the first inclination, first thing that flashed through m' mind was a tanker has gone off on the A74. Knew nothing, no idea. So there is a side road, which is not now there, because the motorway doesn't allow it— But there's a side road, through Castlemilk to Kettleholm. So we went that way—Yeah— up past [inaudible] well we took a long, roundabout way round.

"What's going on?" Because the last thing that crosses your mind is an aeroplane has crashed, I mean, it doesn't, they don't, you know, but later, we approached our house which is end Dumfries Road from the Dumfries direction, whereas normally we'd've come through Lockerbie, and approached the Lockerbie direction. We turn into the house, and people were out in the street, and we could see flames in the Sherwood area by this time, so I remember we— the first person we spoke to Sylvia Porteous and she said a plane has crashed. Now that juncture, we didn't know what kind of plane, and I think there was the odd rumour going round, plausibly, it was an RAF jet, because we do have all this low-flying, we had it at the time, that was the first thing. So I put the car up the top of the driveway; got the house opened up with the lights on, and really, because by that time I was a local councillor, I set off up to see what was going on. I had to talk my way past one policeman, and when I got as far as [pause] far as St Bryde's Terrace, I decided to try to go along and see what was happening, in Sherwood, because nobody really knew— I get quite irritated sometimes at news presenters: "There is chaos here," well of course there's chaos, you' no' expecting a jumbo jet to— and it wasn't chaos—

There was no panicking and screaming, not at all. When I walked along to go to Sherwood, and I met two families that I knew, David Edwards and his family, and he said, "We're all here, tha's the main thing." I remember that, and then I met Colin Gardener, and his family, and he said, "It looks as if the kitchen's gonna be gutted." The entire house got burned down, because it turned out that, although the fire service was there very quickly, there was no water. I think it fractured pipes. So it was extremely difficult for them to deal wi' it.

There were I think twenty-four ambulances that turned up. But I don't mean this brutally at all, but people were either dead, almost dead, or okay. I mean, I can think of just a couple o' people who were injured and maybe had to be treated, other than that, the rest of us were walking about, or whatever. But your suggestion that there was no panic is absolutely right. So realising, you could see the fire hoses trailed across the street an' all the rest o' it, there is no merit in trying to go in there. I went up to the town hall, where the staff already had opened very quickly, which I don't remember them getting credit for, they stopped what they were doing, they went up there and they opened the town hall, just as a focal point.

Well the one I remember was Sandy Welsh. Sandy was in the housing department at the time, and quickly worked out, There's going to be a housing issue here. Y'see. So we got up there. At that juncture, there were no plans, I don' think anybody had made a plan for a seven-four-seven to land in Lockerbie. I think they'd made plans for a big explosion at Chapelcross, or something; So I'm no up for very much criticism o' local people; I'm no' up for it at all. [Dave chuckles] So the town hall was open; the other officers of the council, Ian Smith, Director of Technical Services, who's dead now, Bill Davidson, Director Finance, Donald Bogie, Director Environmental Services, they were on the spot, they were there very quickly, but it was one o' those situations where they were on the spot, and they were willing, but what is it they're going to do. But they were there and they were ready for action. After that, by that time I think I'd met Hugh Young, the other Lockerbie councillor, who— that was actually his constituency; mine was over the railway and away towards Eskdalemuir. So we took a walk up, 'cause by this time we'd heard the rumours, and so on. We took a walk along Sydney Place, up as far as Alexandra Drive, where there was an air engine, lying embedded in the road, guarded by the police and y'know, up Rosebank.

Yeah, so I think we'd a wee walk up Park Place and Rosebank because by that time again we'd heard that the fuselage, basically— Well we were getting new information all the time that it was a wing that had, all the kerosene that had landed on top o' Sherwood. The fuselage was in the Rosebank Crescent area so we went up, and by this time, you're starting to see things, you know, the back of an aircraft seat stickin' out somebody's window, and you think stupid things like, How did that get in there?. 'Cause the aircraft seat was wedged in a *window*. Somebody could have been sittin' in it, lookin' out the window, and that was one of the houses on the left-hand side, the top o' Park Place. And the fuselage was in the gardens, parallel to two rows of houses and, God, it was a bad night, but they say that it could have been worse! How it landed in the gardens, parallel to the houses, more or less without hittin' any of them, I've wondered ever since. But equally, you also quickly sort out that it's a job for professionals, you know, there's nae—the emptying of it, the lifting of it, all this kind of stuff, is a way beyond anything that's available locally. So basically we went' back to the town hall. By this time people arrivin' from all over the place, the regional authority—

Americans got here astonishingly quickly, and the social work department pulled in its people and they based themselves up at the school; they had a media thing up at the school, and so because they'd all the classrooms and everything. So the focus of, not the effort, but the focus of, if you like, the administration of the aftermath was really the school. 'Cause again it was thought, Well just let the town hall be the town hall; people can come in and pay their rent, because you're also thinking, maybe it's amateurish, but you have to try an' think something, so, psychologists would be able to explain it, but you start scraping your way back to normal as quickly as you can. So you think that, Okay, we'll leave it open for the rents. So if there's a coffee morning on Saturday we'll have— [both chuckle] just, I suppose some folk would look at it as a serious smile, but it certainly wasnae funny at the time. And after that, people were sayin' to us, honestly, there was nothin' you could do, there was not a thing. So went back home and discovered many years later, it was actually my cousin's wife who took the first phone call at six minutes past seven at the switchboard at Dumfries that something'd landed in Lockerbie—

Exposure to the enormity of the situation – Dave witnessed acceptance and denial

But an immediate— I remember too, that my sister later on described how desperately she was trying to get through from Melbourne, because by the time the reports got to Australia, very quickly, *very* quickly, oh that the town had been wiped out. That was actually the headline in one of the tabloids: "Town wiped out."

Came home and started to watch it, and just the following day and everyday thereafter it was a case of almost being seen, and tryin' to talk to people and find out what was goin' on, how they were all fixed because there were some anxieties—really the Flannigans, the Somervilles, they were just removed from this Earth. But people like Campbell and Cara Brown next door, and Mister Smith, and [pause] she was the depute— *Adamson!* The Adamsons: their houses on the face o it were ok, but they're starting to discover that things willnae fit where they used to fit, and there were a lot of people like that who wanted a survey of their house, so very quickly there's things you have to start fixing up, and where do you get the personnel to do it, was, you know, an on-going issue.

There wasnae— I don't recollect that there was any exceptional council meeting as such, but— a combination of the officers and elected members of the councils made up a committee, and the councils sort of *endorsed* the formation o' several other things that would allow decisions to be taken quickly and on the spot, et cetera, et cetera; cause there were things that were very immediate and there were things that were not immediate. I mean, it's a massive, mighty, great big huge scene of crime: you don't start sweeping up debris, you gottae painstaking, so it has to be done. And people sort of say, "When are they going to get that? When are they gonna? When are they gonna?" Well it's a police operation, they *can't*, they've got to do it in a certain order; so there were tensions and everything. Having said that, most people, figuratively if not literally, shrugged their shoulders, and started to get on, and I think it was probably because the loss of local families was bad enough, but I think people thought how much worse it could've been, you know, a great plane— wing-load of kerosene land a hundred meters from a petrol station, it doesnae hit it, goes past it. The fuselage is sitting up there, but Rosebank has no water, nae power—there's all kinds of things that have to be sorted, but there are other things that cannae be sorted, because you've got to do them, got to follow the proper procedure. And these were awkward, these were all—people that [pause] they just wanted things sorted, and could get a bit impatient about it.

You almost have to go into some type of denial, sort of say, Well it's not a case of what can I do, everybody was wantin' do something, but in very practical terms, you know, by this time there were American voices, some were relatives, some were the FBI, and people are starting to put two and two together and get about fifteen, and let's not forget that the debris was scattered over fifty-five miles, away intae Northumberland. Folk decided, in quite a lot of cases, I think, to keep their children in, cause of what they might see outside. It's too tabloid if I say there were bodies all over the place, but a lot of the people had fallen out of the aircraft, and in Rosebank, in a sense neither better nor worse, but you know, people could look out their kitchenette windows and see people still sitting in the fuselage. And they had to handle that, they had to deal with that, in whatever way they choose to do it. Fine, if that's what, you know. I can think of one resident who always answered this from behind a closed door. "No. I'm fine, son," and that was his way of dealing with it. I don't think he had power or so on, but he was just rationalising it and sortin' in out and so on.

Community efforts to inform and support each other

The person I remember who was involved with community education who I called Mike Coombe, he was sorta seconded—what happened was the council started to second people, and that's what they did. And Mike, I think, did the community newsletter, and they organised a network of deliverers, and they brought it out as often as they could whenever there was anythin' to tell; but there's always a time lag, and on occasion, by the time—it was gone through wi' a fine-tooth comb, I don't think anybody was ever mislead by anythin' they read in there, but in the sense that by the time they got it, something else had overtaken it. You know, [inaudible] , Why are they telling us that? So it was— had we had emails: but we didnae, and by the time you printed it, and distributed it, you know—and big Jimmy Pagan: he must've delivered tens o' thousands o' those, you know, a *great* effort, and they did their best, the residents' groups an' everything did their darndest to get these things through people's letterboxes. But even at that, you're just no' gonna be as up-to-date, in that people want information yesterday.

I think that the first thing: [street committees] provided some sort of focus and forum. I think they were extremely helpful in identifying, for example, maybe, who would need particular help, because an incoming outside officer, however professionally trained, and however well-meaning, cannae work some o' these things out; so I think that was the really big value, and if there was an issue, they could be told about it, they could raise it at the meetings, and so on, so I think it was very much a worthwhile exercise. Once things started to get sorted, I think that if they were gonna continue, they had to almost metamorphose into something else, because the immediacy of the disaster— you know, after, let's say for the sake of argument a year; they maybe had to look round for other functions, because the houses were being refurbished, et cetera, and I think that was the focus of most people's interest.

You know, I think that just by existing, I think that one of the main things was it existed, and simply by being there helped to create the feeling that things are in hand, we are being listened to, things are in hand. And I don't think anybody necessarily—in fact, I've got a clearer recollection: it was not any o' the residents' groups, but it was a wee bit like helping the elderly across the road, only to discover they don'want to go. And I can remember, a *very* small number, with some degree of resentment, did not want the support that they felt was always being foisted on them. Maybe wee notices through the door, saying, you know, Oh there's a chap at the door, and everything. And I'll emphasise, not by the local residents' groups, because they all knew each other, but maybe other groups who were desperately trying to help. Absolutely no' harm to them, but I've a clear recollection that it wasnae always welcome. We just sort it out, We'll get on an' do everythin'—we'll do it and that'll be fine.

Dave's role on the council team

Goin' tae meetings! I think, shortly— When the school went back in January, Neil Mackintosh, who was the chief executive of the Dumfries and Galloway Regional Council at the time, called Hugh Young and I aside, and said, "You're just not going back to work." And they got a replacement teacher for me; they got a replacement for Hugh, because Neil Mackintosh could see that it was just gonnae grow; there were gonnae be all kinds of things happenin'. And again, it's one of these figures that sticks in your mind, but I remember sayin' to someone, because by this time— you know, by the middle of February, Lockerbie's recovering, and they're asking me, asking all the kindly questions, like, "What the hell are you da'in aff yir work?" and I was able to—in the space of I think it was three months, I was at a hundred and thirty-five meetings, and many of them are just to be at the meeting, because you're a local councillor and you *ought* to be at the meeting. There were several residents' groups; there were all the council meetings still tae go to; there were the other things that were started as people started tae send money, and the trust got set up, and I was involved in a limited way—[pause; chuckles] They called me in to do some counselling—And it was only about twenty years later I started to think to myself, Wait a minute, the plane crashed in me as well! [both chuckle] But all kinds of things: just goin' round, and sittin' in folk's hooses. But it mostly seemed to be meetings, and, och, there were shedloads of all things: oranges arriving from Florida or somewhere and, you know, the Christmas gifts: Lockerbie wasnae big enough to store them, cause people sent things, and it was—

It was an absolutely wonderful reaction. But I think, again, maybe what they'd read in the press, it wasnae really a war zone, it really wasnae, and people were goin' about their business, and I think it was maybe the library, the service area, but also at that time, they had to think about what they were going to do with the victims. So over the weeks the town hall got more or less converted to a mortuary, the ice rink was used, it was suitably cold.

Dave needed to prioritise his time post-disaster

Well I have to say that I've personally had minimal connection with American families. My colleague at the time, Hugh Young: he was more closely involved in the friendship group; now this was nothing more, *nothing more* than a feeling that there was plenty to do, and there were enough people interested in it, literally they didnae need me. Well I mean, the American relatives, just bewildered, just bewildered, were coming off the planes, and they really needed somebody just to look them in the eye and welcome, you know: it fulfilled a great need in— As you say, friendships that were made then are carried on. I know Hugh's been t' the states a couple o' times, Stan Waslowski, I think it was, has been over a couple of times Father Keegans was involved in it. I think I went to a couple of meetings, 'cause I was asked to go to particular meetings,, and some o' the people who emerged, if you like, as the spokespeople, they were tremendous, tremendously sound people, I mean, they're really very solid, and you could see why they were the mouthpieces, very measured, very logical, and quietly emotional about their loss, very impressive people but certainly it wasnae dislike of anybody or whatever: I just decided I wasnae involving myself in the American dimension. So it certainly wasnae—it was nothing other than the fact that, Well if you involve yourself wi' that, I'll do something else.

Dave was also on the housing committee: financial struggles, contractors and placating tenants

There was somethin' else I was gonnae— [pause] I was the housing chair o' the local authority, and the issue that was arising is the refurbishment of the Rosebank houses. So early on, we started to work up a scheme, to renovate them all, new kitchens, central heating an' so on, because there would have been massive repairs, and the day-to-day things like making sure people had somewhere to stay, and that's no' always as— you know, if you're the person who's been blown out o' house and home, you're a priority, but the person whose place on the housing list you're taking, doesnae see it as quite the same priority. So things have to be smoothed out, and quite a lot of them had to be smoothed out; so there's that, and at the same time, we're in close collaboration with the design department down at Annan, just working out how, what turned out, what was the biggest scheme ever undertaken at the Annandale and Eskadale district council, how we're gonna do this, because before you can refurbish housing you got t' get people out. That's how we did them, I think we did them four at a time, and we always put people into another house, not a caravan or a bed an' breakfast, we shifted their furniture an' everything. We *always* did, not just for the disaster, but that's slow, you know, you rewire somebody's cooker, you lay their carpets down for them an' so on, and we thought it was a very good service, but it's slow, so we had tae work out a way of doing this, God knows how much— And the other thing was that the council is constrained by government spending amounts, so we had to get special permission to spend more. *All of this takes time.* And *time* is not what the public is willing to give you! [Dave chuckles] So all o' this is goin' on—And I think that part of the circumstance, some of the circumstances surrounding it are, that for their own reasons, and it's their prerogative [pause] people don't—they don't always rush t' tell their pals that in fact you have been sittin' in their house for an afternoon, you sort of talk to them about things, y'know the rest— I dunno why, but maybe it's just the way of things, so we got round a load of people.

I'm no' painting the picture as well as I should be, because all the while, there are all the other things for example that the council's doing. The housing in Annan, the housing in Moffat, an' so on, and that's got tae go on, so while you're busy trying to build up a method tae get all these houses done in Lockerbie, you know that it's going tae be out of the proper batting order. So you've got tae find a way of doing it that doesnae disadvantage Annan or Moffat or, indeed, other houses in *Lockerbie*. Yes? Yeah, so it takes so much time. I mean, all the other councillors, and again, crystal clear that the phone never stopped ringing, they were on quick support, and they were smashing, but there does come a point when you're talking about, you know, a housing area, the fact is that some o' those houses werenae damaged and they're going to get new kitchens an' so on. That will not go down well with somebody who's waited, you know— So there's all these kinds of wee things that start t' come into it, so you have to try and head them off at the pass, and everything, and it's extremely *time consuming.* All the while, you're in touch wi' Edinburgh to see if they'll give you the money.

This is one of the cleverest things I've ever been the victim of: we had a meeting in the council chambers at Annan, the director had come up with the plan, the timetable, the batting order, so it was then a case of meetin' Lord James Douglas Hamilton. So he comes down wi' the head civil servant, and we had a meeting in Annan, and Lord James mentioned Scottish Homes, cause the government had just formed, really to try and partly to muscle out councils, 'cause this is parenthesis, but the problem for the conservative party in Scotland was, it's always the same, Labor always wins. And y'know, really unable to beat them at the ballot box, I think they were trying to think up some other ways o' doin' it, and Scottish Homes was going to be building houses all over the place, and Lord James suggested, "Well, why don't we use Scottish Homes?" And we were arguing, Look, our houses are pretty decent. We've done all this on our own and it's local firms that get the business. Just give us the money. *Well*, there was a press release, which must've been made up before the meeting, which said that the government has released the money to allow this to take place. What that meant was, they allowed us to *borrow* it. It was local taxpayer that still paid the whole thing. But you'd never have convinced anybody in Lockerbie ever again, "Oh the government gave you the money for that." They didn't! They let us borrow it. So the Director of Finance has to get on the phone and work out, for years in advance, what this is goin' tae do to the finances. So there's all kinds of things going on. And it sometimes took a bit of [inaudible] to keep all the place goin'.

Once we got the money for the Rosebank Park Place refurbishment, the most contentious thing surrounding it was the order in which the houses were done, because the folks that lived up there; the people who'd been there the longest, clearly thought, Oh well, we'll do ours first. But that's not what contractors do, and it is the prerogative of the contractors to determine the order.

What usually happens is—it's by law, what happened, was that the jobs go out to tender, and the lowest tender wins. Once the contractor wins the tender, that's really when they try an' start gettin' the electricians an' the plumbers an' everything, 'cause they don' have them at the *time*. And I think, I think really the fact is, or the fact was, that whichever contractor won, you're goin' tae get the same plumbers anyway! [both chuckle] I mean, that's an exaggeration, but it's no' far away. But whoever won it, you'd get somebody saying "*Oh them!*" but little realising that if their favourites had won, they'd still be getting the same joiners! [Dave laughs]

I remember we had tae have the town hall to have the tenants' meeting, and in that situation, by definition, whoever's first is going to be *delighted*, whoever's last is going to wonder what we've been doing. But somebody, *somebody* is going to be, and finding fairness in that kind of situation, literally impossible. It just so happened that, my recollection again is that, at least, one couple who had been up there a long time, had come near the end, and [pause] they were unhappy, they were unhappy. And that's the kinda thing, ultimately, that's just a deep breath, because there's no' much you can dae about it, because the contractors have said, We will refurbish these houses over this time period. Ye cannae start telling them, Oh don't send plumbers in there on a Thursday, you know, ye cannae start interfering. Ye cannae start phoning them up and saying, "Mrs So-and-so at number fifteen's no' very happy wi' 'er bath taps." You've got to let them do it then go back for the snagging, and so on. And there were some awkwardnesses there.

There were blips, and there were things that were much bigger than blips, you know, but underlying it all, if I went up the street or anythin' like that—it was far, far, far more positive than the negativity, which tended to relate not to overall performance, but to individual disappointments, and ye can handle that because somebody's always goin'a be disappointed. Some of them had a bloody good case for being disappointed, but ultimately, most people are smiling, and they're making it clear they're still quite well-disposed towards the way things are goin'.

Certainly would be, aye. I mean, there must have been economic spin-offs, must've been, all those visitors and people stayin' here, an'—Oh aye, there must've been, but nobody at the time was really thinking about that, naeb'dy was too bothered. So I think it was about April before I went back tae work: I was gone for that length of time. I was pleased to be back, at the end. The woman who stepped in for me was exceptionally good, I was really pleased it was her that we got.

The school was on alert and ready to respond to its community's needs

I don't think they were doing too much, the word they use nowadays is *proactive*, I think the word should be *prophylactic*, but that's sort of just my age. [Jill chuckles] I don't think they were diving in, forcing help upon the pupils, but I think they were highly geared-up to reacting to—they were watching brief, you know, if something seemed to be a bit iffy, then they were all geared-up to step in; but I don't think they were in classes one at a time, nor should they have. I think, Okay, they may have been fifteen rather than thirty-five, but some of them will handle things better than many a thirty-five. If they can handle it, fine. Of course, other things that—there was Ed's party, which involved a lot o' school kids and teachers an' things like that, and these were symptomatic of the fact that things were getting *better*.

Dave considers the big picture – bereavement and the perspective of history

Paul Somerville, who was a smashing example of a wee boy: the school uniform, the tie, hair combed, unfailingly polite, and it's particularly hurtful for somebody like Paul, cause, not that other people— I'm not suggesting somebody else *deserves* it, but it was particularly poignant that I'm sorta standing there an' there's an empty desk where Paul should be, and it's the one I remember, partly because, not long before the plane crash, Grace Hind, first year guidance teacher had organised a trip for the whole first year on the train, so Motherwell depot sent down an electric train t' Lockerbie, and I had Paul and two other boys, and John Clark, who was the manager in Motherwell depot: these guys were rail enthusiasts, so Grace said, "You'll look after these guys." So John had them in the cabin. We got to Motherwell: bring them down to the depot, and then he phoned up Edinburgh Haymarket, and we went across to Edinburgh, and we go round the depot there as well. See now, I *know* that that was one of the days in Paul's life, he was just so so pleased that it had happened, you know. I'm sure that within his family they had better days and great days, you know, but I know, in terms of what he did at school, that was getting round these things, engines and everything, and intae the *cabin*, it was a great day for him. And I've been fair pleased about it ever since, that we managed to fit that in.

And [pause] there are people who till the day they died wondered why they werenae dead. You know, so it's a friend of mine who's dead now: her granddaughter should have been at the Somervilles' for tea that night, but for whatever reason, they didnae phone, so she didnae go, and her granny wondered, for the rest of her *life*, how her granddaughter had managed to get out.

And these are the kinds of things—that's why, you know, when people stick a microphone in my face and say, "Has Lockerbie got over it?" Well, in a communitarian sense, Lockerbie *has*, because there are people who are at university now who weren't even born when the plane crashed, but in a lot of individual cases you actually don't *get* over it. I don't always buy this closure thing. I don't think it ever closes, and it's just a greater or lesser extent, every December. I remember, I wake up in the morning and remember it, in December, you knowSo I'm no' sure you can shut the door to this, although it appears to have a man in jail who, who did it, an' all the rest of it, I don't think so. But we will, those of us who were there at the time, we will all die off. But I do think now, like the Gretna railway disaster, it's historical.

I think it's historical. [pause] I hope nobody is thinking and making the mugs, the keyrings and everything, because it'd be too soon for me, but eventually, I'm sure that commemorative items will appear. But for the sake of people I knew, I just hope I don't see them.

Ah it's just a creeping osmosis, you know: people die, new people come in. Then all of a sudden, it's a new Lockerbie, it's a different Lockerbie. It's normal, but it's a new and a different version o' normal. Because there's any number of people who would—I think our population, it changes by a quarter in a relatively short space o' time. So the twenty years since the disaster, the coming and going has meant that as seriously diminishing number of people were here at the time. And I think that there'll be a tipping point there, and you'll have a majority of people saying, "What happened when the plane crashed?" as opposed to situation where everybody knows what happened. But I don't think you can say, Oh it's five years. Five years and that's it. I don't think. It just creeps up on you and suddenly it's historical, and I think it's been there for a few years now: I don't think that people will have pangs, people will have memories, and I dunno, maybe the folk that made the scones and washed the clothes, maybe they still meet with each other, and everything, but that's almost out to the side, that's a camaraderie that derives frae the disaster, y'know, if they're still all goin' out for a dinner every year, or whatever. But a lot o' people've moved on Donald Bogie, oh, he went away to Calderdale, way tae Halifax, to another job, and Donald was involved in formaldehyde and everything at the mortuary: tough! Tough! And I went in a couple o' times, and the smell of formaldehyde and the— I'm just full of admiration for people who got up in the morning and went and did that, and Donald was one o' them: he was off work for a while, and I suspect because of it.

But the sight, in the town hall, of rows and rows of coffins, waiting to go back to the States, and when you see some of them are that length, it reinforces the bigger picture, you know; you're so focussed on, Oh Mrs So-and-so's back door's leaking, that's terrible, well it is terrible, but no' half as terrible as that child that's goin' back to the United States, and that kinda stuff, and up the ice rink as well, it was the same. And the dignified way in which the whole operation was conducted, you know, these things, they came and went. No under cover o' darkness—, the deeds were done, the lids were screwed down, they were removed, taken away and put in planes and so on and so forth, and it was just quietly effective, and just what the situation needed at the time. So there was so much that reflected very well on the people that were doing it, that unless you were the person concerned, you could say that the balance sheet was very much in the black. But, as I say, if you wanted your house done quickly and you didnae get it done for nine months, you'll probably still be annoyed about it. But the bigger picture, there was a huge amount that was really good about it.

Attitude to council authorities: the town hall scenario

The town hall, it was Hugh Young and I who were responsible for the— obviously not personally, but historical fact tends to be a casualty, sometimes, the refurbishment in the town hall was started before the plane crash, there were traffic lights in Bridge Street, and what was happening was that the downstairs part of the town hall was being done. I don' know if you remember, off the street you used tae go down steps, well we were puttin' the floor up in pillars to make more useful space, puttin' in a kitchen, so that the coffee mornings would be a bit less dank and dark, an' that had started before the plane crash. So the town hall refurbishment was underway, but I can safely say a lot o' people either didnae realise that or have forgotten. So what had to happen there was the same as the Rosebank Park Place houses; there had to be a speeding up of it, and once again, you've got tae speed it up without leaving every other community, because the councillors'll no' vote for— it, so it's got tae be done in a particular way. But again, that got the go-ahead. Ye remember silly things, like the radiators, the radiators so that they could be in the old, cast-iron style, came frae Italy, they were *ordered from Italy*. [Jill chuckles] Because there were, in the main town hall, there were marks on the floor. Some of the staff— now we are not talking, we're not talking about sort of drama kings or drama queens. We're talkin' about people who'd worked there for decades. They'd served the community for decades. They couldnae go through the doors. So the floor had tae be stripped, re-done, re-painted, the lot. And it wasnae quite finished when Hugh an' I gave up the unequal struggle in 1996, but the last thing that needed to be done was the lift. The money was passed on to the new council so that the lift could be put in. So I think that was the very last thing that was done at the town hall refurbishment. I think it cost about 700 000 pounds. And yet, you listen to local people and you look a' the papers an' all the rest o' it, and you'd think it'd never happen'. But it did and it cost a quarter of a million pounds. But you would think, Oh! *nobody's* ever done anythin' here. It's actually no' true.

I don' think there's any malice in it, I just think mibby we've got into a groove, you know, Oh Lockerbie gets nothin'. More recently I cannae speak for, cause there was nothin' wi' do. You remember the caravan park in Bridge Street? [Jill acknowledges] That's gone! There's houses there now. Crown Motor Works went, and Summerfield's, or Templeton's, went in there, you know: there actually were quite a lotta— the old egg packing station down a' the station: that became council houses. There actually was quite a lot went on. Down on the other side o' the railway, the first sheltered houses in Lockerbie were built, but I suppose basically people are, and quite rightly, ye didnae want tae get complacent, they're never satisfied. Amenity houses were built down where the mill used t' be, past your dad's shop, that was amenity housing for elderly people as well, that was the *last* thing that as convenor of Annandale, I signed off, an' the new local authority wanted us t' not do it, so that they could look a' the overall picture, and I remember, I went to the council meeting and I said, "Look, it's on the same side of the street as a grocer's, the police station, the post office, if they keep walking on there's the town hall: it's damn near as good as you'll get for the elderly." So to the council's credit, friend and foe alike, they voted for it. So that's why—I don't know what the new authority did wi' them, that was housing for the elderly. So I think, ach, I think it's just what people say. *All over Scotland* they've got an attitude to the coonci, and it's not really a very positive one.

Dave doesn't hanker for his days on the council

There are *no* circumstances under which— but it's the same attitude that I hinted at before. Once you go, you go! And effectively, it may've only been a small ship but I was the captain, and you don't go back on the crew. And that's no' snobbishness, you just *don't* tell or start telling other people who have other responsibility how they should be doin' it. I have *had* my day, so not doing it again.

I got particularly irritated because we'd heard allegations that [pause] people were announcing [pause] that they'd had awards fae the Trust, and we knew they hadn't had, and we're thinking, Why's he goin' into the pub and sayin' he's had this fae the Trust when he hasn't, and there were these—you've no idea how hard it is, because, the doings of the Trust, because it concerns people's financial affairs, are 100% confidential, so ye just have to take the egg. Ye' get pressed into these—again, I would have to say, I never got too upset or too—for whatever reason, I think it was maybe my upbringing, I was able to roll with it – never shed many tears, never got upset or unhappy, and I think [wife] would tell ye', I didnae come home miserable; I didnae come come *laughin'*, but it just didnae get on top o' me because ye' just keep thinkin', Well, if this beats *you*, you'll be fat lot of use tomorrow. Stand up, dust yourself down, and move forward again. That sounds almost like John Wayne, and I don't mean it to, but that's, that's what ye have to do. As I say, I don't look back much; don't reminisce too much about the school days.

Interviews and reportage: Dave's anecdotes on the Media Group

The first interview I did was with John Sargeant, BBC, in a car, down at the police station. Stopped. The morning after it was, and after that, for all kinds o' reasons. There were interviews with, oh, CNN, God knows, and so forth. But slow but sure I built up a [pause] really a high opinion of the local people, particularly Willie Johnson, and, a lad on Border I think he's still in Border called Tim Bagshaw, who, for me, for what I was looking for, they brought the right attitude, they didnae [inaudible] soft soap or ask namby-pamby questions but nor did they ask stupid questions. And, just over the piece, I just found them more *in tune* wi' the Lockerbie situation than some of the others who, y'know, in the field they were quite big names but they were parachuted in, and I don' know—they were probably as well briefed as they could've been, but in some situations, they really hadnae been talking for very long before they realised they werenae really au fait wi' what they should be talking about.

So that wen' on, and the press were something else again; I actually didnae do too many interviews wi' press because [pause] really some o' them just made up things for me to say anyway; I mean that's actually perfectly true, I mean you get quoted [pause] I even once got a [pause] quite a nasty letter from Pan Am's lawyers because somebody had said that I had said something. Now it as ineffectual because all I had tae say was that, well he was mistaken, which he was, coz he'd made it up as well but that kindae thing's just unnecessary hassle whereas, wi' Willie, in particular, I built up a degree of rapport which I hope is still goin' on, and, I think it was the first anniversary, and Willie commentated fae one o' the buildings overlooking the Flying Angel, the war memorial, and I was up there as the sorta summariser, and so on, and then, much later than that, he phoned up and said, " How would you like to do a half hour jazz programme," and so and so forth, so obviously I've gotta lota time for Willie: I live in the hope that he wouldnae have asked if he thought I was gonna make a mess o' it, and Tim Bachelor, he was the guy—we were down in Sherwood, filming, and he said, "D'you'like to just do this yourself?" :, you know, and that kindae gesture is no skin off his nose, etc, etc, but it goes a long to make—it certainly made me feel as if I was *part* of the operation as opposed to just being *interviewed* by the operation, and some of them were just not good: aggressively—I don't mean aggressive in deliberately forcing you into a corner wi' awkward questions, but you just get the feelin' that they—you know, they had a job to do, and it was maybe just a wee bit tedious, being in the sortae one-horse town, and so on. Not a, not an opinion shared by most of the American visitors because I do—we had a chap from the Syracuse operation in London, he came up to the School, to do some stuff – he was an English lecturer – so we had a—Betty and I, we had him for a meal in Lockerbie, and he said, "No American town of this size would raise the sophistication of Lockerbie." Eh?

How did the media handle the issues, in Dave's opinion?

I wish, I wish they had been able to assume we perhaps understood their requirements better than they thought we did, in other words, we wouldnae take a week to say something; we'd give them something and they would get their job done, but I do—it was the patronising attitude [pause] and I don't know anybody in Lockerbie who leans on a dry stane dyke chewin' straw, you know, it's quite a cosmopolitan town. Hugh and I, just as a matter o' interest, after the disaster [pause] we found twenty three people of different nationalities living in Lockerbie; twenty three, aye! So, Australian, Polish, Ukranian, Lithuanian, English, Scottish, Welsh, French, Irish, German: we ended up wi' twenty three so is probably mibby no' as sophisticated as we would like it to be, but it certainly is not the hick town that, you know—they painted this almost as the sleepy wee Scottish village; its *no'* sleepy at all! This is the town that bought and paid or its own ice rink; its own squash courts; this is the town where the Scouts have their own dedicated headquarters, so have the Guides. You know, they get off their knees in Lockerbie and do things but they prefer this picture of some rural backwater where we woke up, desperate for help; well, we didnae!

Well, it was more—you would learn more fae the articles aboot what the situation was [pause] I wouldnae comment on any o' the literary merit, but if you picked up The Annandale Herald and read the comment there, ye'd be pretty close to the way people were feelin' oz it was—the vox pox were definitely local and so on. I thought they did well, I did, and [pause] course I write for them as well noo, co I s'pose I'm biased but—

Dave was not fazed by cameras and interviews

I wish you could find a way to double check this wi' somebody else, but there was no point at which I found myself nervous, concerned about what I might say, or that I'd said anything stupid, I, I just did *not* feel uncomfortable, I was fine; and I found that [pause] the words just came out and, when I watched it later—I didnae like watchin' it, I don't think I've got a good voice, but some of the stuff I said was [pause] Spot on. So spot on that other folk repeated it later and [jill chuckles] that's actually true. Desperate! Some of the figures of speech to hear, you know, the local community council chairman would be interviewed and he'd say the same bloody thing, you know, which I suppose means you've got it pitched just about right. But I was never nervous, honestly; the thought of these umpteen million—sometimes it was live [pause] aye, och, they've a' been here at one time or another - Kirsty Waugh, Ben Brown, the whole bloomin' lot o' them – and I found at that level, official and courteous and so on. Didnae hing aboot. It must've been one o the anniversaries; was up at McJerrow Park at God knows when in the morning; was doing the camera and Ben Brown was daein' the interview. Turned up, shook hands, asked the questions, and that's it, and that suited me perfectly well: he wasn't brusque or patronising, just efficient, and that's, that's really what ye're looking for whereas I think—on one other occasion, I'd an interviewer frae one of the independent, ITN substations, said she as gonnae ask me five questions then asked me different ones, and I've wondered ever since, it that a tool o' the trade when they're talkin' tae politicians? But I really didnae—I've no explanation why, coz I used to get nervous about three foot putts and things like that, but I just didnae get nervous aboot that so, there you go. Sometimes its just one o' those positive things that you said in your previous visit, that basically, its no' a' bad and I found that, backed into a corner sometimes, I found that I could get out just dint o' havin' the words so you're always learning; I wouldnae suggest for a minute that the events leading up to it justified me learning *that*, you know, but—

The positive aspects of living through the process of accepting the situation

I'm sure they did, I sure that, that, some of them are still, still [pause] up the ladder that they climbed to join in to do whatever they had to do, you know, whether it was through the WRVS or the women who washed all those, all those clothes, so carefully, it wasnae a rush job and the folk who—I'm a great believer that a wee success, even if you're a big fish in a wee pond, if ye win the local monthly medal at the gold club; if ye win a prize at the Sunday school; if ye just do something well and people recognise it, I think ye stay up there, and I think that a lot o' people, who had just been goin' about their daily business, doin' the messages at the weekend, suddenly found, within themselves, that the felt themselves to be more worthwhile human beings and that stayed with them; I mean, I don't think they're still necessarily makin' scones, you know, but I think if ye just get the feelin' that ye're more—within yourselves because other popel have made it obvious, you value yourself more highly as a human being and I do think we all do better if ye can—and I think a lot of people found something within themselves that just jerked their life to a halt and the thought, I can do better than this; that's good, that; I like myself better, and their shoulders have been a wee bit straighter ever since, so it's a disastrous way to get it, but I saw some more genuinely confident, as opposed tae mouthy people, genuinely confident people because somedae had stuck a microphone in their face and they'd come oot ae it quite well; all of a sudden, they'd found the words [pause] and, Fine, quite pleased wi' masel, and—yeah, positive effects.

Sit back and enjoy your flight?? Not likely for Dave

I didnae step intae one till aboot two years ago. I would not get on. I would not get on the plane! And the follow-up was ma sister in Australia started to save up to come here after the crash, direct result, coz he'd been gone since she left college [pause] and you know, we've moving into the twilight of our lives and I think she suddenly realised, if that plane had landed—which really's just a quarter o' a mile further over which is really another thing ye never think of: I was standing at the front window, looking at the ruins of Sherwood, never thinking that that is 0.25 o' a second, hits our house, spirals down slightly differently, and [name of house] is history. That takes once to dawn on you. Oh, its away over there, it missed by quite a lot! God know what your folks felt like, coz one over there and one down there and they're in the middle! Anyway, so eh, what did you ask me?

JH: Air travel and how your sister saved up.

DW: Aye, so she saved up and on the way here, her baggage went missing at Frankfurt, and when it got here, it had been opened wi' a Stanley knife in Frankfurt! The same bloody airfield; so that was *not* an encouragement, I'll tell you, but eventually I stepped—there was a school trip going to Paris and it was plane or nothing so I thought, Ach, well, time to do it, so I've been on tota of six flights but when we go on holiday this year tae Switzerland, it's the train, all the way.

I don't like it and in truth, no many people on the plane like it because [laughs] I remember the plane is quite happy to give *Y Viva España* big licks [Jill laughs] when you're taking off. It goes deathly quiet when you're landing: nobody talks when you're landing; nobody makes a sound, and I noticed it, Here wait a minute, why have they all gone quiet? Coz this is the hard bit but we got down safely though.

Well, I actually thought, when we first went on I thought it was the B flight entertainment, when they were showin' us—I thought they were doin' YMCA, you know [both laugh] You're headin' for the Irish Sea at 400 miles per hour and they're seriously tellin' you to strap on this stuff [both laugh]. Naw, naw, naw.

JH: And how helpful it that whistle really gonna be? [laughter]

DW: And if you're stugglin' for oxygen, reach up! [Jill laughs] Help yourself! Naw, naw. I can thole it; it wasnae as bad as I thought it might be, but it was the direct result of the crash that I didnae get intae a plane.

Mentioning the 'L' word

Well, now, I just say Lockerbie because I know they'll recognise it but, they've started to recognise it less in recent years now, because some o' them wernae here when the plane crashed. I mean, you have to be twenty something now tae—allowing for a couple of baby years when ye'd nae idea what was goin' on.

So, its not—it used to be—people's faces used to change, and you used to think, Och, no, don't have a collection for us [both chuckle but its okay now, its never a—but its just one f the things that never *bothered* me. Just never—there's a lot of things never bothered me to the extent that they seem to bother other people. Aye, I'm fine [inaudible] . Again, probably what they read in the paper, there was a wee bit of figurative mollie-coddling; Oh, we better watch what we're saying!, you know.

Dave has toured venues in the UK, presenting the Lockerbie experience of disaster preparedness

When you think of the geography, Britain's biggest ever air disaster and Britain's biggest ever rail disaster within fifteen miles o' each other! My goodness we've qualified for it, haven't we! I went away tae a couple of things, they're all Geographical Society; I went down tae Leeds, to tell them about it, but another one I did was the Emergency Planning College in Yorkshire and, I think, in the light of experience, was able to point out one or two things, you know, namely that the water mains being fractured can shatter your emergency plan, you know. The fact that you either have hundreds o dead people and everybody else okay can ruin your emergency plan because its dependent on getting doctors there and so on; and the other thing was that most local authorities, at the time, had an Emergency Planning Officer, on whom expectations suddenly fall but he or she doesnae really have the clout tae start telling the Americans what tae do or the British Secret Service, you know? So I said to them, "Look however you do it, get your head honchos involved right away, because the others don't have the clout if its that big an emergency," and this *was* that big an emergency. So people started appearing from Downing Street and the local guys, what are they supposed to say and do? But I think maybe lessons were learnt bout how high up the planning has to go; ye cannae just leave it to the Fire Brigade, who, as I say, when they were there and quite ready to go, and all the rest of it, couldnae. And what do you do them? What do you do it if the water's off and the place is on fire? *That* is worth thinking about as well, so I don't know if good came out of it, but maybe change came out of it, yeah.

The writing was on the wall regarding the Twin Towers attack: Dave explains the need to strike back, and global hypocrisy

Ah, I really—I couldnae believe it. I working at Moffat Academy at the time; the Deputy Head, Donald Hastings, came round to tell us what had happened. I just find it [pause] I cannae get inside the heads o' people who get involved in that kindae thing and I wish I could, you know, but I just don't understand where they're coming from; it seems so random and so on. One o' the, one o' the *marginal* disappointments has been that, apart from telling us how terrible they are, which I'm happy to believe, I still hadnae *read* any kind of dispassionate analysis of how this has sprung up and spread and so on, and I just hope the people who are responsible for dealing with this, know a lot mare aboot it that I've ever read. But in the global geo-political context, I wasnae entirely surprised coz there have been hints at this kindae stuff, especially Osama bin Laden; you know, some of the papers had been writing about him many years ago, saying, Look—and maybe we didnae take the threat seriously enough or whatever, but attacking aircraft is an extremely cheap way to cause a lot o' damage. One thing that surprises me still, I don't really know why, is why a cross channel ferry, frae Dover tae Calais of whatever, why nothing's happened there because I think that would be another really cheap target to go for.

 I've actually got wee anecdote about that. A friend of mine, who also workd at Moffat Academy, [name of friend], her brother worked for Collins the publisher, and they'd just finished printing some year book. One o' the pictures was a jet, flying towards the Twin Towers, not part of the attack, and he had gone rushing to the manager, said, "We cannae send this oot, after what's happened!", you know, and it was withdrawn. He doesnae work there now, but he was a printer who does the checking. Twin Towers! Aircraft in the sky! Maybe not a good idea! So it was withdrawn.

JH: So, what is interesting to me was, you know, the reaction of the Americans to the Twin Towers was, Okay, attack! Let's attack! Just imagine, you know, which is in stark contrast to the Britain, you know, dealt with the Lockerbie thing; imagine if we had said, Okay, that's it! We're just gonna have to go and attack Libya now. The dichotomy of that attitude is really interesting.

DW: For all the emotional impact of the crash on Lockerbie, it wasnae in America. The thing is that throughout the—well, ye cannae discount Hawaii, but the mainland o' America has never been bombed by anybody, and that makes a difference. Somebody did it, and I think that would jerk them up by the ankles; and they are—don't suppose it's a problem but, the difficulty for the United States is that they are geared up to beating an opponent who stands in front of them and fights on their terms; you know, they have massive hardware, sophisticated weaponry and a' the rest o' it, but if the other guy – it happened in Vietnam as well - if the other guy just hides up trees and throws things at you, saps the morale over a long period o' time, and ye've all yer hardware and really nobody to fire it at. And I think they're slowly coming to terms with that now; its taken them a long time and really, the temptation to lash out after the Twin Towers is huge and, ach, aye, understandable, tae a degree, but the problem is, what direction dae ye lash out in? [pause] Course, there's always the conspiracy theories as well.

JH: They must have conveniently forgotten about all those years of arms-dealing with Afganhistan that they were involved in.

DW: Yes, aye, its—geo-politics is laced with hypocrisy, I'm afraid, and [pause] off-hand, I cannae think of any country that's guiltless, whose slate is totally clean. I think Sadam Hussein was probably gassing Kurds with oor gas, so you know.

And even the current furore over China, let's not be too hasty; there's too much money involved now. 40 years ago, we might have announced a buoycott already.

After a decade, the media reminded the masses about Lockerbie

I think, two television things for the tenth anniversary. I've actually got them on video somewhere, just to—two T.V.s and a radio I think, something like that, but it was, it was, it was starting to—it was starting to become not quite as meaningful to a larger number of Lockardians then. I sometimes wonder what would have happened if the media hadn't mentioned it; if somehow, the television stations in particular had just not mentioned it, I'm no' totally sure what we would've done here; no totally sure.

You know, you were getting news; this year is the tenth anniversary! Oh, so it is, and it [pause] starts to take on an momentum, you know, a sort of internal dynamic which means that once the ball starts rolling and ye start tae, yes start tae get a wee touch o' the emporer's new clothes; it's no' easy to stand up and say, Well, I don't think we should do anything, and just let it go at anybody who wants to make it personal—recognise it personally should do it personally; once it starts, that's no' a popular message so—and I think the twentieth, to some extent, will be the same thing. I mean, 19, 20 21; what's the difference? The situation is still the same, we havnae learned anything more.

I mean I, I—I'll go down to the memorial each December and I'll keep on doin' it, just the same as I go to the Armistice Day service every November and I'll keep on doin' it, but [pause] there's still just a few—I'm finding it harder and harder to remember the less striking things; if I pull out minutes of meetings, many of which I've kept, I remember *then*, but I'm sixty five; that's what people do when they're sixty-five; ye' start to forget the stuff that's run-o-the-mill, but I can jog my memory

What commemoration means to Dave as time passes

I mean, ye' wonder—the participants of the twentieth one, some of them, and it's not a pejorative term, will be outsiders, coz they wernae here. I know what happened—its like a science fiction movie; a bloody great aero engine, smoking gently, burning up in the sky; its like *The Day the Earth Stood Still*, the nineteen fifty three movie, and *I* remember that. I remember the figures on the rooves, and that, but the majority cannae possibly so they will be doin' a historical commemoration; I'll be doin' a personal commemoration, and some o' the others, a community commemoration, but the balance next time will probably be gone; its just interesting the way [pause] ye've got all these clichés – more than a grain of truth; Life moves on, and the can sound so callous, but there's nothing callous aboot it; I'll never forget Paul Somerville, ye know, he's in there; I'll never forget [grandfather of deceased victim] , you know, standin' there wi' his hands behind his back, jist bubblin', and that's where—I remember the enormity of it. Not in the fact that the jumbo jet—but it'll never go away, its locked in there and I don't mind, I'll look after it, but at the same time, each December, I *feel* it, you know its probably still spiritual and emotional but a bit of the immediacy has gone. I don't just walk down for the sake of walking down and I'll always do it, but its mibby no' as sharp as it used to be; still the same size, but no' sharp. So.

You grief for you town, you grief for your friends, you grief for whatever, and [pause] I mean I even remember the day of my grandmother's funeral. We're driving along to the cemetery, and I'm thinkin', Why are those people looking so unconcerned? Don't they know my grandmother's dead! Why are they smilin'? But then as Time passes, ye still remember the same people but in a way, its more positive, ye' can talk aboot it and so on; it's the same as [inaudible] Never did get upset about talkin' about it, never ever did, even less so now. Matter of fact, that's not in a negative way. Its like my Mother died fae cancer so that happened tae me; I remember it and I talk aboot it, but I don't get upset aboot it, and that's the zone I'm in, and I have been for more than ten or twenty years and it was helpful at the time so I could stand up and answer questions and so on. Other folk couldnae dae it! They had a story tae tell, but the minute they saw a T V, they went away some other way, and they'd have been able to put in such a lot but didnae feel it was their bag.

Contemporary Lockerbie: Dave sees the public grievance procedure has changed over time

Well, I just think in changes, shifts in commercial and retail operations has put Lockerbie in the same position as every other small and medium-sized town; its not by nay stretch of the imagination specific to Lockerbie, and [pause] as far as I can see, its actually thriving. There's plenty o' factories; we don't any longer have Jackie Gardner's with your old man down at the other and Templeton's in between, and Boots the Chemists is gone but, ye' get far more out of the pharmacies we've got than you ever got out o' Boots. We don't have a shoe shop and that's very regrettable but things have moved; I mean I remember the local fruit shops: however much ye' deprecated Tescos, there's a far bigger range o' fruit in there than we ever got in Cameron's fruit shop, and people don't always sort o' take into account, things that have got better. Now, I'm no' sure about Tescos taking over the world! I wish they weren't as powerful but, at the same time, if you don't want them to be as powerful, don't go! [Dave laughs] Spend the money somewhere else.

But I don't think, when you look at what we have got, okay there's takeaway food outlets; its not the configuration of shops that I would like to see. You know, [name of local retailer] has his [name of shop] and just about makes a living, although I think probably still does some electricianing as well; I don't think its easy but the [name of local shop] done okay; [name of local shop] doin' okay, it's the food shops that really suffered ; I don't like the—as I say, I'd rather have a difference balance; but in terms of employment and everything like that, we've got the local station, more trains stopping, I like its goin' like fair, but as I say, I wouldnae like to be a trader, tryin'tae compete wi' the heavy squad, because they have the option, you know, for example, Margaret Wilson has done very well, and she has a paper shop, so she has managed somehow to keep her clientele and because she's just up the street from [supermarket] who can sell all the popular papers, ignore all the ones that don't make much money, sell all the popular magazines and so on, and it must be very difficult to compete wi' that but she's managed it. The people who came to the Lockerbie Jazz Festival, one of the sales—one of the ticket outlets was Margaret's, and she got a 100% rating for friendliness and helpfulness and a' the rest o' it. Now there's a key there; there's something there

The Butchery's still there; the Butchery is still there in the same street as two supermarkets so they've found something, and I don't think its hopeless but I think Professor Harvey, what you really were referring to, there are one of two premises in Lockerbie which are a disgrace, and I'm no' surprised he looked and said, Och, that's a dump, but it was a bit superficial, his analysis, I thought. There are some places I wish they'd either paint, refurbish of knock down or something, but over the piece, four thousand, five hundred people! Look at it not fae the point of view of someone like your father; two supermarkets! [dave laughs] Two supermarkets in a town of four and a half thousand! That actually isnae too bad but. If you're lookin' for something a wee bit different, ye've had it.

One of the other things that's improved for the better; when I was young, if you went into many, many shops in Motherwell, they gave you the impression they were doing you a favour. I remember I bought a record player – I saved up and I saved up; a Bush record player. I didnae like the way the dance set players dropped the records; my precious jazz records could get broken here, so I wanted a single player wi' a better speaker, so I saved up the eighteen quid and I went to a shop called Bryson and Graham, and I had to give them eighteen quid, they would order it, and I had to keep calling in, to see if it had arrived and then carry it home. Now, that has changed, for the better, but mibby one of two people involved in the retail side havnae worked that oot yet. Even when I came tae Lockerbie, you could get the feeling you were bloody lucky to get served, you know, and just occasionally, you still discern it. You go in; a couple of assistants; they finish their conversation. I don't think they need to come and lick your boots, but if the plan is to end the financial year with a profit, you really have to sort out the customer. There's still just a wee element of doing you a favour, and it doesnae work; people just go somewhere else. It's interesting.

And, I think people too are—I don't know if they're more prone to complain, but I remember thinking during the Thatcher era - I was not a supporter of Mrs Thatcher – that, I remember thinkin', Thank God for pressure groups, because these people getting' out onto the streets and wavin' placards are keepin' Democracy alive, because this government are not, but now, I wonder if people are too quick to have recourse to pressure groups, coz they've worked out, Wait a minute, we don't need to bother with our elected representatives, let's just put the pressure there, and I'm sometimes astonished to discover how much some charities have got in the bank. Here, wait a minute, what is this for, and people, you know, have just learned to bypass the parent whose no' happy, straight to the Director of Education, at the same time, same phonecall, And if you don't, I'll go to the papers. You know, people have worked out shortcuts which, however well it may work for them, is not good for the community, and I think there's a lot of it about; I mean, big business worked out a while ago if everyone of the political parties, never mind the local planning committee, I wonder if folk, and of course, they're forever looking for somedae to sue, but not big business. Public institutions! They'll sue a health board, but they'll no sue their local—you know, paper shop, coz we know them. And there's a shift in the balance that I wish would go back a wee bit again so that, you go to the local councillor; he's nae good, so you try the M.P; that's nae good, or you get satisfaction or whatever. Instead o' that, its straight to the papers; I mean, that's a favourite. So, poor sausage open up his local paper; here's this person on the front complaining about something that, the guy who's reading it, didnae know was even wrang, coz she's never thought to mention it to him, and I just—I'm no' putting it very well, but I get a bit—the last laugh is, the very number of people complain there's too much read tape, but then it they don't fancy a wind farm, they reach for a huge ball of red tape; as much red tape as they can get their hands on, and there is this double standard a' the time, and you know, I sometimes think to myself, Why are you throwing rotten eggs at the Planning Committee? Why not throw them at the landowner who's making a mint outta this! Terment him, so that he won't sell them the land! No, but that's the harder target; let's go for the easy target. Instead of complaining about the police, why not lean on the fence and ask your neighbour if he'll dae something about his dog, but they phoned the police,;nacks and routes have been lost, I think. Maybe I'm thinkin' back to good old days that existed.

On the topic of Margaret Thatcher and her presence at the Memorial Service, 1989

I don't know, I never met her! —this makes me sound so bloody moral, and its no true, but I thought it would be hypocritical! I disagreed with nearly everything she did and I thought, I'm no' gonnae stand there and leer and smile, so actually, I spoke to Cardinal Winning instead, most of the time, whose fae Motherwell – he was, he's dead now – he was fae Motherwell; he was Archbishop Winning at the time; Catholic Archbishop, and I talked to him coz he's fae Motherwell too. We were having a good craic; he asked me what school I'd gone to, coz that's the big West of Scotland question; What school did you go to? The proddie school or the catholic school. He says, What school did you go to? but he was joking, you know, so I didnae meet Mrs T; I as in the same room; the convener at the time, Frank Park, he was tryin' to get me—Hugh met her but I couldnae; I just felt it—you know, when I'm sittin' after tea-time, watchin' the news, swearin' at the woman, you know, and I just disagreed wi' her and that was it, and two years later, Ravenscraig closes, and some of the stuff at the heart of the miner's strike as a disgrace to Democracy [pause] there would have been other ways to achieve the same ends; some of which needed to be achieved, you know; I was never sure why we needed to be crawling around three miles underground in the 20th century – something else couldae been done – and I prefer to think of her as the woman who lost the Falklands. [Jill laughs] Well, she did! She was the Prime Minister!

JH: It was quite ironic, though; I don't know what statistic of Scottish voters could stand her, but there she was representing, on the international stage, Scotland, and okay, she can be labelled British Prime Minister, but, for me, that in itself was just [pause] all mixed up.

DW: Yes, it was, it was a bit uncomfortable; she didnae seem able to recognise that [pause] some people, you know—harking back to earlier stuff – have great unearned advantages in life, you know, so how does her wee boy become a millionaire, with no discernible talent, eh? Coz that's his Mother!

Dave remembers a lie he told to an old man's tears

The things that still stick oot are these; I don't drink, I don't smoke, and I try very hard no' tae tell lies, and the disaster caused one. There's a commemorative stone down at the remembrance garden [pause] to [name of deceased passenger] and his grandfather came over [pause] and I cannae remember how it cropped up but I took him down, you see, — there's this elderly man [pause] tears coursing down his cheeks [pause] and he's looking at the stone, and he said to me, "And it this where my grandson is buried?"

There was only one answer: it was, Yes! But it's the wrong answer because those stones commemorate people who wernae found, you know, and it sometimes—now I don't think God'll send me to the bad fire for that, but it's just illustrative of how—well, what do you do here? Yes, again, you're a hostage to Fortune, because he could be going' back in the plane and some American could say, But that's no'right! And he'll be thinking, Why did that man tell me that?

Damage to the ceiling of the Haldane shop, caused by flying debris from the crater in Sherwood Crescent. (© James Haldane 2008)

Pieces of detritus from the crater on the shop floor. (© James Haldane 2008)

Marjory McQueen, March 31 2008

Retired Councillor, Housewife, Superstar

The agent, on her own admission, is happy to wear each of these labels in describing her multiple roles that constitute her busy and very successful life in Lockerbie. She knows her community inside out: before retiring, she was involved in vital decision-making to shape the Lockerbie landscape and infrastructure. In addition, she has been the local GP's wife for those four decades and that position does not come without in depth knowledge of the composition of families' identities. So she knows the stakeholders and the environment very well.

Her husband was our family GP but I couldn't recall having spoken to her before, although I knew her son in our senior years at school.

I approached this narrator because I knew she had lots of experience of interviews: she became a councillor after the disaster but she was part of the Media Group, like John Carpenter and Dave Wilson – prominent members of the community who were willing to speak to the press and take the pressure off the wider public in Lockerbie. She has been featured in local and national newspaper and on television – I read her opinions recently in an archive piece from the Glasgow Herald about the tenth anniversary.

We met on the afternoon of March 31st, in a small and cosy back parlour. Her husband popped in after the hour-long interview was complete. Before she represented the local authority for twelve years, she was in children's special needs and, prior to that, radiography – she continues a hectic schedule which involves an elderly parent and grandchildren.

Her name in Marjory McQueen. She is personable and quick-witted: the brevity of the subject was often lightened by some laughs. She admitted she had many other stories but confidentiality restricted their telling.

Marjory's immediate and distant family

Right; I have a husband and we'll be celebrating our ruby wedding next year. Never ever have we ever spoken about divorce [Jill laughs] ; murder several times but divorce not; I've got two children and two and three-quarter grandchildren. Son who's thirty eight this year and living down in Poole in Dorset and daughter who'll be thirty four this year and living in Perthshire.

I'm local to Collin which is about ten miles away from Lockerbie; just a wee village; it's much bigger now; I can always get lost when I go back there. Yes it was a very very quiet wee village yes […] a lot of farms round about and, it's very difficult I can't even remember now, :but there was one local shop I think, and a post office.

I attended Collin public and primary school; and then went to Dumfries Academy. From Dumfries Academy then went to Edinburgh and was a student at the School of Radiography at the Royal Infirmary.

My mother is still very much with us; yes she lives in Dumfries. Mum was county secretary for the Red Cross for about thirty years. I'm an only child of an only child. My father came from Wales.

My father worked at the Royal Infirmary in Dumfries and actually was on the commission team for the new hospital which was built about 1970's. He was at the new infirmary: he was at the old infirmary as well, but then transferred to the new infirmary, in the admin side.

Moving to the city and her first job back in the area: Marjory loved her work

Yes I enjoyed the student life; I enjoyed it much more than I did my school days. I really really enjoyed being in Edinburgh and having a bit of freedom; freedom I never really had; and also I suppose I was very fortunate in that I got a job right away; I came back to Dumfries to work once I had qualified, in fact they took me on before I had my exam results [Marjory laughs] , which was a bit of a risk but they did it.

I never had a strong bent for anything really; no, I think I got there by accident to be honest [Jill laughs] with you; I didn't have much of a clue what I wanted to do; but its a job, that given my life over, I would do again. Never got up in the morning and thought, Oh, this is awful, what a day; always looked forward to my days at work.

Meeting her husband

We met—he was a resident, he did his second six month surgery at Dumfries; he'd never been in Dumfries in his life, arrived in this place and didn't know anybody; I think I first met him down, looking at some x-rays in casuality, in the old infirmary. That was Sixty Eight.

He's a Glasgow boy, really the first thing; our first conversation he told me a downright lie. I was always ticked him off about that because after work—if there were any new staff they all had to have chest x-rays to make sure they weren't carrying about any infections about with them; and when he came, he started a the first of February, and we he came, a clerk came in before I did the x-rays and I'd to get his date of birth. I asked him how old he was and he said "Twenty Four" and when I got his date of birth, he was only twenty three. He wouldn't be twenty four until the twenty ninth of February; a leap day boy. Yes so he told me a deliberate lie. I think he was [trying to impress me] with his expedience and maturity.

Marjory remembers improvements in the field of radiography.

Ah yes I worked at the Cumberland infirmary because Ken had moved there, he was an S.H.O. in orthopaedics so I worked in Cumberland infirmary, and then he moved to Edinburgh to demonstrate anatomy at the university, so naturally I followed, and I was a radiographer at the Simpson Maternity Hospital; that would be up until June of 1970, when was Geoffrey born in the August so I stopped worked and by that time we were back in Dumfries

We were like; yes; junior doctors in those days were like horsemen; we were never off the road. I remember when I worked in the Simpson a professor from—Professor Donald from Glasgow, coming over to Simpson with a box of tricks and nobody had seen the likes of before and that was the very start of sonograms [pause] He was the man who invented the sonogram. And we never thought it'd catch on [Marjory laughs] not going to do much I don't think.

JH: And do you sort of keep up to date with how things are going in radiography now?

MM: I'd be completely lost I think; we had a reunion and we were shown around the new x-ray rooms in Edinburgh and I mean the machinery was absolutely incredible and but—cos' the days we started; we were wet developing everything; we had to go and develop in; in a dark room and then huge driers you had to stick things in; now you can have the images in about five seconds.

Coming back to the region and Lockerbie: the history of the doctor's residence in Arthur's Place.

I knew the area; yes I knew the area; and it was quite handy for babysitters I suppose; although Ken's parent's at the time were in Glasgow and he had about seventy three aunts and uncles in Bearsden as well; so we were quite well done to babysitting-wise; but it was quite nice to get away from; from the city. It was nice, you know, I knew Lockerbie was a nice place to live.

Yes, yes it was quite a small town; I remember, now we have West Acres and Vallance Drive and all these places and there are hundreds houses down there; we wanted to build a new house and there was one house there; there was one house built; so that's all been in the last thirty six years, that huge estate.

We lived in Sherwood Park to begin with; in a rented house and then we built a house down in Glenannan, and we were there for five years, and then Ken's senior partner retired in this house that we're in, The Green, had always been the doctor's house; it was built for a doctor, and it was handed on, and the surgeries used to be here

So when his senior partner wanted to leave the house he offered it to us; and we accepted it; and my husband's parents came and lived in the upstairs flat because it's flatted.

And we've been here ever since; that'll be thirty years past.

The house has never been on the market. Never been sold.

It's gotta be 1870's I would think, and we have had a visit from a grandson of one of the doctors that was here in the thirties: he wanted to come back and see the house now.

Well it's just my husband and myself now. Well the grandchildren might come in here, that's the next thing of course; it's handy to have a big house when you've got family here.

Working in not-for-profit and local politics

I had been involved in everything I think; you know I think you just have one of those faces with sucker written on it [both laugh] and you don't work so you can do; you know; although I was the wife of a busy GP so I had phone duties and what-have-you, and taking up a job was never really on; because it was a full time job when we started; because we had one receptionist at the time, that was surgery, so whoever was on call had to do the phones at lunchtime sorta thing; so it was pretty full time job; and I just kinda got involved in various charities and things like that; anything that was going, I'd help out; and eventually it came to McMillan Cancer Relief; a big one that I was involved with and didn't—sat on the Scottish board of that; British as well, the UK; so that was the big charity that I was involved in, but not for any particular reason; I can't come out and say that all my family have died of cancer; I always thought it was a brilliant charity in what they did and the fundraising that they did and the use they put to the money; I was very pleased to be involved in that

The previous chairman asked if I would take it on; she wanted to retire and I took it on and that's what happened then; no they didn't ask for any CV's; I sure you wouldn't get away with it now [both laugh] and now you need Disclosure Scotland before you can join anything, just about anything.

Also became the last thirty five years been involved in politics in a very minor way and cumulating in the last few years being a local councillor, fought three elections and won [laughs] ; at the time, and I had nothing to do with the council at the time; they worked magnificently; the local council and the regional council at that time, there was a double layer, and I think they had to be congratulated in the manner in which they dealt with the situation; a very small council, a very small police force; I think they were absolutely magnificent; and I; and I wouldn't hear a word said against them.

Marjory's busy days on the district council

After twelve years I really was beginning to flag a bit; I was twelve years older than when I started it; let's face it, and every night, practically Mondays to Thursdays, anyways being out, and having to come in, get a meal and be somewhere else at seven o' clock; I was beginning to pall and that was it.

[I gained] huge amount of experience over lots of; lots of different fields, yes; I sat in the Education Committee and the Social Services Committee, Police and Fire Committee for twelve years; and I learnt a huge amount; I was Chairman, Joint Chairman of Planning and also area chair for the last four years. All hugely enjoyable

Memories and anecdotes she can and can't share

Well, I remember being soaked several times, standing at the cross during the Gala when I was a councillor because, obviously, they all quite liked that, and

I was immensely proud when my daughter was Gala Queen the year following the Lockerbie disaster.

That was a big thing because there was a lot of people wondered whether we should celebrate or not and give them their due, they said, "Yes we should celebrate," and that was the year of Ed's party; that was an American boy that came over. So that was, that was very enjoyable; I haven't any really, sort of, that I can think of, to be honest; none that I can tell you see; so many I can't tell [...] remember I was a doctor's wife.

Marjory's was anticipating a busy Christmas 1988: nothing changed

Yes I was expecting a lot of my husband's relatives coming down to stay with us as well. [Ken] always worked Christmas Day, I think as long as I remember he's worked Christmas Day. and had New Year off

It was Wednesday which was always my husband's half day and he always golfed on a Wednesday, but the weather was such that the boys decided they wouldn't golf as boys termed loosely [Marjory laughs] so instead they went to club in Dumfries to play snooker so they were away; Geoffrey was listening to music as was hit wont, in his upstairs bedroom; Victoria and I came through at seven o'clock to watch 'This is Your Life' which is a programme; and we were sitting in this very room here, which of course you can't see, but it faces north and we were sitting here watching telly and somebody had just come out, I think Michael Aspel had just come out in a sooty costume or something, that was a costume because Harry Corbett was This is Your Life, and [pause] there was a noise like thunder. I looked at Victoria and she looked at me and I said "Thunder?" but when thunder rumbles in, it then rumbles away again but this just kept coming [pause] and it, and it must have been coming for quite some time because I got up and went out the back of the house to see if it was a boiler upstairs; we have two central heating systems in the house with it being flatted and there's a boiler upstairs, and I began to think, I wonder if there was a problem with the boiler upstairs; and I went to the back of the house where I could see [pause] and it was then obviously—I didn't know what it was then that was when part of the aircraft came down onto Sherwood Crescent

It just was a noise and then there was a crump, not an explosion, not a—well I don't remember a huge explosion, I remember just a crump sound and flames and the debris and stuff, hundreds of feet into the air [pause] and even then I wasn't sure what had happened; but I came into the house and got the kids and at that time we had a lot of resuscitation equipment in the car which was parked outside as my husband was away in somebody else's car so we then carried the stuff around to the surgery. I presume there must have been some sort of delay while we got ourselves together because, by the time we got round to the surgery, it was open and there was a receptionist in and Dr Sloane, I think, from Lochmaben, was there; and there were people coming in cars, asking if there was anybody needed taking to the infirmary. It was amazing, in such a short time.

I remember Louise from the Flowerpot, standing at the bottom of the driving saying "Do we need blankets, do I need to get blankets?" and I said "I haven't a clue, I really haven't a clue at the moment but I would make for the town hall", because by that time, I think the town hall had been opened up.

I don't remember panicking straight away but then, yes: one of my friends - I'm not going to name her because it would embarrass her - came round and her husband had a shop in town and he was, was in the shop and she didn't know what had happened to him and she was hysterical, absolutely hysterical, and it was very difficult to try and find out what had happened to him because, of course, by then we were starting to get police cars and all sorts coming in

I did go round and went as far as I could to the local chemists house, Tom Carson's house because Tom was golfing with Ken and I knew that Brita and the three kids were there, so I went round there and brought them back to the house. We couldn't get much further than their house actually because there was a car burning on the road outside their house and they had a bit of debris through the roof; so I brought them back here and then I can't remember what time it was; it would have been about nine o'clock; this happened three minutes past seven and by nine o'clock Ken got back; he walked in the front door; he walked straight through the house, out the back door and got pea sticks and stuff from the garden and then just disappeared and by then he was going up the hill to look for bodies, because you're not dead until the doctor says so; so he had to go around marking them. The sticks were for marking

I thought it was two of these trainer jets had crashed mid-air onto somewhere and that was what the fire was, because there had just been a lot of low flying and the joke was when we were golfing in Lockerbie which was on a hill, when you got to the top of the hill the trainer were coming so close we used to laugh and say "There was that ginger guy with the moustache and bad breathe again"; you know it was so so low that everybody, you know would say the cliché that an accident was waiting to happen. So I kinda assume that that was what it was, but I can't remember how—we must still have had a phone line because, Jimmy Hill, my husband's partner phoned back to say that he had been called up to Tundergarth and when they opened the gate into the field, he saw the nosecone and, so word came back round about - it must have been round about nine o'clock - that this was a passenger jet, and I remember we all tuned into the news [Marjory laughs] to see what was going on, the nine o'clock news.

It was a jumbo jet has crashed on the town of Lockerbie, on the petrol station it said; I've still got the tapes of it somewhere.

Well, we knew that that wasn't so, we knew it wasn't so, and I think we got Bert Houston, the local reporter, on the phone; a lot of people on the phone, guys from the hospital on the phone as well because they'd started an emergency procedure, and they'd called in all the blood donors and extra workers and I remember Smith Syme who was the consultant at the time appearing, and said sadly in many ways—you were either very much alive or very much dead; there was not much in between. I think there was an elderly couple who had burns, Mr and Mrs Smith, and I know that Alan Wilson, one of my son's classmates, rushed out to see what had happen tripped over a bit of engine and broke his leg; so there were those kind of subsequent injuries rather than injuries at the time

Marjory's husband had a long, arduous night

No. He came home about; five; when did I catch up with him? About five in the morning; he had been back and he had some policemen with him, and he said "I had to bring these guys home, they had just seen too much" and I remember a bottle of brandy disappeared, quite quickly; well he said, "Don't go looking for the brandy at Christmas!" [laughs] They really needed that; and then he then; he'd came back, just got showered and started a surgery; didn't sleep at all; but he didn't; he didn't go to bed at all.

Before Ken got from Dumfries - some of the doctors from Dumfries had arrived here, sort of asking "What do we do?" and I said, "Well, I really don't know"; so the police station's across the road, so they went across there; one of them was the police doctor from Dumfries. After that there were loads of other doctors arrived from all over; the population went from three thousand to ten thousand; I think in 24 hours, with the army, police, rescue; all the people that came in to help.

The next day, the media descended on Marjory's place

I do remember I went about five o'clock, got a newspaper; and basically just got ready for visitors coming; they were a lot of reporters and people at the door; I remember I gave an Australian reporter breakfast; he had to driven through the night and—I think it was just the central house; he just knocked on the door: I don't know, it just seemed unchristian not to say—he looked absolutely whacked, you know, and I said, "Have you had anything to eat?" and he said, "No!" so I said, "Come in"; so then he had some breakfast; and I do remember later, on in the day, or maybe the next day, he came back with a huge bunch of flowers and that was the first time I cried. I think that was just too much. Yeah, and; Richard Yallup was his name, I still remember his name.

Well I have no idea what brought them here; I didn't have a flashing light outside the door of any kind [both laugh] red, blue, green or yellow [both laughing] that said, "Come here, come here". No I think they just came to the door; I remember Christmas Day as well they must have been taking a service at the church or something was happening, and we had a lot of reporters – the houses is right next to the church - and my husband's aunt was, you know, a very friendly person, insisted that we make scones and take them out to all the people that were waiting; so did that and ended up taking out Christmas pies, mince pies; well it was a pretty rainy day it wasn't very nice so she insisted that we do that [laughs]

Marjory's teenage children adapted to the deaths of friends as best they could

Seemed to be alright; they actually seemed okay; they take it in their stride. [pause] I don't remember them having any reaction; I know later on when it came to Joanne Flannigan's funeral, Victoria had to carry the flowers in; and she was really worried about what was going to— she thought the coffin would be —m, you know she thought she'd seen of telly sort of thing; it would be an open coffin and I had to explain that that certainly would not happen; she just had to take the flowers in.

Well, we all knew Joanne; my son and Joanne's big brother were best friends. And the Somerville, Paul Sommerville, was in her class, and Joanne's brother, Steven, was in Victoria's class as well. Yes yes [pause] : In fact, talking to Geoffrey, my son; the number of people who died in his year or about his year seemed quite to be quite out of proportion.

A priority head-shift for Marjory

Absolutely; and also it's turned me from—well in some ways, I think, a better person; because I tell you, if you break a cup or drop a plate in my house, it doesn't matter; it really doesn't matter, and pre nineteen eighty eight I think I would have got very upset with myself or with anybody if something like that had happened; it would be a tragedy [laughs] and now, so what, you know? Crashed the car! Are you alright? Fine. I think there's been a big sea change in the way I look at things.

I wouldn't say that it has; my own personal life, obviously you enjoy being here; you realise that a nanosecond, you might not have been here and that's got to make a difference and yeah I do; you know, life's for living, enjoy everyday as if it's your last because one of these days you'll be right.

Like many other townsfolk, Marjory volunteered at the incident centres

I actually went and worked up at what used to be the primary school which was turned into the procurator fiscal's office; so I did; I did a lot of work to allow policemen to get out onto the street; I mean what I was doing was just menial stuff photocopying and things like that; but I worked there for; it must have been three or four months at least. I think everybody wanted something to do rather than sit at home and contemplate your navel; it was, it was good to get out and make yourself useful

I think obviously having worked in hospitals was helpful, I mean looking at post-mortem pictures was not the greatest thing I've ever done but you had to do it; because I had to open up files for two hundred and seventy people, and at the time, I have no idea why everything had to have seven copies for every single thing, had to have seven copies and I never ever asked why so I don't know why; that; that had to be done for absolutely everything

Yes, that's right, because at that time, when I went to work there it had gone from a sort of terrible accident to what was actually mass murder; terrorism and mass murder; so, had it remained an accident I think the two hundred and seventy people would have been lumped together as a terrible accident; it became two hundred and seventy separate murder investigations so each body, each body part had to be found, annotated you know, what, where it was found; exact spot, everything had to be gone through for every single person.

We started off with a filing cabinet with two drawers and by the time we finished there were seven filing cabinets, maybe more, because the files were so big, you could only possibly get half a dozen in a big draw if that: it was huge

Marjory extended the hand of friendship

I can't actually remember why they came; I think they were on their way to visit the police station, and whether they ran into Ken or not, and he said, "You must come in for a cup of coffee". One of whom was extremely bitter about the whole thing and subsequently—there were two women, the one who was extremely bitter about the whole thing, and her friend; — when I was in America — when I went to Washington — I met her friend; we were at a do and she was there; and I always had a theory about the woman who was very bitter; I don't know why, I don't know why I even considered it; I thought, You'll be married in a couple of years, you'll have a new husband; and I just remember thinking she was just so bitter and you're trying to, you know, you're trying to say, This is a terrible loss you've suffered, but, Yes you'll be having Christmases and I'll never be having Christmas again, and, I'm really really sorry you feel like that but maybe in time you'll feel better; and I don't know, there was just something, something and I thought, You know what? You'll be married within two years, and when I met her friend back in; in Washington in two thousand and I asked her and she said, "Oh she's got a new husband, a new family", and I just; I don't know why, I don't usually judge people like that: I don't know; out of all the people I met: she; she was one to me who was—yes; and couldn't be, couldn't be given the hand of friendship and just didn't want it.

Marjory recalls the agendas of the press: her husband reminisces at the tenth anniversary

I can't remember about the first because I wasn't involved in it probably would have stayed in and I don't think I would get myself involved with going up town; I think I'd make sure I was away from that because it certainly wasn't what I was looking for, but it suddenly got thrust on me seemingly, as someone who was willing to be part of the media; we actually formed a media group because by then there were so many people who didn't want the intrusion; we thought we'd try and find people who wouldn't mind being interviewed; and we got about a dozen; and we gave them out; out to the media and said, "Look these are people who can tell you practically everything you want to know from every angle, from police, from the schools, everywhere; and that will save you having to go up town and point a camera at people who really don't want to see you"; and that actually worked quite well but it turned against me because I think I had thirty or forty camera crews in the house that day. One at a time, obviously.

Well they seemed to believe this was the first time Lockerbie had celebrated Christmas and we put—they got the wrong end of the stick coz I do remember doing a live interview with Sky News from the park, when the lights were being switched on, and I said "For goodness sake'", beforehand; before, I said, "This has nothing to do with the disaster here, it's just community council bringing lights to the town, it's got nothing to do with anything other than we should have Christmas lights; and we don't want to talk about the disaster".

These were new lights and the press got the wrong end of the stick. And I remember doing this interview and they said, "Thank you, can we now ask you about such and such", and I said, "'Could you just let us have our night please when we don't have to discus the disaster; just let's be happy for a night". So yeah, it had nothing to do with it at all.

Yes there was; yes there was; there was a ceremony in the afternoon, and there was a, a service at night because I remember, Donald Dewar attended it, and speaking to my husband, they'd had a set-to as students [laughs] on a traffic island. They'd had a punch up [both laugh] […] when they were at Glasgow University, from their university days; they'd had a punch up on a traffic island somewhere on Meal Monday, which is one of these university days when they all get dressed up [Jill laughs] and they were reminiscing, I remember that [both laugh].

Bereaved families and the Visitors' Lodge

A few years back, Donald Bogie, who had been very instrumental in helping during the disaster; he was a council officer, an environmental health officer and became Mr Fix-it during the Lockerbie disaster, said that the lodge down by the cemetery was coming up for sale and might it not make a fitting little museum. So he planted the seed and I watered the seed [laughs]; and nine of us got together as trustees and we opened a little; actually Donald opened it for us; we got him back to open it and I think that's about four years ago now. It has about three or four thousand visitors a year which is very good because we're not open everyday; and it's seasonal.

It's not just our disaster; there were twenty one nations involved in the Lockerbie disaster; and all these people who lost their loved ones here obviously want to come back from time to time and there's got to be a place for them here.

Everybody that I've taken time out to do something with has been very kind and been appreciative; I think one that stands out fairly recently was; a widow of a chap who died here; and she brought her son; who was, I think he'd be nineteen because he was a year old when his father was killed and she had never been before but he brought her; he wanted her to come to where his father had died; and that was done on a night when the lodge wasn't open and we took them down there; and that was quite moving and I think she was pleased she came, she couldn't bring herself to come before that and the son was the one who brought her.

I mean since I became a councillor, I couldn't tell you the number of times I've taken relatives there or visitors or you know, people from America, dignitaries and what-have-you.

9/11 – Marjory's personal experience too close to home

Well I was sitting in this very room we're having this interview an and I was making up an agenda for the minutes of a meeting with the trustees of the lodge we were talking about; we were having a meeting at three o'clock and I was so organised that at half past two, I was making the agenda; [both laugh] I had the television on and then this news flash came up; and of course it; it interested me because my son and daughter were in New York and where due to fly home that very day; and we watched it unfold and when the other members of the committee arrived we all just gathered around the television and looked at it; and of the nine people, two of us had relatives in New York that day.

I mean the first one could have just been a horrible horrible accident, but not the second one, no; And I think, obviously if you lived in the United States you'd be wondering where the next one was going to be and would there be another and another.

Certainly my daughter was quite traumatised by it; my daughter was saying, yes, as you went out to the back of the house she was staying in; all the helicopters flying over again, yes, brought it straight back; especially with all the helicopters and all the stuff going on overhead.

Getting back [to Scotland], they'd taken them onto the plane, then they took them off again for some reason; and she had kind of freaked out because they were due home on the Tuesday and this was the Saturday; so they had no money left; this was the end of their holiday; they had been to two weddings in the States so they were kind of spent up; and if my son had not over indulged the night before they wouldn't have been done there doing the last minute shopping.

Victoria was waiting for her brother who had such a sore head from all the milkshakes he'd had the night before that they didn't get down; they were staying on Staten Island and they didn't get down into Manhattan to do their shopping before they came home.

I think my feelings were just; wondering what had happened to the kids, selfishly, I suppose but what else would you do? I mean if the kids hadn't been over there; well yeah, it was a shock anyway just to see it unfold, but there was a part of me saying, Goodness, it's a city of millions of people for Heaven's sakes.

Lockerbie: the terrible accident!

What happened here was not against Lockerbie; nobody set out to destroy the town of Lockerbie; we just happened to be collateral I suppose in some way; it wasn't meant to happen here obviously; the plane was meant to come down in the Atlantic somewhere. So we can't actually say that somebody; somebody sat down and said, "We'll destroy this small town", and I think it was all very unfortunate because, if you look at a map of the south of Scotland and the route this plane was taking, it was like hitting an oasis in the desert really, when you see so much land round about that isn't inhabited.

Positive gains for Lockerbie

There's certainly been, as far as the town's concerned, the links with Syracuse, the university that had thirty five students on that flight; there's been a big link between Lockerbie and that, and I became involved in that through the council and choosing two students every year to go to Syracuse, and so I had twelve years of that which was very pleasurable I have to say, to watch their faces when I had to go and tell them that they were the ones that had been chosen; so I'm very pleased that out of something awful that has; that has grown and flourished and I hope that continues for a long time; and we still have Syracuse students who have a campus in London who come up, usually have a bus tour, and take them round and I enjoy doing that a well. We took them round and up to Tundergarth, showed them the sights. So that's, that's been a positive benefit to the town; I think, the link with the school; I think; I think; population's a movable feast here, its fairly fluid and I think, you know, you know the students for the Syracuse scholarship, you could see as the years went on; I mean last year; the last year I interviewed, they couldn't even tell me how many people died; and why should they; well maybe they should if they were going for that scholarship, perhaps they should have put some thought in it; but why should any kid in that town, really, have to remember that because, I mean there isn't anybody in the school now who was born when that happened. So you know, you've got to weigh it up; it's part of the history of the town; but; it's fading. Definitely fading; there's more to Lockerbie than the disaster - a lot more

Decision-making about the commemorations in December: Marjory is realistic about expectations of the town and beyond.

Having attended the first meeting about the twentieth anniversary I was delighted; round the table, low-key came from everybody around that table; the churches, the Queen's council, and I sincerely hope that's that's what it is; I'm a bit disconcerted to see Alex Salmond say he would like to be invited to

Lockerbie [pause] ; on the twenty first; maybe he felt that would be the right thing to say when he was *in* Lockerbie – he was opening the EON wood burning place; and he said he would—he hadn't received an invitation, and my heart kind of sank because I didn't think it would be; would be that kinda day; where people would be invited for what? And I sincerely hope, and my own personal view is, that it doesn't happen; it's just a day the churches - I believe it's a Sunday - so the churches would have their own service, there may be an ecumenical service; *fine!* but the thought of a streetful of cameras! Its not what the people of Lockerbie want; well the ones that have spoken to *me* anyway and the ones that have asked; it's not what they want

JH: And; who drives; who'd driving what's happens on that day?

MM: Well it seems to be the committee that we're sitting on, but if people like Alex Salmond are starting to say, "Where's my invitation?"', I think we've got to send back the word, invitation to what? You know? I mean I'm sure in a way he didn't mean anything by it: he was just showing interest in the place he was at: I'm sure it wouldn't break his heart if he didn't get an invitation to something [laughs] . The thought of, you know, the first minister comes; the prime minister comes, you know? Who comes? [pause] So, it's very difficult; Well it's the organisation: who wants to organise that? And then the bickering starts, Well, why was he invited and she wasn't: I don't think we need that; I really don't think we need—and I hope it doesn't happen; I hope we don't follow that route; but the next meeting of this committee will be later on in April so, we'll see what they say. Bit disappointed in the community council too, asking people what they want. But, fair enough, if they want to organise it; but I'm sure they won't.

I would imagine what Lockerbie would like, being a resident and having asked around is absolutely *nothing* to happen, but we know that can't happen; but hopefully in the twentieth anniversary, there'll be a few cameras here and this is Lockerbie twenty years on, bla bla, but the last thing I want to see is the razzamatazz, you know [pause] all singing, all dancing. They were talking about open air services and things like that. Well, that's fine, that's all great but they all have to be organised [pause] you know, and who's going to do that?

Marjory believes the façade of Lockerbie is not equivalent to the fabric of the underlying community: sharing economic expenditure in the region.

I think there's a lot going for Lockerbie; I do know that; that there are buildings in the town that could do with tarting up, but I mean there's the big co-op building close to me: well, there's that's planning permission now; that's going to be a retail store . What I don't know but at least somebody's going to *use* it and I know; I know another big building up in Townhead Street which *is* an eyesore but someone has bought *that*: but there are buildings in town that I know belong to various families and the council have absolutely no jurisdiction over how *they* look. You can't *force* somebody to paint their windows or put glass in the windows if they don't want to so; you know, the council get a lot of slating but there's not a lot they can do about some of these places and if nobody wants to buy them—but I don't see anything different from Lockerbie than an small town I go to. They've *all* got their good and bad sides; but invariably I think the people who live here are fairly *happy*; about living in this area, than throwing amenities at something and expecting that to improve

I wouldn't imagine; and I may be terribly wrong; but I wouldn't imagine that this wouldn't be the sort of place where somebody would die and nobody would noticed. You know, you hear horrible things about a body has lain for so long; I would hope that's not the type of place Lockerbie is.

No, we have our Tesco [Marjory chuckles] now - I was on the Chair of Planning for that [chuckles again] - but I for one think it's been an advantage to the town, because if Tesco wasn't in Lockerbie—there's Tescos in Dumfries; and I used to go to Dumfries; I used to shop in Tescos in Dumfries, but you couldn't get shopping because you were meeting people from Lockerbie; who were spending their money over *there*. So its as well to keep money in Lockerbie; the jobs in Lockerbie; and I have to say that the other supermarket that everybody said would be closed in a fortnight; nearly a year *on,* it's still *there.*

And certainly I remember seeing; when I was on the council planning, seeing all these fast food—Goodness, does nobody ever *cook* in Lockerbie? Size of the town. We rejoiced when the Chinese restaurant opened, the Chinese takeaway opened; but, at one time, we had a Chinese takeaway, we'd two Indian takeaways, we have a kebab shop and, I'm trying to think what else? Two fish and chip shops, you know, suddenly [laughs] I think people have less time. "Specially, I would say, the twenty, thirty, fourty year olds. They're too busy, you know, both partners having to work. That's the way life is; if you've got a mortgage; very rare you can get one person to pay the mortgage; so there isn't the *time* that the likes of my mother would have. You know, I remember as a wee girl going with my mother shopping; stand for an hour in the street, you know. Just about fainting [Marjory chuckles] , chatting to people; I don't think that happens. I used to laugh when I was a councillor; I couldn't buy a loaf of bread without somebody saying your name; poking you in the sternum [laughs]; and certainly, since I've retired, I have a little bit more time to stand and have a chat; I almost got out of my way doing it be cause I was always focused on getting what I needed and going home and getting out again somewhere else.

No but I think the pace of life is certainly faster, and, yeah, I mean, you zip too the supermarket with your car, you load it up with goods and you zip back again. I think walking about the streets; oh there's certainly a certain amount but not as much as there used to be. Some of the afternoons here especially; I find Tuesdays and Wednesdays, by two, three o'clock in the afternoon, there's hardly anybody on the street.

Bad experiences of a Scottish airport terminal

> We *do* mind queuing at security [Jill laughs] especially *Glasgow Airport*! [Jill laughs] ; which is just *so* bad. It's got worse but even *before* the incident, they were just so bad.
>
> We're trying to avoid Glasgow Airport now! [both laugh] We're going away in May, we're going away from Manchester. They don't seem to be as bad as Glasgow Airport

JH: Well that's interesting that it's not standardised

MM: No; we find Manchester; we quite like Newcastle as well but we couldn't get the flights we wanted. It just seems to be Glasgow Airport.

Marjory is very content with life in Lockerbie

> Wouldn't even consider leaving this spot to be honest cos, although we are in the middle of town, when you're at the back of the house you could be anywhere; we're not overlooked at all and yet it's so handy; you can have a pint of milk back in the house in thirty seconds almost -if you run! [Marjory laughs]

The legacy of the Lockerbie trust

> Anything Lockerbie does they have to do for themselves: we don't even have tennis courts here.

JH: No I saw they'd been pulled down, why did they disappear?

MM: Lack of interest, lack of money. We never seem to get the investment we deserve here. Goes elsewhere. That's from a local government perspective as well; fought long and hard for things for Lockerbie. And it seemed to be a long hard fight.

> I kinda think that that was part of it; there's so much money washed about in Lockerbie; and maybe so, maybe they could have had their swimming pool, but there were other things to do at the *time* as well. I think it was given away to people who needed it.
>
> I mean I sat in the Lockerbie Trust for twelve years as well and they were always applications in for things, and we tried to be fair and give it to help— Pump priming really, you know, to get things up and running then they get on with it themselves.
>
> Helping the ice rink; I mean they opened that Ice Bowl in Dumfries and that should have been the death throes for Lockerbie, but I was determined that when I was a councillor here it would not: we'd try and support them as well. It's great; it's *fantastic* what Lockerbie's done; and I don't think they get the recognition that they deserve.

The Eon Power Station, a couple of miles north of Lockerbie. It uses willow as a renewable resource to power the facility and was opened in early 2008.
©James Haldane
The boarded-up building of the old Cooperative supermarket chain. This property sits at the main intersection in the township, leading West, South and North.

Jimmy the horse, pulling the Gala Queen's float, mid 1950s. (© Helen Fraser 2008)

Helen and her two children, Neil and Helen, in the garden of their Lockerbie home, Mossbank, in the early 1980s. (© Helen Fraser 2008)

Helen Fraser, April 1, 2008

Distant Memories — Long-Range Projections on Guilt and Fear

This female narrator has the status of being one of two participants who no longer live in Lockerbie. She has been an ex-citizen for almost 20 years now, and regards herself as in exile from her hometown. The family on her father's side has a long-established name in Lockerbie - Scott - and family members still occupy the familial home in Lockerbie, the façade of which dates back to 1783. She also lived for a time in the small hamlet of Corrie, before moving back to the township in the late seventies.

The narrator has been involved with the community through the Gala celebrations and with the schools in the area, as a teacher. She still maintains close links with family and friends in Lockerbie. She gets The Annandale Herald sent by post every week to her home in Aberdeen shire.

She was severely affected by the disaster: her house, on Sherwood Park, was at the entrance to Sherwood Crescent which was the site of the crater area, and she and her family had to endure the trauma of the experience from a distance. Her narrative of the disaster evening is unique in detail but common in happenstance

She is a friend of my parents and mixed socially with them during her married years in Lockerbie. I also knew her, when growing up, as the aunt of my best friend. Before doing the interview, I hadn't seen her for about 18 years, when she put me up for a few days while I looked for a flat in Aberdeen. Prior to that visit, I recall that she sent me a letter of support as I struggled with decisions about college courses in 1986.

I approached her to participate in the project primarily because she lived away from the town and would provide an important perspective to compare with mine, as the other non-residential participant. I figured she would be willing to openly recount her experiences and we could have talked for more hours than we did, that day in late March.

The circumstances surrounding the interview formed a pleasant trip away from Lockerbie for me and my parents. We drove North on the motorway, getting lost briefly on the contraflow on the outskirts of Glasgow — well, it wouldn't it have been a trip otherwise. The drive to Aberdeen takes 4 hours, travelling to Perth – home to the historic Scone Palace which housed the Stone of Scone until 2000, when it was removed and vaulted with the Scottish Honours on the Castle Rock in Edinburgh.. We by-passed Stirling, with its mighty fortress and The Wallace Monument in the background. Dundee's northern by-pass was decorated with a stunning display of daffodils nestled sweetly in the shadow of one of the enormous giant Tescos stores that I had heard about.

The narrator lives about 40 miles in land from Aberdeen, on the tip of the north east coast. Some of the sand-blasted granite buildings were glinting in the watery sunshine as we drove through the northern-most city on the mainland

We greeted the narrator, after missing her lane end and driving past, and rendezvoused at the village castle, a sturdy construction of 800 years standing, lunching in the café at the castle and catching up on Lockerbie chat. It was my parents' wedding anniversary too so there was a wee air of quiet celebration

The narrator has a lovely old house with an extensive garden. Her daughter was home that day, in the other room, nursing a cold. We made ourselves comfortable in the kitchen parlour area – she is a soft furnishing designer and the walls were lined with books, movies and photographs - while the dogs snuggled on the ample sofas and the cat took up residence on my knee. It was a typical Scottish day outside, damp and grey. We spoke for three hours, until my parents arrived and the interview ceased. She replied by letter to my missing questions.

There was a lot of laughter and sadness during the interview but we came out 'balanced' at the end. I was impressed with the detail of the narrator's memory in comparison to my own and, as an ex-citizen, I found her to be generally more reminiscent about the disaster than the resident citizens.

I found an affinity with Helen's narrative post-disaster that I didn't share with the Lockerbie residents. She, like I, had deconstructed her feelings that she shared with her two children on a scale that was not made apparent in most of the other participants. She pulled them apart and examined them closely, to ascertain the constituent parts. I am interested to know if this practice is as a result of spatial distance from the physicalities and personalities of the common disaster experience. Without exposure to verbal and actual repetition of events, agents spatially removed should perform this procedure in their head, with a deconstruction of remembrance and a relative temporal skewing of actual perceived memories as they feature daily in the conscious thought of the agent.

Her name in Helen Fraser and she lives in the village of Fyvie, near Aberdeen. She had just turned sixty a couple of days before the interview.

I hope she gets her wish, to go back to live in Lockerbie again one day but, like most true exiles, the desire to return is equalled by the awareness that the return in real terms would not fulfil their nostalgic expectations.

One can never go back. If I did go back home as it were, it would certainly not be with any idea that it would be as it was. I never wanted to leave Lockerbie, but having had to, I don't think I could return on a whim. The reason would have to be compelling. To be nearer Neil and Geraldine, Christeen, Eilidh, for example, because I could no longer afford or was not able to continue at Fyvie. Going back would underline all those who are no longer alive there who were friends.

Helen shares details about her Mother and Father

HF: [laughs] Well, I was born in Lockerbie, in 27 Main Street Lockerbie. I was born at home. My mother was originally from the Highlands, she was from near Inverness, and she was teaching in Dumfriesshire when she met my father; and my father was born and bred in Lockerbie, and his family had a coal agents and contractor business in the town; he had local connections yes, I mean it was, he was an old old Lockerbie family, and you know, his father's father; I'm not sure if its father's father - his father I think was brought up by his uncle - but that was in Main Street you know, in the 1850s or 1840s; so they had been there quite a long time.

So I was born in the same house that my father was born in, and my sister now lives in it: its still in the family; so and I grew up in Lockerbie; went to school at Lockerbie primary school Lockerbie Academy, and left when I was 19 to go to college in Glasgow.

JH: And did your mother ever return back to the highlands for visits or see family

HF: She went home ever summer for about a month or two, to stay with her mum and dad, and she would take Christeen and I with her; and then, when Christeen was older - cause Christeen is 8 years older than I am - when Christeen was working, it was just mother and I that would go. I hated it of course, because I would have no ponies, but looking back on it, of course I wish I had appreciated it more cause it was a lovely, lovely wee village, and it was lovely; now its just ruined cause its all built up and horrible. Its not far from Culloden Moor.

JH: Oh very remote.

HF: It was, it was—my mother used to cycle to school in Inverness: she cycled 7 miles to the station at Culloden Moor and then got the train into Inverness every morning, and then did the same coming home *every night*

JH: Yes the things you do. And your mother was a great sewer wasn't she?

HF: She did sewing yep, mhm.

JH: Yes, so did you get most of your clothes growing up stitched by your mother?

HF: Oh aye, she made them and knitted things and made things, cause there wasn't any money to buy stuff; and I suppose, if you had plenty of money, you could buy stuff, but there wasn't nearly so much affordable clothing around then; probably partly because people did sew, it was more affordable to sew things; so oh yes aye, everything was homemade, everything; I mean if you went to wedding, my mother would make the clothes; you know she would make—she made my sister outfits to go to weddings, she made me things to go to weddings, she made her own things to go to weddings; so really, the only thing that you would probably buy would maybe be shoes and a hat; and that was it, she made everything

Primary School memories

The sandstone building that Helen attended in first year was originally built in 1875, for primary and secondary students. A new secondary school was built in 1961-63, to house the baby boomer generation. This is the building I attended as a primary. A new composite level school is currently under construction in 2008.

HF: Um the old sandstone building at the fork in the road was the secondary school; my sister went to it. The primary school that I went to was behind that building, and where the new school that I went to as a secondary was, which has now been rebuilt again, there was a building there that was the primary school building; and, I went to that, but it wasn't big enough, because we went to four classes in it I think: primaries 1, 2, 3, and 4. Primary 5 we were taken by bus to Lochmaben school because there wasn't enough room at Lockerbie. For a year; There was two classes, maybe it was classes 4 and 5, that went every day by bus to Lochmaben and then came back for lunch and went back in the afternoon. One of the years at primary school, we went to the English church hall, which was behind the English church on Ashgrove.

Well there was a hall behind the English church, I don't think its there anymore; but we had a year of classes in there as well; and looking back, it was probably just before they started building the new school I think but—and then they built the art block for the new school the one they built in the sixties, and it was three classrooms and we moved from Lochmaben, I think, into these three classrooms on the art block and we were in there, still in primary school, but we were in those classes until I finished primary; and by that time they were building the two sort of tower blocks, you know the four story high buildings, and I started off in first year of secondary education in the old sandstone building.

Helen shares some anecdotes about the conditions and the characters of her schooldays. Were they happy?

I think so; I don't remember an awful lot about it, but I think it was happy enough; there were one or two teachers were horrible, I mean nowadays they would be locked up you know, but you didn't expect anything else; I mean the toilets were all outside; and when we were in the English church hall, we were frozen because there was a fire and that was it - if you weren't near the fire you were frozen - but nobody thought much about it, there was no fuss; most people lived in houses without heating; you know just a coal fire in the living room so it wasn't a big deal. So yes, I think it was quite happy: as I say, primary one was Miss Mackay was very very nice; Miss Oliver, Hazel Oliver, she was my primary two teacher and [...] Miss Oliver; Mrs Robertson was primary three; Primary four was a horrible woman, she really was obnoxious [...]

Anyway; yes, so primary school was—very nice teacher in primary five; primary six was Miss? Mrs? Oh I've forgotten her name, she was awful; she was a drunk; and, we didn't know it, but you could smell it; and I always remember, one morning, she didn't turn up and then she came into school late and her hair was matted with blood, because she had got drunk and fallen over and knocked herself out, and when she came to, she came into to teach with this hair matted with blood

She was the, she was the—that was her last year of teaching cause she retired at the end of that; she wasn't sacked; she retired. And she taught Christeen, my sister, before me, and she was horrible to her, so she was a horrible woman; a really horrible woman. And primary seven was very nice, *very* nice woman

Free-time for Helen meant outside

      Probably [pause] outside with the horses; you know, that sort of thing; didn't do very much to help my mother. No, don't remember doing that at all; I do remember *friends* who helped their mothers, but *I didn't*; my mother was very laid back, she never made anybody do anything

JH: Aye is that right; you didn't have to cook a meal; you didn't have to help with the cooking?

HF: Oh no, oh no!

JH: No? Oh that's nice

HF: No, no no no; never did any of that [laughter] It's not really; when you get older it isn't nice; I wasn't a housey person at all.

Helen recounts birthday memories

Gwenda is Helen's schooldays friend. Gwenda, whose Father managed the shop that my Father subsequently bought and ran as a grocery business, is a good friend of my family

      Gwenda and I had been—we'd had a birthday party, and we'd gone to the shop and we'd bought, which was very new then, a sponge, a frozen sponge cake with real cream in the middle, and we'd bought that from her dad, it was half a crown, two and six pence, and we went back to my house, Gwenda and I, and we had that for my birthday tea; we weren't having a party or any, but Gwenda and I had that for my birthday tea.

Christeen is Helen's elder sister

      For instance a birthday treat would be go to Dumfries to and maybe get a new frock or something, and then we would go to the pictures, with you know Christeen, and my mother would go to the pictures; that was, that was Dumfries.

The shops in Lockerbie had changed in the generation between Helen and her Father. Helen's favourite shop was the saddlers.

      Aye and the strange thing that I had as well, which isn't what everyone else had, was that my father knew these shops by different names, because they were different from when he was young; so he would talk about a certain shop, and I would say, "Where's that?" you know, and he would say, "Sich and sich a shop"; but you know, it was the name that he'd known it as when he was young, you know, and then, well I remember the saddlers shop, which is kind of where Alistair Moffat's music shop is: I don't know if it's still there, next to the Blue Bell? Well, that was the saddlers, and they had a horse in the window: the whole of the window was this grey dappled grey horse, and—

JH: Not a real one obviously?

HF: No, it must have been a stuffed one there or something, aye, cause it was a real—I'm sure it looked—sure it was real horse.

      Oh aye, it was a real horse: it was big! It would be the height, you know—it would have been about 15 hands high; and it was in the window, grey- dapple: maybe it was made out of wood I don't know; but it was in the window all the time.

    I don't know how well it would have been patronised, but ah , I mean he sold harnesses and he sold grooming stuff, you know dandy brushes, curry combs, body brushes, hoof picks, combs, you know its all that kinds; so I used to go, save up pennies take the bottles back, take the empties back, get the pennies and go and buy a dandy brush and riding gloves that sort of thing

JH: Is that right? And where there any shops that your father—whose names hadn't changed, that were the still the original owners from your father's time?

HF: Well the saddlers would have been I think, and there was one up in Townhead Street, which was—oh what was the name of it, now? See, I've forgotten, but I think it was—not an opticians, but a kind of place that you could get your specs fixed: it was an opticians; what was the name of that place? Ah see, I can't remember; I think it would have been the same; what other shops?

JH: I mean, my dads shop: was that, was that McMichaels or something?

HF: Aye that was my mothers—my father's sister's husband. He was my uncle; although it was his brother, John McMichael that lived in your house and managed that shop, kind of.

Travelling out of Lockerbie was a rare treat

    Dumfries or Carlisle; Carlisle was kinda special: Well you had to go that wee bit further; It was a foreign country. [Helen laughs] International, international shopping.[Jill and Helen laugh] We didn't go to Carlisle very often, but going to Carlisle was quite a treat; my father used to take us to Carlisle for a run on a Sunday, cause all the shops were shut; [Jill and Helen laugh] we used to get to walk up deserted streets and look in shop windows and he was quite secure in the knowledge that no body would be able to spend anything, cause the shops were all shut. But for shopping, you know for a day out, for instance a birthday treat would be go to Dumfries to and maybe get a new frock or something, and then we would go to the pictures, with you know Christeen, and my mother would go to the pictures, that was that that was Dumfries

JH: And was there a picture house in Lockerbie operating then?

HF: There was, yeah, the Rex cinema; it was there as long as I can remember; it was very cold if my father hadn't delivered the coke; which was quite often [Helen laughs]

*The Rex Cinema is one the blots on the landscape in present–day Lockerbie. Built in 1933 by the Lockerbie Cinema Company, it stands behind the Town Hall. It was converted to accommodate the popularity of bingo in the 1960s. We used to call it 'the pictures'. It has had a salubrious history, playing host to opening nights and concerts. Fulton McKay, the irascible Prison Officer from the hit BBC series, Porridge, attended the opening night in Lockerbie, of the movie, Local Hero in 1983. **A Night Out** concert, to fundraise for the Gala and cheer* *up the town, was held on 21 March 1989 and featured rock artists Fish from the band, Marillion, as well as a line-up of Celtic rock and ballad bands, including the Battlefield Band, Dougie Maclean, Capercaillie, and Carlos Arredondo. The cinema welcomed 525 members of the community when the Memorial Service of 4 January 1989 was broadcast on a large screen monitor with sound relay. It was a focal point of the community for decades and it sadly now boarded up after operating unsuccessfully as an Indian restaurant.*

An anecdote about her Father and the ponies

The family and that were very involved; and in those days - I think it wasn't very long after the war, in 1953, when they had the first—it wasn't really a gala, it was a celebration of the coronation but it *became* the gala the following year; and looking back, it was only eight years after the war had finished; and, so there was a great deal of effort that went into making the gala- the celebration of the coronation; I remember that: I mean I wasn't very old, but I *do* remember it: My mother spent *hours* and hours and hours decorating the—we had a wee gig - not a gig - it was a governors cart; sort of square wee cart, and you opened the door in the back and you stepped down, and there were seats down each side; we had a pony who was trained to pull: he was a harness pony: he was trained for pulling, you know, carts and things; and—she did, she got wire, very heavy wire put over this thing to make it look like a crown, and she decorated it cause in those days, you didn't get anything like that you had to make it, and it was all crepe paper wrapped round and flowers made out—and this crown and this was to go in the fancy dress parade you see; and Major, the pony, who was the harness pony who was to be pulling this was quite flighty and [laugh] my father was leading him up the street, to go in the parade, to go in to the judging for the fancy dress, and father suddenly decided he needed to go to the toilet, so he gave the reins to some man, I don't know who it was, and said "Haud on tae the horse for me, I'm just goin' to the toilet", so, he crossed—there used to be public toilets just across from—well, kind of where the post office is now, and so he nipped across there, and something came past and terrified the pony, and he got such a fright and reared up backwards and sat on the shaft and broke it. [Helen laughs] And they were only 200 yards from home, you know. So that was it, he just had to take it home again.

JH: What did you mother say?

HF: She wasn't happy, she wasn't very happy at all. And that same year, the big Clydesdale cart horse, Jimmy, he was pulling a flat cart, you know one of the coal carts and they had a wee tree on it and they had the anvil on it and it was Robin Thompson Smiddyo. You know, it's a song, Robin Thompson Smiddyo; and Ackie was on; hammering the anvil. Yeah, I think I was a circus girl in the parade; I was on a pony.

JH: Is that right?

HF: It was wonderful.

On the Riding of the Marches and the Gala

There wasn't a riding that year; the *next* year they started it; and they had to put the riding of the marches; but Lockerbie wasn't an ancient common riding like, Langholm and Hawick, and all these other ones that had been actually being going since you know, Flodden Field or something you know: they had been going a long long time; Lockerbie was a kind of a copy really, of these; I mean the bits—there's bits in the riding were fairly accurate, you know, and some bits -the quarry and things like that, but the make up of it was a copy, really, of other ones, or so I understand it to be anyway.

They went around the boundaries of the borough, yes they did that, but there wasn't—it wasn't part of a hundreds years old tradition of riding round the boroughs boundaries as it was in Langholm; you know in Langholm, they'd ridden the borough boundaries for hundreds and hundreds of years, and Selkirk and Galashiels: they did that, and in Hawick; these places had a very old tradition of doing that, but Lockerbie didn't.

I mean one of the instructions was, when you got to the top of the Mains Hill and you were going along the top there, you had to stop and look south, to see if there was any incomers [Helen laughs] heading up frae Carlisle. Yeah, and I think they had to collect a stone from the quarry on the Hart Hill and they had to cut a sod on the golf course cause that was the old common ground for the market, the lamb sales were on that hill, where the golf course is now; so it was common ground: they'd to do these things on the ride round; but they must—I don't know where they got all the ideas for that; I don't think it was rooted in any local thing particularly; I think it might have been kind of copied from other places; but the, the, you know, the hill was definitely where the lamb sales were and that's why Lockerbie was there, because of the sales, cause it was a big *big* market at Lockerbie and they drove sheep from all over the country to it.

Major, the horse

I remember as a child, Major in the back garden of 27 Mains Street. . He is reputed to have enjoyed almost 45 years equine years.

My father got him; my father's father got him during the war. There was a couple came down who had relatives in Eaglesfield, and they came down from Coatbridge on holiday, mother father two wee kids, and again - petrol rationing - they hired a pony and trap in Airdrie and the pony and trap came down on the train to Lockerbie goods station, which is where the coal agents yards were. And this couple were going to use the pony and trap to get around when they were on holiday you see; and the pony was Major

My father—my grandfather saw him coming off the train at the goods station, and I mean he was a bonnie pony when he was younger he would have been wonderful; and he was very proud you see, and trotting; he was born as a trotting racer, actually, but he wouldn't trot in hobbles so he was no good for racing, but his father was the champ- the British champion racer

He was called the Ace of Spades, and he was the champion trotting race pony in Britain; that was Major's father, but Major wouldn't go in hobbles, so he couldn't race, and my grandfather saw him and that was it, he had to have him, so he got in touch with the couple, and negotiated with the guy in Airdrie and the bought them, he bought the pony and trap.

It would be during the war; forty-three maybe, and Major was six years old when they bought him, so [pause] trying to think [pause] how old that made him, but I mean we did count it up, and [pause] thirty [pause] two, thirty-eight. He died—well they had, I mean he was put to sleep eventually: it was when I was away, and I think we were away on a ship one winter, and I think that would be '80, '81. No I'm sure he was over forty, so maybe it was earlier than the war that they bought him, because I do remember once he got out in Lockerbie, and he wanted to go to the field, and we were trying to catch him and Howard phoned and said, "He's gone, you know, down past Mossbank, maybe, so look out for him", and here he was, of course, trotting down the road and there's two policemen after him, and Howard came round, and the young policeman had got hold of him and was holding him, and Howard said to the young policeman, "Be careful with that pony, he's older than you" [both laugh] and the policeman was looking at him as if he was crazy; Oh dear, but that was Major.

Helen remembers the joys of Latin at secondary school

Well I started out in 1A, class 1A, and because it was streaming in those days, there was A B C D E F G H, and 1A, you did Latin and French, 1B you just did French, and all the other subjects, 1C, you did what they called, you know short hand typing, commercial subjects. Oh no I'm wrong! In C, I think you did French as well, but maybe at a different rate, D was commercial subjects, and it was only girls; E was boys only, and it was woodwork, metal work; F was girls only, and it was sewing and cookery cause the boys didn't do it and the girls; and G was the absolute drongos. It was a mixed class, G, but the boys would go to metal and woodwork work, and the girls would go to sewing and cooking, so that's—so I started out in 1A and I didn't like it, so at the end of that year I changed to 1D, because I didn't want to do any languages; we started out—I don't think—Yes, we *did* do French, we did French and Latin that first year, I quite liked the Latin, but I didn't like the French; I didn't like the French teacher either.

But I liked Latin, I liked Latin, but you see my mother was—she was a Greek scholar, she would hit me for saying that, but she had a classics degree, her degree was in Greek and Latin so I think that probably made it a bit easier for me, because she knew if I was stuck on homework or something she could help me, and I don't supposed many folk would have had that help, and so that was easier for me, and although she had French, she had studied French at university, and she was good at French, but I didn't like French, and I didn't like the teacher, so I just hated French in fact, and he was a bit of a pain.

So I couldn't do Latin without French, so and I thought, ever looking for the easiest way, that I would just go into class D and do commercial subjects - short hand and tying and book keeping - so I had to repeat a year; I think I had to repeat first year or something; I can't just remember how old—maybe I did just first and second year: maybe did first and second year in class 1A and then I was—1A and 2A, and then I would have been going into 3A; that must have been it; and I repeated a year. It doesnae matter! No, I didn't, that's all wrong; I didn't like it, so I went into the class 2 D, and I did that 2 D and 3 D and then, you would have left at the end of third year then. And, as I was in third year and it was getting nearer to the end, I'm thinking, You're not going to have long summer holidays, you're going to have to get a job; Oh no, I don't think I like this very much, so I decided I would try and go back. By that time, of course, it was a fully comprehensive school, so I thought, Right I'll go back and see if I can get onto some O level courses. *That* was when I had to repeat a year.

Art versus Domestic Science – a choice regretted

I did think I would maybe like to be a sewing teacher; I don't know where that came from I quite fancied that I think; but I was quite good at Art, so my art teacher was keen for me to do art, and the headmaster was keen for me to do art, and they were sort of pushing me to do Art, and I had applied to Glasgow art school; but unbeknownst to them, I had applied to Dough* School in Glasgow; cause I thought it would be easier you see at Dough School, cause it was only three years for a teaching diploma at Dough School; but Art school was a four year diploma course and then you had another—really, if you wanted a job, you would have to do another year of teacher training, cause there weren't many jobs that involved Art outside of teaching, unless you were Monet or something, so, and that wasnae going to be happening; so I did, ever again taking the easier option; I thought five years on a grant, no I don't think so, three years, mm, so and of course in those days, you could get a job anywhere it was very easy to get a teaching job; so, it came to sending away applications and all that, and I was sent for by the headmaster, Willy Anderson; you know used to live next door to us; and he demanded to know why he had been sent a form for a reference from Glasgow Dough School, because he had no idea that I had applied to Dough School [Helen laugh] and I'm trying to explain to him without saying that I thought it would be easier [Helen laugh] Yes, but really, I thought that maybe I would go there; he said, "I thought you were going to art school? [Helen laugh] Oh dear! So, he said, "Well, I will write your report, but I can promise you a job today, if you go to art school." He said, "You can come back here to a job *in five years time*, you can have a job here in five years time." Yeah; they were desperately short of art teachers; but—So I didn't go to art school

JH: So did you kind of regret that then Helen?

HF: Well I did regret it sometimes, well I regretted it when I started Dough School
       for a start cause it was hellish, oh it was awful! It was awful; cause they treated
       like you were, oh, about 12? And they were *so* strict, really strict, and you weren't
       allowed to do this and you weren't allowed to do that; and—I mean, the way
       they taught me, I'm very glad of, because they taught me how to sew properly,
       and I know how to do it properly; that probably usually involves taking it out
       10 times, but I do know *how* to do it, and I'm glad of that, because you know,
       nobody can tell me that I don't know what I'm doing, because I do, but I hated
       every minute of it; and there was no artistic licence: you did that that way, you
       know there's just no—I suppose, in the course, there was just no room for any
       kind of *thought*, actually: you just did what you were told, and it was all practical
       work; and we did have one lecture a week on—I think broadly, it was English,
       but I mean, she was a very nice lady, and we discussed books and plays and films
       that were on at the time, which was good; and I *loved* that, and I so wished
       then that I had gone to university and done *English*, because I loved English
       and I loved writing, and I dunno why I never thought of doing that, you see;
       but then I was stuck in Dough School. I tried to get out, I tried to leave, at the
       end of first term: Oh no, I can't stay here, its horrible; so I wanted to leave and
       switch courses and go to university and do English, but you couldn't—they
       wouldn't let you leave in those days; I had an appointment with the principal,
       and I explained to her what I wanted to do, but she looked at me as if I was a
       piece of shit on her shoe, and she said, "Well that's all very well, Miss Scott,
       you can leave tomorrow; but you will repay you grant for last term"; so. I knew
       I couldn't repay my grant; I had no money, and nobody I knew had any money,
       so that was it, I just had to stay.

       Well, I resigned myself to it, it was just as awful as it had been I think;
       second year it was a better, because it was a wee bit more interesting; you know,
       we did tailoring in second year, and we did millinery, so that was much more
       interesting stuff, but it was still very much rote; there was no using your brain
       for anything; and there—we did art classes, but even they were very disciplined:
       there was no, no really much art about it; but then they were teaching people
       to sew, that was what there job was

       We were taught to draft patterns, so we were taught that if we sketched an
       outfit, we also had to know how to cut a pattern to make that outfit; so that was
       a design element if you like; or sometimes, we would be given a dress, a picture
       of a dress or a jacket or a coat or whatever, and we had to cut the pattern to
       make that, you know, so that was—it was design, but it wasn't really, because
       it was very practical.

       Third year was a bit more fun because we did two years and one term at
       Dough School, and then two terms at Jordan Hill Teacher Training college;
       so the third, the forth term if you like at Dough School, the first term of third
       year, was quite good fun, because we'd made stuff toys, and we made jointed

stuffed toys, and we did all sorts of craft work, which was quite good, and we did weaving, and we did, you know, interesting things like that, and we did a big you had to do a big embroidery panel, you know, and that was free design, so—

I started studying Hotel Catering and Management after sixth year, at an institution in Aberdeen, and I hated it, wanted to quit and start at Art College. Helen heard of this through the family and was supportive in sharing her experiences in a letter to me. I stayed on the course until the end of the first year and then went to Art College.

Moving away from Lockerbie for the first time

Oh I hated it! Oh God, I was terrified to put my nose out the door in case I got lost! Oh aye, huge change, and it felt as though it was a million miles away. Cause I had never really been to Glasgow, never been to any city, and I didn't know Glasgow; and it just was—it was scary, and I was in a hostel out in Anniesland Cross, which was—the college itself was on Park Drive, in Glasgow, which is just up from Gibson street, and I think now that the whole building is incorporated in Caledonian University, but I haven't been back to see, but I'm sure somebody told me that; I think that they knocked down the original building; so that was fairly central, you know not far out from Charing Cross, but we had a long way on the bus to Anniesland Cross which was way out on Great Western Road, so I was just terrified going in and out to begin with: I had to make sure I was attached to a group of people that were going, cause I didn't know what bus to get; and of course, you didn't know anybody when you went, you know; and we were none of us street wise, shall we say?

Aye aye, ever the adventurer; I never wanted to leave Lockerbie, *ever*, and all my friends did, all my friends couldn't *wait* to get away; oh they hated it and they didn't want to be there, but I never wanted to leave, *ever*, no. I would never have left if I had had my own choice.

[Written submission: I regard myself as a Lockardian – I was born and bred and spent 40 years of my life there, so it has the superiority of time in my Life, i.e. I haven't had time, yet, to live anywhere else on long.]

Life at sea

Helen married a merchant navy officer from Castlemilk, Lockerbie and accompanied him on sea voyages.

I could travel with him at sea as long as we paid my airfare; so it really had to be a northern Europe port you know, for us to be able to afford that; and so when I went away with him after we got married in January, we joined his ship in Rotterdam and we had to fly to Rotterdam from London, and we took the sleeper to London, I had never been in a sleeper; and we had to get to the airport, and in those days it was still B E A and B O A C so we flew B E A from London to Rotterdam, and it cost 8 pounds. [Both laugh]

248

Oh, dear, and joined a ship there and we were away for five months, aye, about five months or six months usually; not just, I mean you were going into ports, but we would be away from home for five or six months, it would be a five or six month tour of duty put it that way. They did what they called four on two off, so if you were away four months you got two months leave, if you were away five months, you got two and half months leave, six months three months, you know, so that was what it kinda worked out at.

I enjoyed that you see; cause it meant I didn't have to leave Lockerbie; but um yes we went; and I loved ships, I always wanted to be on ships, just loved ships and the sea and the whole idea of being on a house that floats; it was a wonderful idea; didn't like it when it was rough. But no, I quite liked being at sea; it, it was a bit boring.

I mean the cabin would be maybe this size, maybe slightly bigger, and there would be a bunk sort of built in, a double bunk, in a corner and there would be like a built in sofa and a desk and a chair and then off that, there would be a private, you know—your own shower and loo and sink and that sort of thing; that was the third mates quarters; that was what we had when I joined: when I married him, he was third mate; and then second mate was much the same, and then mates, chief officers quarters; you would have a bedroom and a bathroom, well not a bathroom, a shower room, toilet, and also a sitting room; and an office; and then a masters accommodation would be similar to that but bigger; it was fine, it was all you needed; and then for social functions, there would be the saloon, the bar, and saloon, which was just like a bar in a hotel with tables and chairs around it, sofas, and the officers mess, which was just a dining room with long tables really.

Neil—when we married he was with P&O, so there was always a choice, there was European food and a curry, cause the old P&O hands liked curry; the Domestic staff, if you like, on the P&O ships were all Indian. The stewards were all Goanese Indian, and the cooks, I'm not sure if they were Goanese or some other part of Indian; but they might have all been Goanese when I think about it; so the like the chief steward and all the stewards who cleaned the cabins, and people who served at table, and the people who cooked, they were all Indian, and I think probably the greasers in the engine room and things, although they might not have been Indian, but they would have been some other race which—that's how it was in those days, you know: the Brits, they didn't do the inferior jobs, although you know, the junior cadets and the lower officers did quite a lot of nasty work, but there was other, you know—and it wasn't actually because they were regarded racially, although a lot of men in the merchant navy were racist - a lot of people were racist in those days - but it was because they were cheaper labour, that's why they used them, which is kind of a form of racism, but they would be cheap, so that's why they would be used.

Cockroaches and oranges constitute memorable occasions at ports of the world.

Oh gee, favourite place we visited? There's a lot of place, most places that I was very thankful I hadn't spend money to. Just about everywhere we went [laugh] if you go on in a ship, you see, you usually go in on the nasty bit, like you know you go in on a railway to somewhere, you always go through the horrible bits, its kinda like that with ships, the docks are never the nicest part of the country, you know; and I remember we were in West Africa, Dakar, Senegal, or was it the Ivory Coast, doesn't matter cause they are next to one another, and we were going ashore for a meal, cause it was such a treat to get ashore for a meal, and the dockside were moving, it seemed to be moving, and it was cockroaches, it was just masses with cockroaches.

You had to walk through them aye, oh they scuttled away when you walked, oh aye; and then we went and we went for a meal, it was beautiful place, it was a pier, a jetty that was built right out into the ocean, and that was the restaurant, you know, and you sat out on the jetty in the water. It was lovely, very nice; it was beautiful place but then we had to plough through the cockroaches when you got back.

[Another time] Neil was up in the Baltic somewhere, and by that time he was on fruit boats, refrigerated cargo ships, and we joined him in—we flew to Hamburg? It doesn't really matter, but we flew somewhere in Germany and we joined the ship and went up to the Baltic to Reiga, and, was it Lithuania - its one of the Baltic states anyway - and it was February and it was really icy, you know it was iced; it's a great big bay Reiga, huge bay, and we got in, and there was about 20 ships at anchor waiting to get in to the port, the port wasn't handling very many ships; it was all, it was all Eastern Bloc, you know, it was under control of Russia, nothing worked particularly well; and we were in a queue to get in, and I remember all the freshwater tanks froze up, and we had no water, and I remember the sailors chipping out big blocks of ice and putting them in the sinks [Helen laugh] to melt, so that we could get, and I had two babies, in nappies, and it was—I can't remember how I managed, but I did; because I mean you couldn't take disposable nappies I mean they were only kind of new then anyway, but you couldn't take them, cause you couldn't take enough nappies to last five months or whatever; I mean we were only going for a week, but even at that, you couldn't *carry* enough; so, Oh gee, and it was cold, it was very cold, very icy; never got above minus six or seven through the day. Oh it was warm in the ship, but it was cold outside; so we were there at anchor for quite a long time. That must have been a different trip! That couldn't have been the first one we did with the, with the children! I mean the children were very *small*, but we were in the ice, waiting to get alongside for a long time, maybe a week or so; and the current used to carry the ship up, and you would hear the grinding as the anchor trailed up, and then they just let it drift you see until it got so far up the bay and then they would just pull up the anchor and put on the engines and sail back Down and drop the anchor again, you know, cause there wasn't any problem with drifting; but the *noise* when they started sailing back down, because you were actually going through ice, you know along the side of the ship I mean, the ships going North to Leningrad and things, after a certain time, they couldn't, that that would be frozen in; they wouldn't be able to go up there, no, they couldn't get up there: and I could understand why, cause it did freeze; we were there quite a while, maybe a week or two at anchor there; and then we, they took us alongside for fresh water, because as I say the water had all frozen up; so they took us alongside, we were only hours getting the fresh water tanks filled, and I took the chance to take the kids for a walk along the jetty, you know, the dockside, and there was a ship behind us, and there was a forklift truck helping with the discharge.

There was a train, there was a railway line, so a train came in there and they were just discharging this cargo from the ship straight into the train, and wee Neil, you know, wee boy, thought forklift truck, you know, he'd stand and watch it for about 15 hours, you know, "forklift truck mummy", "yes", "Oh forklift truck", so we're standing watching this, and the driver, quite a young chap, and he stopped eventually and he spoke to wee Neil, you see, and I was amazed, I mean this guy, in Lithuania, Latvia or whatever the hell it was spoke perfect English, and we could no more of spoken his language than fly in the air [laugh] and he said, you know, "Where are you from?", and we said, we were from Scotland, and he wasn't just too sure about Scotland, but you UK yes, you know we were on this ship, Oh yes, yes, yes, and we spoke for a time, and he told me that they were discharging oranges from this ship, and he said, "We haven't seen fresh fruit here in Reiga for 18 months", and he says, "All this, all these oranges are going into the train for Moscow"; and we chatted for quite a while - he was a really nice you man - and then we were going to turn around and go back, and he took a bag out of is cab, you know, and he sort of stuck it in the buggy with Helen, covered up, and he said, "For the children, for the children, Don't say anything", and I though, Oh, you know, and so I went back to the ship, and it was a bag with three oranges in it. And he had obviously stolen them for his wee boy, I think he had two wee kids, and I thought, "How kind!", you know; and the fact that we were on a ship with seven thousand boxes of oranges [Helen laughs] we were sick to death of oranges, but I mean, it was *so* kind! That was really kind, I've never forgotten that.

The day of the 21st December 1988

Neil was Aberdeen, and we were in Lockerbie, and Neil was coming home for Christmas; he would have been coming home on the Friday, I think of the week of the disaster, so yes. So when it happened, of course, he just heard of it on the television; he didn't know what had happened. Yes, he was still in Aberdeen; and I was teaching at Kirkpatrick Fleming School, and the school had just finished on the, the Tuesday. And the Wednesday was the first day of the holiday, it was the first day of the school holidays.

I mean, the day, we didn't get up very early, it was school holidays: I had to go and sign on, because I was a temporary teacher, so I didn't get paid in the holidays, so I signed on for the two weeks, and that was always such a performance, we had to go to Annan to sign on. And I did that, and then we went up to Dumfries to collect some Christmas presents and things, and then we drove back to Lockerbie and plittered about. I think we put the tree up, did the decorations, that sort of thing you know.

It hadn't been thundery weather so why the rumbling?

So it was while I was in the bath that I heard the noise, just like thunder, it sounded like thunder, and I was lying back, kind of relaxing in the bath, with this long rumbling noise, and I remember thinking, I didn't think it was a thundery day, you know, it wasn't like thundery weather, it had been dour and it was kinda windy and miserable, but it wasn't thundery. I was just, you know, thinking about that, [Helen chuckles] and then I remember thinking, I better go in next door to see Mrs Mac, because she was terrified of thunder and lightning, *really* terrified, so I thought, Right I'll get out of the bath, I'll get dressed and we'll pop in to see if she's ok.

And then the next thing was this—but I don't remember an explosion. I don't remember *hearing* an explosion, just the, the, the noise, the noise didn't seem to get louder, but there seemed to be, you could *feel* it, rather than *hear* it, and it looked to be as if the house was moving, that was the kind of thing. I thought, What the hell's going on? And then— I'm still in the bath, I thought, maybe I better get out of the bath [both laugh] ; so I'm just getting out of the bath when, I mean the curtains were shut in the bathroom, but there was this *blinding* light came, you know, right round about the edges of the curtains, a *brilliant* light, and I thought, Oh my god, and I thought, It's either a petrol tanker on the dual carriage way, or maybe its Chapelcross, cause I couldn't think of anything that would be big enough, and, I just ran into the bedroom and pulled on whatever I could find, you know, and ah, I was, no—I ran down stairs with the bath towel. What was it? I didn't go—I ran down stairs, and as I was going down the stairs the two windows on the stairs, which were frosted glass but no curtains on, they just, it was white light, *white light*, and I thought *then* it was *definitely* that Chapelcross had blown up.

And the kids came running, "Mummy mummy what is it, what is it?", and I just grabbed them and I sat in a chair in the corner of the hall and we're sitting like this, and waited for—well I suppose we're just waiting to die or something, cause you didn't know did you, what was going on; and said the Lords Prayer, and I couldn't remember it, and in the middle I was getting all muddled up, but wee Neil, he finished it [Jill laughs] ; and we got to the end of the Lords Prayer, and we still weren't dead, and we hadn't been blown to bits and nothing had fallen down, and we thought, Oh right so, and I said, stupidly, "Go and see if it says on the television what's happened" [both laugh] , and we went into the sitting room, and the Christmas tree was, the lights were all on, and the curtains were shut, and it looked lovely, and we switched the television on,

Terry Wogan was just starting his talk show, and he did, he never mentioned it [both laugh] , never mentioned it, and I opened the curtains in the big bay window, and it was like something from Dante's Inferno outside, there was all over the lawn, there was fires; big fires, wee fires. What the hell has happened? And *then* I ran upstairs to put on some clothes, and went into the bedroom which was immediately above that room and it had a bay window and I opened the curtains there, and then I could see nothing but fires all over, the streets, the gardens: big fires, wee fires, and it really looked like the end of the world.

I couldn't think what the hell had happened, and then I looked out the window at the *side* of the house, towards the Andersons' house, and I could see the black outline of the Andersons' house, and beyond it I could see nothing but a wall of flame as high as I could see, and that of course was where the crater was, but I couldn't—I thought, My god, what the *hell* has happened. I had no idea.

Couldn't make sense of it; I think you go into, into a sort of automatic mode. Wasn't feeling panicky, just, what the hell is it? And how the hell have we not been killed by it? was my first thought, and looking out the window, I couldn't see another soul, and of course all that side was in darkness, cause unbeknown to me the power had gone out there, and it just looked as if we were the last folk in the world, you know, that's immediately how it looked, and couldn't think what it was, but you're not asking those questions at that time somehow; and then adrenalin kicks in I think, and then you just do what you have to do, cause, I remember I just pulled on the first clothes I came to, ran down stairs, got the kids, and said, "Come on we're going next door to see if Mrs Mac's okay", and we went out, and I don't remember this, but Neil in one of the essays he wrote about it, said he remembers hearing nothing but flopping noises, like heavy rain and things falling; I don't remember that at all, but it was all the debris still falling from, you know, the explosion, so we were very lucky we weren't hit. There was lots of fires in the garden; there were fires under— there was a fire under the tree at the front, there was one or two bushes on fire, that set the hedge on fire.

Well you couldn't have done anything, I mean you didn't even think about firemen, not when you saw the fire beside us, cause it was higher than those trees, I mean you couldn't *see* the top of the flames.

The immediate aftermath

Howard is Helen's brother-in-law and Archie is a schoolfriend.

We walked down to the gate, and then we met up with—Howard and Archie were there, and they'd come to see if we were alright, and of course,

253

Archie was very very friendly with the Flannigans, and he was trying to go and see if they were alright, and I said, "Oh well, sure they're alright, cause we're alright". And he didn't say anything, you know, and we walked back down, the police moved us then back to the Dumfries—to the Carlisle road, you know back down that hundred yard bit from, you know you come up from the Carlisle road and they moved us back to the Carlisle road, cause they didn't really know I think either; so we were standing there, everybody who had been moved out, you know, kind of cold, but you weren't too cold because you were in shock I think; and I remember Archie saying again, "I'm going to see if the Flannigans are alright", and I said, "Well look", I said, "they're next to Cara Brown, and I've seen Cara and Campbell and they're fine, you know they had to climb out of their window, but they're okay, and the Flannigans are right next door Archie, so they must be alright", and he says, "I don't know"; and so we sort of hung around there for a while, and then, it seemed as though they wanted us to move out: they wanted to evacuate the area, and I said, "Well I want to go back and lock the house then", because I thought, well if it hasn't been blown up, it would be a shame if, if somebody got into it or something, I don't know why I was thinking about locking it, but, I went to get the dogs as well - that was it - so the policeman came back up with me, and Archie took Helen, and Howard took Neil, and they went off.

I ran upstairs to check that the upstairs windows were shut, because I was frightened then, that some debris that was alight would come in and set fire to the house, and while I was upstairs I saw on the digital clock 7:28 and I thought, God, it seems like hours and hours and hours ago since seven o'clock, you know.

Helen's anecdote about the dogs and the parrot

The policeman came to the door and he said—he was all covered in soot and streaks, and he said, "Come on Mrs, we're moving out", and he said, that you know the petrol station's burning, and we're frightened its going to blow up, so you'll have to leave, and I said, "Oh I'm just coming", so I got the dogs - two dogs - and my handbag, because I'd been the bank that day and got ten quid out of the bank Jill, and I wasn't leaving that [JH laughs] Honest to god, the things you think of [Helen laughs] : me with this bag round my neck and two dogs, and I had to leave the parrot outside, because I couldn't catch him in the dark, and had nothing to carry him in, and I was so scared that he would be killed, so I thought, Well I'll just have to do it, I'll just have to leave him, and we set off, and the older dog had had a stroke two days before, and I thought, Gosh she's going to die! so we got out of there, and we walked down to the Carlisle road, by this time there was one or two people walking but most people had been moved out, so I headed—started heading up towards Christeen's house, and I got as far as the petrol station, which was *indeed* burning, when the old dog collapsed, and I sat down on the wall beside him, and I though, Oh I don't know what I'm going to do now, cause I couldn't carry her, she was too heavy, and I thought, Well I'm not going to leave her, can't leave her, so I just *sat* there; and I remember the smoke was getting thicker and thicker, and you couldn't see anything, and there was a couple walking up, and I said to them—I had no idea who they were, I said, "Could you stop at 27 Main Street, and ask somebody to come and help me carry the dog, cause she's collapsed", cause it wasn't very far if you think about it, and I didn't realise that they had excluded people beyond that, but, they said, "Yeah, we'll do that", because they were old, they couldn't of helped me anyway; so I still sat, and I remember a police car going past very slowly, with a speaker on a claxon, saying, Please clear the area, you know, Its not safe. We think this is going to blow up, and then they disappeared, and then I was left. Nobody: nothing: smoke. Oh my god, what am I going to do? and nobody coming: nobody came from Christeen's house, and, Oh jeez, and then I thought, Well I really can't stay here, I'm going to have to move, because, you know, I'll try and carry her. So I got up, and when I got up she sort of came to, and she got onto her feet, so we managed to sort of struggle up, and we got to the corner, where it turned, and as we got there, there was firemen coming Down, and one of them was Sandy Fleming, John Fleming's brother, and he knew me well, and of course, I had the bag round my neck, and I'm like this with the dogs, and he thought I was injured [both laugh] Sandy saw me, and he came—cause they thought there was nobody there, they thought everybody was evacuated out, you see; he came *running* down, he said, "Helen, Helen, are you alright, are you alright", and I said, "Yeah I'm fine, I'm fine", and he said, "But look at you!" and I said, "No, no, it's just the dog, " and he says, "Oh thank god you're alright", so the fireman, I think, were then trying to work out what was happening; so I managed to get to Christeen's, but of course there was nobody there because they'd been evacuated out to beyond the police station, so; I mean, probably the old couple did knock at the door and nobody was there.

The dogs survived the disaster, with one of them finally put to sleep only last year..

We needed the medication for the dog who was—the one who'd had the stroke, so Neil said, "Well we'll just go to the police station and say, you know, that we have to get medication", we wouldn't say its for the dog [Jill chuckles] so the police escorted us in, you know, and the house was okay, and the parrot was alive, it was a miracle.

We were walking up towards the house and I could hear the parrot screaming, and I said to Neil, "he's alive, he's alive!", and the policeman said, "You mean to tell me there's somebody in that house?" [laughs], said, "No, oh no, it's a parrot!".

Realisation of the extent of the disaster

I remember seeing Jim Thomson's wife, cause her sister lived just down from us, two doors down, and she saw me and she said, "Oh is Anne alright, is Anne alright?", you know, and I thought, What's she worried about? and then I thought, she doesn't know, if anybody down there's alright or not, you know, and I said, "Yes I saw her", cause you know I'd seen her when we'd been evacuated out, and she said, "Oh thank god for that", you know; and then I did begin to think then, Are there people *dead*? you know, and all we could see up the Mains Hill in the darkness was blue flashing lights going up the Langholm Road, and I thought, I said to Archie, "Why are the lights, why are they going up there", and he say, "Oh there's an awful", he says, "There's an awful lot of trouble in Rosebank", I mean he wasn't talking about that road at all, he said, he says, "There's bodies everywhere", and I thought, Oh my god, what the hell's happened? You know, and I thought he meant Lockerbie bodies, you know, I mean it didn't matter, but I thought something had happened to kill people in Lockerbie, and he says, "there's bodies all over the streets; they canny—they're walking over them", and I thought, Oh Jesus, and then I thought, How many folk I know am I not going to see again?, you know, it was such a funny feeling, you know, how many people are dead, and why, and what's happened?

Helen's husband's story

I think it was just after 8 or so, and there was a news flash, and it said there were reports that a civil airliner had crashed near Lockerbie, but it was unconfirmed. And we were going, Oh my god; that was the first we knew what it was, we hadn't a clue before that; and that was the first that Neil knew, cause he watched the Channel 4 news in Aberdeen, which was on from seven till eight, and at the end of the Channel 4 news at eight o'clock, they said, We have unconfirmed reports of a 747 crashing on the town of Lockerbie, and he thought, Oh, you know, they'll say that, but its probably up in the middle of nowhere its crashed, you know, but—and he didn't have a phone, cause there were no mobile phones then, they didn't have a phone in the flat, so he went out to find a phone and phone us, just to *see*, you know, kind of for interest, you know see what's happening. He just thought well as they do, you know they'd say it had happened at Lockerbie and it was away in the middle of the moor or somewhere, you now, and so he phoned the number, but of course there was nobody there, and so he began to kind of wonder then, and he thought, well I'll wait for the main news at nine o'clock, and I'll see what they say, and of course the main news at nine o'clock said that half of Lockerbie was blown up, and then he thought, Oh shit [Helen laughs]

So, well, there was no point in phoning then; he got the, he was on, there was a sort of pooled car, he didn't have a car: there was a pooled car with the company he was with, and some other guy had it that night, so he walked across town to his door, and said, and the fella says, "Don't say anything, I know, I've seen it on the news", so he said, "I'm going down", so he just left and drove down. But of course he couldn't get—he said, all the way down every news report was worse, because they said that the petrol station in the south end of the town had exploded, which wasn't true, and he thought, Well if that has exploded then the whole of Sherwood Park, you know, that'll be gone; and he got as far as Beattock and the road was closed there so the policeman stopped him there and he said, you know, "I have to get to Lockerbie, my families there and I don't know if they're alive or dead", and they guy said, "Well you can't go down this road", he said, "for a start there's debris on it", but they put him down the A709 to Dumfries, you know, down the back road; so he actually came in from Lochmaben and I think it was about midnight before he got there, and of course once he got there he wasn't allowed to go anywhere near Sherwood Crescent, so he couldn't see if the house was there or not. He was told that survivors had been sent to the town hall, which we had gone to the town hall and we handed in our names, but he got to the town hall and they said, No sorry, this is a morgue now, we don't have any people living here; and well—so then I think he'd seen Frank Gibson, who was a Special Constable, and Frank had said, "You can't go along there but your house is okay I've seen it", so then he—not sure if he went to Archie's house, you see of course he couldn't go to Christeen's either, cause it was—eventually he went to—he phoned from somewhere, maybe it was Eileen's, it might have been Bryce and Eileen's up at the north end of the town, and we were at Liz and Peter's by then; you were there too weren't you?

Lines of communication were scrambled: Helen's survival was met with surprise

I remember my, my sister-in-law from Perth phoned on the evening of the disaster, you know, the emergency lines, to ask, you know, to find out if we were alive or dead, and they asked for our names, and address, and she gave them the address, and when she said Sherwood Crescent, there was a silence, and then they said, Would they have any distinguishing jewellery or anything, do you know? and that was all, they didn't say any more; Cause everybody thought that everybody in Sherwood Crescent was dead. That was the initial—that was the information that all these people had, and it wasn't until we phoned her, you know, the following day that they found out that we weren't. So I don't—you know, when they give out information, you know, Phone here! just —and it's not their fault, I just think, I say to people if they ever involved in anything like that, don't believe what you're told initially, because nobody will really know initially what's, what has happened; it takes time for the dust to settle; and yeah! There was one or two folk that phoned in and you know, they didn't say them dead, but; and then I though, well that's a bit off, because we had handed our names in at the town hall as survivors, you know; the police said, go to the town hall and register, you know, that's where you have to go and tell them that you're alive, you know; so we did that, but then they didn't want us to stay there, because there was no room for us, and people were going to the hotels and the hotels were opening their doors and all that kind of thing, so we went to Archie's house, and then, when we heard the news at nine o'clock and it was so bad.

I found one or two people, who couldn't believe that there was anybody alive in Sherwood Crescent, because they'd been told that everybody there was dead. I mean, this is two days afterwards; it was just so little communication; of course the town was full to bursting with complete strangers, so you didn't know who anybody *was*, you know; all the soldiers came in, and all the press came in, and you didn't know anybody that you saw, and—they, you know, somebody sent for somebody else, and then somebody else came along and said, "What do you mean, you're in Sherwood Crescent, everybody there's killed", and I said, "No, no we're not", you know, I said, "There's me, and there's the people next door to me, and the people across the road", and I said, "we're all in our houses, but we don't have water, and I'm not *complaining* that we don't have water, I'm just asking if you think there will be water on in the next 48 hours then we won't make arrangements to move out, but if there isn't going to be, we'll have to go and stay somewhere for Christmas", and they said, "Oh", you know, "really sorry, we didn't think there was anybody there, we've been told everybody was dead, and—"

They were council officials, they were, you know. But there was no communicating, nobody knew anything. That was one of the strangest things, it would have been like if something had happened in the middle of Fyvie, and up here you wouldn't know what was happening down at the castle; they didn't—nobody knew what was happening everywhere, and streets were closed, and people weren't moving around, and everybody was in *shock* I suppose But they didn't know; and then they sent a tanker, you know, with a standpipe, but they got the water on before Christmas, they did, yeah. But we had water that afternoon, I mean there was a tanker of water there within a few hours, cause they just didn't know that there was anybody living there

There were reports of depleted uranium contamination in the water on January 8 1989, but the supply was given the all clear by the Air Accident Investigation Branch, the Scottish Office and the National Radiological Protection Board [NRPB], following water samples being drawn from two local sources on 6th January and tested by NRPB, Glasgow : "any small amount of radioactivity detected is due to the natural radioactivity present in all waters."

Damage to Helen's property and Sherwood Park

I remember getting into the house and I went into the dining room with French windows at the back, and I couldn't get the door to shut. Well that's funny, it wouldn't have been open anyway, but what had happened was, it was a bolt, you know, that shut the window, and the bolt was bent at right angles, it must have been, the house must have moved, and the window must have moved, because the bolt had been bent completely and the window was just waving open. [other than that] the house looked okay, because we miraculously had no damage, but the garden was full of, like, smouldering fires big and small, and pieces of debris, and I remember one was like a spear, five foot long, sliver of torn metal, and it was *buried* into the ground, I mean, you know, and there was a another big block of stone that had—you could see it had burned straight across the Anderson's lawn and across our hedge and across our lawn. Just things like that, and the *smell* of aviation fuel *everywhere*, real stink of that, *everywhere*. And the roads were thick with, with mud and rocks, and you know everywhere, I mean you wouldn't have been able to drive on the roads anyway, and, and debris everywhere: there was a bit of an engine housing or something lying somewhere about near the place, and—it was very difficult to take in.

The unquestionable luck of Helen and her children was hard for friends to fathom in the light of the disaster's portrayal on TV

They thought we were dead, and lots of people—well you must have had the same thing: lots of people thought you were dead, cause the news reports were, you know, confusing, and they had seen the fires and people had said there's no way anybody could have come through that, and [pause] one person I phoned, she wouldn't speak to me because she thought I was dead [laughs], and it wasn't that that, it was that she was so shocked when she, "Its you, but your dead", and I said, "No I'm not dead actually", you know, but she just couldn't speak, she put the phone down; so strange [laughs]; she just couldn't cope with it, oh definitely, I mean when you saw Rosebank- how it came down between the two rows of houses, and didn't kill anybody in Rose Bank, was a miracle: I mean, I mean the reason really, not the complete reason, why people died in Sherwood but, it was the fire that killed most people, apart from the Flannigan's, because it landed right on *top* of them, and their house was just *obliterated*, there was just nothing there, and yet the garage was there, - was it the garage or the green house - I mean right at the edge of the crater, not a pain of glass in it, but it was there, and you thought, how could that be there and the house just be a hole, there was nothing, just that huge hole in the ground and just—gone

When the dust has settled, Helen's reaction to the disastrous events in her street.

I think there was just a numbness. I mean I can remember I just stood at the gate for days on end : I just stood at the gate, and watched things. People coming and going, and there was a police—there was a policeman and their police dogs down there, and I just remember, and we didn't know any of them, they were from all over the country. You couldn't—I just couldn't sit in the house. And if you sat in the house, you put the television on, it was on the television *all* the time, and, because it was such a gift to the media, this awful thing happened at Christmas, what a wonderful gift, you know. And I couldn't get it into my head that that was just out there, you know. And then I just stood at the gate for hours and hours and hours on end; and [pause] I don't know why I did, I just did.

An eventual need to see the epicentre

Remember, the crater site of the disaster was roughly 500 metres from Helen's house yet she hadn't seen it expect on television.

They showed on the news one night, further round the crescent, and the crater, and of course we'd never seen it, cause you weren't supposed to go past our house, you didn't go further than that, that's where the police were stopping people; well they were stopping people at the Carlisle Road, you were meant to come up, but [pause] I said, I said, "Well I have to, have to go and see it now, because I've seen it on the television, I have to go and see it, I just have to see it," and it was like all of these things where you hear people, you know they have to see disasters and things, and I used to think, How awful, why on earth would you want to see *that*, but I know now, you just have to see it, and so we walked round the next day.

Evidence of human suffering

—there was a bible, and it was open, and the pages were rifling in the wind——there was this kind of big sheet of stuff about this size, and it was funny looking, it was kind of pinkish-grey, and I was kind of studying it, and I realised it was a huge piece of skin—I mean, this is, What is that? you know, I just couldn't, because I was looking at the bible, and thinking, Oh gosh I wonder what book it's open at? you know and that—and I thought, What's that? and it was about that size and it was rolled up at the edges a bit, and I thought, and What's that then? And black round in a circular—Oh Christ, almighty, its skin! And after that, if you saw something, or if I saw something, I thought, Not going to look very closely at that, I really don't think I want to know what that was it.

I had a Christmas rose that was blooming, so I picked a bunch of them and I put a rose down on each one. It's silly, but it just felt, these are people, you know [...] or you know, you just felt this was so awful, and what could you do?

The post-disaster triggers of Helen's anxiety

I had started teaching again at Kirkpatrick Fleming in the New Year: they had a vacancy, I'd been teaching there on and off for a year or so, and I thought, yeah, I'll go back to work, because it's better than sitting in the house, and I did, and I was fine at school all day, and when I came up the road at night, there was road work signs just as you approached the sidings at Castle Mill on the south of Lockerbie, and as soon as I saw the road work signs, my knees started to shake, and I felt sick, and I had a panic attack, and it was just because it was triggering what you were, cause the road work signs meant you were going to go back into the, and by the time I got home I would be shaking and, you know, you know, horrible, horrible, and until one night I came up the road and I didn't have any of that, and I realised when I got into Lockerbie that they'd taken the road work signs away, cause the road was open again, but it was as I got nearer to Sherwood Crescent, there were signs that you couldn't go, and it started then, and I was thinking, Oh I'm getting better, but it was just the trigger wasn't there; and, you know, they'd open the road again, traffic was able to go through, freely through, and then—but it, it wasn't until I got nearer to Sherwood crescent that I saw the signs up that the road was closed; that was when I started having the shakes and the shivers and the panic attack, so. But no, I think [pause] I think moving up here we did, it was the wrong time, but you can't choose, you just have to do things.

The children's reaction

Helen's son, Neil Junior, was eleven and her daughter, Helen, was 9 at the time of the disaster.

Well they didn't talk about it a lot; Helen: I mean afterwards, Helen had a lot of problems, a lot of problems for years; she had counselling for many many years; I mean, she still has unresolved, issues unresolved I think; but partly, because of course was wrapped up with all of this was the fact that we left home as well and moved up here, so that kind of stopped the healing, you know, because when we came up here, nobody knew about it

Neil didn't talk about it much, Neil junior, but what he did do, was he made models of jumbo jets: he had a cardboard cut out that he made, and he had the bit where the thing, the, the cockpit fell off marked, and he had—I think he used his intellect to try and cope with what happened, to try and understand what had happened; he constantly made plastic models, Lego models of aeroplanes, and *crashed* them, and all that kind of thing; that was—he did that, over and over again, and see how it happened, how did that happen, what happened, you know, why did that wing come off; just a way of coping I think, that was how he did it; not in any—he didn't know he was doing that, he just did that; and so it was his way of dealing with it I think. And of course, being a boy of that age, he was so excited with this, Oh Lockerbie on the telly! Oh how wonderful!

But you know, it was the excitement! Oh great, you know, this is, we're on the telly, it's world news, and just typical: typical kids really; but then I remember when we were out walking at the crater and we met some kids that Neil knew from school, and of course they hadn't seen each other, because the schools didn't open, and so they were kind of getting together in a hunch and having a talk you see, [...] you know, and they're saying, What did you have in your garden? you know, and Neil said, "We didn't have anything in our garden", you know, [Helen laughs] and they were so disappointed, they didn't have anything [Helen laughs]. And of course, we'd said there was nothing in the garden, there was nothing recognisable, there's nothing they needed to *know*, you know?

The seismological effect on Helen's house, Mossbank

We couldn't get a survey, cause everybody needed, well everybody wanted surveys for insurance companies and God knows what, and as far as we knew we had no damage, but *we* of course were in the unfortunate position that we were trying to *sell* the house, and so they employed a formal surveyor to come, from Edinburgh or somewhere, and he was supposed to survey our house and Mrs Mac's house and about four or five houses were supposed to be surveyed, and the problem was, that they'd never actually had anything like that before, so nobody actually wanted to write down on a bit of paper and put his name, professionally to it, saying it was okay, because it wasn't war time, they didn't have any idea what *effect* the jumbo jet ploughing the crater into the earth would have on any of the houses around, and they didn't want to say, Its okay, or it isn't okay, and so it took quite some time to get the surveys done. And the survey just said it looks okay [laughs] it might or might not be okay; so we ended up having to sign a sort of waver thing for our insurance policy saying that if the purchaser found a damage, or damage that had obviously been started or caused by the disaster, that our insurance company would pay for it, so we did that, signed that.

They said that's what they would *do*; cause it was an exceptional case; nobody knew what was going to happen, how it was going to affect anything; but we were lucky, because our houses on that edge there, were actually built on rock, I mean it was earth, but it was a rock, whereas down in—further down the crescent and where all the houses that were burnt out were, that was a bog, that was a fairly boggy area, so it was difficult to know how they would have been effected you see; but, yeah

The statistics show that the seismological impact of the crash measured 1.6 on the Richter scale. In the Sherwood Park and Crescent area, the wing section, weighing 100,000lbs and carrying 200,000lbs of fuel, could have impacted at speeds close to 650 knots.

Moving to Aberdeenshire and leaving the disaster behind – beneficial or inhibitive to healing?

It was difficult I think, because there was a mixture of things, it wasn't just the disaster, it was, you know, we were leaving Lockerbie, and I didn't want to leave Lockerbie, never wanted to leave. So I didn't really want to come; no' didn't want to come, and that—but it was a two-fold reason, I suppose there was an unrecognised reason of not wanting to leave because it wasn't resolved, and there was also the reason I didn't want to leave home *anyway*, which had nothing to do with the disaster; but lots of people did ask me when we moved up here, And is that why you moved up here? To get away from it? And, no, that wasn't why we moved up here to get away from it; I did, there was times when you felt you wanted to get away from it maybe, there was times when you thought, oh god I don't want to stay another day in this.

Helen couldn't cope with air travel

I mean before I never particularly liked travelling, air travel, I used to find it so boring, and the only exciting bit is getting up in the air and coming down again, the rest in between is boring and uncomfortable, so I was never that *fussed* about air travel, but after the air disaster, I mean, it was, I didn't think, consciously, I am terrified of flying so I'll never do it again, although I did have thoughts like that, thinking to myself, God, I would never want this, this would be awful, I never—and then I said to myself, Well there's one easy way of this never happening to you, don't ever go on a plane again, and that was a sort of rational thing that I thought about, but the emotional thing was difficult, because, I remember we were in a car wash in Aberdeen and [pause] you know the rollers start coming forward and the noise, this noise, it was this rolling noise, and it, I was right back in the bath the night of the disaster, and I was terrified, and I was shaking, and screaming, and [pause] that was, it was the noise that frightened me the most; and the same with flying, I couldn't fly to begin with, couldn't of done it, and then we did fly, we went on holiday to Majorca I think, and I thought, Right, yes I'll be alright, we'll just fly, you know, we'll do that, but Oh my god! Got on the plane, and taxiing along the runway. Alright, and then the engines started rolling for take-off, and I just lost it, completely lost it, and everybody on the plane was looking [laughs] That was it, I just had it. I couldn't—I didn't care where I was or what was happening, I just went doolally; and then spent the whole time we were there, frightened about coming back, you know; Oh it was horrible

For years I couldn't fly. I thought, Not going to put myself through that, or anybody else through it [Helen laughs] . And Neil wasn't very sympathetic, cause he flew already, didn't—you used to fly already, just get on with it, and I thought, Oh I know you're right, and then I thought, No, hold on a minute, you weren't there, you know; his experience was horrible, but it wasn't the same as mine, and he'd had no idea of what we'd been through either, so you know, it's alright to say, just get on with it, but I don't know if he would have been able to, cause I *do know* quite a few folk that don't fly anymore as a result; and some of that is fear of that, and some of it is because the noise terrifies them, or they're back in it and they just, you know; I mean Howard wouldn't fly for years and year and years, he wouldn't fly; so, no.

It was—I think we went to Spain in ninety-six, ninety-four, ninety-five, something like that, and that was it, I didn't like it, but I actually ended up— the doctor just gave me valium if I had to fly anywhere, and I just swallowed valium until I got to where I was going; and [pause] I did go out to New Zealand in ninety-six, so it must have been ninety-four we flew the first time. I went to New Zealand because Neil was working in New Plymouth, and it was all booked last minute, so it was the most awkward way to go, but I flew Aberdeen - London, London - Los Angeles, Los Angeles - Sydney, Sydney - Auckland, Auckland - New Plymouth, and it took—I couldn't tell you how many days [Helen laughs] , it was fifteen hours from Los Angeles to Sydney, I know that, I think it was twelve hours from London to Los Angeles, and I just took two valium before I got on every flight [Helen laughs] I remember telling the doctor, who's a close friend—when we were out there, I had to phone him about something, he says, he says, "What did you do?" I said, "I took two valium before I got on every flight", and he says, "Are you sure you're in New Zealand?" [both laugh] , "you could be anywhere"; so I didn't feel any pain that time, I can tell you [both laugh]

Commemorations and anniversaries from afar, and the homecoming on ten years

No we didn't! Not the first, no we didn't It wasn't looked on—it wasn't viewed with favours, shall we say. Neil didn't think: "No, put it behind you, forget about it", you know, which is silly, cause you can't

And so we didn't go back, but on the day of it, I really wished I had been there, I felt like that was where I should be; and—I don't know about Neil, but for Helen I think it would have been better to go back

We watched it on the telly and everything, I actually went to church that day, it was the—the school was breaking up for Christmas, and they had a service, and the Minister was a nice guy, and he said to me, "Why don't you just come along to the service and sit in church for a wee while, and maybe it will help", and I did; and I remember, he actually made a mention, he said, you know, "This is the first anniversary of the Lockerbie air disaster, we shouldn't forget that, you know, everybody that died there."

No, we should have gone back, definitely, it's silly to say put these things behind you, because if they wont be put you can't, you know, and they'll go behind you when you need them, when they're ready to, when you're ready for them to be behind you but, we didn't no.

We went back for the tenth; the ten years; it's funny, Helen and I went, and it was kind of—it was very divorced from, from the, from the, the disaster I think. I felt it was a bit—there was a lot of space between it and the disaster, I think.

First of all there was a service at the cemetery in the afternoon, which Prince Phillip went to: very short thing, at the, you know, the Garden of Remembrance thing, Prince Phillip was at that; I think he came and laid a wreath behalf of the Queen of something; it was a very short service, and of course the Royal family were kind of in disgrace at that time because of the—you know, everything that was happening with Charles and Diana, and the divorces, and I think they wanted to keep a kind of low profile. Certainly the feeling in Lockerbie was that they wouldn't be welcome, but Lockerbie's very petty like that; a lot of it anyway.

So Prince Phillip came to that, and then he just cleared off, quite wisely, in the afternoon, and then in the evening there was service in Dryfesdale Church.

Let's say it was seven o'clock or something, so Helen and I went up, cause we wanted to get in and get a seat, so we were in a queue from about, oh, half past six or something; well, there was nobody there, I'm not saying there was nobody at the service, but there was nobody in the queue, we were there on our own for ages [Helen laughs] , you know, ages and ages and ages, before all the people arrived, and we got in and sat down; it was a bit odd somehow. It was *fine*, it was.

Divided feelings about commemoration in Lockerbie

I don't know, cause Lockerbie's a funny place: I mean, I can never get past the fact that people were stepping over bodies to go to the bingo, you know, that was kind of the stories at the time, and I could believe it; I mean there was some people I know who would not indeed give up the bingo for anything, and [pause] you know, there would be folk, oh, what a lot of fuss, they want to forget about it, which is—no I don't think you should forget about that, I think you should commemorate these things, and I think people should be allowed to mourn, and do whatever they feel the need to do, and give them the space and opportunity to do it, and not be made to feel guilty or wrong, or any of these things, because that's how they feel, cause if that's how you feel, that's how you feel, and it doesn't—what harm does it do to those who say you should forget about it; you know

A piece of the plane consoled a young widow

I did correspond with a girl whose husband was killed on the plane, 'cause her photograph was in the Lockerbie paper, and she'd just had a baby, poor girl, and I felt so sorry for her, your heart went out to her, and I've never done anything like that in my *life*, but I thought, I must write to her, and I wrote a note to her—I mean she was American, I must have sent it to the paper or something, anyway, she got the letter, and she wrote back, and we corresponded for quite a few years, and she was a really nice girl, and she came over [pause] maybe four years after, two or three years after: she came over to Lockerbie anyway, and she said she would really like to meet me, so, I arranged to go down and, I can't just quite remember how it worked out, but she said she wanted to go to all the places and everything, and she asked did I know about them? And of course, I didn't, because I'd been away, so I got in touch with the friendship group, remember they started that?

And they said, Oh well, look, you know, seeing as she knows you, and she's coming down, would you be her guide instead of somebody from our group? So, I did that; so I went a day or two earlier and I went to the, you know, they had all the investigation thing in what was the school, you know, in the community place, and I went up there and met the policeman in charge, and he took me through all the things that they would tell her or show her, and all the things that they showed to visitors who came, and told me all about what they'd done

265

and how they'd done it; took me to where her husbands body had been found and—so that I had all that, so I could take her and show her, and; but the most horrible thing to me was the porta-cabins that they had, full of their clothes, and the shoes, and it was horrible. Felt as if you were walking through ghosts, and—but they were all there, cause they had to keep everything as potential evidence I suppose in the murder trial, which hadn't happened *then*; and, it was horrible. Just felt as if you were walking through shades of peoples lives, and the Christmas presents that they'd never found, you know

But she said that she'd kind of been struggling with it and, for years, so and then I think her psychiatrist or whoever had said, Well maybe you should go and visit Lockerbie, and she said that she felt it was if like, you know, she said, if you, if your husband goes into the other room to get something, and he says he'll be back in a minute and he doesn't come back, you want to go and see where he is and why he didn't come back, and that was her sort of, you know, take on it, and [pause] well obviously it was very moving for her. Her brother and his wife came with her, and the wee—well the baby would have been about two then. And she was a nice woman.

And I had—I'd cleaned the car out because they were going to be in my car, and it was filthy, and I'd found—we had one or two bits of debris from the plane, which the investigators didn't want, because once they'd got enough bits to work out what bits were there, the other bits they didn't need, so as we found bits, they just said, Oh just keep them or throw them out, so we had one or two bits that we had just kept, and there was one wee bit, and it was in the car, and I was cleaning it out and I thought, wonder if I should offer it to her, it was a funny thing, maybe she wouldn't want it, maybe she would like to have it, you know, so we were driving up to Tundergarth, and I said to her, I said, " I don't know if you'll want this or not, but", I said, "this is a piece of the plane", I said, "it was in our garden", and I said, "we've kept it, they didn't—the investigators didn't want it or need it", and I said, "I found it yesterday, and I just wondered if you would like to have it", and she said, "Oh I would really like to have it", and she took it, and I don't think it left her hand after that, I suppose it was maybe a link somehow with his last moments, or where he'd been or, cause there was nothing else, nothing else physical, you know, cause his body was gone, and you know, the hole in the ground that he'd fallen in was gone, everything was gone, you know, but maybe this was a link, I don't know, a link of some kind, but, and she always had it in her hand after that. So I was glad that I had given her it.

Vision of Lockerbie on return trips

[Written submission: I don't have a vision but what I have seen on my return visits is the same sad gradual decay that so many other small firm are suffering – encroaching supermarkets which planners have allowed, are sucking the life blood from small communities. I don't think Lockerbie is any different in this respect from any other small town. I find it sad though that when people visit "Lockerbie" - the disaster town - what they see is still a bit of a disaster. There have been improvements – e.g. to the cemetery which the whole communities can enjoy – if that's the right word!]

What could be done for Lockerbie's façade?

[Written submission: At the moment, I can see it only deteriorating unless something major is done. What to do? Encourage more small business, shops with something which supermarkets can't offer. Make much more of the two oldest hotels- the Kings Arms and the Blue Bell. Their history alone is interesting. Insist that the disgraceful premises on the Main Streets are tidied and put to some use. How can a community have pride in itself with the ' Happy Garden', festering away or the old Co-op building boarded up.]

Survivor Guilt

I do remember there was a very early meeting of the residents in Sherwood Park, Sherwood Crescent, and I can't remember why we were meeting, but we were meeting in somebody's house, just maybe three or four days after the disaster, maybe the week after, and, we go together and it was, it was actually great because we were all—we hadn't seen each other, we'd all been spread to the four winds, you know, and some folks houses had been blown up and they'd had nowhere to live, so they weren't there, we were lucky we were there, but, you know so we were all together in this house, and we were all saying, Oh what happened to you, and where were you, and you know, talk talk talk, and then one of the people, can't remember who it was, but he said, "Now", very officiously, "I think that we should all be quiet and have a moments silence in memory of those that are not here tonight", and of course everyone just went, Oh, and I thought, you stupid bugger

I thought, I really wish I had said it, I felt like getting up and saying, there isn't one of us that hasn't spent many many, many silent moments remembering those who weren't there tonight, you know, it was such a pretentious thing to say. Cause everybody had spent I'm sure 25 hours a day thinking about the folk that weren't there, thinking, Why wasn't I one of them? you know; it was such a strange thing, it was awful that they were gone, but there was that horrible, sneaky feeling of thank god it was them and not me, which you couldn't *not* have, you just, I mean I looked at my kids and thought, I'm, I'm desperately sorry it was the Flannigan's, but—or whoever, the Somerville's and—but I'm awfully glad it wasn't mine, and it was difficult to be—to, to sort of say, I wish it hadn't been them, cause if it hadn't been them it might have been mine.

There was definitely more of a questioning on [pause] ah [pause] maybe why, why we were here, there was a lot of guilt, there was an awful lot of guilt, I mean before that I had read about and heard about survivor guilt, but I had never understood it, used to think it was stupid, same as folk that wanted to go and look at accidents, I mean, it was stupid, but I know exactly how it feels now. I don't know why, but I know how it feels, cause guilt—the emotions I remember immediately afterwards were numbness, which went on for quite a while, and the principle emotion after that was guilt, and you had to sort of dig away to find that in yourself; you sort of think, how am a feeling? What is it that I'm feeling, now that I am feeling something? What is it that I'm feeling then, why do I feel so awful, what is it? and when I analysed it, it was guilt: I felt guilty, really, really, really guilty, because the kids and I were alive, cause I was alive, and these people were dead, and other people around the town made you feel more guilty, because they said things like, you know, You're so lucky, or, you shouldn't be smiling, you shouldn't be laughing, you shouldn't be happy, so many people are dead: No, hold on a minute, we're not dead, we're alive, but then the unsaid thing was, Well you should, not you should be dead, but there was a guilt thing, you weren't dead so why should—why weren't you dead? you know, why, why, why should you be the ones that are lucky enough to survive? There was that, but nobody meant that, but that's what it felt like; that's what it felt like, that[pause] just [pause] and eventually I did say to somebody that was kind of going on about, oh so and so's dead; Flannigan's are dead and, and I did said, "Look, I know its hellish and I know its awful, but don't ask me to feel sorry that its not me, because I can't do that, I cant feel sorry that its not me and my children that was blown to bits", and maybe that's where the guilt comes from, because you can't feel sorry, its not you, and you should feel sorry, because they're dead, but then them being alive might mean you're dead, so.

JH: But unfortunately there's no justification for,—there's no rationalisation for, I mean, for that is there, because, because it was just such a purely chance, you know

HF: It's just, aye, completely random

JH: There's no way you can rationalize that feeling, I mean

HF: Not at all; you do feel guilty, if you survive, you do definitely feel guilty, because you don't know why you survived

JH: So at this point in time, twenty years on, do you think you've packed that guilt away now, or are just dealing with it?

HF: I think yes, I think it's gone, but, maybe it hasn't gone, maybe it has gone somewhere else and all the other guilts that you accumulate through your life, [Helen laughs] which are many and varied; so, yes, I don't sort of question quite so much now; why?

Helen's feelings about being safe at home.

I think to begin with there was a—there was a definite loss of innocence, because you began to think everything was potentially a dangerous thing. You'd no longer have—for instance, a car back-firing is a car back-firing, a car back-firing was maybe the beginning of the end of something, you know, there was that, that you no longer sort of thought things were all sweet and simple in the world, cause people died for no reason whatsoever; and also there was no security to be found in your own home, that was a completely stupid idea: there's no place you would be safe. I mean, the concept that we would murdered, in, in Mossbank by Arab terrorists was ludicrous, you would *laugh* at that, but we very nearly were; so to think that you can be safe and make yourself safe, anywhere in the world, is a fallacy, and everything is in Gods hands, or if its not gods hands its in the hands of fate, not a bloody thing you can do about it. So I think that was the first thing that really, I thought seriously, was it doesn't matter what you do and where you are or what you think, it can be gone tomorrow, as quick as that, and you'd—in the first few weeks afterwards, I was terrified to let the kids be out of my site, or to be out of their site, in case something happened, you know, cause, for instance very often on a Friday night, or whatever, I would go and get fish and chips for our tea, and the children would stay at home for the two or three minutes that it took me to go and get the fish and chips, and all I could think of was, what if I had been out getting fish and chips when the plane had crashed, and they'd been in the house and blown to bits, and I wouldn't have known, I couldn't get to them, even if they hadn't been blown to bits, I wouldn't have known, because I'd be at the wrong end of the town. I wouldn't have been able to get to them, that's the sort of thing you're very aware and frightened and so you were—can't ever do that, but you cannot live your life at that pitch, you cant go on functioning at the pitch of; the heaven is going to fall on us any minute now; so you just have to sort of put it at the back of your mind, and, well it eventually finds it way to the back of your mind, and you just go on; but I think maybe the one that stayed with me, would be that [pause] don't think you're ever safe, cause you're not safe; so the best thing to do is try not to worry about being safe, cause you can't do anything about it anyway.

No. I am a complete and utter pessimist, so there's no way that anything is ever going to be good. I would never be positive about anything; but, I did—not so much for myself, but I did think for other people, Don't think you can make yourself safe, because you can't.

Strength of Faith and Trust in God

I mean if you believe in God then you trust in God, but maybe the Flannigan's trusted in God too, I don't know; you just don't know; and so you just—you just have to[pause] if you had a, if you had a very strong faith, which I did have, you would question what had happened, but I do remember immediately leaping to defence when somebody said, "I'm not speaking to God anymore, he killed all these people", and immediately without thinking I said, "No he didn't, it was *men* that killed all these people", it wasn't God that put bomb on a plane, it was men that did that, whether an all powerful, all seeing god should allow that to happen I don't know, I don't think that's part of the deal actually but, it wasn't god that did it, it was men that did it: it always is, it's always humans that arse things up, so, for whatever reason;

I think—it's a very difficult thing, because your questioning, questioning all the time, why the hell did this happen, you know, but then good things happen to bad people all the time, and faith has absolutely nothing to do with belief and understanding, faith is just about, Faith, its not something you can see or touch or prove; so, no I don't think it got, stronger, but—and I would have said I was questioning until that person said, "I'm not speaking to God", you know, and immediately I said, "No, it wasn't god that did it"; so whether or not you believe in anything it still wasn't a God or anybody that did it other than terrorists, people with different bloody ideas, that's all it was about; and certainly I suppose they meant it to blow up over the sea, and all that sort of thing, but that doesn't really matter. So, no I don't think it affected my faith very much that way really.

The Twin Towers Disaster and Lockerbie – Helen shares her feelings on the political inevitability of the Trade Centre

I didn't see it initially; Neil junior was staying and he—I was out cutting the hedge and he came out and told me about it, he said, "A plane has just crashed in—been crashed into the Twin Towers", the first one, the World Trade Centre he said, not the Twin Towers, and then he came out again and said, "A plane has crashed into the *second* one, and it's a terrorist attack", and I said— I didn't think of Lockerbie. I said, "Well I hope to hell now that the Americans start listening, because people don't like them, and they're gonna have to start listening", and it was after that, I started to think about Lockerbie, because they didn't listen at Lockerbie either, and I'd started to think if they had taken on board, I mean I don't think it was Libyan terrorists for a start, I don't know who the hell did it, but it was a wee bit too pat to me, but if they had taken on board what was done then and sort of tried, instead of saying, This is awful what they've done to us, said, Why do they hate us so much? What can we do stop the hatred? What can we do to even things up? What can we do to make their lives better or whatever the problem is, can we look at the problem? instead of saying, Oh we'll just go and blow *them* up then, you know, which is all they've done in, in the twenty years, and will continue I suppose, is, when they do something, we do something worse, or then they do something worse and then we have to do something back, and that's no the *way*, that's not going to solve it, I mean god knows how you solve it, but to my mind it has led to—I mean, it wasn't Osama Bin Laden that did Lockerbie, cause I don't think he was around, certainly he wouldn't have been in that kind of position at that time I don't think; but the kind of dissatisfaction that the Muslims and the general people in the Middle East have with the Western way of life and governments has *fed* Osama Bin Laden I think; has made him able to do what he does, because they haven't been happy with the West for so long, and people like him have fed on that, and, and honed it into a whole *other thing*, you know, whereas, but I, and I also after the Twin Towers there was a woman that I heard interviewed in the street in New

York, and she said, you know, well she said, you know, "It's awful", but she said, "At least maybe we can understand what has happened to other people in other countries where they've been bombed", you know, "because it hasn't happened to us before"; it was mostly their fault, but it hadn't happened to them before, and I did *hope* that maybe they would have a— but then you see, it was George Bush, so, you know, he's not going to do anything except going to be jingoistic, you know, they bomb us, we'll bomb them.

Helen's thoughts on 20th anniversary commemorations

I think there should be a commemoration, I think there should be—I don't think it should by, oh there'll be plenty of folk that say they don't want it, you should just let it alone, let us get on with it, and what is not said is, let us get on with being the miserable *buggers* that we've always *been*, cause that's what they *mean*! There should definitely be some sort of commemoration of what happened: in what form? I suppose a Church service is about the only thing that you could do; nowadays of course it would have to be of several faiths [Helen laughs]

The one after it was, they had the, the Roman Catholic Bishop was there and the senior Jewish guy, senior Rabbi was there, at the one after the disaster they had—didn't have a Muslim there, but—I don't think, no I don't think they did, but I don't know there were any Muslims on the plane actually.

There were Jewish people and there were Christians and there were, you know, but I don't know that there were Muslims on the plane, because, if there had been they would have been represented because it was a non-denominational service really, that one, the first one. But I don't know; it's difficult because, you know, there's no anywhere big enough to hold a *big* service in Lockerbie, ideally it could be outside, but the weather won't be good, it's December. Maybe just a —,don't know; do you know, I could see being nice, no nice is the wrong word, what I think, I would feel, would be something like a candle-light thing in, in the Garden of Remembrance. I think that would be really nice, I think that would hit the bit somehow. No big fuss, just maybe, maybe just a prayer or something, maybe just read the names, you know. There's so many of them, but read the names; I used to celebrate the disaster by reading the names myself.

[Written submission: This may be the 20th commemoration, but that will not matter to those whose who were bereft that night. However, their wish to remark their own anniversary is their own concern. Perhaps nothing official in the future, first private grief. Perhaps in the future, a wreath on Poppy Day -they died in a war after all.]

Celebrating the Moment

Much later on when it came to things like that kids 21st's and things, I did think we had big parties for both of them, big dressy parties, and I, my thinking was, we very nearly weren't here, so let's have things to remember, it wasn't so much daily things, but I did have things like that, let's go for it, spend the money, do things, because you might not ever have that: next year you might not have that; so that was more, that took a long time; and I still think that way about things: don't not do something for silly reasons, because you might not get the chance to do it again, so, you know, celebrate, do that, enjoy

Just after our interview, Helen's daughter, family and friends threw a party for her at Fyvie Castle, to belatedly celebrate her sixtieth birthday.

Helen and her dog in the early 1980s.
Acknowledgment: Helen Fraser

Helen, with her baby daughter, on a trip to the Baltic States, around 1978/79. Helen's ex-husband was a merchant naval officer. Acknowledgment: Helen Fraser

Jill Suzanne Haldane, a.k.a. Sonia Satellite at the annual Armstrong Road Garden Party in Opotiki, New Zealand, November 2006.

My Story

This interview was performed by Hugo Manson, oral historian, at my parents' home in Lockerbie, one Friday night, 5 April 2008. It was my final full day in Scotland and I was exhausted after two hectic weeks of interviews and full immersion in the Lockerbie project. Hugo was kind enough to make a special trip down to Lockerbie from Glasgow; I picked him up from the train station around 7pm. We drove round to the crater site, up to Sherwood Crescent and down to the Memorial Garden, to allow Hugo a real perspective on the layout of the town.

We settled ourselves in the back room, as the twilight descended and the gloom fell, contrasting the illuminating orange glow of the streetlights, much as it appeared that evening in January.

He was full of positive comments and supportive words regarding the unquantifiable work that lay ahead of me. His parting words to me, as I dropped him at the station, were inspirational and yet I can't quite bring to mind the individual letters as they shape into meaning. It is a seminal point, reinforcing and underlining a cumulative thought that has been bothering me throughout the interview: when listening to the detail of others accounts over the two weeks, I understand I have a shocking memory for recall.

Of course, people say that but its not entirely the full story. Like other Mums, I remember with complete clarity the day my children were born - every detail, and the milestones they reached. Of course, these are much anticipated events which we prime our consciousness ready to identify and then relish with utter focus on that event and no other: it gets parcelled away in the treasure box of memories. Sudden shock like the disaster catches us off-guard. We are not prepared and the nature of impromptu events are inherently spontaneous.

Hugo's questions focus on my thoughts and feelings about the town of Lockerbie; the nature of the community dynamic and the significance of my identity as a native of Lockerbie-born but not bred. He asked me about the glue that binds the Lockerbie community and the typical characteristics of the townspeople. I have lived for more than half my life away from the town so I was found wanting in response.

My paternal and maternal grandparents:

My parents are James Haldane and Elizabeth Yvonne Haldane, nee Wardlaw. They're here in Lockerbie because they came in sixty-six, probably sixty-six, 1966; purchased the grocery shop on Main Street, and they were working in that grocer's shop – owned it and ran it – until 2006, when my Father retired. My Father originally is from West Linton, just outside of Edinburgh, a baker to trade; my Mother was originally from New Galloway, a school teacher.

Well, my Father's father was James Haldane; he was a baker to trade; he ran the bakery in West Linton; quite a successful little bakery after the war and up until his death in sixty-three, sixty four; and my Father's mother was Isabella Cobbin, and she was from Haddo House, well, she was born and brought up in Haddo House in Aberdeenshire and she was a school teacher and taught at

Romanno Bridge [near Nine Mile Burn outside of Penicuik, Edinburgh]

My grandfather was dead before I was born; my grandmother, yes, I knew her well; she only died about 6 or 7 years ago.

My grandmother's father, who was James Cobban, he was the factor on Haddo House estate. [My great grandfather was an architect] The dates of that I'd need to check with Mum and Dad, I'm not entirely sure, but it would span somewhere between the late eighteen nineties and going into nineteen ten or so; yes.

Mother's side: my Mother's mother was Isabelle McLaughlin. She was from Glasgow, but she obviously wanted to forget [chuckles] about that quite quickly, and—because she did everything she could to get out of Glasgow— I think she—she was one of seven children and her Father had died when she as young and her Mother had struggled to bring up these seven children and to give them the education and the future that would remove them from Clydebank in Glasgow, according to my Grandmother. But my great-aunt Meg lived in Clydebank all her life and had a wonderful life, but I think my grandmother wanted to get out as quickly as she could. So she took elocution lessons and went to Tennis Parties and met my Grandfather [chuckles] and he was a teacher so they married in 1911, I think, so my Grandfather was David Wardlaw.

Well, I think they were all kind of encouraged to do likewise. My [great] aunt, aunt Nan: she was a dress designer and rose through stitchery and dress-making circles to be a dress designer – ended up in Shanghai during the war; she'd a really interesting life and ended up in a concentration camp. She had these gorgeous little Chinese bracelets that Aunt Nan managed to smuggle all the way through her three or four years in the concentration camp. They survived and came back to Scotland.

I don't know what she was doing out there but, there they were, just caught in there at the wrong time. So she, yeah; so I think they were all quite encouraged by my great-great grandmother to *improve* themselves and yeah, get a good match, and it kind of showed in my Grandmother's attitude; to be perfectly honest, and,[back in New Galloway], she was driven to do good works in the community and went out into the community and, you know, helped the *poor* ladies and showed them how to stitch and sew and bake, and be a typical [pause] yeah, probably, typical wife.

Yes, yes, so when my grandfather retired, in the early sixties, they knew a couple of people, a couple of families here, so decided to come and live here and, yeah! So this was their house and when they moved in here, there were no houses on either side; this was just all paddocks: paddock this way, paddock that way, with the Manse and some older house adjacent; but, no; it was one of the original houses in this stretch of the town. Yes, because of course, this is The Lea. This house is called The Lea.

Early days of my life

[We lived] to the side and above the shop. My father was a worker: an eternal memory of my Father is him with his overall on, with a fag hanging out of his mouth, fixing the bikes – our bikes or the shop bikes – taking orders out of the shop; deliveries were coming – it was a very busy little place – bread deliveries, grocery deliveries and, yeah! People coming and going obviously all the time.

It was kind of—it was a house to the side and then above as well, so we had an upstairs area too and also downstairs to the bathroom so it was kind of an L-shaped kind of property and, we had a yard with some out-houses, but pretty much the ponies—we had a small Shetland when my sister was just small, and then the ponies grew bigger as we grew bigger, and we were very involved with everything pony-wise – pony club, and cross-country and point-to-point [and hunting] – latterly, my sister was a point-to pointer – but it became very clear early on that I didn't have the horsemanship that my sister had, so she kind of took that further and I kind of dipped out of it a bit more; ended up being sort of, you know helper and, you know, doing some of the [supporting]

Yes, what were my interests? Well [pause] the ponies, they were an interest of mine, and I liked painting – I did a lot of colouring in and drawing. Tennis, I played a lot of tennis. Well, when I say tennis—well, no we did; as a teenager, I would go to the courts and play; the courts, sadly, are no longer there, but I remember, we had a wall at our old property there—whitewashed wall which was quite high, and we used to hit the tennis ball up against the wall, hundreds and millions of time; we also used to construct jumps in the yard out of cardboard boxes and pretend we were jumping them. I had a friend across and we spent a lot of time—we would just go—there was a farm—there used to be a farm at the end of our street – Mains Street was so-called because of the Mains Farm – there was a farm there when I was a kid and we used to go and play [in the buildings in the farm] and, we just dossed around really. There wasn't sort of the river, we didn't go down the river much, and the sea isn't close so I don't really remember doing that; as an interest, I think I really just fitted in with whatever was going on really. I can't remember having any—I was in the Brownies and—I don't remember having any distinct—you know.

My Mother did a bit of supply teaching when we were just small, but she gave that up and so I recall her always being—you know they were always around when we got home from school and so on.

Childhood memories of a royal visit.

The one memory I have to do with the town and the community was when the Queen came to open the new cheese factory that we saw smoking from the graveyard there, and that must have been about seventy five, and as a small Brownie, we were all instructed, well, we trooped down to the Station car park to meet her off the train, and I remember her big car was waiting, with huge big glass windows, and we were all standing round, in our Brownie uniforms, and she got off the train with Prince Philip, and she came *up* to me, and I can remember her coming towards me, and was thinking, What am I going to say? And she said: "And which pack are you? she said, meaning the pack of Brownies, and I replied with—can't remember which pack, division we were. "Oh," that's very nice," she said – she had a blue dress on – and then she walked off, and that's really one of my major memories about living in the community of Lockerbie, but we also have Gala Day:

Now, we have a Riding of the Marches tradition here, which is quite a borders town tradition, and each June, we have a week of festivities, which culminate in the Gala Day, which is a float parade, and a riding, so they go round the boundaries with the horses, and check that no *nasty* English people have come into our area, and it is—it's not a hugely long tradition – not as long as Galashiels and Hawick and what-have-you – but—so I have a lot of memories of that: being involved in that; never in the floats but we took the horses there, and we always knew people in the riding because we were that way inclined: horsey people.

My father's diverse roles as a shopkeeper

I s'pose most people knew me because of my Father and so it would be because of, I didn't know who they were, in terms of—I'm not talking about my peers but older people, but they would be aware of who I was.

Jimmy Mace, they called him, Well, his name is Haldane but the shop was called, The Mace shop, so they renamed him, Jimmy Mace, as opposed to Jimmy Smith or Jimmy Brown or Jimmy MacDonald. Yes, but, I mean, I had friends – I had a friend across the road – and I went to the local school, and it certainly was—I mean, when you're a child, your immediate community is your world, isn't it, so.

Correct, aye that's right, and that was quite a strain on my Father, talking about moods and modes […] and if they wanted to stand there and chew the fat about how their drainpipe was burst, then he basically had to stand there and listen. That was hugely tiring for my Father.

Yes, and he had to absorb all this gossip and nonsense that, in actual fact, he just didn't even care about, but in the customer service role, you have to be Joe Interested all the time, and of course, he'd come home and: Oh God, Mrs Dooda's just driving me crazy!" So it could be a stressful job for my Father, just trying to maintain that cheerful demeanour. He definitely would get *a lot* of community information which meant that he was actually was in quite a privileged position, and he'd to be careful who he recounted it back to, you see; so, yes, I think he had a lot of, a lot of responsibility to his customers.

And he was also the DIY man, I mean, the people who lived around, if they did have a problem with something, and they were usually the elderly people who were living alone, then Jimmy'll fix it: so when Jimmy went in with the messages, it was, Oh, Jimmy, can you look at this? And, "Hello, what's wrong with ma' TV, Jimmy?" so he served several roles in that small Mains Street community, and also wider still.

My Mother's ambitions

My Mother: she was much more the—probably the boss of the household, so she was more—my Dad would do the practical stuff and she was a lot more [..] pragmatic, and caring, but not you know, not emotionally compassionate, but caring in a practical way. Yes, yes, and probably a little bit unfulfilled in her—you know, did a little bit of teaching; had the kids and then just worked in the shop, ands he had probably, you know, ambitions that she would have liked to attempt; tried, but didn't manage to do that, but—wasn't allowed to: she had to go and be a teacher, and that that it; and she wanted to go to the Barony, which is a horticultural and agricultural college on the west coast there, so she always wanted to do that, but she wasn't allowed to, and she ended up being a teacher, and she didn't really like it: you know. But certainly, my Father, his family came first, and he was a complete family man and got up in the morning and went to bed at night, thinking about his family, and if he had to deal with the shop community in the interim, well, so be it.

A work ethic pervades the individual, the family, the community and region.

Well, from a work perspective, you know, knuckling down and getting on with it: yes, that would be correct

I don't know if that came from the generational era into which he was born and brought up in or perhaps working in, but it was certainly a type of entrepreneurial attitude that, you didn't wait for the welfare, you know, the State won't provide: you get our there and so it yourself, and if there's initiatives to get you out there and doing it, well, they come from the conservative side of politics rather than the labour side, but no, he definitely was not a Labour man.

Well, in my working life, yes, that's right; and we were very encouraged— well, I don't actually remember being *encouraged* at school, but I remember being very studious, and having to work hard, as opposed to my sister who didn't and still got good grades; and I enjoyed working hard at school, and I wouldn't have considered *not* working hard at school, and we were never forced to do that, so I suppose that did come quite naturally in school work.

Feelings of belonging highlighted

I always had the feeling, growing up as child, that I wasn't Lockerbie born and bred: a lot of that was because – I don't know if I mentioned this before, but my accent was different, so because I didn't speak Lockerbie vernacular at school, it was very much like, Oh, you're really snobby, and [I hated having to say my name out in the class]

I think *now* my parents probably speak much more with a Lockerbie accent—you maybe hear it maybe more, and I think their accents changed over the years, but definitely, my Father had quite an Edinburgh accent and my Mother, a lilting soft rolling Galloway type accent, and us children didn't speak Lockerbie, and I didn't have a strong accent, which is very distinctive here in the town, and I kind of got slated for that so I maybe just picked up that label and wore it, and kind of, Well, if that what everyone thinks I am, then I'll just be that [Jill chuckles]

I don't remember it being a deliberate thing: I don't recall that. We were certainly, yeah—we were living in Lockerbie but we weren't Lockardians and I think that was instinctively there with us. I couldn't quite say where it came from because, like a lot of things cultural, they just are and it's hard to say what their source is, but we certainly weren't: we did go to Brownies but, you know, we weren't right in the thick of it, I would say. We did the Pony Club thing, and that was also looked upon as needing money to do that, and Lockerbie, socio-economically, is challenged to a degree, and people – children – probably thought that we were well-off and my Father has his own business, so in that respect, we weren't typical of the Lockerbie community.

Public characters of Lockerbie town

I can think of a particular individual whose Mother worked in the papershop and whose Father was a plumber, and they went to Silloth for their holidays in the caravan, and they would be third or fourth generation Lockardians: they would be typical. And, yeah: and the farmers are typical Lockerbie, from round here. They don't own their farms – well, some of them do- we have a large estate, Castlemilk estate, just down the road there, about four or five miles, owned by the Buchanan-Jardines, so that kind of class structure very very firmly was embedded in Lockerbie people: that, we had a laird down there, and everybody had to work hard because they were on the laird's farm, so always paying rent—rental is reality for a major proportion of the Lockerbie township and countryside .

Well, we owned *and* we had a business so we that looked a lot more up the ladder than was typical. Yes, there was a man who lived in the flats just round the road from us and he was a widower had been in the war, I think, and risen to a certain rank in the army and thought himself quite debonair he was probably quite eccentric so he dressed in a posh way, with a waistcoat and a cravat, but he was living in the council flats, and he used to come in the shop, and I think he was involved in the hunt – the hunt is—was very string here so he was a huntsman of some degree and dealt with the hounds, and he used to trap pigeons in the kitchen window of his flat, cook them and eat them [Jill chuckles] and this was maybe a throw-back to his military days, so he was quite a character.

There was also another character called Durty Wullie who lived in the cottages opposite out house – they're flats now – and I have a faint memory of Durty Wullie and he was obviously living alone and I don't really remember much about him but when he died, they cleaned out his house, and he had empty milk bottles and newspapers strewn all over the place, and I remember my Father going over to Durty Wullie's house and filing up milk crates, coz in those days, you took back the empties and got a few crates filled up. So, these are some of the characters I recall from my upbringing in the town.

One individual; he is variously classed as the town's eyes and ears, or the street patroller; or the town's chronicle; his family is well-established in the town; and he knows everything that's going on in the community—he spends his day—he doesn't work—spends his day going up and down the high street, in and out the shops; he speaks to everybody and anybody, so he knows everything that's going on, and he'll know who was down the town that day and who wasn't, and who's granny's in the hospital, and what time the buses run out of Lockerbie. And people never deride him because he is an important person in the town due to the amount of knowledge he has amassed on local comings and goings. I'm sure the public mandate would put this individual as the most *weel kent* in Lockerbie, because he is internally one of them, and he does not have the external prejudices that others have This individual is surely in practically every image taken of Lockerbie He has great *mana* in the community as he knows everything that's going on and its like he earned the right it

Schoolday reminiscences

School? I remember the boys lined up at one side of the building and the girls on the other side. Indeed, it was carved into the Victorian sandstone: *Boys* and *Girls*. What do I remember about it?? I remember having to do country dancing at Christmas time and having to hold hands with sweaty boys, and I remember reading- I liked reading – so I remember standing in the reading circle and doing that. We didn't many trips or anything; it was quite a kind of Presbyterian type of schooling – you went there to learn and— my mother was a school teacher so I was encouraged to read, yes, we did—I don't recall we went to the library often, or ever, but I think my Mother bought quite a lot of books for us, and my Grandmother had a lot of books so we were certainly encouraged to read.

Sunday was just another day!

It seemed only well-to-do people went to church; well, I don't know about the Catholic church coz we weren't brought up Catholic, but—we – my parents, sister and I weren't church goers— but my grandmother went with my grandfather, and they got all poshed up to go to church on a Sunday, with their bible and their gloves, and off they went, to sit in the same pew. It never really came back on us for not going, and I don't recall my Mother being put upon by the grandmother to attend, but we were still Presbyterian nonetheless, and we were Church of Scotland, but we never went to church. I had a small stint at Sunday school but I remember not liking it very much and I didn't have to go back, which was great. My mother would say that she would rather be in the garden on a Sunday and communing with nature, that being in the church, and my Father had never been a church-goer although his Mother was a regular attendee every Sunday, but it didn't seem to be a matter of issue for Mum and Dad, and I must say religiously—in religious terms, there certainly was some, what would we say? dissention towards the catholic church, that they were in some way in opposition with the Presbyterians, and that came very strongly about the English; I was brought up, and my parents and grandparents that, we wouldn't really be entertaining the English very well, so there were quite a lot of prejudices, I suppose you could call them, both in terms of nationality and religion [both of which were historically founded]

National identity?

No, no, that was never something I was inherently aware of, and still frankly don't. I sort of sometimes don't want to have to out British on that airline— customs form you fill in. [British is equivalent to English, as far as I'm concerned] It was never a strong feeling—although my parents were conservative voters, they had a strong work ethic, and they were Presbyterian by they didn't attend church so it's almost as if they did one thing but perceived themselves another way, and

I wonder if that comes back to my grandmother's influence, I'm not sure.

The vision of their town by most of its residents

Think they would look askance at the rest of the world, with a little bit of suspicion. There is a term for people who leave Lockerbie and head south, and they say: they've gone doon sooth! which is a generic way to describe somebody who's gone bad and had to leave. People who come in: well, they'd be incomers, so: suspicion. Suspicion really is the—I know its got negative connotations, but askance: definitely not up! It wouldn't be a case of—I mean they would think that we would think that what we had was pretty good, and I've heard that said by most of the people that I've interviewed; I mean, it might be depressed and a bit run-down just now, but it's a good little town.

My teenage expectations to move on

I was young, and I wanted to live a little; well, live a *lot*. Yes that's right, [but maybe I wasn't willing to be accepted] and its interesting that, when we came here—well, mum and dad had only been here for a matter of ten years or so before I was in school, and that kind of thing but of course, now, they've been here for forty years, well, forty-plus years, I would say, coming back and doing this project, there had probably been more acceptance for it because of Mum and Dad's longstanding in the community, not for who *I* am

Yes, oh, yes, because my *family* was here, so this *developed* sense of identity really only came later, when of course, I *left, so as a child; yes,* I was perfectly happy in my little space.

But also, as I was saying, with my Father having the shop, you couldn't do anything but for everybody knew about it, and I found that really really stunting and—I mean; yeah! I remember my friend and I used to stand on the dual carriageway bridge, watch the traffic going North and South, and say, Oh, where are you gonna go when your eighteen? you know, and maybe that was also one of the reasons I worked hard at school so that I could precipitate myself about of here. But it was never considered that I would stay and marry the farmer down the road. I would never have done that. Never

The people that moved away—like myself that moved away, we didn't come back and marry people from the *area*; we stayed away. [None of my cohort that went to uni came back to marry and live here, not one that I know of] But the people who didn't go off to pursue recognised higher education, etcetera, etcetera, etcetera, stayed here and now live down the road, and I don't say that with any amount of value judgement attached – it's just a fact

Whilst I always identify myself as being Scottish, and definitely proud to be *that,* I don't generally consider my identify as a Lockardian and I don't feel any sense of pride, or *otherwise*; I don't feel ashamed about coming from Lockerbie, but that sort of regional identity doesn't really affect me.

Pre-disaster. [pause] I suppose my attitude was quite a negative one of Lockerbie, pre-disaster; however, my parents lived their and I was from there and it was the only hometown I had.

My experience of death and loss

Not of people but we had horses die and that was very upsetting, like a death in the family. One of them got knocked down on the carriageway and I remember great tears and crying and grief, but I mean, that was quite a shock to me. I can't remember being particularly upset but I remember being aghast at the way the family responded – my sister and my Mother. And, yes, so I think I must have been about six when the horse got run down; but human death: no, no, I hadn't experienced that, and I still have only *been* to one funeral, and whilst my three grandparents have all passed away, I've only attended one of their funerals. So its not something I have a lot of experience in.

Hugo asks what has held Lockerbie together through that period of devastating loss of life

Homogeneity, I think, makes Lockerbie what it is: its strength lies in its internal machinations, and the way it works internally.

The people who make up the core of Lockerbie culture are very old families who've been here for long time, or people who have come, like my Father, or one of the policeman I interviewed who became, through their work initially, very involved in the community and were accepted therefore they begin to work through the community groups and do that and form part of the circle; you know, I always thing of communities as being quite circular [organisms] with kind of threads running through the thing, or maybe like a mat, a circular mat; but it doesn't work by opening itself up to the outside world; it certainly isn't looking for any—it works fine as a machine of Lockerbie with the people who always keep it going – [its internal cohesion] and its strength lies in the fact that they all understand each other, but as we've seen; when the Lockerbie disaster happens, outsiders come in from outside and Lockerbie pulled itself in from the outside, a bit like a hedgehog that pulls its head in, and that's what kept them sane—It was heightened, almost; the essence of what the community was, was heightened as they retreated into themselves.

Lockerbie friends

I think—well, my friend, Janie Hannah; we were friendly from six years of age, onwards, and she was—I mean, I remember we made our plans for the future together, and she came from an old Lockerbie family, actually; well, Lochmaben and Lockerbie, and, yeah. She was quite influential but I couldn't exactly say why. Maybe she just mirrored what I was thinking and I did the same to her, therefore consolidating what we felt about things. Yeah, and [pause] who else?

Ambitions then and now: still unsure

I have no idea; you see; I *have* no idea. No, I kept oscillating—well, I did always fancy something with writing and I did think about journalism, but I thought about a lot of things. I went to Art College for a little while in Carlisle; they did a Foundation course there and I did—but that's only because they did that course [and I didn't go *way* doon sooth] But they did a Foundation course specifically; go for one year, do that, and then get onto a degree course which was my plan, but I was just so—I was really *stupid* because I didn't—I wanted to go into second year of the Fine Arts course in Aberdeen, and they said, Well, we'd really like you to do first year again, and just stuck my heels in and said, "I don't want to do that though!" and, perfectly reasonably, they said, Well, I'm sorry but—, and that was that. I didn't go! So I went to university instead.

I would have been—well, actually after I left school, I did a year—well, not quite a year on a hotel catering course at Robert Gordon's in Aberdeen again, but I hatred that and—I don't really know—I think I did have an interest in that but wasn't driving me and it's funny because I've been doing a bit of careers advising in Levin and I realised that I had absolutely no careers guidance and I would never have advised somebody like myself to go Hotel Catering, but I went and it wasn't me. And then I spent a year down there so that would've been—19, 20—oh, I'd've just started at Aberdeen, in the first year, in English Lit, Moral Phil and History of Art [in 1988] .

Setting the scene: during the day

It was a Wednesday! I don't remember that: I've just read it; I had forgotten it was a Wednesday.

December '88; I don't recall when we finished up atAberdeen, but I certainly was home for the holidays.

I think I may have helped Dad a bit, delivering orders probably because Christmas was one of his busiest times, so while he was in the shop, busy doing that, it was really helpful for someone to be out, delivering orders, specially on Christmas Eve, it was very busy although of course, he disaster happened before that, but there was more stock in the shop, so I may have been helping for only a couple of hours a day. I did have a boyfriend at that time down in Carlisle, so we had been going out together about two years. So I think I was hanging out with him; he wasn't at university, he was working at 14MU which is military ammunitions place at Carlisle, so I think I had been done to see him that day because I came back on the train, the day of the disaster.

[A typical] Winters day, I believe; bit grey and wet; usually is at the end of December. I don't recall really, but no snow or freezing cold, as I remember.

I think [I got back] late afternoon but again, hard to remember: I'm just guessing really. I had my evening meal with Mum and Dad so, yeah—I certainly don't recall—in fact, until somebody mentioned—we were talking the other evening, just quite informally with my auntie Mary about the disaster: until they said to me, Were you in Carlisle that night, or—?, I had actually completely forgotten that I had even *been* in Carlisle that day, so that was a big—my memories came rushing forward when she said that; Shit, that's right, I was. And I was, and I think I had been doing some Christmas shopping but, again, we get into the realms of, you know, perceived memory or—I do funnily enough remember what I was wearing, though: this long, steel grey, man's overcoat type-thing which my mother hated, and I do remember that, I was wearing that, coming back in the train, and I don't remember anything else about what we did, if we had a meal in the town, or—I really can't remember. But I *do* remember that we weren't going to be seeing each other again over Christmas;, I was gonna stay here and he was gonna do stuff with his family, yeah, so that, that was distinctly what happened, and of course, that all got completely changed; yeah.

I do recall that we had made coffee and were upstairs in the lounge where the Christmas tree was – the tree was obviously up – and my Father was downstairs and he was going to be going round to the shop to do some work after tea; so, Mum and I took our coffee up the stairs, and we didn't actually often go up to the good room, as we'd call it, of the upstairs lounge, you know, as usually, we sort of sat down and had our coffee downstairs in the living room; so anyway, we went up and put the Christmas lights on, and the rest of the room was dark, but with a nice glow of the lights and curtains closed; about quarter to seven maybe; quarter to seven-ish, and I remember we were discussing Christmas presents, and what we were going to do and who should get what.

Memory jogging: strategies for recall

I haven't told it often but I have been thinking—I was a bit concerned, when I came here, and I realised—I felt—I actually felt very guilty about the fact I was talking to people who seemed to have very clear memories and I, in fact, could not remember much about the night at all. But, as couple of years ago, I wrote a short story, and I wrote one about Lockerbie, and it was at that point that I began to reflect on the night of the disaster, and to be honest, in the intervening 16 or 17 years, I had just not thought about it at all, and that—without any exaggeration, apart from recognising the date on the calendar *and* on the day, I just hadn't thought about the chronological happenings. So when I wrote the short story, I cast my memory back and made some deep efforts to try and recall—bring to the front what had happened.

HM: Do you feel in that story, you were able to do it accurately, or did you have to make up—?

JH: No, no, no, I didn't make it up, but it was quite a short short story, and I wrote it—what was the style? I wrote it in like a newspaper article, you know, with content words only and no articles and pronouns, like you know, Father put on shoes, so you know, it was kind of [pause] detached voice, yeah, abit like that, and I specifically left it staccato with incomplete sentences, probably to reflect the fact that I couldn't actually remember much about it.

So, no, whenever anybody asked me, I would say I came home for Christmas, sitting upstairs having coffee and then, fireball: bla, bla, bla. So I never went into detail because it was never the right circumstances to go into much detail about it really; yeah.

The crash punctuates a pleasant Christmas evening

It was around seven o'clock because the Terry Wogan show had just come on; he had a chat show, and it had just come on, and I do remember it was Terry Wogan; I was sitting on the sofa; my Mother was sitting on the chair; we had a fireplace and the TV was in the corner. The TV was on the same wall as the window and the tree was over there.

The fire was on but it was an electric fire: we didn't have a coal fire up the stairs; it was electric, so there was generally quite a lot of red, orangey light going round the room, which was actually quite atmospheric, I suppose. Then often, when a large truck or lorry went past that street, the windows would shake a little bit: you know, articulated lorry would have to slow round to get round that bend and a bit of shaking of the window, and that's indeed what began: the shaking of the windows, except it got louder and more intense, with a deeper rumbling, and I suppose that must have gone on—and this is the part I do remember clearly, it must've gone on for about six or seven seconds, and at this point, I was shouting to her, "On Christ, what the hell is it?" and she went to the window and she pulled the curtains—you know, she stood right in front of the window and pulled the curtains, and there was this *huge* ball of fire: just this enormous orange light and it really looked as if the windows were going to come in, because in my mind, I can see my Mother, at the window, you know, with arms stretched out wide, and this huge ball of fire in the sky, and I shouted to her, "Get away from the window!" coz it really looked as if the glass was almost changing its texture, you know, against the glow of the orange, and—I can't remember if she did or not, but she stepped back anyway, and we just stood there, looking at it, and it wasn't like a mushroom cloud, it just continued to shoot up into the sky, so it wasn't really, you know, like a fountain or something of light, or a fire, and so, down we rushed because my Father had been going out to the shop so he had to go out of our back door, and into the yard, and round to the shop at the back; he would be going round to work after the shop had shut, because it was coming up to Christmas so he had bread orders and cream orders and things like that.

Well, then there was no noise; after the booming—after the rumbling and the deep rumbling—I don't recall there being a crashing sound: certainly, there was movement and things were shaking, you know; there was shaking, but I don't remember an explosion type sound. There possibly was but I don't recall it. I can visually recall how it looked, but after that initial rumbling, which made us think, My god, what is it? and a shaking: something like an earthquake really, you know, and then the fire, so I don't actually recall any more sound that that.

So we ran downstairs, we ran downstairs because we were a bit concerned—well, we just ran downstairs, I suppose, and my father was standing in between the doorway of the living room and the kitchen, and the fire wasn't on because during the day, we had an electric fire and at night, we'd put on the coal fire so, I had been during the day; we'd just been working with an electric on, and often we lifted that one off the hearth, you know, instead of putting on the fire, so we went downstairs and my Father was standing there with his shoes in his hand - we had gone out yet, and all this soot had come down the chimney and the soot was al over the hearth and the rug, and my Father was looking very *anxious* and I remember we had his flat cap and his coat on, and he's going, "Just wait here!", and my Mother pulled the curtains in the downstairs room— opened them wide, and there was all this—I mean we had to stay inside till he found out more, so we were peeking through the venetian blinds and there was all this rubble all over the street, and there was a man over the other side of the street with a head injury; he was sitting on a wall area, sitting with this head injury; and this fire is still there, and we're going, Oh—I can't really remember what we said to each other, to be honest, or that's what I recall seeing.

Mains Street after the crash

We just went outside because my Father didn't come back after 3 or 4 minutes, and the huge smell of this fuel just completely filled the air.

Aviation fuel! Pieces of concrete and rubble and mud, as we were walking up the entry of our yard to the street: concrete and rubble everywhere all over the street; mud, and the destruction of my Father's shop windows: the glass everywhere—no, it had only been the plate glass; funnily enough, there had been no damage to the house windows, just the plate glass that was damaged. So, people were beginning to come out of their houses, and collect in the street, and very very quickly – probably about 10 minutes or so after the initial rumbling, then police in jackets were walking down the street; couple of police cars, and the we initially thought – I don't know if you noticed: I should have drawn it to your attention. There's a petrol station just down the hill from where we are now, but its past our house, the one at Mains Street, so midway between here and the old place, and they thought it had exploded, so they were going to see what had happened there, at least that's what they told us, as they walked down, and so we just kind of hung around, and people came out and speculated as t what had happened, what it could be, and Mother wanted my Father to come along here, to see it my grandmother was okay - she was in this house - and he walked up here, and she was quite [pause] infirm at the time. She was quite shaken though, thinking it was the end of the world, she said and it was Armageddon and she had just sat down and prayed, and he has said, "Come with us down the street," but at that point, the police were moving residents from this area along to the local hotel: using it as an evacuation point, and at this stage, they knew it wasn't the petrol station, although there was a small fire burning at the back of the petrol station and they were very concerned it was going to blow up.

The demeanour of the residents at this early stage

Well, I've asked that question [Jill chuckles] to my participants, because I'm interested to know what they recall. Nobody was panicking! There was no panic! We weren't panicking; we were—I think—well, I—everybody seemed very concerned, obviously, but doing as they were told, and there was much instruction from the police as to—we were told that we had to go to the Town Hall and we had to vacate the place; my Father was quite concerned because he had to leave the shop with the windows broken and he was really concerned about that.

So [pause] my mother and I, we—well, I think, we—quite honestly, we just had no idea what had happened, as we were just in shock, I suppose.

Well, we heard—I didn't, but we heard, as we make our way up the street, we heard people saying, Oh it could be a jet; we get a lot of low-flying jets round here, or we used to. And you didn't get the noise until the rounded the Haas Hill, for example, and it was right there [I remember, when we had the ponies, if a jet came over, it was like, the sky was clear and the next instant this—and the cracking noise of a sonic boom was on top of you, often just clipping the tops of the trees they were that low; and the horses, although they weren't flighty, did bolt on occasion]

So people were talking as they were walking up the street, and people coming out of their houses; and saying, You wouldn't get that kind of fire with a—and [puase] almost a sense of excitement: I mean, I can remember feeling quite excited; like it was, Wow, what on earth! I mean, yes, I didn't have any feelings of dread or, or—it was quite exciting really—

My memory spikes over convivial circumstances and blocks out the upset – it selects what to remember.

No, no, but, it was very slowly coming through, and by the time we got to the pub, people were saying, It's an airliner, this kind of thing, but still there was a complete *mis*comprehension, if there is such a word, you know; Well, that can't be true coz how come the whole town hasn't been obliterated?, you know; your mind is trying to make sense of it.

In the pub—no, actually not in the pub, the TV wasn't on in the pub, no, no. My boyfriend had arrived anyway and, I don't know how he found me in the pub; he probably explained how he did but I can't recall the story, and we were there, and then they said—but nobody had any—my Father recounts the story that he was the only one with any money out of 2 or 3 families, so he had to stand the round of drinks, and then we went to our friends—

[At the pub] ,well, I think we were telling our own, What-had-happened stories, you know, but its funny because my Mother had recounted memories of meeting relatives of a deceased family killed in the crater, and I just don't recall that' I had no memory of that whatsoever, The relatives of these people, and they had said, You know, I wonder if Dora and Maurice are okay? And somebody else can along and said, No, they've been hit by the plane!" and my Mother recounts this relative breaking down, and I don't remember that at all: you'd think I would; that's a powerfully dramatic scene for someone who, like myself, hasn't had much connection with death or tragedy, but I don't remember that; just don't recall it, really don't. I remember being in the pub, and what seats we were sitting at, and we were around, talking about what had happened but with some excitement about us being collected round this table and discussing what had happened to us on this otherwise ordinary night. . I can't deny there was an air of excitement, but, of course, we hadn't seen the pictures or knew the full extent of things then.

There would be maybe 8 to 10 of us sitting there, a and we were all just very engrossed in the stories that were being told there, so we didn't talk to people we wouldn't normally talk to: we wouldn't normally go in the pub; my father and mother had never—question if they'd been in the pub before or since. They might go a hotel for a drink, but not the pub in the High Street. But we did and I must have thought, Wow this is really strange? I mean, my mum and dad never went up the street to the pub- never ever, and here we were, friends and family assembled in this social situation, and in an environment that was out of character for them usually: it was a unique experience; hadn't occurred before and probably won't again. Strange, too, that I remember the pub but not the relative breaking down.

Maybe reporters coming into the hotel, and it was quite a small room where the pub is, and again, this is selective memory: I'm not even sure if this is true, but I have a vague memory that that's why we left, as it was beginning to fill up with reporters, but we still hadn't seen anything on TV at this point.

Details were sketchy but we knew it was beyond our control

I don't remember walking but we did walk – to Mum and Dad's friends house which was over the motorway area; the way we came in, as if to go to the memorial garden – they live down there, and we went there because they hadn't been evacuated or anything

All the people assembled at Peter and Liz's [...] didn't really know what was going on, we really didn't, and it as quite odd that we were sitting watching the TV to do with the town that we were living in, but it was pretty much a case of, Well, if its something of this magnitude and on this scale, then there's nothing we can. So yeah, we stayed through the night there and I remember dozing on the sofa, and a lot of whisky was consumed, I think [we didn't] go off to find out where the fire was coming from; there was nothing like that; [w] e never—[w] e didn't go near, or go inquiring or anything

The trauma of the night's events brings dreadful feelings

They had, yes, it was a kind of nightmarish dread, I think, especially having to say away from your own home; that as really quite horrible, and—, nobody was in tears, no, nobody was; just stunned, I think; not a lot of silence; a lot of talking about what had happened so not stunned silence, but I didn't see anybody breaking down in tears, no. And I certainly didn't feel that, but a feeling of dread, really: I remember waking up the next day, feeling, Oh God! just quite depressed.

An anecdote to illustrate my lack of coping with subsequent dramatic periods

But, its quite interesting, I must tell you; when there was the flood in the Bay of Plenty [New Zealand], two, three years ago, we were coming back from Rotorua maybe; somewhere, and we couldn't get from Ohope through to Opotiki, because it was flooded, and we had to spend the night in Whatakane, so got a hotel which was amazing, but the hotel was evacuated because they were concerned about a slip from the rock in Whakatane, and we had to end up coming to the Salvation Army Hall. Well, all my partner will say is, "You didn't' handle it very well, Jill!" And I didn't handle it very well at all, and we had two small children too: thankfully, we had blankets because we had been staying at Ohakune and it had been cold so we'd taken a lot of stuff, but I didn't cope well at all with that type of evacuation situation and I just really got my blankets, found a space to lie down out the way, and went to sleep; just shut down, and my partner had to deal with the children; so. And I didn't really realise until I was in that situation and had to do that—and I often found myself avoiding having to do any communal sleeping in the marae and that kind of thing. I'm not comfortable doing that, and it's not because I'm—I mean, I don't consider myself to be prudish or conservative or anything in that way, but I don't like that kipping down, communal muck-in.

My father, I remember, tried to maintain his routine but it was thrown to bits; there was much cleaning up to do in the shop; people were coming in, and journalists too so Dad was getting anti and getting a hard time from them. The girl who worked there—that was the first of the emotion; heard about it from Dad and Mum; much coming and going, and my Father recounts some upset with journalists and shoppers, and Dad was getting cross with them,[the journalists] telling them to get lost, and people were coming in with various first-hand accounts of how—and by this time, we knew about the crater, and who had been killed, and we knew about Rosebank, so we were pretty much fully aware then, coz they were coming in with some horrific accounts in full details; and I remember that my boyfriend and I did go and look at the crater site but we had to go around by the country lane, the Quaas Loaning, and up round that way, and I remember, yes, it was just this huge enormous hole, and it was incredible because you haven't got anything to reference that against, but we didn't take pictures or anything; we just—you know, now I think, Well, why didn't I take a picture, but there must have been a reason I didn't.

Anyway, yes, and just cleaning up, and then after that, I don't really recall very much until Christmas Day, when I don't really remember much except it was cancelled; we weren't having Christmas as such, no decorations; I'm sure there were presents, but I don't recall them, or if my sister was there. I remember it appeared very grey and dull in our living room for the Christmas meal, and I remember the man from the Salvation Army in Glasgow came during our Christmas meal, and it was all very dark, and a wet day, and it was really dark it the room, and he came to the front door, which was really unusual, as they usually come to the back door, and at the door was this Salvation Army man from Glasgow, and he had been sent to the house—we'd come down to Lockerbie anyway, and he'd been sent to the house by my Mother's cousin's son, John, and he'd asked the Salvation man to see if we were okay, and I remember him, sitting down, but I don't remember anything else except it was very dark and very depressing, and then some silence began to kick into our routine. Silences increased generally, in contrast to all the talk, talk of the proceeding 3 days.

Disaster details – I have avoided the sites and memorials of Lockerbie

I never saw any nasty bits, any human remains, things like that I never witnessed that personally. My father didn't want me going to look coz I remember my boyfriend was quite keen to go and see the crater so we had to keep it from Dad and I had a curiosity too, so we went to look at the crater but I—in fact, before today, I probably haven't been up to Rosebank for—yeah! Twenty years.

Yeah. I haven't been up there for years and years and years, and my Father was saying, "Oh, there's a plaque on the wall," and I was: "Was there?" I must tell you about the other day, and this will surprise you: there's a little dedication room at the church where the nose cone fell, up at Tundergarth, so-called coz that's the name of the farm, and I have not been up there ever since the disaster. We used to go to Tundergarth Mains a lot because my sister used to ride with the girls who lived there, but that must've been twenty five years ago and I have not been up there since, and I've *never* been up to visit that wee room.

Yeah we went up to take some pictures, but not since our riding days with the Wilson girls, and so that's maybe some indication that we didn't do homage to the disaster at these memorials *at the time*, but of course, it's a bit different now.

Hugo asks how people in Lockerbie reacted – my response is plain

Well, people will tell you—you see, this is quite interesting because I don't feel in any way equipped to answer that question, honestly, as I don't know because I wasn't here.

HM: [But] I hear what people say, and people say that it brought the community together. Brought them together; Dunkirk spirit and all that, you know, brought out the true nature of the Lockardian; out there with the blankets and the scones, helping, helping, gotta do something, can't sit around.

JH: Well, it's true in the fact that there was a huge army of volunteers who variously washed and ironed clothes, formed search teams looking for this, that and the other, photocopied resources for the investigation, social worked from door-to-door: just went out there on mass, doing whatever they could, that is definitely true, that's true.

But it also caused a lot of—I think in the early days, the people who were predisposed to *be* like that, *were* like that, and they would lay it all on for the services and the army and the helpers and volunteers - the grafters. But, at the same time, to the journalists and the media who came in, the boards were up, and they would not allow penetration of the inner sanctum of Lockerbie, the town and its people: they couldn't see them and the like far enough. So, on the one hand, do anything we can to help individuals who come to the town; take the scones, here's the blankets, but the to the media broadcasting to the world, well, they may be present in the town, but they would get no more than a surface impression of the place, in order than the firmament of the community wasn't ruptured and was held in tact. You know, and they came up with the profile of, *sleepy little market town*, because it was suitable oxymoron to catch the jingoistics beloved by media and public like . And there was as many people who didn't drop everything and go and help, but just carried on as best them could, with work and family commitments. But it's the local heroes that made that news stories; unlike this project where it's the ordinary experience that tells the complete picture.

1989 and my New Year departure

I had exams actually, in the February, and I remember if being rather surreal, because I was just walking around the campus, and it had all just happened, and nobody asked about it or mentioned it and it was in stark contrast to what I had just left. The people in my Hall knew I was from Lockerbie – up at Hillhead Halls – and so—and I got a call actually from an American girl who had been with me in halls the term before, and she was in Israel, and she called me when the disaster hit the media, so that as quite amazing, and I think that sticks in my mind, but I don't recall telling my hall mates about it, or their response or anything; its quite bizarre, you know. And I really don't remember having any long, drawn out conversations about it, I might have done but I don't remember it.

HM: You don't recall your overall feelings about it? Did you feel that you had been assaulted in any way?

JH: Quite alienated, I think, that's the truth; having to go back to the university, certainly I left alienated a bit from what was going on in Lockerbie, and I—yes; and I think I quite hankered to be back there, to see what was going on. But I don't know it that was because I felt I should, for support, or to maintain that level of drama in the unfolding events

I still harbour vivid feelings about the memorial event in January 1989

I certainly didn't think it was okay for Mrs Thatcher to be represented at the memorial service – I didn't like that and I was young and opinionated about her – I was anti-poll tax and the Miners Strike was a recent event then, in 1988 – she was a anathema to me as a student, and this harks back to what I said about being British – that she should represent me and my town, was an insult in my regard: I felt aggrieved that she'd come and what comfort would she be, and that wasn't what helped me. I understand now, with maturity, that it was a requirement of national etiquette in the face of disaster, but the fact that it was *her*, in full sail, while the public had to stand outside of their local place of worship to make room for her! I still get irritated, thinking about that.

Downplaying Lockerbie: for me, the stigma perpetuates

I think I have since then—since the disaster, I have been quite reticence to tell people where I come from, because of the stigma that it now has.

HM: It's a stigma, is it?

JH: I think it's a stigma. I'd call it a stigma: that Lockerbie is known globally for only that; it is a stigma; having to downplay it all the time to everyone that always asks, and I do *try* and avoid saying where I'm from, but if they ask me, I don't lie, but it does irritate me that I have to downplay it, and say, Well, there you go! More Chardonnay? I don't like having to do that, but you don't rationally think, That's irritating me! It's just a layering of over the years, but certainly I do feel very strongly, and this fits in this the whole ethos of the project; that my hometown has been violated, and I'm annoyed about that [Jill chuckles]

Whether I'm proud to be a Lockardian or not, it's the only hometown I'll ever have., I hadn't rationalised this until the lady who lives away from Lockerbie said it; an essence of guilt about survival about the disaster, and I feel that quite strongly too, but that rolls into other layers of guilt that people—well, that I, have acquired in my life [Jill chuckles] , and I think I would agree with that, as—well, a concept, Why wasn't it me? and I feel a bit guilty about coming from Lockerbie and well, I wasn't killed, so maybe guilt was the wrong—semantically, the wrong way to describe it, but— a bit of a phoney; I had an experience but then it was snatched away from me, and I haven't had the same experience as all these other people, my mum and dad included, so, as I mentioned earlier on, probably that stolen memory thing; yes, like I had the experience but it got stolen away from me. Robbed; I feel a bit robbed.

What the disaster meant to me: the big picture

A kind of lack on control; it was a period of time, in those minutes, hours, days, when it was completely out of control and everything was all turned upside down and I had no prior experience of that to relate it to, so that time is unrelated to anything since or prior. Like I was hanging in a vacuum. I think that, prior to Lockerbie, I was quite a rebellious type and certainly wasn't conforming; had three attempts at higher education and nothing was really sticking, then I think it really made me become a lot more serious; I became a bit less erratic and knuckled-down; quieter probably and a lot and more focussed on what I was doing; a reality check, I suppose: Oh shit, that could have been me. And that time of no control was a feeling that was not good and it took a lot of getting used to. But these words I've said to you are really inadequate to describe how earth-shattering it was to have a thing fall on your home environment out of the sky.

Yes, it would. Yes, it would, and people have said that so often and they're right, but I think you can apply that to all aspects of anyone's life. I must just tell you, I did go ad see Anita Harris as she played Peter Pan in a pantomime back in 76 maybe, and we went to a theatre in Edinburgh to see it and the next day, the theatre burnt down. Now luckily, no-one died, and then one time, we always used to go on holiday to Girvan and Turnberry and we went on the Waverley, which was the last ocean-going paddler steamer, out of Ayr, and the next day, it ran aground [Jill chuckles] And I suppose, then there's Lockerbie, and I sure I could be much more fatalistic than I am about things; if I did have any feelings about being religiously faithful, that all went out the window after the disaster and I don't keep any religious feelings whatsoever.

I don't and I never did [feel angry with Libyan people]

I don't think [Al Magrahi] did it, and that's because I've made an effort to become informed about what's going on, but at the time, there were no feelings of anger from me.

Footnote: My parents received a few hate calls after the disaster. I recall I picked up the phone one evening and a voice made a statement along the lines of that Gadaffi would get us yet or finish the job off. I never found out if my parents received any more calls or if they reported them

My experience aside, I can listen with fresh ears to the stories of the participants because of my physical distance and the time lapse.

Well, currently, I'm standing back from the whole thing because I feel I'm quite capable of doing that because I have not, over the twenty years. I know fewer people now, that's true, and the town has definitely changed in the five years since I was back last: it looks different and I think it looks *busier* actually, than it was, and until I was in the paper last week, I could have walked down the street with quite a lot of anonymity, so, yeah.

I haven't been living here on a daily basis for [more than] twenty years, and going down and seeing the same people every day and the same folk for saw the day after the disaster, and the day after that and the day after that, so I have been completely removed from the *site* of the disaster and the people involved in it, and therefore you almost can become—fool yourself into believing that it didn't happen to *you*, and especially when I was recounting it to you now, I had the feeling that I was creating a narrative for someone else, so the feelings and what they meant have become very fragmented in my memory over the past twenty years, because I never consider it except for a fleeting though on the date; I *hardly* ever talk about it with anybody, I usually never have to confront it, so up till this point, when I've been speaking to you, I have been completely *removed* and distance from the grouping of those involved in the disaster, except tonight I'm classed as one of them. But that has also been easier because none of them have got upset except one of the participants was quite emotional and that made me quite choked because I could relate to what she was saying about being removed from the homogeneity of Lockerbie and removed from the environment of being able to share and support. So I was drawn into her narrative quite strongly and my kind of guard of sitting back and being the interviewer and historian kind of slipped, which was interesting, and it wasn't till it happened that I realised how detached I had been with the other people.

So, yeah, I do feel quite strongly that I have a different dynamic with everyone that I'm interviewing, and if probably given half a chance, and my interviewee was in floods of tears, I probably would be as well, but that hasn't happened. So I feel at this point I've been quite detached *but* I'm waiting for the right time—not the right time: I'm waiting for the point that will come in—you know, as the project rolls on, for my story to kind of wash over, if I can say, the other narratives.

My role as narrator and historian

I've read accounts many time, and you know, I haven't read the literature on Lockerbie cover-to-cover coz I don't need to cos its all very formulaic, and I have found myself thinking, I've read that bit somewhere, and the recounts detail things that I obviously knew but none of them asked me if I was here that night, so why should they be aware that I knew anything about it. They're not treating me in the way that I thought In fact, maybe they reckon I don't and that's why I'm doing the project; or they become so involved in remembering that I am a dispassionate audience for their oracy and not treating me in the way I *thought* they would treat me, which is someone who has had a similar experience: they're almost treating me—responding to me as a relative outsider, and they've gone, click, into their stories and that is great, as far as I'm concerned because it means they have no expectations on me as regards prior awareness, so I can slip under the radar. I don't know how a historian's supposed to feel, doing these interviews; or how I *should* have approached it, or how I'm going to feel. There have been a variety of unspoken responses from me to the interviews I have done, and I have no idea how that it going to make their accounts informing on the different factors of the whole disaster.

Finding comfort and security in the ordinary

HM I remember talking to people about the Piper Alpha and it's the same talking to you about this, the significance of very tiny, unimportant detail, you know: if an aeroplane hadn't just fallen out of the sky, what you are talking about it so ordinary, really; going up to the town hall, having a drink in the pub, and—so, finding a link between that and one of the world's greatest aerial disasters is quite difficult, isn't it?

JH: Yes, it is and I'm no psychologist, but I'm wondering if in the ordinary, we are finding comfort, or the people involved in Piper Alpha would find comfort in the everyday because, suddenly, that ordinary everyday was potentially blown out of existence, so its also like, Thank God I can go up to the pub! or, Thank God I can walk up my own street! Maybe that's why: those ordinary everyday things suddenly become quite heightened in your consciousness, in contrast to the extremely surreal thing that's just happened. And of course, for those who did lose loved ones, the mundane and ordinary was possibly a way of focussing on something tangible and knowable; like a frame of reference, as opposed to the dark abyss of grief and uncertainty induced by the disastrous events that had just taken place.

And I think, too, it's the site of that, I mean, you know, because this happens in your town, or your workplace community in the case of Piper Alpha, I— you know, its not like we were on holiday in a foreign climate; I'm thinking about the Boxing Day tsunami in Indonesia; you know, imagine lying on the beach, quietly on the beach and then suddenly that happens, but I wonder what the memories and feelings of the tourists, who were in an unknown environment to start with, and when you're in an environment you know really well, and something completely bizarre happens, like the plane; well, how are you supposed to respond to the things that are *around* you; probably finding the everydayness very heightened; it's a, it's a strange one.

Details of the profile of Lockerbie post-disaster

I think Lockerbie had irrevocably changed since the disaster, but how much that is to do with the disaster and how much is to do with the natural passing on time, that would be hard to quantify and I'm certainly not about to do that in the book, but I think what will come out in the book, through the stories of the people, is how on the one hand, Lockerbie is the same as it *ever* was, but on the other hand, it will be the same as it *never* was because fellow Lockardians; well, some lost a lot – everything - and some had cause to gain a considerable amount; that created personal grievances *internally*, on the inside, while the community was strong and cohesive *externally*. So, there was physical and psychological damage; the first was easy to evidence but the second wasn't, and that caused a rift in community life, because, just as we discussed before, the strict hierarchical structure here and not a lot of money, some people suddenly *had* money, and, Were they entitled to that money? some asked; so there was now suspicion, which has previously been reserved for outsiders coming in, being applied to neighbours and citizens on the inside. And that had not been an issue prior to the disaster. And there are some sad sad stories as a result of those matters. If you imagine the community to be organic, like an organism, the nucleus remains unchanged, but there were some divided cells that were Amidst the awful lost of life or destruction as it *was*, I think we would all have a case for mental trauma and stress, but how awful to accuse someone of *not* having suffered as a result as well, so it was a very mired and murky issue; contentious and not openly discussed; it was quite shameful really, and the knock-on of these matters still pervades today, as a legacy and reminder of that black time for Lockerbie. People still say, 'That's Pan Am money, that is!" So whilst the disaster pulled the community together, it also cleft division too, amongst their *ain folk*. And I believe people don't really want any more public commemorations and they don't want to think about it, because it is a personal and communal reminder of the black times for the communion of Lockerbie – to go back to the body metaphor, when the symptoms of the disease began, and best to draw a veil over, and deal with it as its in remission now.

Yes, I think, on the one hand, they are just the same, but if you scratch the surface and look underneath, as I've tried to do, you can find, you know, that there is a real need to move on, once and for all.

Dad's shop front – mud and aviation fuel blew outwards from the crater.(James Haldane)

Jane and Jill Haldane at the Market in Sydney Place for Gala Day Riding of the Marches, 1978. Jane is riding Paint and I am on Pebbles

Tundergarth Church and Dedication Room. ©James Haldane, 2008

Signing the visitors' book on my first and only trip to the Dedication Room at Tundergarth Church, Lockerbie, in March 2008 ©James Haldane, 2008

Memorial cross near the Golf course, marking the site where a passenger was found.

Lightning Source UK Ltd.
Milton Keynes UK
UKOW041005260911

179301UK00006B/5/P